ASPEC
OF RELIGIO
IN WALES,
c.1536-1660

Leadership, Opinion and the Local Community

J. Gwynfor Jones

© 2003 J. Gwynfor Jones / CAA

ISBN: 1 85644 824 X

Published by the Centre for Educational Studies, Faculty of Education,
University of Wales, Aberystwyth

Cover and Design: *Enfys Beynon Jenkins and Andrew Gaunt*
Printers: *Cambrian Printers*
Cover illustration: *Mallwyd parish church, Merioneth.*
Photographer: *Eric Hall*

The author, formerly Professor of Welsh History at the University of Cardiff,
has published several books, chiefly on early modern Welsh social, religious,
administrative and cultural developments. Among his main works are *Concepts
of Order and Gentility in Wales 1540-1640; Beirdd yr Uchelwyr a'r Gymdeithas
yng Nghymru c.1536-1640; The Wynn Family of Gwydir; Law, Order and
Government in Caernarfonshire, 1558-1640; The Welsh Gentry 1536-1640; Conflict,
Continuity and Change in Wales, c.1500-1603*, and a modern edition of Sir John
Wynn's *History of the Gwydir Family and Memoirs*. He has also published a
large number of articles in Welsh and English journals.

CONTENTS

PREFACE

This book has gradually evolved from studies, which I undertook over many years, of aspects of religious life and activity in Wales during the Reformation period. Preparing single essays on individual Welsh bishops during the latter half of the sixteenth century led me, in due course, to consider examining more closely aspects of the course of the Reformation down to the restoration of monarchy in 1660, in the light of contemporary texts which highlight some of its main features. Although many of these texts are already well known to the historian of early modern Welsh religious history, it is hoped that applying them to the immediate context may add a dimension which gives them a more personal significance, particularly when associated with individuals who were lay and clerical apologists of the new faith in the reign of Elizabeth I. The studies extend into the first half of the seventeenth century and include a discussion of the role of Welsh bishops in consolidating the Protestant Church in a period, before the Civil Wars, when the religious order demanded strong leadership, an age when new challenges threatened its solidarity. The continued abuses in church government and administration, the survival of Roman Catholic communities and the emergence of a nonconformist movement were causes of serious concern to church leaders who were constantly aware of the need to reinforce its inbuilt sources of strength. Also the impact of civil turmoil and an unpopular Puritan regime added significantly to the strains and tensions which Protestantism endured in the 1640s and 1650s. The volume aims to use original sources to uncover some of the stresses which prompted religious leaders, Anglican and Puritan alike, to advance the faith according to their own convictions.

I am deeply indebted to Sir Glanmor Williams, whose researches and publications I have admired and benefited from over the years, for his continued friendship and support. His numerous works, particularly *Wales and the Reformation*, the *magnum opus* which appeared in 1997, has been a source of inspiration for me. I also wish to thank Brian Ll. James for his kindness in reading the whole work in draft and for very valuable suggestions from which I greatly profited. I am indebted to Professor Emeritus R.Geraint Gruffydd for his expert help with the translation of some of the more abstruse poetic extracts in Chapter 3. Furthermore, the assistance given by Dylan Foster-Evans, Peter Keelan, Tom Dawkes, Aled

Cooke and Dr E. Wyn James of the University of Cardiff, Ms. Vivienne Larminie of the *New Dictionary of National Biography*, Bryn Jones of the City of Cardiff Public Library and the assistants at the National Library of Wales at Aberystwyth is also appreciated because they all, in various capacities, were very helpful in seeking information, setting the format and enlightening me on various aspects of the work. I am particularly grateful to Mrs Helen Emanuel Davies, Director of the Centre for Educational Studies in the Faculty of Education at the University of Wales, Aberystwyth, for accepting the work for publication and wish to thank Mrs Enfys Jenkins and the staff for their care and expertise and Mrs Eleri Melhuish for her assistance in compiling the index. Mrs Eirlys Roberts deserves special mention because of the thorough manner in which she edited the work. Needless to say, I alone am to blame for any errors or misconceptions that may appear. As usual, Enid, my wife, has given me the support that I needed when preparing the work, and my appreciation of her patience and forbearance cannot indeed be expressed in words.

Cardiff, April 2003

ABBREVIATIONS

AC	*Archaeologia Cambrensis*
BBCS	*Bulletin of the Board of Celtic Studies*
BL	British Library
Cal. State Papers Dom.	*Calendars of State Papers Domestic, 1547-1660* (London, 1856-)
Ca. MS.	Cardiff City Library manuscript
DNB.	*Dictionary of National Biography*, ed. L. Stephen and S. Lee (London, 1885-1900)
DWB	*Dictionary of Welsh Biography*, eds. J. E. Lloyd and R. T. Jenkins (London, 1959)
GAS	Gwynedd Archive Service
HMC	Historical Manuscripts Commission
JEH	*Journal of Ecclesiastical History*
JHSCW	*Journal of the Historical Society of the Church in Wales*
JMHRS	*Journal of the Merioneth Historical and Record Society*
JWBS	*Journal of the Welsh Bibliographical Society*
JWEH	*Journal of Welsh Ecclesiastical History*
JWRH	*Journal of Welsh Religious History*
LlC	*Llên Cymru*
NLW	National Library of Wales
NLWJ	*National Library of Wales Journal*
Rhagymadroddion	*Rhagymadroddion, 1547-1659*, ed. G.H. Hughes (Cardiff, 1951)
TAAS	*Transactions of the Anglesey Antiquarian Society and Field Club*
TCHS	*Transactions of the Caernarfonshire Historical Society*
TCS	*Transactions of the Honourable Society of Cymmrodorion*
TDHS	*Transactions of the Denbighshire Historical Society*
UCNW	University College of North Wales (Bangor)
WHR	*Welsh History Review*
X/QS	Caernarfonshire Quarter Sessions Records

ILLUSTRATIONS

ACKNOWLEDGEMENTS

Illustrations in this volume are reproduced with the kind permission of the National Library of Wales. No.7 is from J. Steegman, *Portraits from Welsh Houses* 1.

ILLVSTRISSIMAE,

POTENTISSIMAE, SERE-
NISSIMÆQVE PRINCIPI ELI.

ZABETHAE,Dei gratia, Angliæ, Galliæ,& Hiber-
niæ Reginæ,fidei veræ,& Apoſtolicæ Propugnat.
&c. Gratiam , & benedictio-
nem in Domino ſem-
piternam.

QVANTVM Deo optimo ma-
ximo Maieſtas veſtra debeat(Auguſtiſ-
ſima princeps) vt opes, potentiam, &
admirabilem ingenij ac naturæ dotem
taceam:nó ſolũ gratia,qua apud pluri-
mos pollet rariſsima, & eruditio , qua
præ cæteris ornatur varia,& pax , qua
præ vicinis fruitur alma, eiúſque nun-
quam ſatis admiranda protectio, qua
& hoſtes nuper fugauit atroces , &
multa ac magna pericula ſemper euaſit fæliciſsimè.: verum etiam
cũ primis eximia illa pietas toto orbe celebrata, qua ipſe V. M. im-
buit,& ornauit,nec non veræ religionis & propagandæ, & propug-
nandæ ſtudium propenſiſsimũ quo ſemper flagraſtis, clariſsime at-
teſtantur. Nam(vt & gentes alias, & reliqua præclarè à vobis geſta,
iam præteream) quàm piam curam veſtrorum Brytannorum ha-
buit V. M. hoc vnum (quod ſacroſancti Dei verbi inſtrumenta v-
traque , vetus ſcilicet & nouum) vnà cum illo libro , qui precum
publicarum formam,& ſacramentorum adminiſtrandorum ratio-
nem præſcribit, in Britannicum ſermonem verti non modò benig-
nè permiſerit, ſed ſummorum inclytiſsimi huius regni comitio-
rum authoritate ſolicitè ſanxiuerit) ſemper conteſtari valet. Quod
idem noſtram ignauiam & ſegnitiem ſimul prodit , quod nec tam
graui neceſsitate moueri, nec tam commoda lege cogi potuerimus,
quin tam diu res tanti (qua maioris eſſe momenti nihil vnquam
potuerit) intacta penè remanſerit . Nam illam liturgiam cum
nouo Teſtamento duntaxat reuerendus ille pater Richardus
piæ memoriæ Meneuenſis Epiſcopus (auxiliante Gulielmo Saleſ-
burio,de noſtra Eccleſia viro optimè merito) annis abhinc viginti
Brytannicè interpretatus eſt. Qua re quantum noſtratibus profue-
rit,facilè dici non poteſt. Nam præterquàm quod vulgus noſtrum

✻. ij.   quæ

First page of William Morgan's *Latin Dedication of the Bible* (1588)
to Elizabeth I

INTRODUCTION

This volume proposes to examine aspects of the early period in the development of the Protestant Reformation in Wales, principally from the reign of Elizabeth I down to the close of the years of Puritan government. The main aim is to adapt original sources to reveal the progress of Protestantism and the perplexities of its leaders as reported in the published works of clergy and laity involved in the promotion of the new faith. Their comments in prefaces and dedications of religious translations often focus on central issues which affected the advance of religious reform. The study is designed to evaluate the opinions and reactions and to dwell on the ambitions of individual leaders of religious life in Wales as revealed in contemporary sources.

From the Elizabethan settlement down to the decades of Civil War and Puritan government, Wales saw the advancement of the Protestant Church. New generations at each social level were less familiar with the Roman Catholic Church and more prepared to accept the official religious establishment that the majority of gentry families, as community leaders, were eager to uphold. Despite its shortcomings and the problems which threatened its progress this Church, by the early seventeenth century, had established itself fairly securely among the Welsh people. The new faith was more rapidly embraced in the towns, particularly in areas which, in the seventeenth century, saw the growth of Puritanism, because commercial interests attracted a constant flow of Protestant ideas and opinions.

The first chapter examines the contributions of published religious texts, in Welsh and English, to explain the manner in which the Protestant faith was introduced and established during the reign of Elizabeth I. In this context the contribution of a series of Elizabethan bishops to the establishment and progress of the Church is noteworthy, despite the limitations imposed upon it by internal and external factors. These threats to the new institution delayed the impact of the new faith, particularly on isolated rural communities. Despite such problems ways and means were devised to initiate reform, all of which was considered insufficient by the Puritan John Penry whose scathing attacks on the failure of the Elizabethan Church to introduce radical reform and the inadequacy of its

1

preaching ministry gave him ample opportunity to lament its deplorable condition. Discussion proceeds to examine the concerns of church leaders faced by Roman Catholic threats, Penry's invectives and the traditional abuses inherited by the new Church in 1559. These challenges engaged Elizabethan bishops at a critical time when political relations with Spain and the Papacy and the weakening position of the reformed churches on the continent caused serious concerns for church and state.

The chief features of the Elizabethan Protestant Church are broadly identified with its structure, its personnel and its mission, all of which were essential to its success in a period of bewildering religious change. In addition to the Acts of Supremacy and Uniformity (1559) the legislation which laid the basis of the Protestant faith in Wales and England, the role of propaganda and the way in which it shaped Protestant and Roman Catholic opinion in Wales need further investigation. It contributed fundamentally to the making of the Reformation in Wales, for it was initiated by a small dedicated group of lay and cleric humanist scholars who were painfully aware of the inadequacy of existing printed books and sought to remedy that by publishing a small number of religious works, many of them in translation. Among such scholars were some of the most conspicuous of native-born and resident bishops who became increasingly conscious of the need to enhance the Anglican faith in their respective dioceses in an age of economic tensions, clerical negligence, secularisation of church tithes and properties, Roman Catholic opposition and, in the 1630s, the emergence of Puritan nonconformity.

The Elizabethan Church in Wales emerged into the seventeenth century in many respects as a curious blend of the traditional and innovatory, for it retained close affinities with the Church in England. This explains why there was such strong support for the Tudor and Stuart monarchies. There were a number of factors responsible for this strong bond of affinity and among them political ambition, administrative skill, cultural affiliations and the transference of loyalties from the Tudor to the Stuart dynasties based on patriotic sentiments. Religious factors were also significant in this transference because the Church, as formally established early in Elizabeth I's reign, was regarded, in scholastic circles, as the true heir to the primitive 'apostolic' church of pre-Saxon times in Britain. Thus the Welsh gentry and clergy gradually associated themselves with this institution which they accepted as having strong spiritual and cultural affinities with their past. This implied that the labours of church leaders and lay gentry, representing broadly the intelligentsia, whose contributions to maintaining the reverence for the new Church into the seventeenth century, merit more attention than has hitherto been given them. They were foremost in 'selling the Church', and their written testimonies illustrate their concerns. Lay support for the Church was a fundamental feature of the Church's success in the early Stuart period. Religious affiliation also revealed clear traces of nascent Puritanism. This was reflected in the preaching and published works of a small band of clergy and laymen who were dedicated to the Church as a state institution, but who also publicly revealed their own personal convictions. Puritan trends, which appeared among clergy and laity alike in the early seventeenth-century Church, served more to strengthen rather than weaken its very existence, for it gave it a body of opinion in print which enabled it to reinforce its defences down to the Civil War period. Ruthless though John Penry's violent comments were against an institution which he considered to be totally inadequate to 'save souls', they did serve to alert church leaders to the need to assume responsibility for an impoverished Church.

The attention given to scholars in the context of the Protestant settlement dwells principally on the reactions of humanist scholars to the progress of the new Protestant Church and to Roman Catholic opposition to it down to the eve of the Civil Wars. Emphasis is placed on information gleaned from original sources which reflect the opinions of eminent church leaders and lay scholars, of whom Richard Davies, Nicholas Robinson, Sir John Pryse, William Salesbury, Hugh Lewis, Maurice Kyffin, Gruffydd Robert and Dr John Davies (Siôn Dafydd Rhys) were doubtless the most prominent. Each of them is concerned with the condition of the Christian faith and its adherents in Wales. Consideration is given to the way in which these learned individuals viewed the quality of spiritual life and expressed their desires and plans for reform, and their zeal was maintained in the early decades of the seventeenth century when Protestant apologists, such as Rowland Vaughan, Robert Llwyd and Dr John Davies of Mallwyd, were actively engaged in advocating knowledge and understanding of the faith in their translations of standard English Protestant works. Their literary achievements displayed the methods adopted to consolidate the new religious order in an age when it was gradually but firmly being established. These exponents of Protestantism were aware of the need to bring the faith to the nation, to make it understood and accepted and to overcome the difficulties which prevented them from achieving their aims. By the eve of the Civil Wars the Church had laid solid foundations but was frustrated by problems of communication, which continued to hinder its progress before war and Puritan rule caused further confusions in religious life.

Bardic composition has been a valuable vehicle by means of which religious opinion has been exposed, dwelling as it often does on religious conservatism, change and adaptations in worshipping practices in isolated Welsh rural communities. Sources of this nature reveal the progress of the Protestant faith, and hindrances to its progress, and gauge the Roman Catholic responses to it. The content of bardic material also reveals the amount of support found among gentryfolk for the Elizabethan settlement and the nature of their firm allegiance to church and state subsequent to the Acts of Union. These sources are richly endowed with comment and reflection on the extent of the concerns and bewilderment in communities subject to religious change, and the degree of support for the Old Faith which persisted. They expose features of popular culture which thrived among an illiterate peasantry whose opinions were represented by free-metre bards who defended the old faith or promoted the new. Religious poetry was also composed by the professional strict-metre bards, principally through the agency of the popular *cywydd* metre. In addition to addressing religious themes, these exponents of the traditional bardic order saluted heads of families who adhered to either of the two faiths, and thereby expressed their own convictions. The latter decades of the sixteenth century, before and after the translation of the scriptures, together with the years down to the 1640s saw a flourishing period in the composition of strict-metre poems addressed to major Protestant leaders in the Welsh dioceses, which illustrated their most salient contributions to promoting the faith.

Although the Church was abolished as a state institution in the 1640s it is undeniable that its spirit survived among a predominantly royalist governing class in Wales who, at heart, resented the stringent religious impositions of the 1650s. Apart from the overwhelming support given to the monarchy in the 1630s and 1640s it is evident that literary work evoked a strong awareness of loyalty, such as the publications of Rowland Vaughan, John Owen (*Epigrammatist*), Edward James and Lewis Bayly.

The most significant factor which retarded the growth of Protestantism was the ignorance and illiteracy which continued to be widespread, particularly in rural communities, into the early Stuart period. Although the progress of the Church in the reigns of James I and Charles I down to the 1640s revealed a distinct adherence to its doctrine and showed that it had by then become more firmly entrenched in isolated Welsh communities, the problems created by poverty in deprived areas far from urban centres continued to cause apprehension among high-ranking clerics. However, the bonds which attached the ruling gentry to monarchy and the law and to their social inferiors also strengthened their affinities with the Protestant Church. These links also bound such leaders to the rule of a parliamentary monarchy, inseparable in their common interest, a phenomenon which, in the early seventeenth century, formed an alliance which had to be defended. The forces which bound together the monarchy, the gentry and the law were reinforced by religious considerations.

Thus the Elizabethan Church maintained its mission to regenerate spiritual life in the Welsh countryside. Although popular religion continued to impair the Church's objectives the institution was established by law and imposed stringent demands in the quest for uniformity. In England this led small dissenting groups to leave the Church and abandon conformity, thus pursuing their own modes of worship based on preaching the gospel and their own personal spiritual experiences. Social deprivation prevented Puritan tendencies from blooming in Wales before the 1630s but individual clerics who possessed preaching and literary skills did reveal more extreme traits. Puritan influences revealed themselves, not only in the literary output of a small number of clergy, some of them high-ranking, but also through the agency of 'feoffees for impropriation'. Tithes were bought up so that Puritan preachers could be installed in livings, particularly in and around market towns. It was an unsuccessful plan of campaign, revealing a nascent Puritanism which did not adversely affect the progress of the national Church which was in the process of consolidating its position.

Moreover, despite the shortcomings of the Church, attempts at reform continued. In this sphere the quality of the clergy should not be undermined because their educational standards generally were showing signs of improvement by the first half of the seventeenth century. They had been trained to conduct sacerdotal functions as well as to pursue pastoral duties and a small increase occurred in those who were prepared to reveal their thoughts in print. Their academic skills varied but, judging by the publications of a small group, their interests extended into the fields of history, antiquity and lexicography. Although material restrictions affected their commitment to their duties, particularly the effects of pluralism and non-residence, the parochial system remained intact and in many parishes local clergy functioned, giving the Church in the early decades of the seventeenth century a means of deepening its roots.

The pastoral role of bishops is central to the progress of the Stuart church in Wales. The early decades of the seventeenth century revealed how English and Welsh-born bishops, some with moderate Calvinist leanings, proceeded to defend and promote a Church dogged by past problems and persistent social and economic drawbacks. Despite the valiant efforts to place the Church on firm foundations, the policies aimed at restoring its properties and revenues were continually frustrated by lay and clerical impropriations and persistent papist threats. Situations arose which placed some bishops in perplexing situations. The career of Richard Parry at St Asaph, for example, revealed the difficulties which arose when attempts were made to recover tithes and properties which had long been impropriated by lay families and higher clergy. The poverty of the lower orders and the depressed illiteracy in Welsh communities were also factors which prevented the Church from achieving its full potential.

Progress in the Church was further initiated by episcopal visitations, the use of church courts and the drive to restore church livings and endowments and to give the preaching ministry a higher profile. Improved educational standards led to a better quality ministry and, in the 1630s, high-church Laudian policies proved to be more popular among bishops, higher clergy and even some heads of families than has generally been acknowledged. On the eve of the Civil Wars, the Church appeared to have secured for itself a more solid base than it had at the close of the previous century. Arminianism was supported by a small but significant number of clergy led by bishops such as John Owen, Morgan Owen and Roger Mainwaring, all of whom were specifically associated with imposing discipline. Theological differences between the Calvinist and Arminian prelates, however, caused very little stir in Wales, for the activities of early seventeenth century Welsh bishops were mainly directed towards the Puritan practices of preaching and religious instruction.

Of greater danger to the establishment of a vibrant Protestant ministry were Puritan methods of promoting the gospel initiated during the 1650s, the godly approach based on the inter-relationship between 'the magistrate and minister, the Word and the sword'. Such a programme gave the Protestant Reformation an added and deeply resented dimension, unacceptable to the rank and file in Welsh communities who were accustomed to less demanding religious practices.

Aspects of the religious fortunes of Puritan rule during the 1650s are abundantly revealed in local government records, principally those of quarter sessions, and in those of Caernarfonshire, the only county in Wales for which such records have survived in this period. Its records reflect attempts to puritanize one of the most conservative and isolated of Welsh regions. The small band of administrators eagerly sought to impose strict religious laws but encountered insuperable problems which sprang chiefly from social conditions and firm opposition among a people traditionally loyal to the monarchy and its institutions. Sources focus on the failure of Puritan authorities to achieve their aim, chiefly because of the lack of a preaching ministry, the arduous physical features of the terrain and the negative response of the general populace. All the pent-up frustrations of an unpopular regime are encapsulated in the short career of Major-General James Berry, the well-meaning military governor, who failed to make much headway when trying to impose a moral code and to appoint loyal and reliable officials.

The main weakness of the religious policies of the Cromwellian regime in Wales and England was the fact that its policies failed to have any meaningful impact at all levels of the social spectrum. It has been considered that 'the *Interregnum* completed the penetration of the English provinces by the Reformation'. To what extent the Puritan movement achieved any lasting success in traditionally royalist communities, it is difficult to tell, but evidence suggests that in most Welsh rural areas the full force of Puritanism was not felt and was almost non-existent because the peasantry failed 'to appreciate the requirements of godliness'. The policy of creating patterns of godly worship was followed by the emergence of Puritan sects, whose extremist views on religious practice and social standards hardly touched a credulous and ignorant peasantry.

Once the Church had been abolished they were forced to accept the religious whims of Puritan agencies who disregarded traditional ways of worship and social customs. After the Civil Wars Puritan governments reopened old wounds in such communities and they soured relationships between them and the central government, especially during the two years when the Major-Generals ruled Wales and England. The leaders of this regime were only able to affect a minority of zealots in the Welsh countryside, nor were the policies imposed as zealously in some remote and conservative areas as in others. Also the inadequacy of Puritan preachers, particularly those proficient in the Welsh language, hindered what success the mission might otherwise have achieved in the hinterland. The Puritan regime failed to reform communities traditionally attached to a way of life far removed from the sobriety and discipline which the new preachers and government agents and officials advocated. A rural population determined to continue its traditional practices and to cherish the Elizabethan state Church deeply resented a harsh and intrusive regime bent on changing lifestyles and promoting its own spiritual programme.

CHAPTER I

Prelates, Priests and the Concept of the 'Christian Magistracy', c.1559-1603

In his speech to the prebendaries of Llandaff in 1575-6 William Bleddyn, Bishop of the see, stated as follows when reprimanding them for the negligent manner in which they attended to their tasks:

> This is the labour, this the toil; since I have reached Sparta, may I, as much as I can, adorn it...For behold Elizabeth, our most gracious queen, will be at hand...and some most illustrious men, the best patrons of learning endued with every virtue..[1]

His letter was a stern warning to those in office to pay more diligent attention to their spiritual duties and responsibilities. The words reveal some of the major complexities and features of Elizabethan episcopacy in Wales, the frustrations which they suffered and the enormity of the task which confronted them. In the above words Bleddyn draws attention to his awareness of the weaknesses of the Church, his consciousness of his own duties within his diocese, his respect for Elizabeth I as head of the new church and a symbol of unity, his erudition and, most significantly, his belief that the reformed Church had to develop from within the existing institution.

The Reformation bishops were appointed as leaders of a Church fraught with problems, many of which they had inherited from their predecessors who had served their diocese, with varying success, in a period of religious turmoil and instability during the decades before Elizabeth's accession to the throne. She wished to establish a religious settlement which she could control through the agency of archishops and bishops. In Wales on her accession she was faced with Roman Catholic bishops, all of

---

[1]   J. Bradney, 'The speech of William Blethin, bishop of Llandaff, and the customs and ordinances of the church of Llandaff (1575)', *Y Cymmrodor*, XXXI, 1921, 257-8; J. G. Jones, 'The Reformation bishops of Llandaff, 1558-1601', *Morgannwg*, XXXII, 1988, 49-50. For a discussion of Bleddyn's motives see T. J. Prichard, 'The Reformation in the deanery of Llandaff, 1534-1609', *Morgannwg*, XIII, 1969, 28-30. The reference to Sparta in the above extract denotes a leading cultural and military state, the meaning here being that Llandaff is a citadel of ecclesiastical power.

whom, excepting the time-serving Anthony Kitchin at Llandaff, refused to subscribe to the Acts of Supremacy and Uniformity of 1559. The queen's power rested on what her father had accomplished in establishing a church based on statutory law. She was a 'governor' of the Church rather than its 'supreme head' and was thus essentially placed in a different position from her father. He had involved himself in episcopal matters and had assumed the position of the highest-ranking among ecclesiastical personnel. Elizabeth, on the other hand, chose to govern by means of archbishops and commissions. She denied being a 'lay pope' but regarded herself as a 'queen governor'. The papal power (*potestas jurisdictionis*) had been transferred to Henry VIII, which allowed him to govern the church in temporal affairs. The *potestas ordinis*, that is, the spiritual functions of the Pope, were never claimed since the king could not assume priestly powers. With Thomas Cromwell as his Vicar-General he took over episcopal rights but refused to exercise sacerdotal ones. Elizabeth assumed the same powers but transferred theological matters to church hierarchy. The *Ecclesia Anglicana* was in the making; the Thirty-Nine Articles, the bases of the Church's public teaching which omitted Zwinglian tendencies, were issued and were passed in Convocation in 1563, to become statute law in 1571. Now that the Pope had excommunicated the queen, it was the bishops' duty in their sees to enforce uniformity, as incorporated in the 1559 injunctions.[2]

One significant aspect of the role of the episcopacy was the extent to which it was able to uphold the royal supremacy in ecclesiastical affairs and the extent to which it demonstrated bishops' loyalty to the Elizabethan state. There are four broad spheres of episcopal activity which commanded attention, namely the enforcement of the new religious dispensation, combating Roman Catholicism, maintaining hospitality and discipline in the Church and performing pastoral duties. All four aspects reveal the formidable task which lay ahead of them in a period when enforcing the new settlement was no easy task, when loyalties to the 'old faith' persisted very strongly in many parts of the country and when the condition of the clergy left much to be desired and their activities needed constant supervision. These major responsibilities taxed the Welsh

---

2   St. 13 Eliz. I c.12. *Statutes of the Realm*, IV (Pt. i), 1547-1585 (London, repr., 1963), pp.546-7. For background see C. Cross, *Church and People, 1450-1660* (London, 1987 ed.), pp.124-33; G. Williams, *Wales and the Reformation* (Cardiff, 1997), pp.216-25.

bishops to the full. Despite some unfortunate misgivings, as a group of first generation Protestant bishops they were remarkably active, eager to promote the faith and reform the clergy. But the Welsh dioceses were among the most impoverished in the realm, and to reform the church to the level expected was seen by them to be a daunting task.[3]

During the Elizabethan era sixteen bishops were appointed in Wales, eleven of whom were of Welsh birth and closely associated with the local communities which they served. This situation was in sharp contrast to previous generations when, in the period c.1500-1558, for example, only seven Welsh-born bishops were appointed, some of them for short periods. The quality of the majority of Elizabethan bishops was altogether impressive. Nine of them were educated at Oxford and the other seven were products of Cambridge. Some were educated at both institutions and eight of them held doctorates of divinity. Of these bishops eight also held livings in Wales prior to their elevation, but not all were resident. The majority had close links with Welsh scholarship and learning and a proportion were fervent patrons of the professional bards. The English-born bishops, namely Hugh Bellot of Bangor, a Cheshire man, Gervase Babington (Llandaff), Francis Godwin (Llandaff), Marmaduke Middleton (St David's) and Anthony Rudd (St David's) were themselves no mean scholars, Godwin, for example, being a notable antiquary and a reformer of his clergy. The scholastic interests of Richard Davies (St David's), Nicholas Robinson (Bangor) and William Morgan (Llandaff/St Asaph) are well-known and well-documented, Davies being among the most ardent of Protestant propagandists and a translator of parts of the scriptures.[4]

---

3   G. Williams, 'Landlords in Wales: the Church', in J. Thirsk (ed.), *The Agrarian History of England and Wales* (Cambridge, 1967), pp.381-93. For individual dioceses in Wales see J. G. Jones, 'The Reformation bishops of St Asaph', *JWEH*, VII, 1990, 17-40; idem, 'The Reformation bishops of Llandaff'', *Morgannwg*, XXXII, 1988, 38-69; R. Houlbrooke, 'The Protestant episcopate 1547-1603: the pastoral contribution', in F. Heal & R. O'Day (eds.), *Church and State in England Henry VIII to James I* (Basingstoke, 1977), 78-98.

4   For studies of individual bishops see G. Williams, 'Richard Davies, bishop of St David's', in *Welsh Reformation Essays* (Cardiff, 1967), pp.155-90; A. O. Evans, 'Nicholas Robinson (1530-1585)', *Y Cymmrodor*, XXXIX, 1928, 149-98. Much has been published on William Morgan in recent years, such as R. G. Gruffydd, *The translating of the Bible into the Welsh tongue by William Morgan in 1588* (London, 1988); I. Thomas, *William Morgan and his Bible* (Cardiff, 1988); G. Williams, 'Bishop William Morgan (1545-1604) and the first Welsh Bible', in *The Welsh and their Religion* (Cardiff, 1991), pp.173-229.

The educational achievements of the bishops, their experience as priests and their skills as preachers made them men of some standing in their community. What they achieved in terms of their service to the Protestant cause is altogether admirable despite the limitations placed on their activities. In that context their role in Welsh society as a corporate entity needs to be reassessed in view of the complexity in which the new Church found itself in an age in which discipline, order and quality of leadership had become crucial features of ecclesiastical life. Each bishop in turn referred constantly to the weak constitution of the church and the poor educational standards of their clergy in their respective dioceses. This was clearly manifested in Richard Davies's introduction to his survey of the diocese of St Asaph during his short stay there. The picture he gave was not encouraging for only ten among a hundred priests in the diocese had been ordained. Eighteen were absentee, seven of them residing in other livings in the diocese. The hospitality offered was rare, preachers were scarce – five in all – and the educational quality of the clergy in general left much to be desired.[5]

The average age of Welsh bishops in the year when they came to their sees was about 47 years which was similar to most of their English colleagues. Nicholas Robinson of Bangor came from mixed English and Welsh stock in Conwy but the majority were of Welsh parentage and came chiefly from native areas well-known for their strong cultural links, such as the Llŷn peninsula and the Conwy valley and surrounding districts, all of which were heartlands of the Welsh language. Richard Vaughan and Henry Rowlands were natives of Llŷn, Richard Davies, Thomas Davies, William Hughes and William Morgan came from the Conwy valley, and Thomas Young and William Bleddyn were born to Welsh-speaking parents in Pembrokeshire and Shirenewton, Gwent, respectively. Almost all of them patronized the Welsh bards, some of them, particularly Richard Davies, William Morgan and William Hughes, being most supportive and highly-praised by the most eminent among them who considered ecclesiastical dignitaries to be worthy of the highest adulation.

The prestige accorded to Reformation bishops through their close native connections was increased by means of wider sources of external patronage. Bishop Nicholas Robinson of Bangor, for example, was

---

[5]   D. R. Thomas, *The Life and Work of Bishop Davies & William Salesbury* (Oswestry, 1892), p.15.

supported by Sir William Cecil. He was described as 'an excellent scholar' and able *extempore* preacher who was given praise by Sir John Wynn of Gwydir for translating, at the request of his father Morus Wynn, a Welsh version of the *Historia Gruffyd vab Kenan* into Latin.[6] On the other hand, Thomas Young, after a short stay at St David's, was recommended for the archbishopric of York by Matthew Parker and moved there in 1561, and William Hughes of St Asaph served as chaplain to Thomas Howard, 4th duke of Norfolk. Some Welsh bishops, such as Henry Rowlands of Bangor, William Hughes and Nicholas Robinson, married English women. To make both ends meet they acquired lands *in commendam* but also obtained some substantial preferments. If Sir John Wynn of Gwydir's *Memoirs* are to be relied upon three Welsh bishops died in an impoverished state, namely Richard Davies, Richard Vaughan and William Morgan, while Robinson and Rowlands at Bangor left this life in comfortable circumstances.[7] Despite their limitations Elizabethan bishops in Wales, with regard to their connections and depth and breadth of their scholarly attainment, matched several English bishops, particularly in the northern dioceses of England.

Episcopal endeavours to advance the Protestant faith in their respective sees were characterized by an intense zeal. Even William Hughes and Marmaduke Middleton, allegedly the two most disreputable prelates in Wales during the latter half of the sixteenth century, had some redeeming features, one being an erudite scholar who supplied William Morgan with books when translating the scriptures, and the other, before his actions at St David's caused many grievances and opposition to him, ardently informing Sir Francis Walsingham in 1583 about the state of his diocese, emphasizing its 'spiritual destitution' and his desire to maintain the Church's integrity.[8] It was an age when prelates were transferred to English dioceses, but whether they prospered materially as a consequence is questionable. A case in point is Richard Vaughan who, after having held the canonry of St Paul's and archdeaconry of Middlesex, was installed bishop of Bangor before moving to Chester and then London within the

---

6   J. Wynn, *History of the Gwydir Family and Memoirs*, ed. J. G. Jones (Llandysul, 1990), pp.1. 60, 78-9.
7   Ibid., pp.59-63.
8   *Cal. State Papers Dom.*, 1581-1590, CLXII, no.29, p.119; W. P. M. Kennedy, *Elizabethan Episcopal Administration*, 3 vols. (Alcuin Club, 1929), II, 145 et seq.

space of nine years. Even within Wales bishops obtained ample experience of ecclesiastical administration well before they were elevated. Rowland Meyrick, a scion of a prominent Anglesey family, for example, was appointed Principal of New Inn Hall, Oxford (1534-6), and canon and chancellor of St David's (1550) before being deprived in Mary's reign, and subsequently becoming bishop of Bangor.

Doubtless the tenure of bishops in their respective dioceses varied according to circumstances. The average number of years of service in a Welsh see was twelve, which was a sufficient length of time for a bishop to get to grips with basic problems and responsibilities. While some resided and continued to function in one diocese over a longer period than was normal, such as William Hughes (27 years at St Asaph), Richard Davies and Anthony Rudd (20 years and 21 years respectively at St David's), Nicholas Robinson (19 years at Bangor) and Henry Rowlands (18 years in the same see), there were other bishops who were installed in their first dioceses for incredibly short periods, such as Richard Davies at St Asaph (fifteen months), Gervase Babington (4 years at Llandaff), Richard Vaughan (one year at Bangor) and Thomas Young (again one year at St David's). Episcopal accomplishments in such situations were shortlived and based essentially on the prelate's skill in applying himself to the relevant tasks at hand. At St Asaph, for example, Richard Davies revealed his earnest desire to inform Parker of the state of the church and clergy in his diocese within a few months of his arrival.[9]

Taken all in all Welsh Elizabethan bishops, excepting the refractory Marmaduke Middleton and, to a lesser extent, William Hughes, formed a dedicated group whose zeal, however, was probably greater than their achievement. Doubtless their episcopal skills varied: for example, Thomas Davies of St Asaph was primarily a church lawyer, having become a Doctor of Laws who was eager to establish secure administrative foundations for the new Elizabethan settlement in his diocese.[10] William Morgan, on the other hand, humble and devoted to Biblical scholarship though he was, was often aggressive in his determination to maintain the integrity of the Church against the ambitions of arrogant laymen bent on

---

[9]   Browne Willis, *A Survey of the Cathedral Church of St Asaph* (London, 1720), pp.251-64.
[10] J. G. Jones, 'Thomas Davies and William Hughes: two Reformation bishops of St Asaph', *BBCS*, XXIX, 1981, 320-25.

promoting their ambitions and acquiring church tithes and livings.[11] Whatever their approach to the vital problems of the church in their day, Welsh bishops sincerely applied themselves to the task of promoting the Protestant faith, and so did many of the laity.

Like Elizabethan archbishops and bishops, leaders of the Church in Wales considered that propaganda was of the utmost importance in extending the Protestant faith. In England, Foxe's *Book of Martyrs* and Jewel's *An Apologie...in defence of the Churche of Englande* (1562) are worthy examples of such a campaign.[12] As John Strype has shown, the press was an essential part of the propaganda machine and, in Wales, emphasis was placed on the Protestant Church theory and the restoration of the apostolic church as the correspondence of Richard Davies of St David's and William Salesbury with Matthew Parker amply revealed.[13]

It is difficult to assess whether constant attempts to maintain a life-style befitting the chief ecclesiastical dignitary in the diocese detracted from bishops' more worthy pursuits. Parker believed that the higher clergy should adopt a standard of living equal to their status. In his letter to Sir William Cecil, himself a propagandist, deploring the pluralist activities of William Hughes at St Asaph, he considered that the bishop's unseemly conduct was better than if

> the order of godly mynisters...shuld be brought to contempt, for lacke of reasonable necessaryes...the worlde loketh for post agreable, and wise...men thinke ther is done already Inough toward that state, for brynging sup'fluytie to moderation etc.[14]

---

11 Idem, 'Bishop William Morgan's dispute with John Wynn of Gwydir, 1603-04', *JHSCW*, XXII, 1972, 49-64; idem, 'Bishop William Morgan – defender of church and faith', *JWEH*, V, 1988, 20-30.

12 W. Haller, *Foxe's Book of Martyrs and the Elect Nation* (London, 1963); J. E. Booty, *John Jewel as Apologist of the Church of England* (London, 1963); V. C. Sanders, 'Elizabethan Archbishops of Canterbury and Public Opinion' (unpublished University of Wales M. A. dissertation, 1979).

13 J. Bruce and T. T. Perowne (eds.), *Correspondence of Matthew Parker* (Parker Society, Cambridge, 1853), pp.327-8; D. M. Lloyd, 'William Salesbury, Richard Davies and Archbishop Parker', *NLWJ*, II, 1941, 7-8; G. Williams, 'Bishop Sulien, Bishop Richard Davies, and Archbishop Parker', ibid., V, 1948, 215-9; idem, *Reformation Views of Church History* (Ecumenical Studies in History, no. 11, London, 1970); R. Flower, 'William Salesbury, Richard Davies and Archbishop Parker', *NLWJ*, II, 1941, 7-14.

14 *Parker Correspondence*, pp.207-8.

His reference to 'post agreable' or seemly carriage is underlined:

> I never heard or read, but that al maners of princes...did evermore cherish their ecclesiastical state, as conservators of religion, by...which...people be most strongly knit together in amity, their hearts...won to God; their obediences holden under their governors.[15]

The main source of propaganda was the pulpit, which reached people of all levels in all places. The prelate's image was central and it is evident that each of the Elizabethan prelates had qualities which, in different ways, served to promote the faith. Their strength lay partly in their close attachment to their dioceses and their scholastic achievements and partly in their endeavour to improve the quality of their clergy. In his brief surveys of the north Wales bishops in his *Memoirs* Sir John Wynn of Gwydir was, for the most part, exceedingly complimentary. He regarded his friend Henry Rowlands of Bangor as 'a good and provident governor of his Church and diocese, a great repairer of his decayed cathedral church, and...in houskeeping and hospitality, both to rich and poor, the greatest that has been in our time'.[16] Although his comments on William Glynn, Nicholas Robinson, Richard Vaughan and Richard Davies were equally favourable, doubtless the squire of Gwydir considered Rowlands to be the most praiseworthy.

With notable exceptions the role of bishops was overtly displayed more in their relations with their clergy than in their administrative skills or scholastic achievements. After all, in their sees and, in particular, in the task of offering guidance to parish priests they were expected to maintain and increase the momentum of religious change. They were expected to be the driving force establishing the Church on in-built features which served to consolidate the new settlement. The quality of the lower clergy evidently varied within dioceses. Doubtless the most impoverished were in dire straits and their stipends hardly rose above £5 a year. The Welsh dioceses were themselves materially among the poorest in the kingdom.[17]

---

[15] J. Strype, *The Life and Acts of Matthew Parker* (London, 1711), pp.50-2; *Parker Correspondence*, pp.148,158.

[16] J. Wynn, *Hist. of the Gwydir Family and Memoirs*, p.59; Browne Willis, *A Survey of the Cathedral Church of Bangor* (London, 1721), p.110.

[17] G. Williams, 'Landlords in Wales: the Church', pp.81-93. See also C. Hill, *Economic Problems of the Church from Archbishop Whitgift to the Long Parliament* (Oxford, 1956), pp.14-38, 194-244.

This was made abundantly clear in the letter written by Richard Pryse of Brecon, son of Sir John Pryse, to Lord Burghley when he referred to the many impropriate livings in Wales, implying that they caused hardship to the clergy as well as depriving parishioners of religious instruction. Many churches and their properties, he declared, were impropriate and only a few livings were available to maintain curates, excepting those 'as please the proprietaries and their farmers to give, which commonly will give as little as they can'.[18]

Pryse's words reflect the inability of the Church to meet the requirements of its preaching ministry, thus drawing attention to the prime weakness of the institution:

> ...And therfore it is no mervell that they are very injurious one to another, and live in contempt both of the Lawes of God and man...But this lack of good Teachers doth partly growe by reason the Churches are (in manner) all impropriate...unlesse the foresaid enormities and exactions be spedely redressed, as the people are allready greatly disquieted and impoverished therby, so they will shortly be alltogeather unable to yeld the Prince anie Subsidie worthe the levieng, or to serve her Majesty but with their bare bodies. [19]

Pryse wrote at a time of economic insecurity declaring that if the Church was not reformed then civil disobedience in Wales would be rife. In part, he is of the opinion that the spiritual condition of the country was largely responsible for its material impoverishment.

The Elizabethan era saw financial inflation reach its peak, which made it increasingly difficult for Welsh bishops to maintain a reasonably high standard of living. What they accumulated in income was not commensurate with that enjoyed by their counterparts in English sees and thus the benefits derived from that income were very limited. It is hardly surprising that pluralism increased as a consequence and the quality of clerical life deteriorated and, where the entire fabric of church buildings was neglected, ruin set in. While impoverished curates suffered from

---

[18] *Original Letters Illustrative of English History*, ed. H. Ellis, III (2nd Ser., London, 1827), p.44.
[19] Ibid., p.47.

impropriation and inflationary processes the impropriator benefited from increased prices.

Not only were the clergy ill-endowed, the bishops and other diocesan officers also found themselves at a low income level, hence the increase in livings held by them *in commendam*. William Hughes of St Asaph was considered to be the most notorious among his colleagues in this respect. Besides obtaining the archdeaconry of St Asaph he held *in commendam* several others, making a total of sixteen, admittedly at various times. The archdeaconry was regarded as his preserve together with other livings to the value of £150, but there is no doubt that he reaped many other benefits during his tenure of office.[20] Although St Asaph, according to the *Valor Ecclesiasticus* (1535), was judged to be the second wealthiest Welsh diocese it was still worth less than half the poorest English sees. In fairness to Hughes, of the livings he held, only two, namely Llysfaen and Castell Caereinion, were his throughout his long episcopacy. In addition to the archdeaconry Archbishop Parker gave his predecessor, Thomas Davies, the chancellorship of Bangor, as Strype maintained, 'for the better keeping up the part of a bishop'. And he continued:

> And though he [i.e.Parker] did not like of Commendams nor Pluralities, yet in small Bishopricks and Preferments, he thought them a less inconvenience, than that Hospitality and the Credit and Esteem of the clergy should be lost.[21]

There were many other examples of such acquisitions; the archdeacon of Bangor impropriated the livings of Caerhun, Llandygái, Llannor and Deneio in 1603 and the archdeacon of Merioneth acquired Llandudno. The dean of Bangor held Y Gyffin, and Christ's College, Ruthin, kept its hold on Ruthin parish and its chapel at Llanrhudd.[22] Doubtless impropriators reduced the income of parochial clergy, a common problem which persisted in the four dioceses. Marmaduke Middleton, simonist and pluralist though he was, took a poor view of his clergy's and his own

---

[20] D. R. Thomas, *A History of the Diocese of St Asaph*, 3 vols., I (Oswestry, 1908), pp.99-100; 'Reformation bishops of St Asaph', 31-5; J. Strype, *Annals of the Reformation*, II (London, 1725), 293-4; III (1728), p.467 (see also vol. II, app. xxxii, pp.62-4).
[21] J. Strype, *The Life and Acts of Matthew Parker*, pp.147-8.
[22] M. Gray, 'The diocese of Bangor in the late 16th century', *JWEH*, V, 1988, 36.

circumstances in a report in 1583: 'Very few sufficient men', he declared, 'occupied the indigent benefices and the people were greatly infected (by want of preaching) with atheism and wonderfully given over to vicious life'.[23] Hugh Lewis, the outspoken vicar of Llanddeiniolen, in a well-known passage in his preface to *Perl mewn Adfyd* (1595) – his translation of Miles Coverdale's *A Spyrytuall and most Precious Pearle* – made drastic comments on the condition of religion in his country.[24] The title-page to Coverdale's translation illustrates the deeply spiritual purpose of the work, concentrating on the centrality of the Cross in man's experience and the manner in which it fortifies the soul in adverse personal circumstances. The work, it is said, aims to teach

> all men to loue and imbrace the crosse, as a moost swete and necessary thyng, vnto the sowle, and what comfort is to be taken thereof, and also where and howe, both consolacyon and ayde in all maner of afflyccyons is to be soughte, and agayne, how all men should behaue them selues therein, accordynge to the word of God...[25]

The praise accorded to Otto Werdmüller's work is rehearsed in Edward, duke of Somerset's preface to the 'Christian reader' in which he declared that God's Word is the only cure for man's afflictions:

> This man, whosoeuer he be, that was the first author of this boke goeth the right way to worke: he bryngeth hys grounde fro(m) gods worde: he taketh w(i)t(h) hym the oyle and wyne of the Samaritane: he caryeth the hurt man from the(n)ce where he lay hurt, and bri(n)geth him to hys ryght host, where no dout he may be cured, if he will aplye hymselfe therto.[26]

In addition to attending to the soul's needs Lewis, in his own preface, adds his own purpose and draws attention to the serious needs of the Welsh people and of the Church which served them. When referring to the lack of learning in the Welsh language, principally because the printing press had hardly made an impact, he stated:

---

23 *Cal. State Papers Dom.*, 1581-1590, CLXII, no. 29, p.119.
24 *Rhagymadroddion*, p.100.
25 O. Werdmüller, *A spyrytuall and moost precyouse pearle*, trans. M. Coverdale (London, 1550), title-page.
26 Ibid., preface.

Hynn yw yr achos pam y tyfodd cymeint o chwynn, gwyg, ac efrae, yngwenithfaes yr Arglwydd, sef cymeint o draddodiadae, a dynawl ddychmygion a gosodigaethae yn yr Eglwys, yn gymyscedic a gwir, ac a phurlan air duw.[27]

[This is the reason why so many weeds, debris and tares grew in the Lord's wheatfield, namely so many traditions and human imaginations and ordinances of the Church, mixed with the true, pure and holy word of god.]

This lack of learning and the apathy and ignorance of the clergy, in Lewis's view, retarded the progress of the new faith. He was earnestly committed to promoting Protestantism even to the point of exposing weaknesses in the Christian ministry, and doubting the ability of the clergy to amend the situation.

But why did Lewis, himself a staunch Protestant priest, proceed to censure most of the Welsh bishops and clergy and what would he hope to gain from it? His main objective was not only to publicise the need to improve morals amongst the Welsh people but also to reveal why that task was really necessary. He was an Oxford graduate and aware of the need for reform at parish level if the new faith was to be well-rooted.

Who else would constitute the readership of *Perl mewn Adfyd*; apart from a small band of dedicated clergy and some gentry, it is difficult to say but, in the interests of improved religious standards, Lewis was certainly not the cleric to withhold any criticism of his colleagues in the church if he considered it justified. His comments are primarily focused on a dissolute priesthood whose position was not improved by the dire lack of preaching and religious works published in the Welsh language. His attitude, in fact, echoes that expressed by Sir John Pryse which indicated, in a shorter preamble, that all was not well in the Church. There was opposition to it among ardent Roman Catholics, principally among a small group of gentry and bards, such as Siôn Brwynog and 'Sir' Owain ap Gwilym (Tal-y-llyn), Llywelyn Siôn (Llangewydd) and the curate Thomas ap Ieuan ap Rhys of Hendreforfudd, Merioneth.[28] A more fundamental

---

27   *Rhagymadroddion*, p.101.
28   NLW Cwrtmawr MS.238.37; C. W. Lewis, 'The literary history of Glamorgan from 1550 to 1770', in *Glamorgan County History*, IV, *Early Modern Glamorgan*, ed. G. Williams (Cardiff, 1974), p.567; D. G. Williams, 'Syr Owain ap Gwilym', *LlC*, VI, 1961, 182; L. J. Hopkin-James and T. C. Evans (eds.), *Hen Gwndidau, Carolau a Chywyddau*, (Bangor, 1918), pp.1-44.

weakness, however, was the unavailability of the scriptures among the people even after the translation of the Bible in 1588. Remarkable though that achievement was, Lewis maintained, unless the Bible was used among the people on a daily basis then Morgan's translation fell short of what might have been achieved:

> Ac er bod y Beibl, yrawrhon yn ddiweddar, wedi i gyfieuthu, ai droi i'r Gambraeg, drwy boen a dyfal ddiwydrwydd, y gwir ardderchawg, ddyscedicaf Wr, D. Morgan... eto, drwy fod hwn, mal y mae gweddaidd, a chymwys, yn gloedic yn yr Eglwysi, lle nid oes cyrchfa atto namyn vnwaith yn yr wythnos...mae llaweroedd yn ymddifaid o gyngor, yn amser i ymweliad, ac heb wybod pa wedd y mae ynddynt i ymddwyn ei hunain, yn ei hadfyd, ai cledi.[29]

[And although the Bible, now lately, has been translated and turned into Welsh, by means of labour and persistent diligence of the truly excellent and learned man Dr Morgan...again, since this is, as it is seemly and appropriate, locked in the churches where there is no means of getting to it except once in the week...many are deprived of advice in the time of its appearance, and not knowing how they should conduct themselves, in their adversity and affliction.]

From another perspective and in a more bitter mood, the prolific Roman Catholic writer and missionary, Robert Gwyn of Penyberth, Llŷn, vindictively compared his fellow-Welshmen – rich and poor alike – to animals because of their ignorance of the tenets of the Old Faith:

> ...ond yr owron myfi a glywa fod aml leoedd ynGhymbry, ie Siroedd cyfan heb vn Cristiawn ynddynt, yn byw mal anifeilieid, y rhann fwyaf o honynt...yn dala henw Crist yn ei cof, heb wybod haychen beth yw Crist mwy nag anifeilieid.[30]

[Now I hear that many places in Wales, yes that whole counties have no Christians in them, living like animals, the majority keeping the name of Christ in mind, but without knowing even who Christ is more than animals.]

A grossly unfair judgement perhaps but one which does, however,

---

29 *Rhagymadroddion*, p.100.
30 Ibid., p.52; G. Bowen, 'Roman Catholic prose and its background', in R. G. Gruffydd (ed.), *A Guide to Welsh Literature, c.1530-1700* (Cardiff,1997), pp.222-9.

question the degree to which the ecclesiastical hierarchy had succeeded in improving the spiritual life of ordinary parishioners in Wales. It is evident that Thomas Davies at St Asaph had made a valiant effort very early on in his tenure in 1561 when he ordered that 'after the pistyll and Gospell in Englyshe, the same should be read also in Welshe', that children in the diocese should be educated and that clergy who had not graduated as Masters of Arts should have the New Testament in Latin and English with a paraphrase of Erasmus's comments on it. Moreover, he abolished all relics and superstitions ('fayned reliques and other superstycyons') and assigned the stipend of the office of 'Lady-Prest' to a schoolmaster 'whereby idleness of yowth may be avoyded and the same kept to learning, and browght upp in love and fear of God and knowledge of ther dewties towerd the worlde'. Davies also signed the Thirty-Nine Articles and the bishops' letter to the queen urging her to see that the House of Lords agreed to them as soon as possible.[31] Owing to the lack of a Welsh Bible, that was an effort on his part to use what resources were available to improve spiritual standards, using Sir John Pryse's primer *Yny lhyvyr hwnn...*(1546) and Salesbury's *Kynniver llith a ban* (1551). In fact, he attempted to do much that would improve the quality of his clergy as well, and Nicholas Robinson, who was reluctant to condemn his parishioners outright, was nevertheless obliged, in his letter to Sir William Cecil in 1567, to admit 'that ignorance continueth, many in ye dregs of superstition, which did grow chiefly upon ye blindness of ye clergy', adding that 'the most part of ye priests are too old' and unable 'to teach God's word'.[32] The scarcity of preachers in the church accentuated his problem since a powerful preaching ministry was central to the advance of the Protestant faith. It all had a knock-on effect on the depressed poor for they remained tied to their superstitious practices. Such is the evidence of an anonymously written and undated document reflecting on the religious condition of North Wales. The evidence it evokes is unequivocal:

> Trewlie at this daie yf you loke throwlie to the whole number of gents and others of all sortes in North Wales ye shall scarcelie find anie (the Byshops and some fewe others exepted) yet in anie sorte well instructed

31 *Diocese of St Asaph*, I, pp.89-90..
32 D. Mathew, 'Some Elizabethan documents', *BBCS*, VI, 1931, 78.

in the faithe of Christe...Yf the enemies of God and trewe religion shall ever endevor the disquiett of the setled state, they are in policie to practise the same where ignorance moste aboundeth, and where the gospell hath bine leaste preached, w'ch suerlie is in Wales.[33]

This is a depressing picture of conditions which were all too familiar to the Welsh bishops who found it difficult to get at the roots of the problem and who wished that there might be an easier solution than merely waiting for more advantageous conditions to enhance their mission.

Several other Elizabethan bishops also complained about the lack of preachers. Only five resident preachers – the *'concionatores evangelici'*, as Richard Davies called them – functioned in the diocese of St Asaph in 1560, namely Hugh Evans, dean of St Asaph, Chancellor John Price, Thomas Jenkins, rector of Newtown, Gruffydd Lloyd, rector of Llanfyllin (*'residens et hospitalis'*) and David Lloyd, rector of Llangwm-Dinmael.[34] There were ten (including the bishop) at St David's in 1570 and only fourteen in Middleton's time in 1583.[35] Anthony Kitchin reported in 1563 that only four clergy were licensed and resident at Llandaff, one of whom was William Bleddyn,[36] and Hugh Jones, Kitchin's successor, confirmed it, adding that he had occasionally paid out of his own pocket for preachers from neighbouring dioceses.[37] In 1576 Bleddyn, who was then bishop, admitted that of the thirteen resident chapter preachers available only five were graduates.[38] At Bangor in 1567, according to Robinson's testimony, there were only six, which increased the 'inhabilitie to teache gods worde'.[39] One reason for the initiative taken by Edward James, vicar of

---

[33]   BL Lansdowne Collection 111 f.10. E. Owen (ed.), *A Catalogue of the Manuscripts relating to Wales in the British Museum*, 4 vols. (London, 1900), I, 72(d).

[34]   Browne Willis, *A Survey of the Cathedral Church of St Asaph* (London, 1721), p.102; D. R. Thomas, *Diocese of St Asaph*, I, pp.252, 540; II, pp.165, 233.

[35]   D. R. Thomas, *Life and Work of Davies & Salesbury*, p.38; *Cal. State Papers Dom.*, 1581-1590, CI XII, no. 29, p.119;

[36]   J. D. Evans, 'Kitchin's return (1563)', *Gwent Local History*, LXVII, 1989, 11-18.

[37]   *Cal. State Papers Dom.*, 1547-1580, LXVI, no. 29, p.362; L. Thomas, *The Reformation in the Old Diocese of Llandaff* (Cardiff, 1930), p.128; J. G. Jones, 'Reformation bishops of Llandaff, 1558-1601', 45.

[38]   W. P.Griffith, *Learning, Law and Religion: Higher Education and Welsh Society, c.1540-1640* (Cardiff, 1996), p.314; G. Williams, *Wales and the Reformation*, pp.301-2. The preachers were Lewis Baker, William Evans, Robert Johnes, John Evans and Andrew Vayne.

[39]   *Cal. State Papers Dom.*, 1547-1580, XLIV, no. 27, p.301; D. Mathew, 'Some Elizabethan documents', 78.

Cadoxton-iuxta-Neath and chancellor of Llandaff, when translating the homilies into Welsh in 1606 was to make up for the lack of preachers:

> Fal y galle y rhai ni chlywant lafar pregethwyr ond yn ambell, wrth arfer o glywed darllen y pregethau duwiol dyscedic hyn yn fynych, ddyscu mewn amser gredu yn Nuw yn inion ac yn ffyddlon...am fod pregethwyr mor ambell ynddi, ni ewyllysiodd Duw ini gael neb o'r Homiliau hyn na'r fath eraill yn y iaith Gymeraeg hyd yr amser hyn.[40]

[so that those who hear not but occasionally the voice of preachers, by being accustomed to hearing the reading of every godly learned sermons often, learn in time to believe directly and faithfully in God...because preachers are so scarce it was not God's will that we should be deprived of these Homilies in the Welsh language to this time.]

Edward James was concerned with enrooting the chief points of faith among the Welsh people so that priests who, by reading the homilies, preach true doctrine. In the preface to the Homilies he declared:

> ... yn y rhai y cynhwysir y prif byngciau o'n ffydd ni ac o'n dlyed tu âg at Dduw a'n cymydogion; fel y gallai'r offeiriaid a'r curadiaid annyscedig, y rhai ni fedrent yn amgen etto wrth adrodd datcan a darllen yr homiliau hyn, bregethu i'w pobl wir athrawaeth, ac fel y galle bawb o'r bobl, wrth wrando, ddyscu'n inion ac yn iawn anrhydeddu ac addoli'r holl-alluog Dduw a'i wasanaethu'n ddiwyd.[41]

[within which is contained the chief tenets of our faith and our debt to God and our neighbours; so that the uneducated priests and curates, those who cannot yet, by reciting, declaring and reading these homilies, preach the true doctrine to the people, and so that all the people, by listening, learn exactly and very honourably and worship the almighty God and serve him diligently.]

Richard Pryse's strictures on the lack of preachers in Wales, like those of John Penry, rang true, to a point, but it needs to be emphasized that

---

[40] E. James, *Llyfr yr Homilïau: Pregethau a osodwyd allan trwy awdurdod i'w darllein ymhob Eglwys blwyf a phob capel er adailadaeth i'r bobl annyscedig* (London, 1606), [A2v]; G. Williams, 'Edward James a Llyfr yr Homilïau', in *Grym Tafodau Tân: Ysgrifau Hanesyddol ar Grefydd a Diwylliant yng Nghymru* (Llandysul, 1984), pp.180-95.

[41] E. James, *Llyfr yr Homilïau*, [A2v].

graduate preachers, where they were licensed, were not the only ones who extended knowledge of the gospel for there were many others, unlicensed though they may have been, who left a deep impact on simple parishioners, namely ministers who catechized and exhorted privately although they lacked 'the guifte of utterance, and audacitie to preach in the Pulpitt'.[42] This is a significant point since there were priests who, although they were not given the attention they deserved, devoted their time and energy to advancing the faith. For example, Thomas Powell, rector of Llanfechain (1562-90) and archdeacon of St Asaph (1566-73), and Hugh Evans, the long-serving dean of St Asaph (1560-87), both resident preachers, were also scholars in their own right.[43] Reference is made to the rector of Llanfechain in that remarkable document 'A Discoverie of the Present Estate of the Byshoppricke of St Asaph' (1587) which, in addition to making scurrilous attacks on Bishop William Hughes's outrageous practices in the diocese, also referred to the residence and hospitality provided by the few, namely Dr David Powel, scholar and antiquary and vicar of Meifod, Dr William Morgan, vicar of Llanrhaeadr-ym-Mochnant, and 'the parson of Llanfechain, an aged man about lxxx years old'.[44]

The 'Discovery' is a valuable document. Not only does it reflect conditions in the diocese of St Asaph in the middle years of Elizabeth's reign but also gives specific examples of its mismanagement by the bishop. 'Great housekeepers', it was reported, 'there no longer be'. Thomas Banks, dean of St Asaph, it was reported further, 'never kept house in all his life and is an unfit man for that place and calling, in all respects'.[45] The vicar of Cwm in the deanery, 'boardeth in the ale-house' and hospitality and charity generally had ended.[46] William Hughes was censured for

---

42   M. Gray, 'Diocese of Bangor', 38.
43   D. R. Thomas, *Diocese of St Asaph*, I, pp.248, 320; II, p.225; Browne Willis, *Survey of St Asaph*, p.103, 111.
44   J. Strype, *Annals of the Reformation*, III, p.467 (app., pp.184-6); 'Discoverie...', 53-8: 'There is nev'r a preacher within the diocese (the L. B. only excepted) that keepeth ordinarie residence and hospitalitie upon his lyving but Dr Powell and Dr Morgan and the p'son of llanvechen, an aged man about lxxx yeres old.'. 'A Discoverie of the Present Estate of the Byshoppricke of St Asaph', AC, I (5th ser.), 1884, 56, which adds Dr David Powel of Ruabon and Dr William Morgan of Llanrhaeadr-ym-Mochnant.
45   J. G. Jones, 'The Reformation bishops of St Asaph', 33; D. R. Thomas, *Diocese of St Asaph*, I, p.300; Browne Willis, *Survey of St Asaph*, p.171; E. Roberts (ed.), *Gwaith Siôn Tudur*, (Cardiff, 1978), I, CXXVI, pp.494-6.
46   J. G. Jones, 'The Reformation bishops of St Asaph', loc. cit.; J. Strype, *Annals*, II, pp.293-4; III, App., pp.184-6; F. O. White, *Lives of the Elizabethan Bishops* (London, 1898), pp.196-8.

practising usury 'which thing is a scandal to his profession and an ill example of usury to the laity', for being a misappropriator of ecclesiastical funds, for being an indifferent persecutor of Roman Catholic recusants and for reputedly fleecing rather than feeding his flock.[47] This lengthy assessment is now considered to be harsher than just. Whatever his shortcomings, William Hughes was a reputable scholar who assisted William Morgan by lending him books when he was translating the scriptures. Moreover, his bequests reveal him to be a prelate who had the welfare of the diocese and the Church generally at heart, and for that he was warmly applauded by a number of the prime Welsh alliterative poets, such as Wiliam Cynwal, Wiliam Llŷn and Siôn Tudur.[48]

Wiliam Llŷn's sturdy lines reflect on a personality of some academic standing:

> O codaist yn ŵr cadarn,
> Cefn y fainc mewn cyfiawn farn,
> Nid da neb, ond dyn a'i air,
> Duw a'th godes di i'th gadair.[49]

[You were elevated a powerful man, the backbone of the bench judging justly. Only a man of his word is worthy, God raised you to your seat.]

Hughes's weakness, however, like that of his colleagues, lay fundamentally in the very nature of the system which he served. Owing to those disabilities they were compelled to administer a poverty-stricken institution which, by the close of the sixteenth century, was tightly controlled and weakened by the forces of financial inflation. That poverty did not stem merely from bad management but also from deprivation, age-old religious traditions and the rapacity of ravaging landed gentry.

---

47 F. O. White, loc. cit.; J. Strype, *Annals*, III, App. pp.184-6; J. G. Jones, 'Thomas Davies and William Hughes', 325-6. See also *Annals*, II, pp.293-4.

48 J. G. Jones, 'Thomas Davies and William Hughes', 331-2; E. Roberts (ed.), *Gwaith Siôn Tudur*, I, CXXIV, pp.484-7; , 'Gwaith William Llŷn', R. Stephens (unpublished University of Wales Ph.D. dissertation, 1983), I, XXX, pp.142-4; NLW Mostyn MS, 1.326, 338.

49 J. G. Jones, *Concepts of Order and Gentility in Wales, 1540-1640* (Llandysul, 1992), pp.189-90; idem, 'The Reformation bishops of St. Asaph', 30-5; R. Stephens (ed.) 'Gwaith Wiliam Llŷn.', I, p.143.

In this context professional bardic compositions, which reveal features of the clerical fraternity, are worthy of consideration though unreliable because of their partiality and excessive hyperbole. Many clerics, some of very modest status, attracted the itinerant bards who offered panegyrics in their honour. On balance, the cultural interests of many of them were indeed quite remarkable, the most notable being 'Sir' Arthur ap Huw (vicar of Tywyn and Llanfair Dyffryn Clwyd), 'Sir' Dafydd Owain (rector of Nannerch and Llanddoged), 'Sir' Owain ap Gwilym (curate of Tal-y-llyn) and, in his younger days, the celebrated Dr John Davies of Mallwyd, doubtless the prime Welsh scholar of the later Renaissance period in Wales.[50] Standards were gradually improving among the clergy generally, and some notable scholars appeared among them. Arthur ap Huw was described as being knowledgeable in Hebrew and the classics and a good companion and conversationalist.[51] The versatile David Johns (also of Llanfair Dyffryn Clwyd) was a bard, copyist, Latinist, translator and versifier of some of the Psalms,[52] and 'Sir' Huw Roberts Llên, rector of Aberffraw, composed *cywyddau* applauding members of several north Wales families and, in 1600, published *The Day of Hearing: or six lectures upon the latter part of the third Chapter of the Epistle to the Hebrews.* He added to this work ... *a Sermon against fleshly lusts, & against certaine mischievous May games which are the fruit thereof*, which reveals a strong Puritan trait in his writings.[53] In Monmouthshire, Thomas Jones, rector of Llanfair Cilgedin near Llanofer, celebrated in verse the victory over the Armada and the publication of the Welsh Bible [54] and, in 1606, Edward James, a Glamorgan cleric, translated the homilies into Welsh, a work whose style and diction betrayed the influence of Morgan's Bible.[55] William Evans, chancellor of the diocese of Llandaff, described by Dafydd Benwyn as the 'Ifor Hael' of Llandaff, was a prominent patron of bards

---

[50] C. Fychan, 'Y canu i wŷr eglwysig gorllewin sir Ddinbych', *TDHS*, XXVIII, 1979, 119-28. Davies, C. *John Davies o Fallwyd* (Caernarfon, 2001)
[51] Ibid., 119-110.
[52] *Dict. Welsh Biog.*, pp 442; D. R. Thomas, *Diocese of St Asaph*, II, p.100. His main work is contained in his extensive six-volumed manuscript, BL Add. MS. 14866. G. H., Hughes, 'Cyfieithiad Dafydd Johns, Llanfair Dyffryn Clwyd, o "Weddi Sant Awgwstin" ', *NLWJ*, VI, 1949-50, 295-8.
[53] BL MS. 14892,8b; NLW Peniarth MS. 104,15; Llanstephan MS. 118,25; D. W. Wiliam, 'Traddodiad barddol ym mhlwyf Bodedern, Môn', *TAAS*, 1973, 55, 57, 60, 63-7. B. Rees, *Dulliau'r Canu Rhydd, 1500-1800* (Cardiff, 1952), p.139; *DWB*, pp.864-5.
[54] J. H. Davies (ed.), *Hen Gerddi Gwleidyddol, 1588-1660* (Cymdeithas Llên Cymru, Caerdydd, 1901), I, pp.7-11.
[55] G. Williams, 'Edward James a Llyfr yr Homilïau', *Grym Tafodau Tân*, pp. 180-98; *Glam. County Hist.*, IV, pp. 247-8, 576-7; *DWB*, p.422.

who adjudicated at an eisteddfod held there.[56] Although a large corpus of strict-metre poems in praise of Welsh clergymen who are described as men of stature in their community survives in manuscript, the more reliable official evidence alas gives a more negative impression.

In an age when higher educational standards were emerging opportunities were given to clerics and laity alike to attend Oxford or Cambridge or both and the Inns of Court.[57] The standard of education generally among the clergy, however, left much to be desired. Their inadequacies largely betrayed a marked lack of learning among them. Grammar schools and other educational institutions existed to provide for the clergy but the overall quality of priests, as prelates were aware, revealed serious deficiencies. Attempts were made to improve the situation, usually on a private basis. William Hughes at St Asaph, for example, bequeathed monies for the founding of a free school at St Asaph.[58] If there were no primary beneficiaries then twelve boys from the parishes of St Asaph, St George, Abergele and Diserth were to be educated until it was time for them to attend university. The consequences of this bequest are unclear for it does not appear that the school was established although Sir Roger Mostyn, in a letter to Sir John Wynn of Gwydir in 1613-14, referred to 'an excellent school at St Asaph and the better by much in respect my Lord Bishop [presumably Richard Parry, Morgan's successor] useth once or twice a week to come to the school to oppose the children'.[59] Similarly, Henry Rowlands of Bangor, in his will in 1616 provided the means to establish a school at Botwnnog, described as 'a petty school in Llyn', whereby appointed feoffees were required to formulate rules for its good-running.[60] Doubtless the bishops were

---

56   C.W. Lewis, ' Literary History of Glamorgan', pp.546-7. 549; G. J. Williams, *Traddodiad Llenyddol Morgannwg* (Cardiff,1948), pp.88-9; Browne Willis, *A Survey of the Cathedral Church of Llandaff* (London, 1719), pp.196, 198. 207; L. Thomas, *Reformation in the Old Diocese of Llandaff*, pp.119, 134 et seq.
57   W. P. Griffith, *Learning, Law and Religion*, chap. 7, pp.278-326.
58   NLW St Asaph Misc. Doc. 835-9; Browne Willis, *Survey of St Asaph*, I, p.107; D. R. Thomas, *Diocese of St Asaph*, I, p.338; L. S. Knight, 'Welsh cathedral schools to 1600 A.D.', *Y Cymmrodor*, XIX, 1920, 108. For the background to schooling in Wales see W.P. Griffith, 'Schooling and society', in J. G. Jones (ed.), *Class, Community and Culture in Tudor Wales* (Cardiff, 1989), pp.79-119.
59   NLW Add. MS. 466E.642.
60   J. G. Jones, 'Henry Rowlands, bishop of Bangor, 1598-1616', *JHSCW*, XXVI, 1979, 40-1; J. Morgan, *Coffadwriaeth am y Gwir Barchedig Henry Rowlands, D.D., Arglwydd Esgob Bangor* (Bangor, 1910), pp.62-4; J. Wynn, *History of the Gwydir Family and Memoirs*, p.59; Ca. MS.4.58,54.

involved in supplying books to promote the Church. Books were bequeathed in their wills for this purpose and William Morgan was assisted by the two northern bishops when translating the scriptures.

In a request poem in strict metres, the Merioneth poet Siôn Phylip in 1596, addressed Bishop Richard Vaughan (when bishop of Chester) on behalf of three kinsmen of his from Llŷn, namely Robert Madrun, Gruffudd ap Rhisiart and Maredudd ap Thomas. They wished to obtain a copy of the Bible, the 'communion book' (*Book of Common Prayer*) and John Foxe's celebrated *Acts and Monuments of the English Church* (*The Book of Martyrs*, 1563), presumably to complete the refurbishment of St Tudwen's Church, Llandudwen.

The poet deftly wove references to the three works into his couplets:

> Am dri llyfr medri wellhad
> Sy'n tueddu sancteiddiad:
> Y Beibl, help y bobl ei hun,
> Llai fo'r cam, a'r Llyfr Cymun,
> A llyfr budd, nid llafur byr,
> Mawrwaith eiriau merthyrwyr
> O waith Siôn, gyweithas aeth,
> Fox hen, ddiffug wasanaeth...
> Os da'n ffydd, os dawn hoff well,
> Y tri llyfr a'n try wellwell.[61]

[Three books which can heal and sanctify; the Bible, the people's own aid, and the Communion Book, as well as the beneficial book, a work of no small labour, the words of the book of martyrs of John's authorship, old Foxe, who gave honest service...If we are healthy in the faith, if our fond skill is to be improved, these three books will make us far better.]

These were the types of books which Protestants needed, two of them essential to Protestant teaching and the third which created a martyr tradition which served to promote that faith. It heightened a sense of

---

[61] NLW Add. MS.16129.86; E. M. Phillips, 'Noddwyr y Beirdd yn Llŷn' (unpublished University of Wales M. A. dissertation 1973), p.147.

religious tension and sympathy for the Protestant cause during and after the Marian persecution, and became central to popular mythology, strengthened support for the Elizabethan Church and inspired hatred of Roman Catholicism.[62] The *Acts and Monuments* were based on the Protestant Church Theory, tracing the history and martyrology of the Church from the earliest forms of Christianity to the death of Mary. 'Foxe's basic message', it was said, 'was that the Anglican Church was a 'true' historical Church founded by the spirit of God.' He assimilated traditional and reformed concepts of faith and doubtless his work would appeal to the modest Llŷn gentry.[63]

Lack of evidence prevents the historian from making detailed assessments of educational standards but, judging by the episcopal register for Bangor diocese in the 1570s and 1580s, for example, only 43 per cent of them were graduates, and the preaching activity of the Church obviously suffered as a consequence.[64] In rural areas in particular situations of this kind created many frustrations for church leaders who considered preaching to be essential to the promotion of the new religious movement. William Morgan emphasized this aspect when he accused John Wynn of Gwydir of making a 'stave' of him and driving 'preachers partryges to hys netts'.[65] Moreover, so disturbed was Francis Godwin at Llandaff with the condition of his diocese in 1603 that he instructed his clergy to admonish their parishioners from committing 'many outrages' on preachers 'not only in reproachfull and contemptuous speeches but [also] in laying violent hands vpon them'.[66] The Bangor evidence, however, suggests an increase in graduate clergy since in that diocese there was an upward trend from thirteen in the years 1560-80 to thirty-four in the period 1580-99.[67] To what extent clergy were resident and how active they all were in their parishes is not a matter easily resolved but it can be tentatively

62   P. Williams, *The Later Tudors: England 1547-1603* (Oxford, 1998), pp.115, 468.
63   J. Guy, *Tudor England* (Oxford, 1990), p.303. See also W. Haller, *Foxe's Book of Martyrs and the Elect Nation*, Chap. V, 'The lessons of history', pp.140-86; P. Collinson, 'The Elizabethan Church and the new religion', in C. Haigh (ed.), *Reign of Elizabeth I* (London, 1984), pp.184-7.
64   G. Williams, *Welsh Reformation Essays*, p.301.
65   J. G. Jones, 'Bishop William Morgan's dispute with John Wynn of Gwydir in 1603-04', 74.
66   R. G. Gruffydd, 'Bishop Francis Godwin's injunctions for the diocese of Llandaff, 1603', *JHSCW*, IV, 1954, 19.
67   M. Gray, 'The diocese of Bangor', 31-9.

suggested that the quality of the clergy generally showed some signs of improvement.[68] It can also be said that the numbers of preaching clergy had increased significantly. In St Asaph in 1602, for example, there was a preacher in every three of the clergy, and Llandaff and St David's had fifty and eighty-four respectively, which suggests strongly that the Welsh dioceses were producing more preachers than many English sees.[69]

Having said that, a major deficiency in the Welsh Church was the lack of prominent expository preachers. It did not produce men like William Perkins, the powerful Cambridgeshire preacher, and Richard Greeham, rector of Dry Drayton, in the same county, a preacher of whom it was said that 'his masterpiece was in comforting wounded consciences'.[70] Nevertheless, with some exceptions, leadership among the bishops in supporting a learned ministry and encouraging preaching left much to be desired. In England, church reform was achieved partly through the links forged between local clergy and the laity which led to frequent preaching, and steps were taken by Presbyterians to finance a 'godly ministry'. Because standards had fallen, chiefly because of pluralism and impropriations, lectureships were financed by laity and town corporations,[71] a development which had no impact on Wales chiefly because of economic backwardness and the lack of a Puritan tradition. It is evident that the Welsh bishops were not entirely satisfied with the situation. In his 1603 injunctions, Francis Godwin at Llandaff declared how impoverished his see really was.[72] In addition to complaining about the condition of the cathedral building itself he drew the attention of preachers, who found that they were unable to preach 'quarterly sermons', as authorized by the royal injunctions of 1559, to the need to report to him, and to the fact that clergy were not allowed to preach unless formally licensed to do so. How effective these injunctions were it is difficult to say but it was evident that the new bishop of Llandaff was

---

68   W. P. Griffith, *Learning Law and Religion*, pp.311-26; idem, 'Merioneth and the new and reformed learning in the early modern period', *JMHRS*, XII, 1994-7, 340-44.
69   G. Williams, *Wales and the Reformation*, pp.294-9. For detailed evidence of the personnel and condition of the Welsh Church in the Tudor and early Stuart periods see B. Williams, 'The Welsh Clergy, 1558-1642' (unpublished Open University Ph.D. thesis, 1999).
70   P. Collinson, *The Elizabethan Puritan Movement* (London, 1967), p.128.
71   I. Morgan, *The Godly Preachers of the Elizabethan Church* (London, 1965), pp.27-30; C. Cross, *Church and State, 1450-1660*, p.162.
72   R. G. Gruffydd, 'Bishop Francis Godwin's Injunctions for the diocese of Llandaff, 1603', 17-20.

aware that his predecessors in the see had not attended to clerical discipline in the see as thoroughly as they might.

With regard to the quality of the clergy the humanist scholar Sir John Pryse testified to their utter inadequacy when referring to the 'mass-priests who are in our midst alas some either not able to, or not inclined to reveal to their parishioners the things that they are bound to reveal or to know', a statement which shows a very sad state of affairs:

> Kanys heb ffydd ny ellir rhengi bodd duw, ar perigloryon y sy yny mysk oswaethiroedd, y naill ae nys medran, ae nys mynnan ddangos yw plwyvogyon y petheu y maen yn rhwymedic y llaill yw dangos, ar llall eu gwybod, duw ae dycko yr iawn ac y adnabod y perigleu, pa wedd y gorffo arnyn atteb am yr eneideu elo ar gyfyrgoll drwy y heisieu hwy.[73]

[For without faith God cannot be satisfied, and the priests in our midst, alas either they cannot show, or do not wish to show, to their parishioners the things which one is bound to show and the other to know: God bring them to the right and to know the collects, the way they are forced to answer for the souls who stray for want of them.]

This is accompanied by several similar statements made by other humanists later in the century. Having said that, it would not be accurate to conclude that all clergy were devoid of educational attainment, and evidence does show that there were a larger proportion of graduates in the Welsh church by the end of Elizabeth I's reign than has been recognized in the past, and there were stalwarts among them, such as Dr David Powel, Edmwnd Prys, Edward James, Thomas Huet, Robert Holland and Hugh Lewis, any one of whom might easily have been considered suitable for promotion to an episcopal seat in the Wales of his time. Eligible sons of gentry were encouraged by bishops to choose the church as a vocation and to conduct academic pursuits. [74] It is said that William Hughes, for example, while at Cambridge or possibly later as bishop of St Asaph, urged his contemporary William Morgan, an expert Hebrew scholar, to translate the scriptures into Welsh, but there is no

---

73   *Rhagymadroddion*, p.4.
74   G. Williams, *Welsh Reformation Essays*, pp.22-3.

evidence to prove it.[75] It is also possible that Richard Davies, bishop of St David's, encouraged him to undertake the task of translating when he was sinecure vicar of Llanbadarn Fawr (1572-7), a living that may have been reserved for him.[76] In 1607 Henry Rowlands recommended a Beddgelert youth for the scholarship endowed by Sir John Wynn's father for a place at Friars' School, Bangor. His recommendation was firm: 'I thinke you shall doe verrie well', he declared, 'for my own parte, I knowe none of his kine to be moved, for him more then out of my devotion and care of the good government and supply of those rowmes'.[77] In this respect Rowlands extended his benevolence into educational affairs for he doubtless saw the dire need to furnish young scholars with the means whereby they might take holy orders in due course.

An examination of the manner in which prelates in Wales attempted to advance the Protestant faith requires close consideration in view of the fact that they associated the Church with the concept of statehood since Wales was, from 1536 onwards, assimilated to the realm of England. How did Welsh prelates define statehood and in what respects was the Church considered to be an essential part of it? Moreover, how important to the Church was the establishment of unity and uniformity and how eager were the Elizabethan bishops to ensure the smooth-running of ecclesiastical administration within the parallel structures of Church and state? How far did they strictly apply their authority so as to ensure the advance of Protestantism, and how much emphasis was placed on 'good prelacy'? With the exception of Middleton and Hughes bishops in Wales have enjoyed a good press, although local issues and social conditions limited their efforts to fulfil their spiritual obligations. Doubtless Elizabethan and early Stuart bishops were academically well-equipped

---

75 Idem, *Wales and the Reformation*, pp.299-300; W. P. Griffith, *Learning, Law and Religion*, chap. VII, pp.278-326. It is also argued that Hughes might have been the cleric who opposed the need for a translation and who advocated the introduction of the last clause in the 1563 statute for the translation of the scriptures into Welsh declaring that English versions were to be set side by side with Welsh versions in the churches. See the general comment made by Maurice Kyffin in his preface to *Deffynniad Ffydd Eglwys Loegr* (1595), in *Rhagymadroddion*, p.94. For further elucidation on this point see R. G. Gruffydd, 'Y cyfieithu a'r cyfieithwyr', in idem (ed.), *Y Gair ar Waith: Ysgrifau ar yr Etifeddiaeth Feiblaidd yng Nghymru* (Cardiff, 1988), p.30; J. G. Jones, *Early Modern Wales, c.1525-1640* (London, 1994), p.150.
76 G. Williams, 'Bishop Wiliam Morgan (1545-1604) and the first Welsh Bible', in *The Welsh and their Religion*, pp.187-8.
77 NLW MS. 9053E.459.

and the majority were personally well-endowed to promote the faith, but how successful in fact were they in reality and, moreover, what attracted John Penry to make his unsavoury comments on their office and personal qualities?

The Elizabethan and early Protestant Church is regarded as the pivot of religious life in England and Wales but, in view of dire socio-economic problems, the persistence of Roman Catholic recusancy in addition to the growth of Puritanism, particularly in England from the 1560s onwards, it is hard to sustain such a view. It is an underlying fact that the Church of Elizabeth, alongside the Crown, the law and parliament, formed one of four major bastions of unity and uniformity in the state.[78] The adherence of the majority of the Welsh gentry to the religious settlement was based essentially on the need to maintain the security of the political and social order. This was largely established in a secular context since the gentry were responsible for local government and administration and, despite the friction which often occurred in their relations with royal agencies, that stability was maintained and served to preserve the kingdom's independence in times of political crises in the late Elizabethan period. The same can be said of the new Church for it was erastian and established by statute law; it not only offered so many benefits to the landed gentry but also, more significantly, sought to uphold the principles of good government within itself and the state. In that sense the Church was a pillar of order in an age when the prime emphasis was on hierarchy and stability, features which the Crown and ruling classes considered vital to the welfare of the nation state.[79] The Elizabethan Church in Wales, as Sir Glanmor Williams has amply proved, also had a distinctly Welsh appeal since it was considered to herald a return to the Celtic Church and hailed the restoration of the pristine faith rather than the unwelcomed imposition of a Saxon one.[80] Despite the serious depredations which the Church suffered at the hands of clergy and laity alike, in purely secular terms its defence was considered essential in view of continued Roman Catholic threats and, on a wider scale, increased attacks by extreme Protestants. In this context government used the bishops to guard the

---

[78] G. Williams, *Welsh Reformation Essays*, pp.26-7.
[79] G. Williams, *Renewal and Reformation: Wales c. 1415-1642* (Cardiff, 1993), pp.330-1.
[80] Idem, *Reformation Views of Church History* (London, 1970), pp.63-5; idem, 'Bishop Richard Davies (?1501-1581)', in *Welsh Reformation Essays*, pp.183-4; idem, *Wales and the Reformation*, pp.244-6; idem, 'Bishop Sulien, Bishop Richard Davies and Archbishop Parker', 215-9.

Church against any aggression which might damage its integrity and, in this context, three main sources of the destruction of a fragile and impoverished institution became evident, namely lay and clerical rapacity of the Church, Roman Catholic recusancy and the fear of hostile foreign powers. All three factors, in different respects, made the Elizabethan Church in Wales vulnerable to destructive elements which emerged essentially from the circumstances in which it was initially formed. So much in the Church was a legacy from the past, its structure, organization and poverty, and its susceptibility to attack and abuse.

The high profile of the Welsh bishops demanded that they became primarily occupied with routine administrative tasks and reporting on the conditions of their dioceses. They also referred in their correspondence to the role of the church in the state and to their own role within it. This aspect of their character usually emerged at times of stress when they were obliged to defend their honour as well as the prestige of the Church, particularly after the Papal Bull excommunicating the queen in 1570, usually when harassed by clerical inefficiency or lay hostility. Elizabeth's government was threatened and the bull released her Roman Catholic subjects from political allegiance to her. The defence of the Church is reflected in William Bleddyn's bitter but timely attack on the serious inadequacies of the prebendaries of Llandaff. He urged them to attend more diligently to their duties, to defend the Church's welfare and to uphold the noble traditions of the see. Their gross malpractices, he believed, had tainted the Church's reputation as well as their own. Through making proper use of the ordinances and the initiation of other reforms, together with his own leadership as 'master of the stormy ship', the diocese's reputation might be recovered.[81] Besides this encouragement to the canons to mend their ways Bleddyn believed that the honour of the Church itself as an institution was at stake. He considered himself to be a true successor to Urban, first Norman bishop of the see, who 'united and restored the see's 'usurped jurisdictions' by St David's, and described himself as a restorer of the see's glory who was prepared to defend it and to urge the prebendaries to restore the Church's properties and salvage its reputation.[82] He projected himself as a dedicated Protestant bishop who had the cultural as well as the spiritual welfare of the institution of the

---

[81] J. Bradney, 'Speech of William Blethin' 258.
[82] Ibid.

Church at heart. What he had to say of Llandaff might also, of course, be said of other dioceses. He desired to restore the integrity of the religious establishment, obstructed though he was by private interest and greed. In other words, Bleddyn stressed the 'militant promotion' of the Church which demanded strict control of the clergy as well as the destruction of all its unseemly features. His appeal to the prebendaries was as ardent as that of any bishop of his day:

> Therefore let us awake. It is time to rise from sleep. The night has advanced. But the day of salvation approaches and this is the day which the Lord hath made we will rejoice and be glad in it.[83]

Welsh bishops severely censured lay encroachments on church tithes and properties. In 1577, however, Richard Davies defined the problem in broader terms, rebuking lay impropriators and local officials in his diocese for their high-handed practices in government and administration and for their popish leanings:

> [They] walke after the pleasures and riches of thys worlde, applye all their power to further and continue the kingdome of Antichrist, defend papisterie, supersiticion and Idolatrie, pilgrimages to Welles and blinde chappelles, procure the wardens of churches in tyme of visitacion to periurie, to conceale images, roode loftes and aulters. This is lamentable, that Gods chosen officers in this blessed time of light & knowledge of the gospell of Christ, will neither enter themselues to the Kingdome of Heauen, nor suffer the[m] that would...[84]

It is true that Davies at the time had an axe to grind with recalitrant lay gentry in his own diocese, the earls of Pembroke and Leicester, Fabian Phillips and Sir John Perrott of Haroldston, Pembrokeshire, which may account for such a harsh indictment. However, although not at all times blameless in his dealings in the church, he did point clearly to instability in the reformed Church in the Wales of his day. Indeed, he was among the most ardent of Elizabethan prelates in Wales in drawing attention to the shortcomings of clergy and laity alike and the long-term weaknesses

---

83 Ibid.
84 *A Funerall Sermon preached the XXVI day of November...md lxxvi in the Parishe Church of Caermerthyn ...by the Reverend Father in God, Richard...Bishoppe of Saint Dauys at the Buriall of the Right Honourable Walter Earle of Essex and Ewe* (London, 1577), Dii.

which hindered the Church's progress: [85]

> Here we may see what wofull case they be in that neuer thinke of any reconing to be made howe they behaued the[m]selues in their authoritie. And what shall become of them that in their dooings will neuer consider what the will of God is: but contrarie unreasonably walke after the pleasures and riches of thys worlde ....[86]

Davies, being aware of his status as bishop of the most prestigious diocese in Wales, was always prepared to defend his position and withstand any attack on his rights and privileges. Like others of his contemporaries William Morgan, when at St Asaph, after a relatively peaceful period at Llandaff, strongly responded to the constant attacks on the Church's welfare. In an age of lay rapacity and ecclesiastical despoliation, one of the most hostile disputes in which he was involved was that with Sir John Wynn of Gwydir over the rectory of Llanrwst in 1601. He had previously encountered the opposition of others but his quarrel with the formidable head of the Gwydir family, to whom he owed a debt of gratitude for his and his family's support in the past, is significant for reasons other than the wrangling over the acquisition of church lands. It could plausibly be argued that Morgan, in his desire to retain the living, was primarily eager to supplement his own income by holding it *in commendam* – a common enough practice among prelates of his day – and that Wynn was anxious to demonstrate his power as a landowner at a precarious time in his career as a country esquire, but the fundamental issue, however, judging by Morgan's argument in his correspondence, was preserving the Church's honour. He considered its integrity to be at stake in a diocese torn by political and religious strife. 'One thing moveth me agaynst all these', he declared to Sir John Wynn when referring to his intentions, and proceeded to justify his stand:

> vz. my conscience, w[hi]ch assureth me th[a]t youre request ys such th[a]t in grauntyng yt [i.e. the lease of Llanrwst] I should prove my selfe an unhonest, unconscionab[le] and irreligiouse man, ye a sacrilegious[e] robber of my church, a p[er]fydiouse spoyler of my diocesse and an unnaturall hynderer of preachers and good Scholers.[87]

---

85 G. Williams, 'Bishop Richard Davies (?1501-1581)', pp.167-8, 169, 175-8.
86 *A Funerall Sermon...*, D ii.
87 J. G. Jones, 'Bishop William Morgan's dispute with John Wynn of Gwydir in 1603-04', 67-8.

Such a powerful defence implied that the Church stood either to be defended and vindicated or to be mercilessly exploited. Since he emphasized the need for 'competent mayntenance for p[rea]chers' it was obvious that Morgan wished to install a resident preacher at Llanrwst. 'I wyll not spoyle ye church', he further declared in a letter to Thomas Martin, the London-based lawyer, 'I knowe that God whose church I wold defende, is able to defende me agaynst all enemyes and wyll defende me so farr as he shall see ytt to be expedient for me'.[88] Powerful words indeed which, when put in context, reveal the true role of the institution which Morgan was so eager to defend in the broader framework of the state. He undeniably proclaimed that it was a state institution created to enhance and preserve spiritual and moral values while, at the same time, maintaining the unity of the realm. It is hardly surprising that Wynn, in his *Memoirs*, was less complimentary to him than to other bishops of his time, maliciously describing him as being of servile stock and relying on the labours of Richard Davies and William Salesbury when translating the scriptures.[89] It was a mere afterthought which led to his condescending postscript that Morgan was a good scholar.

The crusade against Roman Catholic recusancy formed a significant feature of this stalwart defence and each bishop, at various stages, reported the state of play regarding Catholics in their respective dioceses. The problem seemed to be most acute in the eastern dioceses, particularly Llandaff where hardened recusants, such as the Morgans of Llantarnam and Turbervilles of Glamorgan, exercised great influence. In such circumstances episcopal residence was essential, and the new Protestant order broke with tradition. Alongside regular visitations, preaching activities and hospitality it implied that they were able to maintain close contacts with diocesan affairs and to instil into them a reforming spirit. Hence, in Richard Davies's and William Morgan's day, Abergwili and Mathern respectively became centres of hospitality where Protestant learning was disseminated as well as sources of spiritual regeneration. The emphasis by most bishops on *de jure divino* symbolized a staunch moral defence against the evils of the time, and doubtless the emphasis on

---

88 Ibid., 76.
89 J. Wynn, *History of the Gwydir Family and Memoirs*, p.63.

preaching was regarded not merely as a means of imparting Christian values but also as a cohesive binding force sustaining political unity within the state. In his Latin preface to the Bible in 1588 Morgan, some years before he was elevated to a bishop's seat, unwittingly declared that establishing uniformity in religion was paramount to securing unity in the state, and he maintained that the availability of the Bible in the vernacular would contribute far more effectively to consolidate unity and uniformity in the state than would uniformity in language:

> Moreover, there can be no doubt that unity is more effactually promoted by similarity and agreement in religion, than in speech. Besides, to prefer unity to piety, expediency to religion, and a kind of external concord among men, to that heavenly peace which the Word of GOD impresses on men's souls, shows but little piety.[90]

In Morgan's view, and that of many of his contemporaries, therefore, the scriptures were not merely a literary accomplishment but an agency of spiritual enlightenment, a means of forging unity among the Welsh people as a national entity within the Tudor state and of establishing uniformity within it.

Any examination of the early stages of the Reformation in Wales reveals that the first two generations of the Elizabethan religious settlement down to 1588, were based on parliamentary legislation. The Reformation was essentially statutory in its character, and those appointed to implement it were royal nominees best able to serve in a Church whose drawbacks would otherwise have been too serious to remedy. By and large it is the native character of the episcopacy in Elizabethan Wales which was instrumental in moving the Reformation ahead regardless of the shortcomings and the modest legacy which it bequeathed to its successors in Stuart Wales. It is the gradual weakening of recusant opposition, a continued zeal among some of the early seventeenth-century bishops and higher clergy, as well as an increase in Protestant literature and publication, and the lack of a strong Puritan opposition to the Church, which served to strengthen the establishment. Added to these factors the

---

[90] W. Hughes, *The Life and Times of Bishop William Morgan* (London, 1891), p.127; C. Davies (ed.), *Rhagymadroddion a Chyflwyniadau Lladin, 1551-1632* (Cardiff, 1980), pp.68-9.

continued support which the majority of the gentry gave to the institution, despite the despoliation of its properties, assured its future. What the Church in its first generations had to offer fell short of what was expected in terms of being able to stem the alienation of Church property, improve the living conditions and education of most of the lower clergy, and tackle the on-going problem of illiteracy in Welsh communities. Albeit the appearance of the Welsh Bible, although its impact at first was not as great as historians have made it out to be, to an extent alleviated what was at best a gloomy religious scenario. However, its true impact was not to be felt at grass-root level for many decades to come. In so far as the Elizabethan Welsh bishops themselves were concerned it is evident that, regardless of their personal qualities, they were confronted by many constraints. While they were pressed to lead a life-style befitting their office, at the same time they were expected to promote charity and support the needy. The added pressures of family life, fiscal demands and their duties to the gentry and the clergy as well as to the Crown and the community, made episcopal authority vulnerable within its own sphere of activity. The best testimony that any self-effacing bishop might give himself was expressed in a letter by Henry Rowlands: 'Neither horse nor mare shall choke me to betraye the church; I have vowed the fidelity of my services that way to the church against kindred, flesh and blood'.[91] He was among the most praiseworthy prelate of his generation, widely renowned for his bounty. This is a declaration which echoes the testimony, declared in an equally forceful manner, by William Morgan on another occasion. It was left for future generations of bishops to attempt to 'settle' the religious framework and to tackle some of the most complex problems that the ecclesiastical establishment had to face in the years before the Civil Wars and the Puritan *Interregnum*.

Although Puritanism had hardly made any impact on Wales by the close of Elizabeth I's reign it is altogether remarkable that a Welshman rose to prominence as an author who contributed to Puritan thought in a decade – the 1580s – that became increasingly critical in the movement's development. This son of a modest Brecknockshire freeholder from Cefn Brith, a farmstead on the northern slopes of the Epynt mountains, was educated at Peterhouse, Cambridge, where he became a Presbyterian and

---

[91]   NLW MS. 9052E.265.

an ardent supporter of the need for extreme religious reform. John Penry ranked among the most dynamic of propagandists.[92] If direct references to his native country were to be taken out of the texts of his three treatises on Wales their content would not be substantially different from the writings of Job Throckmorton and others. Fanatical though Penry was in his views on several issues, he did propose wide-ranging reforms which he considered necessary to improve the spiritual condition of his people. These demands cut the ground from beneath the episcopalian system, one of the mainstays of the Elizabethan religious settlement, and because of his strong Calvinist beliefs he found no redeeming features in any of the Welsh prelates of his day. In fact, it is debatable whether he knew much about the bishops as individuals, but, since his mission principally was to denounce episcopacy as an institution, the human qualities of church leaders were of no concern to him. Evidence suggests that he was also unaware of the conditions in all the Welsh dioceses, with the possible exception of St David's, and probably Richard Pryse of Brecon, who also censured religious leaders in his region, was better placed to pass a balanced judgement on conditions in the diocese.[93]

Penry certainly had a tight agenda to follow, and if his role is to be properly assessed then he is best described as an exponent of the Puritan ethos devoted to reforming the organization and mission of the Church rather than its theology. Owing to the nature of his mission this ardent evangelical revealed himself at heart to be a contentious person, an individual who later, on his conversion to Protestantism at Cambridge, saw himself as God's envoy appointed to save the 'souls of his countrymen'. Moreover, his obsessive and rigid mind revealed his unswerving desire to see the Church of God, as he defined it, firmly established in Wales. It has been proven that his method of arguing his case in his three treatises concerning Wales (1587-8) was in line with Puritan propaganda, whereby the condition of the Elizabethan Church, and the changes needed in it, according to Puritan interpretation, would

---

[92] There are several publications on John Penry, notably W. Pierce, *John Penry: His Life, Times and Writings* (London, 1923); D. McGinn, *John Penry and the Marprelate Controversy* (Rutgers UP, 1966); G. Williams, 'John Penry: Marprelate and patriot?', *WHR*, III, 1967, 361-80; R. T. Jones, 'Mantoli cyfraniad John Penri', *Y Cofiadur*, 58, May 1993, 4-41; J. G. Jones, 'John Penry: government, order and the 'perishing souls' of Wales', *TCS*, 1993, 47-81. Penry's three treatises on Wales are also published in *Three Treatises concerning Wales*, ed. D. Williams (Cardiff, 1960).

[93] H. Ellis (ed.), *Original Letters Illustrative of English History*, (2nd Ser.), III, p.42.

ordinarily be focused upon in a local or regional context.[94] Penry's chief aim was to promote the success of his brand of Puritanism and, in line with his fellow religious leaders, the emphasis was placed on the need for a drastic reform of the Church and the introduction of a learned preaching ministry. At Cambridge he had read the works of Bishop John Bale and Thomas Cartwright, Professor of Divinity at Cambridge, and had adopted a strict Calvinist theology. Although Penry seemed to have little personal knowledge of the condition of the Welsh Church in his day, because of his continued absence from his mother country, he appears to have accumulated sufficient material to draw general conclusions about the deficiencies which hampered its progress in Wales after the Elizabethan Settlement. Where he obtained that knowledge it is difficult to tell for he is known to have visited Wales only once – in 1584-5 – after his departure for Cambridge, and his contacts in Wales, who might have informed him of religious affairs, were probably very few.

The Elizabethan settlement had been imposed by the will of the government. The survival of the new Church depended on the success of the Queen's reign. Parliament had imposed the Thirty-nine Articles based on the Forty-two Articles of 1553. The corporate unity achieved needed to be reinforced and the settlement adopted the south German or Swiss patterns of reform. Thus arose disputes over the degree to which a thorough reforming spirit was acceptable. Attempts were made to keep the settlement intact but extremists on both sides – Protestant and Roman Catholic – cherished divergent theological viewpoints that could never be reconciled.

Penry's treatises on Wales were written in the critical period 1587-8, and it is almost certain that he had not seen or would not have known of any bishops' reports on the condition of their sees. Neither would he have read William Bleddyn's speech to the prebendaries at Llandaff (1575),[95] Richard Pryse of Brecon's earnest letter to Sir William Cecil (1575) censuring the laxity of the clergy in his native Brecknockshire [96] and the anonymous report on the condition of religious life in that shire (1586),[97]

---

94   G. Williams, 'Marprelate and patriot?', 372-80.
95   J. Bradney, 'Speech of William Blethin', 255-8.
96   H. Ellis (ed.), *Original Letters Illustrative of English History*, III, p.42.
97   *Cal. of State Papers Dom.*, 1581-1590, CXCI, no. 17, p.339; G. Williams, *Bywyd ac Amserau'r Esgob Richard Davies* (Cardiff, 1953), p.56.

unless he was its author. Neither would the damning report (1587) [98] on the diocese of St Asaph and its bishop, William Hughes, be probably within his grasp nor Marmaduke Middleton's report on the diocese of St David's (1583).[99] The testimony of church leaders on the condition of their dioceses was depressing to say the least. In Richard Davies's report to the Privy Council (1569) he stated that, owing to lay impropriations, the condition of the church would have serious repercussions on religious practice.[100] It had led to lack of sustenance and inadequate clerical stipends and a general malaise among the less endowed priests. His desire was that 'that smale patrymony of the church which is yet remayning to the maintenance of Goddes s[er]vice, may so styll co[n]tinue to the sustentacon...of preachers and teachers, after that the incu[m]bents now beinge no preachers shall happen to depart'.[101] Despite his efforts Davies could not find sufficient numbers of preachers and teachers unless he offered them more than one living. He had ten ministers in the diocese in 1570, and of these three at least could not preach in Welsh. It may have been the case that Davies, Thomas Huet and Thomas Price, vicar of Nantmel, were the only ones fluent in the language and able in their sermons to make effective contact with parishioners. Some years later Richard Pryse (mentioned above) echoed a similar comment when he said that there were 'scarce ii learned and sufficient pastors' in Brecknockshire and a slender reading ministry, each priest serving two or three parishes, 'whereby the common people are so rude and ignorant in the most necessary points of the Christian faith that over many of them cannot as much as say the Lord's Prayer and Articles of Belief in any language that they understand'.[102] If the Church is not reformed, he declared, then civil obedience in Wales would be at a loss. Indeed, Penry, basing his strictures possibly on what Pryse had said, went so far as to declare that spiritual regeneration was an almost impossible task in Wales. He censured church leaders for being unmindfull of the essential needs of their people, giving

[98] J. Strype, *Annals of the Reformation*, II, App., pp.184—6; J. G. Jones, 'Thomas Davies and William Hughes', 332-5. Hughes's dubious background in his early days is traced in W. P. Griffith, 'William Hughes and the "Descensus" controversy of 1567', *BBCS*, XXXIV, 1987, 185-99.
[99] *Cal. State Papers Dom.*, 1581-1590, CLXII, no.29, p.119.
[100] D. R. Thomas, *Life and Work of Davies and Salesbury*, pp.40-3.
[101] Ibid., p.44.
[102] H. Ellis (ed.), *Original Letters Illustrative of English History*, III, pp.42, 47-8.

far less attention to priorities such as an awareness of sin and seeking salvation. He remarked further:

> Though they graunt it needeful, they think it sufficient to heare one sermon once perhaps in al their life.[103]

Hugh Lewis and Maurice Kyffin were to echo these sentiments in years to come so that Penry's criticisms were familiar to all Anglican clergy concerned about the need for reform. When it is considered that Richard Pryse's father, Sir John Pryse, had translated these scriptural sections into Welsh almost thirty years earlier, the situation in his view must have been deplorable.[104] He blamed the government for not attending to the spiritual needs of the people and repeated the views of others when he declared that uniformity in religious practice, in the context of national unity, would never be achieved unless the Protestant faith was preached and explained more convincingly to the peasantry.

Nicholas Robinson was more specific and sharper in his approach to the inadequacies of the clergy in his diocese. Ignorance and superstition, he maintained, grew out of 'ye blindness of ye clergy...and also upon ye closing up of God's word from them in an unknown tongue'.[105] He continued that many of the clergy were well into old age and no longer capable of being educated. Only six could preach in the diocese, he continued, but the 'poor people' were handicapped by 'want of knowledge' and showed no opposition on their part to hearing and understanding, if given the opportunity. In his report on the state of his diocese in 1583, submitted probably to the Council in the Marches, he declared that public preachers were scarce because 'there are few devynes skill full in the Wellshe tonge' and because there were no general stipends available in the diocese for preachers unless provision had been made through appropriation.[106]

It is evident that the bishops were at least aware of a lack of effective missionary zeal and effective communication in the parishes. Richard Davies, when referring to the inadequacies of Hugh Jones for promotion

---

103 J. Penry, *Three Treatises concerning Wales*, p.7.
104 G. Williams, 'Sir John Pryse of Brecon', *Brycheiniog*, XXXI, 1998-9, 49-63.
105 D. Mathew, 'Some Elizabethan documents', 77-8.
106 A. O. Evans, 'Nicholas Robinson (1530?-1585', *Y Cymmrodor*, XXXIX, 1928, 177.

to the see of Llandaff, in a letter to Sir William Cecil in 1561 declared that it was necessary to appoint men to responsible positions in the Church: in order that they by 'preaching of the Word of God, and living according to the same, may set forth the glory of God and show light in these places of extreme darkness'.[107] It is this line of attack that John Penry took when he overtly stated that 'my brethren for the most part know not what preaching meaneth, much lesse think the same necessarie to saluation'.[108] On the same track Hugh Lewis, the scrupulous vicar of Llanddeiniolen, drew attention to the lack of books in Welsh for instructional purposes, the lethargy of the clergy and the consequent inability to understand the tenets of the faith:

> Yrawrhon, y diffig hwnn o lyfreu sy in mysc (gida bod y Preladieit ar gwyr eglwysig hwythau yrhann fwyaf yn ddiog yn ei swydd ai galwedigaeth, heb ymarddel a phregethu ac a deongl dirgelwch gair duw i'r bobl, eythr byw yn fudion, ac yn aflafar, fal cwn heb gyfarth, clych heb dafodeu, ne gannwyll dan lestr) yw yr achos paham y mae cymeint o anwybodaeth mewn pethau ysprydawl in mysc...[109]

[Now, this deficiency in books amongst us (since most of the prelates and churchmen are lethargic in their office and career, not professing to preach and interpreting the mystery of God's word to the people, but rather mute and harsh, like unbarking dogs, bells without clappers, or a candle under a bushel) is the reason why there is so much ignorance of spiritual things in our midst.]

In view of this testimony, the weakness in John Penry's argument in this context appears in his lack of sufficient evidence to give it more force and an edge which might otherwise have had a greater impact on the House of Commons. This is a key deficiency in all of Penry's writings concerning Wales. Only on occasions, and even then facts appear to be exaggerated, does he venture to display tangible evidence, the main thrust of his argument being a severe and discursive censure of the Church hierarchy rather than an all out attack on the avarice of the gentry.

---

[107] J. Strype, *Life and Acts of Archbishop Matthew Parker*, p.203.
[108] J. Penry, *Three Treatises concerning Wales*, p.7.
[109] *Rhagymadroddion*, p.101.

Richard Davies's report in 1570 deplored the rapacity of the landowners and drew attention to two kinds of parishes which were endangered as a result. They were the endowed parishes and those which had no rectorial stipends and vicarial tithes and, in both kinds, the clergy suffered. The gentry enjoyed the fruits of such livings and it was Bishop William Morgan, during his altercation with Sir John Wynn of Gwydir, who highlighted the problem most poignantly in his correspondence. It is evident that the Church produced several clerics who, besides those in the upper ranks of the hierarchy, were by reputation honourable and learned. Among them were those who also functioned as professional bards such as 'Sir' Dafydd Owen, vicar of Llanddoged, 'Sir' Arthur ap Huw, vicar of Tywyn, Merioneth, and, in Denbighshire c. 1560, it was reported that there were fifteen such vicars.[110] How effective they were as parish clergy is unknown but, despite the dearth of preachers among them, it is evident that they formed a band of priests who deserved some acclamation for their learning and residency, a feature which the professional bards sought to promote. Robert Llwyd, vicar of Chirk, had it in mind to please John Owen, Bishop of St Asaph, in his preamble, in Welsh, to his translation of Arthur Dent's *The Plaine Man's Pathway to Heaven* (1630). Since Owen's predecessor, John Hanmer, had died shortly before the work appeared, it was dedicated to Owen, and in the preamble Llwyd described some of his clergy as being zealous in their pastoral care and others as scholars, while the remainder modestly exercised what skills they possessed:

> ...chwi a gewch weled yno lawer o'ch tan-fugeiliaid yn trin ac yn areilio eu praidd yn ofalus, yn daclus, yn drwyadl. Rhai bywiog a chalonnog...Rhai yn casglu cerrig llyfnion gweithgar o afon Gair Duw...Rhai yn gyrru yn bybyr, yn ddi-rus, ac yn wrolwych yn eu galwedigaeth...Ac eraill yn rhagorol eu dysg a'u dawn yn dwyn i adeiladaeth Eglwys Crist roddion gorchestol o bur athrawiaeth, ffraethineb ymadrodd, a hyfder i guro i lawr bechod a drygioni.
>
> Eto er hyn i gyd, y mae yn hyderus gennyf na bydd anghymeradwy gan eich Arglwyddiaeth chwi weled eraill, eiddilach eu grym a gwannach eu nerth, yn dwyn pwys y dydd a'r gwres yn ôl eu gallu, drwy wneuthur cydwybod o drin yn ofalus ac yn ffyddlon y talentau bychain a distadl yr ymddiriedwyd iddynt amdanynt.[111]

110 C. Fychan, 'Y canu i wŷr eglwysig gorllewin sir Ddinbych', 118-51 (esp. 118-26).
111 H. Lewis (ed.), *Hen Gyflwyniadau* (Cardiff, 1948), p.16.

[...you shall see there many of your under-pastors caring for and shepherding their flock carefully, tidily and thoroughly. Some lively and hearty...Some collecting smooth industrious stones from the river of God's Word...Some pressing on staunchly, unhesitatingly and valiant in their occupation...And others of excellence in learning and ability bringing masterly gifts of pure doctrine for the edification of Christ's Church, witty in speech, and bold to beat down sin and wickedness.

Again, despite all this, I am confident that it will not be unacceptable to your Lordship to see others, frail in strength and weaker in power, combating the pressure of the day according to their ability and conscience, carefully and faithfully exercising the small and humble talents entrusted to them.]

In view of the bishops' concerns it appears that, in some respects, John Penry echoed much that already constituted a serious situation in the Protestant Church. His views concurred with those of his fellow Puritans that reform in the Church should be taken to its logical conclusion, which implied that the individual is totally responsible to God and that the spiritual authority claimed by the episcopacy was redundant. Thus he, like other Puritans, placed emphasis on strict conduct, rejecting the apostolic claim of the priesthood and the Order of Service in the Book of Common Prayer as well as the pronouncements on vestments and other ceremonial features by Matthew Parker in the *Book of Advertisements* (1566), which was intended to impose uniformity in services.[112]

Penry, however, ploughed a lone furrow in Wales and his writings compared well in content with that published by his fellow Puritans in the England of his day. That literature, in fact, achieved much notoriety. So did Penry's, and his comments are exceptionally bitter on the inadequacy of the preaching ministry and the unwilligness of the Queen and her government to attend to the matter. The onus placed on secular government to fulfil its duties in this respect and the displeasure expressed that they had not been accomplished assumes a central theme in his three treatises, even to the point of presenting his case in a lengthy and excruciatingly tedious and repetitive manner. He deplored the over-indulgence of the higher clergy: 'My purpose', he maintained, 'is to shew that all the good politique lawes in the woorld cannot wash awaie these our stains...If it be the wil of the Parliament therfore we shal be bettered,

---

112   J. Marlowe, *The Puritan Tradition in English Life* (London, 1956), pp.27-30.

let the word be preached among vs'.[113] His comment on the condition of preaching is striking for its honesty. For one parish where an ordinary quarter sermon is preached, he declared, there are twenty without any. Since tithes are paid a preaching ministry should be made available. In his examination of the Church's problems, Penry revealed the degree to which they hindered that ministry from being installed.

One factor which was evident in Penry's first treatise was his belief that, if religious reform was to have any success, the Welsh language was essential in several areas of Wales. Although he was eager to see English as the chief vehicle for propagating Protestantism he was well aware that the Welsh language was essential if the faith was to progress in the more isolated areas. He was equally aware that ministers were not able to express themselves adequately even in their mother tongue. This was a fundamental problem, but he advocated the use of a Welsh-speaking ministry which, he believed, would create uniformity in the spoken language. Equally important in Penry's view was the inadequate number of ministers competent to preach the gospel. He estimated that the universities could despatch 3000 ministers, some of whom might be employed to ease the situation in Wales. He was equally aware that a significant decline had occurred in the number of students who desired to enter holy orders, and students who obtained fellowships were prepared to forgo their academic positions rather than be obliged to enter the ministry.[114] He declared that the 'idle' priesthood had undermined the appeal of the ministry and that the minister had no certainty of a living to which he might be inducted. In such a situation Penry appealed to the Queen in parliament in the first treatise, *Aequity of an Humble Supplication* (1587), to ensure that learned ministers might be assured of their living for their lives, and if that were allowed, able men might be attracted to the Church and their less motivated colleagues already in office be made to function more efficiently.[115]

Penry continued further to suggest the use that might be made of Welsh clergy – many Welsh-speaking – who held livings in England and who

---

113 J. Penry, *Three Treatises concerning Wales*, p.36.
114 Ibid., p.38.
115 Ibid.

might be induced to return to serve in Welsh parishes.[116] On a more radical level he observed that there were laymen not educated at universities proficient in theology, and even better than some learned priests, who might also be able to undertake the task of preaching. One university, he stated, had sent out 3,400 graduates since Elizabeth I's accession, of whom 400 were properly trained and might easily have been employed in Wales: alas only 12 were available in 1587 in Wales to undertake the task.[117] The statistics which Penry supplies are doubtless suspect but reveal his enthusiasm in pressing home his case.

Penry even proceeded to tackle the thorny problem of the maintenance of ministers. He wished Elizabeth to install preachers, the sincerest of whom, he stated, 'would thresh to get their liuing, rather than the people should want preaching'.[118] Excuses offered to avoid this service hindered the progress of the Reformation, as did non-residents and impropriations which prevented the priest from living well by the Church. Penry deplored the fact that some gentry held 6 impropriate livings and recommended that one-tenth of every impropriate living in Wales should be bestowed to maintain a teaching minister who would become a Queen's farmer in every one of the impropriate livings owned by the Crown in Wales.[119] Non-preachers, he stated, held three livings, and many livings were held by university students who were non-resident except in rare occasions when they came to 'fleece'. 'Non-residencies', he maintained, 'have cut the throt of our Church...it is the very desolation of the Church, the vndoing of the common wealth and a demonstratiue token that the Lorde will watch ouer vs to euill, and not to good'.[120] A learned ministry could be encouraged if one living alone be allowed each resident priest.

Penry deplored the reading ministry which was often employed. In his view it was inferior to a preaching ministry. The standard of reading was, in his view, unsatisfactory because not all the scriptures were available in the Welsh language. The Old Testament had not yet appeared so that the

---

116 Ibid.
117 Ibid., p.39.
118 Ibid.
119 Ibid., p.40.
120 Ibid.

first lesson in parish churches was read in English to a largely monoglot peasantry.[121] He believed that the whole Testament might be translated by one person in two years and in a shorter time if more assistance could be given. The small prophets could be translated first and read in services to await the appearance of the remainder of the Old Testament. He ardently appealed to the Queen that she should take it in hand to see that the whole work be translated and published as soon as possible. Dialectical differences should not cause any problems for if a preaching ministry were to be introduced parishioners, he believed, would read the scriptures at home and become acquainted with the diction. Ministers could also compare the English and Welsh versions in order that the Welsh might be better understood. Penry's emphasis is again on a preaching ministry, the want of it revealing that 'the high mysteries of salvation' were unknown to parish priests and that consequently non-residents who 'do imprint these skars of spiritual misery...' do not shield parishioners from social and economic hardship.[122] He then proceeded to show that dearth of foodstuffs and increased poverty created hardship in isolated country areas. Normally, he stated, men would sow sufficient corn to sustain the family for a year and would breed enough cattle and sheep to purchase the seed. The poor harvest of 1585, however, was one in a long series of bad harvests in the latter half of the sixteenth century and early decades of the next. It had yielded little corn and less bread-corn was sown because of scarcity.[123] Consequently, many were reduced to beggary and forced to seek all ways and means of surviving: 'the very sinowe of their mainteinance is gone', he declared, 'As long as the Lords house lieth wast in our land, we shal sow but meere salt'.[124]

According to the Calvinist system established at Geneva, the Church's authority lay in ecclesiastical affairs and that of the state in secular politics. The state had a God-given authority and civil magistrates were regarded as 'ministers of divine justice' concerned with setting up and extending justice of morals.[125] The state could not interfere in ecclesiastical affairs

---

[121] Ibid.
[122] Ibid., p.41.
[123] G. Williams, 'The economic life of Glamorgan, 1536-1642', in *Glam. County Hist.*, IV, pp.17-19; C. W. Lewis, 'The decline of professional poetry', in R. G. Gruffydd (ed.), *A Guide to Welsh Literature c.1530-1700* (Cardiff, 1997), pp.48-50.
[124] J. Penry, *Three Treatises concerning Wales*, p.42.
[125] V. H. H. Green, *Renaissance and Reformation* (London, 1956), pp.175-6.

but, at the same time, it was expected to support the Church. Thomas Cartwright and Robert Brown emphasized the Queen's subordinate position as 'nurse' and 'servant' to the Church. Civil magistrates, it was added, were liable to excommunication by Elders if they hindered the Presbytery from executing God's laws.[126]

Penry's censure of the government became sharper in his second treatise, *An Exhortation unto the Governours ... of Wales...*(1588), in which he addressed Henry Herbert, 2nd earl of Pembroke and Lord President of the Council in the Marches.[127] He, like Penry, was educated at Peterhouse, and was a strict governor at Ludlow and a staunch supervisor of public administration. That Council, made statutory in 1543, was the government's most powerful agency in Wales and the border shires, an institution, Penry considered, which should be in the vanguard of religious reform. He scurrilously attacked its negligence, its contempt of God's ordinance to care for the salvation of the people and its failure to identify itself truly as His representative.[128] He considered it urgent that reform be introduced because he was evidently aware that the religious settlement was dependent on the queen's survival and that its reputation was entirely reliant on the subjects' loyalty to the queen and her government. It had taken no action to prevent the induction of reading ministers who failed to convey true doctrine to their parishioners. Teaching and preaching of the gospel was needed by all: 'the worde read', he declared, 'is the same vnto all, whereas the foode of eternall life must bee made milke vnto the weake and tender, and strong meate vnto them which are capable thereof'.[129] The Reformation, it was contended, should be carried to its logical end; its teaching should be based on the Bible as revealed in the divine message imparted to the Apostles in the scriptures.

In a similar vein the *Exhortation* particularly drew attention to Herbert's role as chief magistrate in Wales in this context, whose success in undertaking his responsibilities was considered essential for maintaining the spiritual well-being of the Welsh nation. As magistrate he was to see to it that divine law would be served 'or els the cursse of God wil light

---

[126] D. McGinn, *John Penry and the Marprelate Controversy*, p.18.
[127] *DWB*, pp.350-1.
[128] J. Penry, *Three Treatises concerning Wales*, p.50.
[129] Ibid., p.56.

vpon you, for your carelessnesse in this point'.[130] His address and challenge to Herbert was unequivocal:

> Hath the Lord called you to be lorde president of Wales...to the ende, you shoulde sit still when you see your people runne vnto hell, and the Lord so notably dishonoured vnder your gouernement? The estate of Wales not being amended by your meanes, the poore people shall die in their sins, and be damned, but their bloud will the Lord require at your hands...So, my Lord, with reuerence be it spoken vnto your Honour, if it lie not in you to bring Wales vnto the knowledge of God, or if your leisure will not serue thereto, then bee not the Lorde president thereof.[131]

Herbert's position in public life made him responsible for ensuring that the word preached was made available in Wales. 'For you ought to acknowledge your selfe ruler ouer none', Penry remarked, 'that doe not subiect themselues at least outwardly vnto true religion'.[132] His stand on the role of governors and the honour accorded them in the state is positive:

> Gouernors my Lorde, must gouerne vnder God. They haue no allowance to be rulers wher the Lord is not serued, where he hath no acknowledgement of Superioritie, there man hath no commission from him to beare rule.[133]

Penry reminded him of the fine example set by his family since God had given it, through the Word, its eminence in the state. He proceeded by reminding him that although magistrates considered themselves the maintainers of true religion they were neither godly nor virtuous unless they were able to draw their subjects 'out of the snares of blindnes and ignorance'.[134] If magistrates loved God, he declared, then they should ensure that people in their charge were fed with knowledge and trained by them in the fear of God. The most enduring feature of his message in all three treatises is its urgency in view of the political circumstances of the late 1580s. Penry ardently appealed to Herbert to attend to his religious

---

130 Ibid., p.59.
131 Ibid., pp.59-60.
132 Ibid., p.60.
133 Ibid.
134 Ibid., p.61.

duties as a civil magistrate: 'procure you the woorde preached, for your selues', he stated, 'and obay the same, or els woe woorth you, woe woorth you, I say Magistrates, Gentlemen, Ministers, and people, for otherwise you reiect Iesus Christ, and wil not haue him to raigne ouer you'.[135] In the interests of establishing a preaching ministry Penry desired him to dismiss the existing clergy, and called on him to bestow some of the proceeds of his estates to appoint good preachers.

Moving on to examine what the symptoms of spiritual misery were yet again in Wales, Penry emphasized that reading in the Church was inadequate: what parishioners received was the reading of a few psalms, a few prayers, a chapter from the New Testament in Welsh (the original 1567 version), and they poorly conveyed to the people and not made intelligible to one in ten of the hearers.[136] The reason for that might well have been William Salesbury's linguistic idiosyncracies but also, of equal importance, as Penry makes clear, was the poor quality of the clergy themselves.

In this respect Penry's contempt of bishops knew no bounds. To him they were 'the verye ground-worke of this our miserable confusion'.[137] Whereas vestments and ceremonies had occupied most Puritans in the early years of Elizabeth I's reign, their opposition to the Prayer Book led to their attack on episcopal authority which they considered to be ungodly. Thomas Cartwright, and Walter Travers, both at Cambridge and leaders of the Presbyterian movement, declared that a disciplinary episcopacy was not acceptable in the Bible. On the contrary, it was believed that church ministers should be equal under God. Puritan classes had sought to undermine episcopal authority, the aim being to establish a Genevan system consisting of ministers and elected elders and a hierarchical structure headed by a National Assembly.[138] By Penry's day the anonymous Marprelate Tracts (1588-9), coinciding with Penry's invectives, represented the peak of anti-episcopal literature. Whether they were written by John Udall, preacher at Kingston-upon-Thames,

---

[135]   Ibid., p.76.
[136]   Ibid., p.56.
[137]   Ibid., p.61.
[138]   For discussions of Calvin's organization see W. G. Naphy, *Calvin and the Consolidation of the Genevan Reformation* (Manchester/New York, 1994); E. Cameron, *The European Reformation* (Oxford, 1991), pp.153-5.

John Field, Job Throckmorton or John Penry or any other is less important than the austere message which they conveyed.[139] In his treatises Penry was equally scathing, particularly in the second entitled *An Exhortation vnto the Governours...of Wales* (1588). Bishops, he said, were anti-Christ who allowed rogues to serve the Church.

> Therefore wo be to the shepheards of Wales...which feede themselues, should not the shepheards feed their flocks; you eat the fat and cloath you with the wooll, but you feede not the flocke...And I trust in the Lord Iesus, to see his church florish in wales, when the memorie of Lord-Bishops are buried in hell whence they came...And giue you ouer your places, or doutlesse, the plague and curse of God will eat you vppe. You are vsurpers, you tyrannize ouer the Lords people.[140]

A harsh judgement indeed, and possibly unjustifiable. Yet Penry proceeded with his mission to cleanse the Church. Together with bishops 'dumb ministers' (an often used description by Penry) should be supplanted. They prophaned the sacraments, living on 'stealth, sacriledge and the spoile of souls'.[141] Since the marks of a true church were the word preached, the right administration of the sacraments and the outward form of church government, Penry vented his spleen on unworthy reading ministers who made sinners of those who received the sacraments at their hands. They have an 'outward calling' only, whereas the true preaching minister has an 'inward calling' arising from spiritual inspiration.

'There is no minister but a preaching minister by his institution', he declared, and if there is no preaching minister near at hand parents should seek one from afar to baptize their children. If that is not possible then it is admissible in the sight of God to leave them unbaptized until one is found. Although ministers represent the outward calling of the ministry, the true minister essentially possesses a 'being' or 'life', given only by God, and a birth bestowed by the Church as an instrument of God's ordinance by virtue of his outward calling.

---

[139] For a discussion of Penry's alleged authorship of the tracts see D. McGinn, *John Penry and the Marprelate Controversy*; G. Williams, 'Marprelate and patriot?', 361-72.
[140] J. Penry, *Three Treatises concerning Wales*, p.65.
[141] Ibid., p.66.

> Be a man therefore neuer so godly, neuer so learned, endued with neuer
> so liuelye faculties of the ministerie, yet he is no minister in deed, vnlesse
> he haue the ordinaunce of his God vpon him by his outward calling.[142]

Preaching the gospel is a gift not dependent on ordination. They who
have not been ordained and who have that gift, as well as the life given
by God to the minister separate from the outward calling, constitute the
true preachers. '...Menne not ordained of God for the gathering of the
saints', Penry maintained further, 'are no ministers whatoseuer calling
they haue in the Church'.[143] The preaching of the gospel is a gift not
dependent on ordination. He who does not have the outward calling of
the Church is no minister unless God has given him the life.

In the introduction to John Penry's third treatise, *A View of some part of
such public wants and disorders*...(1588) references are made to Dr Robert
Some (who became Master of Peterhouse in 1589), whom Penry regarded
as 'a godly and learned man', and who responded to his invitation to
reply syllogistically to his fifty-three propositions, contained in an
appendix, which rejected readers as ministers.[144] Some accused him of
being 'an vnderminer of the ciuill State' and of the unpreaching ministry.
Penry, however, obstinately adhered to his belief that the Welsh people
'desire to be watered by the dewe of Christs holy Gospell, and to be
compassed about, with that beautifull wall of his holy gouernment'.[145]
Penry was firm in his view of the role of civil government in protecting
God's Church. He regarded the Queen as a 'Christian magistrate whose
sacred authority I subject my self unto and reverence as the royal
ordinance of God's own majesty'.[146] He was prepared to obey her
authority in the church with a good conscience despite its imperfections.

In the main body of his third treatise Penry then proceeded to examine the
role of the magistrate and defined the difference between that secular
office and the minister. Magistracy was lawful according to the word of
God, he maintained, but, while the life and office of the minister is
prescribed in the word containing gifts and separated from his outward

---

142 Ibid., pp.82-4 (esp. 83).
143 Ibid., p.97.
144 Ibid., p.98.
145 Ibid., p.102.
146 Ibid., 103.

calling, those of the magistracy are neither prescribed nor contained nor separated from his outward calling.[147] Outward calling gives the magistrate his life although the person performing its functions needs gifts to discharge the office. The essence of magistracy lies in the gifts of courage, understanding and wisdom among other virtues, those of the minister are faithfulness. Magistracy is derived from outward calling but the minister is in possession of a ministry bestowed upon him by God. Penry regarded those who served God in civil government to be endowed with gifts and to be His true messengers. Those who do not serve him were they who increased their status and authority through greed, acquisitiveness and oppression at the expense of others. True magistrates, in rooting out all undesirable officials in the Church and who, 'seeing that the worde [is] preached...desire that the God of heauen and earth may be acknowledged, and accounted worthy alone to rule in his Church within this land'.[148] The deficiencies in the Church (the 'disease' and 'malady', as he called them) to which he referred were to be remedied by the authority of parliament. Moreover he wished parliament to promote God's glory by receiving and considering suits and petitions, and urged heads of families to teach their households in the faith, an advantage which, according to his testimony, he had enjoyed as a child in his own home:

> ...the Lord should enioine, more vnto a father, or maister in the gouernment of his family...For a father and so a maister, is not only bound to see, that his sonne bee no Idolatour, or swearer...but also to bring them vpp in instruction and information of the Lord.[149]

It is at this stage, in the third treatise, that he focused on what he considered to be the dangers of Roman Catholic practices. He had been employed in 'plucking vp by the rootes, of these filthie Italian weedes' which had polluted and 'deformed' the state. He informed parliament of its duties in this respect and declared his anxiety not only because of defects in service but also because of the damage that corruption and abuse of the church might incur.[150] The government had an obligation to attend to the spiritual needs of the Welsh people since it was shameful

---

147 Ibid., pp.130-8.
148 Ibid., pp.105-6.
149 Ibid., p.20.
150 Ibid., pp.111-13 (esp. 111).

that a state that was at its most flourishing in maintaining 'outward peace' should be neglectful of a nation's 'want of knowledge'.[151] The Welsh people knew not 'the right hand from the left' and 'governors' unto whom 'he hath committed inferiours, discharge not their duties in his sight, vnlesse they haue great care of the saluation of their people'.[152] Penry proceeded further to warn the government that although it may consider itself to be flourishing at that time, unless it repented, God might destroy it. In his mind a parliament involved in maintaining the security of the kingdom but which did not attend to the 'eternal misery of a whole nation' is inconceivable. And he continued:

> Will it then profit them at all, to haue liued in a kingdome professing true religion, though they haue gayned the whol world therein, seeing they are sure to lose their owne soules: because in this life they haue wanted the preaching of the Gospell.[153]

Corruption tolerated by the laws of the state and supported by parliament, and described as 'most pernicious and dangerous', would surely arouse the wrath of God.[154] Could parliament justify its defence of ecclesiastical officialdom and did it believe that any church government is lawful before God? Penry dismissed Dr John Bridges's argument in *A Defence of the Government established in the Church of England* which considered ecclesiastical government to be none else but a human constitution which might be lawfully changed and abolished at a magistrate's pleasure.[155] Secular government, he declared, was ungoldy because it drew no distinction between that which belonged to the true worship of God (as did ecclesiastical government) and that which appertained to civil policy or affairs.

With regard to papal authority ecclesiastical government, as a human institution, allowed it to assume superiority over all civil magistrates and pastors. Penry believed that the Pope had as good a warrant to function as had the bishops of Wales. They exercised temporal government as civil

---

151 Ibid., 117.
152 Ibid.
153 Ibid., p.119.
154 Ibid., p.125.
155 Ibid., p.102.

magistrates and claimed superiority over ministers more than state legislation had done.[156] They had no right to join both magistracy and ministry together and their spiritual authority over their fellow ministers was supreme:

> ...I demand of you, by what authority you are so far, in respect of temporal things, and the abuse of ecclesiasticall jurisdiction, preferred before many godly and learned ministers in this land; as you by vertue of your places, are Barons of the parliament house, enjoye great revenews, and are Lordes ouer your brethren and fellow ministers?[157]

Since parliament had dismissed papal power why had it not pronounced against itself for its inadequacy in spiritual matters? In his mind, for parliament to allow ministers leave to join the magistracy and the ministry together would bring 'a final destruction vpon the land'.[158] It is wrong to make ecclesiastical government a human constitution which undermines civil government. Penry resented the subordination of parliament in matters regarding religion to bishops in Convocation. Parliament robbed itself of its own prerogative and liberties in this respect. If convocation contained learned and sincere ministers, he continued, its decisions might then be presented to parliament for enactment. Hence church governors might be better placed to advise parliament legally:

> For as in a christian common wealth, where the ciuill state sincerely fauoureth the true worship of the Lord, it is not tolerable...to establish any thing in the church, but by the authoritie of the christian magistrat: so wher there are godly wise and sincere ministers, it is vnlawful for the ciuill gouernour, to order any thing in the church within his domminions, but by their direction according to the word.[159]

Parliament should be advised by a truthful Convocation, but that Convocation should not be permitted to enact upon its own authority. To allow that would 'charge the wolues vnder paine of the displeasure of careful shepherds, to see that the lambes may be fedd, besides the

---

[156] Ibid., pp.127-9.
[157] Ibid., p.132.
[158] Ibid., p.135.
[159] Ibid., pp.141-2.

injurious derogation that thereby is offered vnto the liberties of this house'.[160]

In conclusion, John Penry charged parliament to accomplish two things, namely to abolish all that is a breach of God's ordinance and to place godly and learned men to provide spiritual sustenance for the people. The dangers also extended beyond Convocation. His *Aequity of an Humble Supplication* pleaded the cause of Zion based on the 'evidence of greatest antiquity'. Another work, *Y Drych Cristianogawl* (1586-7), a long treatise on the 'Four Last Things', 'printed in an obscure cave in North Wales', that is at Rhiwledyn or Trwyn-y-fuwch (the Little Orme), Llandudno, was 'published by an author vnknowne' (now considered to be Robert Gwyn, described as 'a learned theologian and a most eloquent preacher', and a prolific recusant author of Penyberth, Llŷn).[161] The printer was Roger Thackwell and six others, and the work proved to be the most important Catholic publication to appear in Wales. Penry scornfully described the work as being based on Robert Persons's *First Booke of Christian Exercise, Appertayning to Resolution* (1582), enlarged as *A Christian Directorie* (1585), a 'booke contayning many substantiall errors...and ...shamful fables'. He feared that the work, of which the prelates had obtained a copy, being 'entertained of them', might lead to serious consequences for the new religious establishment. Penry wrote at a time when anti-Spanish sentiments were at their height and he orchestrated what he had to say about the dangers to spiritual welfare in Wales and England around that theme.[162] He also dreaded what might be the consequences of the foreign dangers from Spain (Philip II), Italy (the Papacy) and the Guise faction in France (the powerful Roman Catholic allies of Philip II and formers of the Catholic League, 1585).[163] Penry's dread that the Roman faith might overrun the realm is a constant reminder of the dangers of external threat in time of war. Had God not intervened, he declared in the first treatise, the situation might have become critical. The Babington Plot (1586) had shaken the government, not only because of the dangers associated with

---

160 Ibid., p.142.
161 Ibid., p.157; G. Bowen (ed.), *Y Drych Kristnogawl: llawysgrif Caerdydd 3.240*; idem, (Cardiff, 1996), xix, xxvii, xlvi; R. G. Gruffydd (ed.), *A Guide to Welsh Literature*, III, c.1530-1700, pp.226-7, 268-9; idem, *Argraffwyr Cyntaf Cymru: Gwasgau Dirgel y Catholigion adeg Elisabeth* (Caerdydd, 1972) pp.1-33; G.Bowen, *Y Drych Kristianogawl: astudiaeth*, JWEH, 1988. p.8. Penry calls the work a 'pamphlet' and probably refers to the first part that had appeared by 1587.
162 W. B. Maltby, *The Black Legend in England: The Development of anti-Spanish Sentiments 1558-1660* (Durham, NC, 1971), pp.76-87.

a Roman Catholic conspiracy, but also because Mary Queen of Scots, who was deeply involved in the plot to assassinate Elizabeth, was poised to place herself on the English throne:

> Howe likely was it, had not he [i.e. God] in mercy choked with their owne raiging spirits, these vnsatiable blood-suckers, Babington, and his adherentes, that we should have had in this kingdome the hand of the vile, against the honorable, the base against the noble, the indigne against the woorthiest of the land?[164]

To prevent further calamity the government attempted to discover the causes of such ungodly acts. That was not possible, Penry insisted, so long as parliament allowed non-residencies, pluralities of impropriate livings, ungodly ministers and so on, which would be useless in any attempt to defend the realm against Spain, France and any other of the 'forces of Rhomish Cain'. His hatred for Rome knew no bounds but led him into believing that they could be agencies of God designed to destroy the kingdom. For its sins, Penry declared, God would pour his wrath upon it and destroy its very existence. If God had meant to call the kingdom to reckoning for its 'great ignorance' and 'wicked ecclesiasticall constitutions' he would not have saved it from the onslaught of the Armada in the summer of 1588.[165] Parliament, he maintained further, must fear God; the victory over the Armada was God's warning that he had spared the kingdom on that occasion, but if the Queen in parliament failed to reform religion immediately then He would seek retribution for their sins. Penry's words at that point were admonitory:

> It is not therefore the Spanish furniture [equipment and outfit] and preparations; but the sins within the land, which we are most of all to feare. For although the army of the Spaniard were co[n]sumed with the arrowes of famine: although the contagious and deuouring pestilence had eaten them vp by thousands: although their tottering shipps were dispersed, and caried away with the whirlewinde and tempest...a navie of winde and weather beaten ships, a refuse of feeble and discomfited men, shalbe sufficiently able to preuaile against this lande: vnlesse another

---

163 J. Penry, *Three Treatises concerning Wales*, pp.157, 159.
164 Ibid., p.27.
165 Ibid., pp.27, 161. Cain was the perfidious elder son of Adam and Eve in the Book of Genesis (iv, 1-16).

course be taken for God's glory in Wales by your h[onoura]b[les] then hitherto hath bene.[166]

Despite their depressingly negative tone John Penry's diatribes do contain burning issues in his day and age when the reformed churches on the continent were in a state of decline. The technique which he used was comparable to that which his English colleagues, such as John Field and Sir Anthony Cope, employed.[167] The first treatise, for example, was presented to parliament by the Puritan Edward Donne Lee, of Abercynfor, Llandyfaelog, Carmarthenshire, son of a Buckinghamshire landowner, a prominent local government administrator and M.P. for Carmarthen boroughs in 1584 and 1586,[168] and Job Throckmorton, Puritan writer of Haseley, Warwickshire, and M.P. for the shire in 1586.[169] John Whitgift, Archbishop of Canterbury, had harassed Puritans and they consequently felt intimidated and repressed. That treatise, therefore, as Sir Glanmor Williams states, appears to be 'part of the elaborate campaign of propaganda and agitation which the Puritan "lobby" prepared for the parliament of that year [1587]' when the Presbyterians also presented to parliament a programme to establish a Presbyterian system in England and Wales.[170] It has been argued further that, despite the attention John Penry's intense patriotism and concern for Wales have received from historians since the early twentieth century, it appears that his chief concern was to disseminate the Puritan message and respect his personal religious convictions. He was essentially part of the Puritan propaganda machine, a fitting companion to John Udall, John Field and their associates in a time of crisis in the growth of reformed churches abroad and of increasing Jesuit missionary activity at home.[171]

Doubtless John Penry was given to exaggeration, purely for effect, and put to good use his rhetorical skills and his discursive style.

---

166 Ibid., pp.162-3.
167 G. Williams, 'Marprelate and patriot?', 374-5.
168 *The History of Parliament: The House of Commons 1558-1603*, ed. P. W. Hasler, (London, 1981), II, p.48. Donne Lee's maternal grandparents were Sir Thomas Johns of Abermarlais, Carmarthenshire, and Sir Edward Dwnn of Cydweli. L. Dwnn, *Heraldic Visitations of Wales*, ed. S. R. Meyrick (Llandovery, 1846), I, pp.20, 199; J. E. Neale, *Elizabeth I and her Parliaments, 1584-1601* (London, 1957), p.153.
169 *History of Parliament*, I, pp.492-4.
170 G. Williams, 'Marprelate and patriot?', 374.
171 Ibid., 374-5; J. Penry, *Three Treatises concerning Wales*, xii.

His often involved and complex method of writing and heavily loaded scriptural comparisons and references, whilst often obscuring the run of the argument, do however emphasize what he considered to be the most fundamental needs of religious life in his native country. Whether the establishment fully deserved the fierce denounciation it suffered is questionable since he deliberately failed to draw attention, as he might, to the more positive contributions of Welsh religious leaders of his day. He gave no tribute to the translators of the Bible, saw no value in their attempts to reform the Church, regarded the religious establishment in Wales as having been anti-Christ with no hope of redemption and paid no attention to the role of enlightened laymen in the production of Protestant literature, meagre though that output was. Also, he seemed not to be aware of the fact that licensed preachers were on the increase in England by the close of the sixteenth century, principally because of the educational opportunities available and the establishment of lectureships. In addition, the degree of practical reform achieved through the links forged between local clergy and the laity in England was less successful in Wales. What he did accomplish, however, and that unawares to him, was to hasten the publication of the Bible in late 1588 through his powerful criticism of the lack of the scriptures in the first and second treatises.[172] Whether this was his lasting contribution is questionable. More significant is the fact that Penry, despite his virtual anonymity in the subsequent annals of Welsh history before the close of the nineteenth century, did positively contribute to the rise of a dissenting movement in Wales which emerged within half a century. He also observed the weaknesses of the Elizabethan Church settlement which, in his view, revealed Laodicean features, and regarded it as being too loose and accommodating for true Protestants. He was well enough known for Vavasor Powell, one of the most dynamic of the leaders of the dissenting movement, to regard him, along with Henry Barrow, as his 'father in the faith'.[173] In his own day, despite his shortcomings, this irascible character stood out among a small but devoted band of separatist leaders, who desired to establish their vision of God's Church on earth. By arguing on the basis of the Genevan structure Penry advocated the creation of a partnership between Church and state in Elizabethan England to realise this vision.

---

[172] G. Williams, 'Bishop William Morgan (1545-1604) and the first Welsh Bible', in *The Welsh and their Religion*, pp.208-9.

[173] *Common-Prayer-Book No Divine Service* (London, 1660), pp.5, 15; R. T. Jones, *Vavasor Powell* (Swansea, 1971), pp.58, 172.

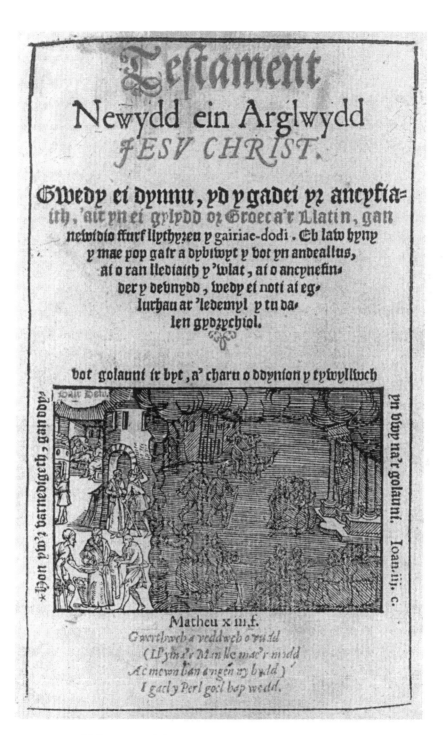

Title-page of the New Testament in Welsh, 1567

CHAPTER II

Scholars and the Protestant Settlement, c.1559-1640.

At the time of Elizabeth I's coming to the throne in the autumn of 1558 religious life and the social and economic factors which shaped it were in the throes of significant change. Her accession also coincided with much political uncertainty. Through the support and leadership of Sir William Cecil, Secretary of State and her chief counsellor, efforts were made to strengthen the government so as to safeguard the realm against uprisings and outbreaks of opposition to the new queen's religious policy. Her main needs at the time were to defend the realm against external threat, to reform religion and to reassert royal supremacy on new Protestant foundations. Although Elizabeth had no deep religious convictions she had been reared in the Protestant household of Catherine Parr, Henry VIII's last wife and, to Protestant leaders, she had become a symbol of deliverance from the Roman Catholic policies of her half-sister Mary. She was denounced by papists, however, as an excommunicate and regarded as illegitimate by the papacy.[1] Her position when she ascended to the throne, therefore, was not to be envied for she was surrounded by dangers she could not easily overcome.

Much that occurred in the religious and political spheres, the two central areas of control which were considered essential to maintain unity and uniformity in the state, depended largely on the attitudes and aims of the queen. If she had adopted the Roman Catholic faith then she would have been forced to regard her mother, Anne Boleyn, as a prostitute, and herself as illegitimate and dependent on the Pope for special dispensation to govern her realm. She certainly was not prepared to establish a Church organization and an ecclesiastical order independent of the state. The royal supremacy was maintained in politics and religion, and Elizabeth herself knew that the past could not be restored. Most of her subjects wished to see the return of her father's religious order, but that was impracticable owing to extreme measures taken in the reigns of Edward

---

[1]   C. Haigh, *English Reformations: Religion, Politics, and Society under the Tudors* (Oxford,1993), pp.235-50; N. L. Jones, *Faith by Statute: Parliament and the Settlement of Religion, 1559* (London, 1982); J. Guy, *Tudor England* (Oxford, 1988), pp.290-308; S. Doran, *Elizabeth I and Religion, 1558-1603* (London, 1994).

VI and Mary, and the conservative reactions to them. Doubtless Protestant missionaries had left their mark on England in the years 1547-53 and well before then. The task facing Elizabeth and her advisers was to devise a middle way which would be acceptable to all her subjects. She herself was essentially secular in mind and spirit, and her response to circumstances which she encountered revealed more her anxiety about maintaining unity within the realm than about her conscience and spiritual condition. Experience had taught her to be disciplined and she rejected any kind of idealism and extremism which might be detrimental to the realm's welfare. Her chief aim was to try to solve her main governmental problems, and organized religion was doubtless the most pressing issue in her first parliament.[2]

When Elizabeth came to the throne social and legal relationships between Wales and England had developed remarkably since the Acts of Union (1536-43). By then Henry VIII's legislation for Wales had enrooted itself firmly to the benefit of all those who considered that maintaining allegiance to the Tudor dynasty was vital to their progress.[3] Well before the dissolution of the religious houses and subsequently at an increasing pace, it was largely the world of the gentry which prospered, often at the expense of the Church. The Church as an institution was there to be exploited and was a means of broadening the material horizons and regional power of landed proprietors. At the same time, they harmfully involved themselves in its spiritual as well as its secular affairs, thus weakening further its capacity to function adequately. Most of them acquired offices and local power and, at the same time, clung tenaciously to the new religious order imposed on the realm by Elizabeth's parliament.

In view of episcopal opposition in the House of Lords and the lukewarm response in the Commons, asserting the 'supreme governorship' was no easy task. Existing church leaders were not in favour of it and, since there had never been a religious compromise before in England, royal policy

---

2   C. Cross, *The Royal Supremacy in the Elizabethan Church* (London, 1969); idem, 'Churchmen and the Royal Supremacy', in F. Heal and R. O'Day (eds.), *Church and Society in England, Henry VIII to James I* (London, 1977), pp.23-34; P. Williams, *The Tudor Regime* (Oxford, 1979), pp.253-67; idem, *The Later Tudors: England, 1547-1603* (Oxford, 1995), pp.229-37
3   G. Williams, *Renewal and Reformation: Wales c.1415-1642*, pp.304-31; J. G. Jones, *Early Modern Wales, c. 1525-1640*, pp.143-8; P. Jenkins, *A History of Modern Wales 1536-1990* (London, 1992), pp.102-10.

was viewed with some trepidation. In this context the role of the Church needs to be considered. The monarchy had been placed in control of the Church, implying that it had a political foundation. The emphasis on comprehensiveness and uniformity was understandable because any dissension would have damaged not only the Church itself but also social harmony which might be established in an age when stability was increasingly hindered by financial inflation and economic unrest. Monarchy therefore relied on the ecclesiastical hierarchy and an actively-engaged gentry devoted to maintaining concord and securely enrooting the new settlement.[4]

In Wales the new Church was accepted without protest. In the summer of 1559 commissioners were sent around all four dioceses, together with those of Hereford and Worcester, which formed the western circuit, to administer the oath of uniformity among the clergy and to receive full acknowledgement of the queen's supremacy.[5] Among these commissioners were Richard Davies, Thomas Young and Rowland Meyrick, three ardent Protestant leaders who were to be elevated to episcopal seats in Wales soon after the queen's accession. Davies and Young had experienced a period of exile in some of the Protestant centres of Europe during Mary's reign, where they met Protestant leaders, and were devoted to the promotion of the faith in their native country.

Three serious shortcomings in Welsh religious life again adversely affected the Church's fortunes soon after the settlement, namely its poverty, its conservatism and the severe limitations placed on its resources, features which exposed the many obstacles which confronted religious leaders in four of the remotest and most inhospitable dioceses in the realm.[6] In a mountainous country with no large towns, no capital city and no university, the Church's resources had always been circumscribed. A short and depressing description of Llandaff appears in Rice Merrick's *Morganiae Archaiographia* (c.1578) where references appear to its ruinous state and 'the absence of the bishops dwelling at Mathern, and the canons or prebendaries, sometime having fair houses and dwelling there, became

---

4   G. Williams, *Welsh Reformation Essays*, pp.26-7; idem, *Wales and the Reformation*, pp.216-47.
5   G. Williams, 'The Elizabethan Settlement of Religion in Wales and the Marches, 1559-1560', in
      Welsh Reformation Essays, pp.141-53; idem, *Wales and the Reformation*, pp.218-53.
6   Idem, *Wales and the Reformation*, pp.19-39; idem, *The Welsh Church from Conquest to
      Reformation* (Cardiff, 1962), p. 461 et. seq.

non-resident, and their houses almost in utter decay'.[7] The benefits of the New Learning had hardly borne fruit among parochial clergy in the Welsh dioceses, and the printing press had made no impact at all before 1546. The Church on the threshold of the Protestant Reformation was very fragile. Its frequently absentee English bishops before Elizabeth's reign, its lethargic clergy, its illiterate and largely monoglot population and the continuous attacks by the laity on church property and tithes had serious effects on the quality of pastoral work. Although the priesthood was accepted for what it had to offer in the parishes the formal language of church services was Latin before 1549 and English thereafter, so that the liturgy was totally meaningless to a monoglot peasantry. The Welsh dioceses were among the poorest in the realm, and continual provision of pastoral care was a daunting task, particularly in out-of-the-way rural communities. The priesthood lacked adequate resources in education and were unable to cater for the spiritual needs of impoverished parishioners. Lay landowners pressurized the church and took every opportunity to exploit it. One of the most explicit attacks on such overbearing behaviour appeared in Richard Davies's preamble to the Welsh version of the New Testament published in 1567, six years after his installation as bishop of St David's:

> Mae'n gymaynt trachwant y byd heddiw i tir a dayar, y aur, ac arian, a chowaeth, ac na cheir ond yn anamyl vn yn ymddiriet i Dduw, ac yw addaweidion. Trais a lladrad, anudon, dichell, ffalster, a thraha: a rhain megis a chribynae mae pob bath ar ddyn yn casclu ac yn tynnu atto...eithr mae chwant da'r byd wedi boddi Cymru heddiw, a chwedi gyrru ar aball pob ceneddfae arbennic a rhinwedd dda. Can ys beth yw swydd ynghymru heddiw ond bach i dynu cnu a chnwd ey gymydoc attaw?...Amyl ynghymru, ir nas craffa cyfraith, i ceir neuadd y gwr bonheddig yn noddfa lladron...Ni chafi o ennyt yma fanegi yr anrhaith a wnaeth chwant da byd, ac anghredinieth i addaweidion Duw ar bob rryw ddyn ynghymru o eisie dysceidieth yr yscrythr lan [8]

[There is much covetousness of the world to-day for land and possessions, gold and silver and wealth, so that only unfrequently wilt thou find one who trusts in

7   R. Merrick, *Morganiae Archaiographia*, ed. B. Ll. James (Cardiff, 1983), p.94.
8   *Rhagymadroddion*, pp.32-3. See also A. O. Evans, *A Memorandum on the Legality of the Welsh Bible and the Welsh Version of the Book of Common Prayer* (Cardiff, 1925), pp.107-8.

God and His promises. Violence and theft, perjury, deceit, hypocrisy and arrogance; and with these as of with rakes every condition of men gather and drag to themselves...the lust of the world's goods has drowned Wales to-day, and impoverished every special quality and good virtue. For what is an office in Wales to-day but a hook for a man to draw to himself the wool and the crops of a neighbour?...Often in Wales, though the law marks it not, the mansion of the nobleman is a refuge for thieves...Time will not permit me to unfold the harm which the lust for this world's goods has wrought, and the disbelief of the promises of God among all conditions of men in Wales because of the lack of teaching of the Holy Scripture...]

Davies's attitude is unmistakably clear. His words appear to prophesy doom for all those who abused their authority or abjured all responsibilities to maintain public standards in Wales. His comments were as biting as those of John Penry but were directed more fiercely towards the laity than those of the Brecknockshire Puritan. Dr John Davies (Siôn Dafydd Rhys), the Welsh Catholic Renaissance scholar, like others of his generation censured the gentry for not attending to their cultural and spiritual duties to their fellow Welshmen, particularly in the use made of the Welsh language. Their negligence in such matters, he maintained, was deplorable, and he further declared that their rivalries and lack of unity perpetuated insecurity and instability:

> Canys heddwch yw y Cyfarwydd a'r Llywiawdr, y sydd yn cadarnháu pôb glân gyfeillach: ac hebddei ny's gall fôd nêb ryw gydfasnach ym mhlîth pobl y byd, na dim cyfrannu meddylieu...A'r anghytundeb a'r anhêddwch bêth a wnâ hitheu, onyd gyrru pawb benbenn, i ymleassu a e gilydd, ac i waethu pawb arr eu gilydd; a hynny o rann cymhell pawb eu gilydd weithieu i fôd yn anghenogion yn ôl treilo yr cwbl: weithieu i adu Gwlâd, a myned arr encil rhag ofn gelyn neu gyfraith...A hynn...y sydd yn rhy aml i'n plith ni y Cymry, ac ynn drygu yn rhy dôst arnam. Canys nynî a'n drycanian yn anad neb, sydd ynn rhoi peunyddiol gynhaliaeth i Lys Cynghor Cyphinyddion Cymry: ac ony bei ni a'n llîd a'n cynhen tu ac at eu gilydd o amser pwy gilydd, ef a allei llawer gwr ynn byw wrth gyfreith, fyned i gylôra; ac o's mynnei i fwyâra, yn lle ei gyfreithwra.[9]

---

9   *Rhagymadroddion*, pp.79-80.

[For peace is the leader and governor which confirms every pure friendship; and without it there can be no co-operate trading among people of the world and no sharing of minds... And what does the disagreement and hostility do except to set everyone at loggerheads with each other, to oppress and harm each other; and to compel each other at times to become needy after expending all: sometimes to leave country and to retreat in fear of enemy or law... And this... is too often in our midst the Welsh, and damages us severely. For we and our evil disposition more than any, give daily maintenance to the Court of the Council in the Marches of Wales; and were it not for our wrath and contention towards each other time after time many a lawabiding man could go to gather nuts and, if he wished, to gather blackberries instead of going to law.]

The author, who was eager to equate peace and security with the order imposed by the Tudors on Wales, was aware that indiscretions among the leaders of society hindered the growth of goodwill and that controversy and contention defeated the end of law. It was the lack of unity and understanding among the Welsh people, the author contended, that made them practice injustice and misuse law chiefly to promote their own interests. This is reminiscent of the situation in the pre-1536 era when the old marcher lordships were constantly regarded as regions where lawlessness and disorder were condoned and where the perpetrators of crime avoided the consequences of justice.[10] Davies's Catholic companion, the author and translator Robert Gwyn, of Penyberth in Llŷn, likewise, some years earlier, censured the more eligible members of Welsh society for not offering their dependants spiritual guidance to the degree that their counterparts did in England. They would pay for their sins and dilatory attendance to their duties on the day of reckoning, he maintained, for the common people invariably took their example from their superiors. They shunned the language and faith which led their English acquaintances to believe that they were ashamed of their heritage.[11]

As expected, Dr John Davies and Robert Gwyn publicized the Roman Catholic viewpoint on the need for spiritual uplift and their comments reveal the instability that persisted, and caused concern, in the

---

[10] I. Bowen (ed.), *The Statutes of Wales* (London, 1908), pp.54, 62; G. Williams, *Renewal and Reformation*, pp.257-69.

[11] *Rhagymadroddion*, pp.52-3.

Elizabethan Church in Wales. Their desire was to expose what they considered to be the most serious lapses in the religious and cultural life of Wales, thus posing the question: to what degree were the leaders of Welsh society in a position not only to introduce the principles of the new Learning into Wales but also to support and defend a new institution designed to promote that learning as well as create uniformity in the realm.[12] Roman Catholic apologists, fully aware of the benefits which most Protestant gentry in Wales had gained from exploiting the church, asserted their reservations as to whether leaders of Welsh communities, regardless of their religious convictions, were able to improve the moral standards of the people.

In theory and in fact the gentry lay at the apex of regional society and the basis of their power derived essentially from the powerful interaction and alliance established between them and the Tudor dynasty. Their virtues symbolized power and authority which combined together strong bonds of political and cultural identities. The ideal of the 'perfect' gentleman, as expounded in Wales and England, consisted of a combination of Aristotelian qualities aimed at cultivating moral virtues in the community together with the Christian attributes of faith, charity and humility.[13] The structure was established on the concept of order in God's creation which was regarded as the foundation of medieval thought on degree, order and status. Society was based essentially on a divinely approved organic unity. Although the virtues attributed to worthy gentlemen – primarily courtesy, humanity and civility – were secular in the sixteenth century, they were associated with Christian principles and attached to them were the qualities of prudence, wisdom, courage and hospitality. The concept of nobility which underlay the role of the 'good man' in his community, was essentially interpreted in Elizabethan England as that of the Christian gentleman appointed to govern according to the writings of Sir Thomas Elyot, Sir Thomas Smith and other social commentators. Government, in its various functions, was defined in a religious as well as secular context, grace (*grazia*), a fundamental feature of the renaissance gentleman,

---

12 G. Williams, 'Religion and Welsh Literature in the Age of the Reformation', in *The Welsh and their Religion* (Cardiff, 1991), pp.146-57.
13 W. P. Griffith, *Civility and Reputation: Ideals and Images of the 'Tudor Man' in Wales* (Bangor, 1985); J. A. Mazzeo, *Renaissance and Revolution: The Remaking of European Thought* (London, 1967), pp.131-59.

theoretically implying that the nobleman was expected to aspire to a position of moral supremacy.

It is not always possible to reconcile religious virtues with the doctrine of the gentility of the Renaissance, since divine law prescribed equality among individuals before God and the ideals of the New Learning placed greater emphasis on inequality, allowing for preference, status and advantage to thrive among the materially prosperous. The Christian values of faith, charity and humility were adapted to enrich surviving ancient pagan virtues, primarily Aristotelian, which were the chiefest features in the making of the Renaissance gentleman.[14] The concept of monarchy, however, represented by the ruler appointed by God to be a viceroy and the lesser mortals extending downwards from the aristocracy, the squirearchy, the gentry and to the lower orders, seemed to approve of God's plan – that the social order was based on obedience and on the recognition and acceptance of one's station in the community. It was also believed that the Almighty had created that order to establish peace, security and a sense of unity focused on the monarch. Christian virtues were flexibly adapted to conform with the accepted values associated with the practical gentleman, and this was highlighted in the relationship forged between the Elizabethan Church and ruling families which had adopted the Protestant faith. In this context, however, religion was largely interpreted in a political context. The Church was there to assist in reinforcing a newly emerging state and proved itself to be the spiritual stronghold of that state, a prime institution on which the monarchy could rely to maintain its power to govern. Since the Crown and its institutions, secular and ecclesiastical, were ordained by God so too were magistrates, functioning below the Crown and appointed to maintain the state's authority and manage its principal functions.[15] Doubtless the politically articulate were becoming increasingly aware, particularly after the Papal Bull *Regnans in Excelsis* (1570), that their best interests were allied with those of the Tudor Crown.[16]

---

[14] R. Kelso, *The Doctrine of the English Gentleman in the Sixteenth Century* (Gloucester, Massachusetts, 1964), pp.31-41, 70-110.
[15] J. G. Jones, *The Welsh Gentry: Images of Status, Honour and Authority, 1536-1640* (Cardiff, 1998), pp.95-132, 164-9.
[16] C. Haigh, *English Reformations*, p.260; J. Guy, *The Tudor Age*, p.296; G. Williams, *Wales and the Reformation*, pp.256-7.

In any consideration of the Christian gentleman, the role of the Godhead in the creation was essential. In view of the Godhead being acknowledged as the essence of creation within the divine plan, the privileged individual, fortified by kindred ties and adorned with skills of regional or national leadership, rose to a position of Christian ennoblement. Whereas in the pre-Reformation period the gentleman practised his virtues in the universal church, in the latter half of the sixteenth century, subsequent to the Elizabethan settlement, he was required to transfer his loyalties and employ his skills in the interest and to the enhancement of the state's new structure and its accompanying creed. It was that Church, established by Elizabeth I in 1559, which gave them the opportunity to redirect their allegiances and presented them with a powerful challenge which tested their own consciences as well as their governmental skills.

The highest in status among the upper gentry, the knight, was described by Sir Thomas Elyot as he who

> hath received that honour, not onely to defende with the swerde Christis faithe and his propre countrey...but also, and that most chiefly by the meane of his dignitie...he shuld more effectually with his learnyng and witte assayle vice and errour...having thereunto for his sworde and speare his tunge and his penne.[17]

That learning was essentially Christian. At regional level the Church was entrusted to the country gentry who, in alliance with the priesthood, upheld its authority. Whilst the clerical hierarchy were held responsible for conducting spiritual duties in the Church, the gentry, under the queen and her government, were to enforce all commandments and edicts relating to its administration and form of worship, thus maintaining unity and uniformity in the realm.

The main prop of gentry support for the Tudor monarchy was the *gravita riposata* associated with the gentleman in action. In practical terms, however, the nobility, in a Welsh context, combined their duties in the state with their allegiance to the religious institution which formed a major component. In that respect politics and religion worked hand in hand, serving to bolster a new settlement which was regarded by its

---

[17] *A preservative agaynste deth* (London, 1545), fo. AIIb-AIIIb., cited in Kelso, *Doctrine of the English Gentleman*, p.50.

apologists as the 'true Catholic church' founded by Christian fathers and upheld by holy scripture. God ordained civil order, law and obedience which were regarded as the basis of scriptural authority for the state. Indelible links were forged between the spiritual and secular components. The essence of order in society was declared in the Homily of Obedience in which it is stated:

> And let us pray for ourselves that we may live godly in holy and Christian conversation; so we shall have God of our side; and then let us not fear what man can do against us: so we shall live in true obedience, both to our most merciful King in heaven, and to our most Christian Queen in earth...[18]

In Wales, the tradition was interpreted within the much publicized 'Protestant Church theory', expounded at its fullest by Richard Davies in 1567. The 'Epistle to the Welsh' at the beginning of the Welsh version of the New Testament beckoned the Welsh people to repossess their reputedly glorious spiritual heritage with which their forebears, the Britons, had been endowed, a heritage that had been gained before any other nation by divine approval.[19] A sense of 'patriotism' among Protestant lay apologists was particularly strong. In the preamble to *Yny lhyvyr hwnn* (1546), Sir John Pryse, referring to his translations of the creed, Ten Commandments and the Lord's Prayer, had it in mind to express national sentiments:

> ...mi a veddyliais er kariad vyngwlad roi yddyn y pynkeu hyn ynghymraeg er dangos blas yddyn o velysper ewyllus duw ac er kadw eu henaidieu...Weithian dangoswch vynghytwladwyr o hynn allan nad o ddrwc anian onyd o eisieu gwybodaeth y byoch veiys kynn hynn...[20]

[I thought, for love of my country, to give them [his countrymen] these tenets in Welsh to give them a taste of the sweetness of God's will and to save their souls...now my fellow countrymen show from this time onwards that you were blameworthy before this because of want of knowledge and not an evil disposition...]

---

18   J. Griffiths (ed.), *The Two Books of Homilies appointed to be read in Churches* (Oxford, 1859), p.117.
19   *Rhagymadroddion*, pp.17-18, 29-30; A. O. Evans, *Memorandum*, pp.83-8.
20   *Rhagymadroddion*, p.4.

Doubtless William Salesbury, regarded universally as the most noteworthy of Welsh humanist scholars of his age, together with Bishop Richard Davies was consumed with enthusiasm for the Protestant theory of the antiquity of the faith and expounded its revival as the old faith of the Britons traced back to St Joseph of Arimathea, a member of the Jewish Sanhedrin and lesser-known disciple of Christ, rather than an alien faith imposed on them by the English:

> ...goreu cydymaith yw'r hen gydymaith: velly yr vn modd yr ei ys y yn dyval ymdreiglo yn yr Scrythur lan, sy yn dywedyt hwytheu may goreu ffydd yw'r ffydd hen...Ac am hyny gwae'r nep ailw hon yn newydd, o ba vodd bynac y gwnel, ai o anwybod ai trwy wybot, yw dwyllo y hun ac y hudo'r bopul.[21]

[...the best companion is the old companion: therefore, in the same way those who turn in the holy scripture, who themselves say that the best faith is the old faith...And for that woe to those who call this new, in which ever it is done, of ignorance or of knowledge, to deceive himself and to enchant the people.]

Salesbury, however, cannot improve on Richard Davies's powerful rhetoric in the early sections of his preface (*Epistol at y Cembru*) to the New Testament:

> ...paid ath ddigenhedlu, paid âth ddifrawy, paid ac edrych ir llawr, tremia y vyny tu ar lle ith hanyw...ystyria sy tan dy law, cowleidia, ac erbyn attat yr anrheg nefol a ddanfonawdd trugaredd yr Arglwydd yt heddiw ... Wele, mi a ddangosais bellach yt dy vchelder ath fraint gynt, ath ostyngiat, ath yspeil wedi. Am hynny...ti a ddylyt fod yn llawen, ac yn fawr dy ddiolch i Dduw, i ras y Urenhines, i vrddas, ac i gyffredin y deyrnas, sy yn adnewyddu dy fraint ath vrddas....[22]

[...do not denationlize thyself, do not be indifferent, do not look down; but gaze upwards to the place thou dost belong...consider what thou hast within thy grasp, embrace and take to thyself this heavenly gift which the mercy of the Lord hath sent thee this day...Behold, I have shown to thee thy pre-eminence and thy privilege of old, and thy humiliation and thy deprivation afterwards.

---

21 Ibid., p.44; Evans, *Memorandum*, p.125.
22 *Rhagymadroddion*, pp.17, 26; Evans, *Memorandum*, pp.84., 98.

Therefore...thou shoulst be glad, and frequent thy thanksgiving to God, to her grace the Queen, to the Lords and Commons of the kingdom who are renewing thy privilege and honour...]

Aside from the bards, who sang profusely to William Morgan, the testimonies of Maurice Kyffin in *Deffynniad Ffydd Eglwys Loegr* and Michael Roberts in the preface to the small Bible of 1630 reveal how highly rated he was as a translator. In 1595 Kyffin praised Richard Davies for his work in producing the New Testament and for his epistle which served 'to lead them [the Welsh] to a revival of the old Catholic faith and the light of Christ's gospel' ('...iw twyso nhwy i adnewyddiad yr hen ffydd gatholic a goleuni Efengyl Crist').[23]

DEFFYNNIAD
FFYDD EGLVVYS
LOEGR : LLE Y CEIR GWE-
led, a gwybod, dofparth gwir Grefydd
Crift, ag anghywirdeb Crefydd
Eglwys Rufain:

Angenrheidiol i bawb ei ddealld, a ma-
dws i ddynion ei ddyfcu, o ran arwain eu bu-
chedd yn y byd hwn, fal y caffont fywyd tra-
gwyddol yn y byd a ddaw.

Wedi ei gyfieuthu o Ladin, yn Gymraeg,
drwy waith M. KYFFIN.

Nefcio qua Natale Solum dulcedine cunĉlos
Ducit, & immemores non finit effe fui.

Richard Field a 'i printiodd yn
Llunden. 1595·

Title-page of *Deffynniad Ffydd Eglwys Loegr*
(1595) by Maurice Kyffin

---

23   *Rhagymadroddion*, p.92.

An ardent supporter of such patriotism was John Penry who considered it essential to tie his arguments to the need for drastic reform of the church with the belief in the church's antiquity:

> It might greeue vs the lesse to be denied the gospel, vnlesse the same were the inheritance which our fore-fathers the Cymbrûbrittons many hundred yeares agoe possessed in this lande...But the impes of that lifelesse and brutish stock of Rome, planted in England by Augustine that proud friar, whose tyranical proceedings our diuines in Wales resisted euen to the losse of their liues. That these trash be but of small continuance among vs in respect of the antiquity the trueth hath had, I proue because the verie mother of them, the execrable Masse, was but yesterday, as it were knowen vnto vs.[24]

How much concern was shown by the Elizabethan Welsh gentry for the defence of the new order is unclear, but a variety of administrative sources suggest that all was not well. On Elizabeth's accession they were certainly divided in allegiance and it was no easy task for the government and new Church leaders to ensure a transference of loyalties. Whatever their religious affiliations, the vast majority had already benefited from the despoliation of religious properties and rights before and after the dissolution of religious houses and were eager to pursue further their secular ambitions through the acquisition of landed and ecclesiastical rights. In his preface to his edition of Gerald of Wales's *Itinerarium Kambriae*, Dr David Powel, vicar of Ruabon, addressed Sir Philip Sidney (to whom the work was presented) as a worthy successor to his father, Sir Henry Sidney, a defender of the queen and the state.

> Y mae gennych chwi...esiamplau 'cartrefol' ac 'etifeddol' o hyn oll yn aros yn eich boneddicaf dad, fel petaent yn cael eu harddangos i chwi mewn drych er mwyn eu dynwared...yn ei ofal am fuddiannau'r cyhoedd...nid wyf yn petruso ei gymharu ef â'r mwyaf cytbwys o lywodraethwyr mewn llawer oes... er budd y Wladwriaeth ac er anrhydedd i'w Frenhines.[25]

[You have 'domestic' and 'inherited' examples of all this remaining in your noblest father, as if they were being displayed to you in a mirror to be imitated...in his care

---

24   J. Penry, *Three Treatises concerning Wales*, p.30.
25   C. Davies (ed.), *Rhagymadroddion a Chyflwyniadau Lladin*, pp.56, 161-2.

for public interests...I do not hesitate to compare him with the most balanced of governors in many ages...for the benefit of the State and in honour of the queen.]

One of the main attributes of gentility was allegiance to the Elizabethan state of which the Protestant Church was one of its most prominent pillars. Its reputed antiquity was proclaimed by Maurice Kyffin in his preamble to his translation of Bishop John Jewel's *Apologia Ecclesiae Anglicanae*, addressed to the 'howddgar ddarlleydd Cristnogawl' ('the amiable Christian reader'):

> Dymma i ti ar les d'enaid, yn hyn o lyfr, sylwedd a chrynodeb y Ffydd wir Gatholic; ith hyfforddi a'th berffeithio yn llwybr gwasanaeth Duw, ag Iechydwriaeth dyn. Wrth ddarllen hwn y cei di wybod hanes, a dealld gwirionedd y Grefydd Gristnogawl, a chyda hynny ddanghossiad a dat-guddiad amhuredd crediniaeth Pâb Rhufain.[26]

[Here, in this book, for your own soul's sake, is the substance and summary of the true Catholic faith to instruct and perfect you in the paths of God's service and man's salvation. By reading this you will come to know the history and understand the Christian religion, and with that a showing and revelation of the Roman Pope's impurity.]

Since the Elizabethan Church was maintained and defended by statute law, it was recognizably an erastian establishment, and the faith it expounded was safeguarded by a firm ecclesiastical structure based on the episcopalian system reputed to be in the apostolic succession.

In this context the gentry were regarded as secular supporters of a state Church. Jewel amply set forth the justification of the new faith:

> But in case we doe proue that the sacred Gospell of God and the auncient Bishops, together with the primitiue Churche dothe make for vs, and that we haue upon iust cause, both departed from these men, and also retourned now againe vnto the Apostles and olde catholike fathers, and that we do it in dede not couertly or craftely, but with a good conscience before God, truly, frankly, clerely & plainely.[27]

---

26   *Rhagymadroddion*, p.89.
27   J. Jewel, *An Apologie or Aunswer in Defence of the Church of England 1562* (Scolar Facsimile, Menston, 1969), Biii.

What can be said of the state as a political concept that was universally employed in official circles in England in the latter half of the sixteenth century? Since the Reformation formed England into a unified political entity it ensured that the Crown, acting through parliament, combined in itself Church and state. What evolved in the 1530s was confirmed by the two major statutes of Elizabeth's first parliament, the Crown, through divine ordination, becoming responsible for governing the Church and defining articles of faith. It was Richard Hooker in his *Of the Lawes of Ecclesiastical Polity* (1594-7, 1600) who drew a distinction between Church and state. He introduced a political theory devised to defend the structure of the Church, and concluded that a Christian state was governed by laws agreed to by the Crown and the clergy in parliament and convocation respectively. He proceeded in his section on the laws of the state briefly to describe the role of the body politic in the preservation of good order:

> Two foundations there are which bear up public societies; the one, a natural inclination, whereby all men desire sociable life and fellowship; the other, an order expressly or secretly agreed upon touching the manner of their union in living together. The latter is that which we call the Law of a Commonweal, the very soul of a politic body, the parts whereof are by law animated, held together, and set on work in such actions, as the common good requireth.[28]

The gentry, who were the lay representatives under God and the Crown in the provinces, played a central role in this political structure, and lay and clerical gentry were required to promote and safeguard the concept of the *imperium* created by Tudor rule. From their standpoint the Church was essentially a vindicator of a political as well as an ecclesiastical order. It is hardly surprising, therefore, that William Morgan, translator of the scriptures, referred triumphantly, at the beginning of his Latin epistle-dedicatory of the Bible to Elizabeth in 1588, to the significance of the unity and stability achieved within the realm. The magnanimity of the Crown was symbolized in her person and she maintained the unity of her kingdom by means of God's grace and favour. Such ideas were not uncommon in commentaries on the role of monarchy in England in that

---

28   R. Hooker, *Of the Laws of Ecclesiastical Polity*, ed. K. Bayne (London, 1907), p.188.

period but Morgan proceeded to express that it was the unity of the kingdom under the Crown, particularly in critical situations, that was mainly responsible for the appearance of the Bible. Elizabeth's victory over the Armada, indicated her loyal attachment to the nation's best interests. By God's grace, together with her virtues, it was possible to establish 'blessed peace' within the realm, all signified by her success in overcoming Mary's threats and by her victory in 1588:

> ... eich cyfoeth a'ch gallu a'ch cynhysgaeth ryfeddol o ran doniau a chyneddfau naturiol, dyna eich graslonrwydd dihafal, sy'n peri fod Eich Mawrhydi yn destun edmygedd i gynifer o bobl; a'ch dysg, sydd o ran ei hamlochredd yn eich addurno mewn dull sydd y tu hwnt i gyrraedd pawb arall; a'r heddwch gwynfydedig yr ydych chwi'n ei fwynhau rhagor eich cymdogion; a'r modd y bu i'r heddwch hwnnw gael ei amddiffyn...pan yrasoch eich gelynion creulon ar ffo yn ddiweddar, a hefyd bob tro y cawsoch ddihangfa lwyddiannus oddi wrth y llu peryglon mawrion a'ch amgylchynai ... 29

[...your wealth, your power and your admirable endowments of birth and intellect is abundantly testified not only by that most rare grace, wherein you so excel, that varied learning, with which you are pre-eminently adorned, that happy peace which you enjoy above your neighbours, and that divine protection...whereby you have both lately put your savage foes to flight, and have ever most fortunately escaped many great dangers...]

One further factor, Morgan maintained, which consolidated the queen's success was her ardent desire to propagate the faith:

> ...a'r sêl fwyaf eiddgar honno dros ledaenu ac amddiffyn gwir grefydd sydd bob amser wedi bod yn llosgi o'ch mewn. Oblegid...y mae'r un ffaith hon bob amser yn ddigon i ddangos maint gofal duwiolfrydig Eich Mawrhydi am y Brytaniaid ymhlith eich deiliaid... 30

[...that most forward zeal for both the propagation and the defence of true religion, which, at all times, has burned within you. For... this fact will always suffice to show what an affectionate care your Majesty has for your British subjects.]

---

29 C. Davies, *Rhagymadroddion a Chyflwyniadau Lladin*, p.64.
30 Ibid., pp.64-5.

This sturdy declaration of political philosophy by a renowned ecclesiastic gives a clear lead to understanding the nature of the defence of Protestantism within a unified state, as revealed in literary sources in the late Elizabethan age.

The gentry were also expected to defend the Protestant faith and to identify themselves with the political doctrines of the state. Since the laity were conceived as those members of the community who possessed virtues destined to strengthen their skills in governing for the common good, secular and ecclesiastical governors shared a common unity of purpose which stemmed from fundamental links forged between the Crown, parliament, the common law and the Protestant Church. All this lay essentially at the base of the new sovereign state. Just rule, based on law, order and obedience, was the objective, and it was in that context that Dr David Powel wrote as follows:

> Ymhellach, pa wasanaeth mwy gweddus y gall dyn da ei roi na'i fod yn ei gyflwyno'i hun yn gyfan gwbl i fuddiannau'r wladwriaeth, gan ystyried unrhyw ennill i'w les personol ei hun yn eilbeth; yn gosod pob llafur, pob gofal a phob meddwl ar hyrwyddo ffyniant pobl yn gyffredinol; ac yn cadw'i feddwl wedi'i hoelio ar yr un peth hwnnw'n unig, y mae'r enaid yn ymorffwys o'i ennill, heb ddymuno dim pellach? [31]

[Furthermore, what service is more fitting that a good man can give other than to present himself completely to the welfare of the state, considering that any gain to his own personal benefit is secondary: placing every labour, every care and every thought on promoting the prosperity of the people generally; and keeping his mind firmly fixed on that same thing upon which the soul rests after gaining it, deserving nothing further?]

Such qualities, incorporated in the concept of gentility, were employed in promoting the duties of the gentry as defenders of the established order. Their reactions to these duties varied as much as did their commitment to the Church and to their leanings towards the Old Faith. Richard Davies's jaundiced view of the Welsh gentry (quoted above) was further reiterated by him a decade later in the *Funeral Sermon* delivered by him on the death

---

[31] Ibid., p.55.

of Walter Devereux, 1st earl of Essex, in 1577. His comments are particularly sharp on their role in local government:

> Then shall appeare that they haue altogither applyed their authoritie and office to pyll and poll the countrey, and to begger their poore neighbours to perfourme that which Esay the prophet sayth...you dresse your houses with the goodes of the poore. Then shall appeare that whereas by reason of their offices they should haue bene *Patres patrie*, fathers of the countrey, they became spoylers of the countrey. And where the part of fathers is to prouide for theyr children, they contrarywyse agaynst order of nature, forced the childre(n), that is, the countrey, to prouide for them and their houses.[32]

Moreover, in his diocesan report of 1570, Davies perceived 'a great number to be slow and cold in the true service of God, some careless for any religion and some that wish the romish religion again'.[33] Since maintaining good order in local government was essential for the well-being of the community, so it was also a means by which the new Church might be defended and supported. Efforts made to comply with the anti-Catholic laws were a step forward in ensuring the establishment of the new Protestant order, but since the transference of loyalties in the Church among the politically articulate was not as clear-cut in all cases, it was evident that the customs and practices of the Roman Catholic faith still remained strong in the localities. Several families became notable for their resistance to the new order, such as the Somersets, earls of Worcester, and the Herberts of Powys Castle. Among the privileged of lower status the Turbervilles and Carnes of Glamorgan, Morgans of Llantarnam, Pughs of Penrhyn Creuddyn and Owens of Plas Du ranked among the most prominent.[34] Even other families, such as the Stradlings and the Salusburys, were not enitrely committed to the new faith in its early stages. They all commanded considerable loyalties among their kinsmen

---

32 *A Funerall Sermon preached the XXVI day of November...md lxxvi in the Parishe Church of Caermerthyn by the Reverend Father in God Richard...Bishoppe of Saint Dauys at the Buriall of the Moste Honourable Walter Earle of Essex and Ewe* (London, 1577), Dii [23].

33 D. R. Thomas, *The Life and Work of Bishop Davies & William Salesbury* (Oswestry, 1902), p.38.

34 F. H. Pugh, 'Glamorgan recusants, 1577-1611', *South Wales and Monmouth Record Society Pubs.,* no.3, 1954, 49-67; idem, 'Monmouthshire recusants in the Reigns of Elizabeth I and James I', ibid., Pub. no.4, 1957, 59-110; E. G. Jones, 'Catholic recusancy in the counties of Denbigh, Flint, and Montgomery, 1581-1625', *TCS*, 1945, p.111-33; idem, 'Robert Pugh of Penrhyn Creuddyn', *TCHS*, VII, 1946, 10-19.

and tenants, and doubtless the early decades following Elizabeth's accession were a testing time for many gentry, particularly after the Revolt of the Northern Earls (1569), and in the following year the Papal Bull *Regnans in Excelsis*, issued by Pius V, denying Elizabeth her claim to the throne and declaring her an excommunicant. From then onwards disloyalty to the throne and its institutions became a matter of treason rather than heresy. It is hardly surprising that fervent efforts were made on behalf of both Catholic and Protestant factions to win over the allegiance of the common people. Protestant writers were as critical as their opponents of the misdeeds of the gentry. Among the most vociferous in his comments was Hugh Lewis who translated into Welsh Miles Coverdale's *A Spyrytuall and most Precious Pearle:*

> Pa faint yw rhwysc cybydd-dod, vsuriaeth, chwant, trais, lledrat ac ysbel, in mysc, fe wyr pawb sy yn dal ac yn craffu ar gwrs y byd...casineb, llid, gelynniaeth, digofaint, ymrysonau, ymgyfreithiaw, anghariadoldeb ac anudonau sy ry aml, ac agos a gorescyn ein gwlad. Ac ni wnn beth yw yr achos o hyn, ond...ein eisieu o lyfreu, in twysaw, ac in llwybraw yn y ffordd iawn.[35]

[How much pomp, miserliness, usury, lust, oppression, theft and spoliation in our midst, all know who see and look intently on the world's course... hatred, fury, enmity, wrath, contention, litigation, ill-will and perjuries are too frequent and close to overrunning our country. And I do not know what the cause of this is except...our need for books, to lead and guide us in the right direction].

Lewis's plea is for more Protestant works to be published which might be appropriately used to deepen a knowledge and understanding of the faith, and it is hardly surprising that the translated work, *Perl mewn Adfyd* (1595), was presented to Richard Vaughan, then archdeacon of Middlesex, who was soon to be elevated as bishop of Bangor and then of Chester and London successively, a staunch persecutor of Catholic recusants.[36] What is equally important in Lewis's preamble is the critical attitude taken towards those whom he regarded as recalcitrant in an age of unashamed acquisitiveness. Edward Kyffin, brother of Maurice Kyffin, a clergyman and versifier of some of the Psalms in Welsh (a work which

---

35 *Rhagymadroddion*, pp.101-2.
36 Browne Willis, *Survey of Bangor*, pp.24, 109, 323.

seemingly remained unpublished), took a more rational approach and, in view of the peace which Elizabeth's reign had brought, desired that goodwill be shown towards the language and that the Christian faith be promoted. In his preamble to *Rhann o Psalmae Dafydd Brophwyd* (1603) he declared:

> A chan eyn bôd yn byw yn yr Oes honn dann archerchockaf Vrenhines o'n gwlâd eyn hunain, yr honn sydd yn canhiadu i ni gael y Scrythur lân yn eyn hiaith eyn hunain, ag oll gyfreidiau eraill ar a ddamunem ei cael tu ag at amlhau Gogoniant Duw, a mawrhâd eyn hiaith...O fy anwyl wlad-wyr, tra fo duw yn canhiattau i ni, y rhwydd-deb, yr heddwch, a'r rhyddid y rydym yrowron yn ei gael, na chollwn yr amser presennol... a dangoswn i'r byd, eyn bôd yn prisio mwy am Ogoniant Duw, am Orchafiaeth a derchafiad eyn Gwlâd a'n hiaith, ac am ddi-dranck lywenydd ag iechydwriaeth eyn Eneidiau eyn hunain, nag yr ydym am ddarfodedig fwnws y byd hwnn, yr hynn nid oes i ni ond byrr amser i'w fwynhau.[37]

[And since we live in this age under the most excellent Queen of our country who has permitted us to obtain the holy Scripture in our own tongue, with all other needs that we desire to increase God's glory and enhance our language...O my dear countrymen, while God permits us the ease, the peace and the freedom which we now have, let us not forsake the present time... and let us show to the world that we value more God's glory for exalting our country and language and for the unending joy and the salvation of our own souls than we do the transitory burdens of this world, these which we have but a short time to enjoy.]

Kyffin was prepared to see the possibilities as well as sense the dangers and considered that the good government of the realm, which provided peace and security, also gave the Welsh people the opportunity to fulfil the essential intellectual needs of their generation. His address is directed mainly towards the landed proprietors, the clergy and the commercial groups, all of whom shared the opportunities of attending to the spiritual regeneration of the people, hence the author's aim in the versification of the first few Psalms to introduce part of the word of God so that they might convey them to their subordinates.

Arthur Dent, vicar of South Shoeberry near Southend in Essex, whose

---

[37]   *Rhagymadroddion*, pp.106-7.

work influenced Robert Llwyd, vicar of Chirk, pronounced on the same theme. He was a victim of serious persecution by John Aylmer, bishop of London. Undaunted, he expounded on the corruption and sins of humanity and emphasized pre-ordination and salvation through God's grace. It was his conscience that led him, in his petition to the Privy Council when in prison, to defend his position:

> ...if a man, then, be condemned for doing a lawful action, because he doubts whether it be lawful; how much more should we incur the displeasure of the lord, and justly deserve his wrath, if we should subscribe, being fully persuaded that there are some things in the book (i.e. Book of Common Prayer) contrary to his word! If our reasons might be so answered by the doctrine of the Bible, and we could be persuaded that we might subscribe lawfully, and in the fear of God, we would willingly consent.[38]

Such strident remarks were made to little effect in his case but his text was translated into Welsh by Llwyd in 1630. In addition to drawing attention to the religious content of the work in his preface, he also revealed the danger which confronted younger sons of gentry who, having left home, were inclined to forsake the virtues taught them and to abandon the faith. His address to the reader in *Llwybr hyffordd yn cyfarwyddo yr anghyfarwydd i'r nefoedd* (1630), a translation of Dent's *The Plaine Man's Pathway to Heaven*, is ardent in its plea to the younger generation of gentlemen to attend to their duties as Christian leaders and to sanctify themselves by reading and meditating upon the work:

> Pe cymmerai foneddigion ieuaingc ein gwlad in ryw gyffelyb orchwylwaith duwiol, a buddiol i dreulio eu hamser arno, ni byddei anllywodraeth, a rhysedd yn cael cymmaint rhwysc: Na gwir Grefydd uniawn-grêd yn cael cyn lleied brî, a chymmeriad; ac ni byddei occreth yn yssu ac yn bwytta y naill ddarn o'u tiroedd, na thafarndai, a mŵg Tobacco, yn yfed y darn arall.[39]

[If young gentlemen of our country were to accept some godly and beneficial supervision, to spend their time on it, there would be no ill-government, and

---

38   A. Dent, *The Plaine Man's Pathway to Heaven* (repr. Belfast, 1994), vi.
39   *Rhagymadroddion*, pp.130-1.

abundance gaining so much pomp; nor true orthodox religion gaining so little respect, and character; and usury would not consume and devour the one piece of their lands, nor alehouses, and Tobacco smoke, drink the other half.]

This testimony is clearly directed against the trends in a society which revealed significant cross tendencies, simultaneously broadening the horizons of the gentry and maintaining loyalty to their nation's heritage. It was an age which tore their interests both ways, for they amply benefited from material gain while, at the same time, a large proportion still clung to their traditions. In this respect the Church served to unite them for, as a bastion of state control, it won their allegiance. Political loyalty to that institution, however, did not at all times imply, as Llwyd observes, a true spiritual adherence to the Church for it appears that material attractions diverted their attention.

That was not so in the Merioneth squire Rowland Vaughan's case for Llwyd complimented him for translating Lewis Bayly's *The Practice of Piety* into Welsh (1630):

> Dyna wr bonheddig yn treulio ei amser yn weddol, ac yn ganmoladwy, gan wneuthur gwasanaeth i Dduw, daioni iw wlâd, a llesâd mawr iddo ei hun drwy gyfieithu y llyfr godidog hwnnw.[40]

[There is a gentleman spending his time well and in praiseworthy fashion by serving God, doing good to his country and benefiting himself by translating that excellent book.]

In another context, but with similar intent, Maurice Wynn, one of Sir John Wynn of Gwydir's younger sons who served his apprenticeship as a merchant in Hamburg, came under Puritan influences there and clearly made known his religious views. In August 1623 he rebuked his father for not attending as much to the spiritual needs of his people as he had to establishing almshouses for the poor of Llanrwst:

> I presume to put yow in mind that there is annother Dearth that w'ch is worse by far w'ch is not soe sensible as the other, but ought to bee far more and we may instead feare to bee the cause of the other, and that is

---

40   Ibid., p.130.

the want of gods word preached amongst yow, by reason of w'ch Diuers soules perrish for want of knowledge non can bee saved without faith and how is it wrought in mens hartes but by heering his word ther wher the words not herd ther cann be noe faith and without faith yt is unposible to please god. [41]

Cultural circumstances, however, were not generally as satisfactory as those enjoyed by Maurice Wynn. Younger sons of gentry were further removed from first-generation Reformation changes and thus more inclined to drift away from traditional family values. Such an instance was the anxiety expressed by William Wynn of Glyncywarch about his son Cadwaladr's behaviour at Oxford (c.1630), and his desire that he speak English only to his friends.

> keepe company with honest students who aphore evill courses as drinking and takeing toebacko to their own losse and discredit of their friends and parents whoe sent them to the University for better purposes...Speake noe Welsh to any that can speake English, noe not to your bedfellows, and therby you may attaine... and freely speake [the] English tongue perfectly.[42]

William Wynn was obviously an anxious father, and his advice reflects the concern which Sir John Wynn of Gwydir continually showed in his correspondence regarding his sons at various educational institutions.[43] He feared that they might become subject to powerful Roman Catholic influences and, in this context, it is hardly surprising that the young Sir John Wynn, heir to Gwydir, had been approached by papist agents during the 'Grand Tour' in Italy in 1613-14.[44] About half a century earlier (1570), Richard Davies expressed his concern for the integrity of the Church when he appealed to the Privy Council 'to consider all the sp[irit]uall sores and diseases of the dioces', and 'to become protectors and defenders of the church... that it be no further troublede spoyled or

---

[41] NLW MS. 9058E 1132

[42] *Clenennau Letters and Papers in the Brogyntyn Collection*, ed. T. Jones Pierce, National Library of Wales Journal, App. Ser. IV, no.1(Pt.1), 1947, no.444, pp.126-7.

[43] *Calendar of Wynn of Gwydir Papers, 1515-1690*, ed. J. Ballinger (Cardiff, 1926), e.g. nos. 180, 457, 473, 539, 736.

[44] Ibid., no.647 (9 March 1614). See also Ffowc Prys's ode to Wynn junior appealing to him to return home. Cardiff City Library MS.4.101, 205a; J. G. Jones, 'Sir John Wynn Junior of Gwydir and Llanfrothen and the "Grand Tour", 1613-14', *JMHRS*, 11, 1990-93, 398.

impoverished'.[45] If that was true of some members of privileged families then it was certainly true of the population at large.

This uncertainty which characterized Protestant writers is reflected in Maurice Kyffin's letter to his kinsman William Meredydd in 1595 in his preface to *Deffynniad Ffydd Eglwys Loegr*, in which he points to the role of religion in the advancement of learning.

His emphasis on the need to establish the new faith was tempered by a fear that the mission would not be accomplished:

> A chyda hyn, petid yn pregethu Efengyl Crist yng Nghymru fal y gwelsoch chwi a minnau mewn gwledydd eraill, diau nad oes genhedlaeth yng Nghred a allai ragori ar y Cymry mewn crefydd a duwioldeb, gan eu bod hwy o athrylith a naturiaeth yn chwannog i ddysgu pob rhinwedd a daioni, ond cael ei ddangos a'i ddeongl iddynt.[46]

[And with this, if the Gospel of Christ were preached in Wales as you and I have seen it in other lands, doubtless there is no generation in Christendom that could excel the Welsh in religion and piety, because they have the genius and nature and are inclined to learn every virtue and goodness, if it is shown and interpreted to them.]

Instruction in the tenets of the faith, he stated, would stem acrimony and jealousy, and the author proceeded by declaring that the establishment of peace and order in society lay in the hands of the gentry:

> ...pe câi gwir grefydd a gwasanaeth Duw ddechrau'i goledd a'i osod allan yn hylwybr, a gweled unwaith o'r cyffredin bobl fod wynebau a llawnfryd pendefigion Cymru y ffordd honno, e fyddai bob Cymro barod i studio ac i wrando gair Duw yn ddyfal.[47]

[...if the true religion and the service of God would begin to be cherished and set out conveniently and if the common folk were to see once that the faces and

---

45 D. R. Thomas, *Life and Work of Bishop Davies & William Salesbury*, p.44.
46 H. Lewis (ed.), *Hen Gyflwyniadau* (Cardiff,1948), pp.7-8.
47 Ibid., p.8.

eagerness of the nobility of Wales were pointed in that direction every Welshman would be prepared to study and listen to the word of God diligently.]

Despite all these reservations about the Church's progress, Welsh humanist scholars appreciated the support of a small but dedicated group of scholar-gentlemen, both Catholic and Protestant, who had assisted them in the publication of their work. 'Sir' Thomas Wiliems of Trefriw praised a number of Welsh gentry, most of them prominent in their respective localities, who had loaned him books to enable him to complete, in manuscript, his Latin-Welsh Dictionary (*Trysawr yr iaith Latin a r Gymraec...* (1604)). In his preface he names Morus and John Wynn of Gwydir, Sir John Salusbury of Lleweni (brother of Thomas Salusbury, the Catholic conspirator), Robert Pugh of Penrhyn Creuddyn, John Edwards of Chirk, Hugh Gwynn of Berth Ddu, Llanrwst, Edward Thelwall of Ruthin, Robert Holland, a native of Conwy, rector of Prendergast (1591), Walwyn's Castle (1602-08) and Robeson West (1612) in Pembrokeshire, and William Gruffydd, probably of Cemais, Montgomeryshire. All of them, he maintained, cherished their language and its culture as did William Herbert, earl of Pembroke, whom Wiliems regarded as 'llygat holl Gymru' ('the eye of all Wales'), the earl of Worcester and Sir Edward Stradling.[48] His choice consists of an interesting variety of both Catholic and Protestant scholars as well as two Anglican clergymen. Dr John Davies was himself a highly-reputed Roman Catholic scholar, and in his preface he also praised Morgan Meredith of Llanfihangel-y-Bugeildy in the vale of Tefeidiad in Radnorshire who, together with his wife, offered lavish hospitality. Among the most prominent of Protestant landowners who adhered strongly to the Elizabethan Church were Sir Edward Stradling (son and heir to the Roman Catholic Sir Thomas Stradling) of St Donat's, Sir John Wynn of Gwydir, Sir Thomas Mostyn and his successor Sir Roger Mostyn of Mostyn, the Mansells of Margam and the Perrotts of Haroldston, Pembrokeshire. Whatever their shortcoming in public life they were intent on maintaining the existing political and religious structures. This public image did not at all times reveal their religious affiliations but the confidence which the Tudor Crown placed in them indicated that they, besides their own private interests, had the welfare of the state Church at heart.

---

[48] *Rhagymadroddion*, pp.114-15.

The famous letter sent by Sir Henry Herbert to the deputy-lieutenants of Caernarfonshire in 1596, reminding them of their duties to the state and censuring them for their inexcusable laxity in performing them, is but one reminder of the pressures upon them in times of war and during threats of invasion which shook the fabric of government and weakened the defences of the new religious settlement. They had always been prepared to demand *cymortha* for their own private gain in their localities, and it was now time for them to exact *cymortha*, Herbert declared, for the good of the whole state.[49] On another occasion Herbert was again obliged to censure the deputies for their lack of control in matters of security and defence whereby 'the whole state may be endangered for no prevention of this disorder'.[50] Spanish hostility threatened the very existence of the nation state, and surviving local government records for the period c.1580-1604 are rich in detail on the administrative complexities of organizing coastal defences. In Caernarfonshire, for example, the inefficiency and frustration which hindered Sir John Wynn and Sir William Maurice, the deputy-lieutenants, from performing their duties involved them constantly in conflict with Pembroke. In addition to the general threat of invasion the two officers disagreed among themselves about the manner in which the defence system should be safeguarded, a deficiency which seriously left the coasts of north-west Wales open to attack.[51] In addition to the use made of the limited local resources that were available, the clergy in the diocese of Bangor in 1595 provided seven light horses, twelve petronels, six muskets and ten calivers (light portable guns) for service in Ireland. Also, Roman Catholics were to be observed and local officials were to ensure that they were kept under close surveillance to prevent any collusion with the enemy:

> Amongst other things, considering how of late years divers of her [i.e. the queen's] subjects, by the means of bad instruments, have been withdrawn from the due obedence they owe to Her Majesty, and her laws; inasmuch as divers of them most obstinately have refused to come to the church to

---

49   *Clenennau Letters and Papers*, no.106, p.31; W. Rees, *The Union of England and Wales* (Cardiff 1948), p.10-11.
50   *Clenennau Letters and Papers*, no.113, p.34.
51   *Clenennau Letters and Papers*, nos.11, 16, pp.3, 5; J. G. Jones, *The Wynn Family of Gwydir: Origins, Growth and Development c.1490-1674* (Aberystwyth, 1995), pp.196-9; idem, 'The defence of the realm; regional dimensions c.1559-1604', in *Conflict, Continuity and Change in Wales c.1500-1603: Essays and Studies* (Aberystwyth, 1999), pp.113-53; idem, 'Governance, order and stability in Caernarfonshire c.1540-1640', *TCHS*, XLIV, 1983, 27-33.

prayers and divine service, for which respects, being so addicted, it is hardly adventured to repose that trust in them which is to be looked for in her good subjects.[52]

The Spanish enemy depended largely on obtaining intelligence from England to inform them as to the most favourable places to attack, and every precaution was taken to baulk such treasonous activity. To take risks would be too dangerous, for coastal defences had never been strong. Moreover, stability was less evident in government and financial resources; the Crown's inland military power was declining and sea-power often depended on the enterprise of privateers and pirates. Although Roman Catholic activity had to an extent been curbed by the end of Elizabeth's reign, those who adhered to the faith were not compromised and drawn within the framework of the national Church, and it continued to challenge the establishment. Since the Tudors had no standing army it was only to be expected that the gentry and their dependants were regarded as vital links in the 'chain of command' which, for defence purposes, attached the central government to the localities.

In the same context the Privy Council addressed Lord President Zouche at Ludlow in 1603.[53] While discussing the rumour that the queen was very ill, it ordered the Council in the Marches to ensure that in unity and common amity Wales and England should proceed to preserve peace in public and private affairs. The danger that younger sons might adopt 'Romish customs' while being educated abroad became a matter of grave concern. In 1593 the Privy Council ordered that information concerning the sons of gentry who had been sent by their parents overseas should be reported immediately since 'it is daily by dangerous experience found that the direction of such in foreign parts bred much corruption in religion among the better sort'.[54] It was declared that they, 'under colour of learning languages', were brought up in the 'popish religion', many becoming seminary priests. Widespread inquiries were to be made on a private and public level to root out any seditious material or activities 'against the state or established religion'. In 1573 William Cecil informed Nicholas Robinson that the examination of the affairs of Edward Mytton,

---

[52]   *Calendar of Wynn of Gwydir Papers*, no.162.
[53]   *APC*, XXXII, 1603, pp.493-4.
[54]   Ibid., XXV, 1593, p.515 (App.); *Calendar of Wynn of Gwydir Papers*, no.144.

the queen's ward, would be entrusted to him as the bishop who was to certify as to his learning, especially his grounding in religion and his status.[55]

One of the most ardent of Elizabethan political commentators who referred constantly to the welfare of the Protestant state was William Lambarde, the most prolific writer in English on the theory and practicalities of regional government. He was the author of a treatise written in 1575 on the qualities expected of juries and regional governors generally. If they attended diligently to their responsibilities, he declared, then they would fully discharge the duties of their calling to God, their prince and their country.[56] He was aware of the need to protect the 'ship of the Commonwealth' which contained the institutions regarded as essential to the realm. He appealed to local governors to be vigilant in ensuring that the law be obeyed. 'The very end of law', he stated, 'is obedience, and the end of obedience is the life and safety of the Commonwealth'.[57] Lambarde was intent on seeing that juries (in his own county of Kent) realized and performed their duties to God, the queen and the commonwealth, three major aspects of one obligation due to the state. They should be men 'having a right eye upon the holy religion of God, the goodly law of the realm, and the bounden duties that you owe to your own country'.[58] In this respect religious ideology had been associated with secular politics within an erastian framework which formed its basis. Such obedience was expected in religious as well as secular affairs, and the *Book of Homilies*, published in 1547, underlined the chiefest manifestations of moral integrity and submission to legitimate authority.[59] Peace and security were symbols of godly government, within a prosperous state considered healthy in its relations with other nations in an age when nation states were emerging. Thus stated Humphrey Prichard, once rector of Llanbeulan, Anglesey, in his Latin preface to Dr John Davies's Latin-Welsh grammar (*Cambrobrytannicae Cymraecaeve Linguae Institutiones et Rudimenta* (1592)):

---

55 Ca. MS. 4.58.45.
56 *William Lambarde and Local Government*, (ed.), Conyers Read (Cornell University Press, 1962), pp.87, 116, 129.
57 Ibid., p.95.
58 Ibid., p.172.
59 *Book of Homilies*, pp.109-13.

Yr ydym ni oll yn trigo ar yr un ynys, yr ydym yn ddinasyddion yr un wladwriaeth; y mae'r un gyfraith yn bod i'r naill a'r llall ohonom, a'r un Frenhines dra hyglod; y mae materion busnes, cyfeillachau, cydgynulliadau, priodasau, materion cyfraith a chrefydd ... yn gyffredin rhyngom ni a'r Saeson.[60]

[We all live on the same island, we are citizens of the same state; the same law exists for the one and the other of us, and the same very glorious queen; business matters, fellowships, assemblies, marriages, legal and religious affairs – are common between us and the English.]

His words were keyed in positively with secular opinions of the age. As a cleric he declared that Christian well-being was identified in the state with the unity of the commonwealth under the Crown. Since royal supremacy was ordained by divine law, the queen herself declared during the Northern Rebellion in 1569 that she was 'bound in duty to God to provide that all estates, being subject to us, should live in the faith and the obedience and observance of Christian religion'.[61]

In *Of the Lawes of Ecclesiastical Polity*, however, Richard Hooker honoured the position of parliament in such matters, declaring that membership of church and state was coextensive.[62] Ecclesiastical laws needed the consent of the clergy in convocation and the laity in parliament. This implied that parliament represented the new church. Although Hooker's views of the church were, in several directions, contentious, to him secular rulers and their subordinates executed their authority by 'divine right' but governed by law. Equitable government was maintained by the interplay between the legislative and the executive and in Elizabeth I's reign local government justices of the peace and their co-administrators rose to positions of eminence as regional executive officers. The increase in the number of justices of the peace and the heavy burdens that were imposed upon them, on the one hand gave them considerable power and, on the other, a sense of responsibility. Their attention to such duties varied according to their private interests and

---

60   C. Davies (ed.), *Rhagymadroddion a Chyflwyniadau Lladin*, p.91.
61   P. L. Hughes and J. F. Larkin (eds.), *Tudor Royal Proclamations*, 3 vols., II, *The Later Tudors, 1553-1587* (London, 1969), pp.323-9.
62   R. Hooker, *Of the Laws of Ecclesiastical Polity*, ed. R. Bayne (London, 1907), pp.187-99.

extended into matters relating to religion and public morality.[63] These features of their work were reinforced by the supervisory power exercised by the Council in the Marches. That Council, for example, was to ensure that justices of the peace and other officials subscribed to the Act of Uniformity in 1559; it proclaimed against 'despisers or breakers' of order prescribed in the Book of Common Prayer (1573), enforced laws against Roman Catholic recusancy, punished those who spread false rumours and executed a variety of commissions and injunctions.[64] In religious matters, the Council's main task was to impose uniformity and to suppress recusancy. It also dealt with wills and allied affairs and heard cases of sexual immorality.[65] The exercise of its power over church courts led to considerable conflict with ecclesiastical authorities late in the century and that power was not curtailed in the instructions of 1602.[66] What is of importance in this context is that membership of the Council in the Marches was drawn from among governing families who were duty bound to uphold the religious settlement. In Wales men like William Aubrey, an eminent civil lawyer of Brecknockshire, Sir Richard Bulkeley III of Beaumaris and Baron Hill, Sir John Herbert of Neath Abbey, Sir Thomas Jones of Abermarlais, Dr David Lewis, Abergavenny, Sir Edward Stradling and Dr Ellis Price of Plas Iolyn were all well-known for their Protestant connections. They also had strong London-based connections.

When associated with governmental affairs many sources contain detailed instructions and injunctions appertaining to religious practice. When describing the virtues attributed to gentlemen in power, the bards appear to be among the strongest advocates of the divine power granted to them to maintain good order. No person of integrity, as the bards would describe their individual patrons, could ever achieve true eminence unless endowed with moral qualities. In this context, but from a secular angle, William Lambarde eagerly expressed his opinions on moral issues in the public role of the gentry:

---

[63] J. H. Gleason, *The Justices of the Peace in England, 1558 to 1640: A Later Eirenarcha* (Oxford, 1969), pp.68-74, 96-115.

[64] R. Flenley (ed.), *A Calendar of the Register of the Queen's Council in the Dominion and Principality of Wales and the Marches of the same, 1569-1591* (London, 1916), pp.58-9, 104-5;

[65] P. Williams, *The Council in the Marches of Wales under Elizabeth I* (Cardiff, 1958), pp.84-105.

[66] Ibid., p.105.

The uttermost and endless end of all our actions ought to be the glory of the High God, from whom... all true both religion and justice do flow and fall unto us. The nearer end is the outward peace and profit of the church and commonwealth of our country...And therefore, for the achieving of all these ends at once and with one same labour...there is only requisite *obedience – obedience*, I say, to the religion of God, and obedience to the godly policy of our country.[67]

At the head of this hierarchy stood the monarchy, hence the tribute paid to Elizabeth I by Siôn Tudur, one of the most celebrated of late Tudor Welsh professional bards. He regarded the Queen as the stalwart defender of the faith.[68] The interaction between Crown and commons in Wales, therefore, is made abundantly clear as well as the glorification of the queen's bounty in allowing the scriptures to be available in the Welsh language. Such munificence had overawed George Owen of Henllys:

...and nowe not three yeares past, we haue had the light of the ghospell, yea the whole Byble, in our owne natyue tongue, which in shortt tyme must needs worke great good inwardly in the hartts of the people, whearas the seruice and sacraments in the English tounge was as straunge to many or most of the symplest sorte as the mass in the tyme of blyndness was to the rest of England...[69]

This extract expresses a prominent layman's tribute, not only to those who made the scriptures available but to the occupier of the throne who initiated it in parliament. Owen would not have praised that achievement had it no connections with maintaining unity and uniformity in the state. Similarly, the responses of Edward, Lord Zouche, Lord President of the Council in the Marches, when reprimanding local officials for not attending as diligently as they might to their duties, to the need to defend the realm against recusants, implied that the religious as well as the secular establishment had to be defended. He sought only good government and the due execution of law, the neglect of which would overthrow the state and the private possessions of those appointed to

---

67 W. Lambarde, pp.146-6.
68 E. Roberts (ed.), *Gwaith Siôn Tudur*, I, XCVIII, pp.388-9.
69 G. Owen, 'The Dialogue of the Government of Wales', in H. Owen (ed.), *Penbrokshire*, III (London, 1906), pp.56-7.

defend them at a time when rumours spread concerning the queen's state of health.[70] Moreover, laxity in administration caused by private interests prevented the course of justice since 'where blood calleth for vengeance, the commonwealth will suffer'.[71]

In a similar vein the Privy Council ordered him to maintain peace and security:

> Assuring you that, as Her Majesty, by whose authority we do this, lyeth with good sense and memory... you shall be truly and timely advertised thereof from us, to the end that we and you and all others that truly love the State may, in unity and common amity, join together in all such courses as may preserve, both in public and private, the peace and tranquillity of the same...[72]

The role of the individual in the preservation of religious uniformity is often revealed in the manner in which persons are viewed by others. Whatever their personal indiscretions might be, when they showed favour through patronage attention was often drawn to their moral qualities or religious attributes. These qualities were identified with those normally associated with the Renaissance doctrine of the 'complete gentleman' conceived of in a religious context. The active public benefactor was often cast in this mould; his private virtues were revealed as manifestations of moral rectitude. In the Elizabethan and subsequent periods the virtue of integrity was associated with the consummate courtier. It was within this moral framework that Sir Edward Stradling was depicted by Gervase Babington, bishop of Llandaff, in a letter which accompanied books he had sent Stradling:

> The Lord hath made you able to doe much good...The Lorde hath made yow a pyller of this country, and yf yo'r godly zeale shall ever make yow soe, allso of his kingdome... [73]

These words evidently underline the qualities of leadership in both religious and secular matters. It is in that context that Stradling was

[70] *Calendar of Wynn of Gwydir Papers*, no.324 (1604).
[71] Ibid.
[72] Ibid., no.240 (16 March 1603)
[73] *Stradling Correspondence*, ed. J. M. Traherne (London, 1840), CCXVII, p.277.

viewed by William Fleming who sought his assistance in gaining a preferment in the church. He pleaded for his patronage as 'one of the chiefest authors' of his welfare.

Fleming went on to censure the church for the manner in which preferments were allocated within it:

> ...but covetousnes raignes soe generallye...amongst men at this day, that the doore w'ch leades men to any preferment, by yt neuer soe meane, can not be opened w'thout the sylver or goulden key...but my trust is soe surely grounded on Godes p'vydence, that I hope He will move the good myndes of worshipfull gentlemen to unite ther helps to worke a scholer's preferm't ...[74]

This was not a new revelation since prospective clergy were often faced by situations which betrayed the avarice of landowners. In an entirely different context the classic example is William Morgan's hardened response to John Wynn of Gwydir, the acrimonious tone of the correspondence between them revealing different attitudes towards church tithes and property as well as a marked clash of personalities.[75]

In Roman Catholic circles the frustrations felt by exiled litterateurs who were eager to see the old faith restored is made evident in their writings, particularly those of Robert Gwyn, in his preface to *Y Drych Cristianogawl*, and Rhosier Smyth in his translation of Pierre Boaistuau's *Le Théâtre du Monde*. It was as much a concern for them as it was for Protestant apologists to emphasize the deeply 'patriotic' element which their religious persuasion enabled them to project, a significant feature which deserves further consideration by literary historians, especially in relation to Catholic humanist activity on the continent and in Elizabethan England. Reference has already been made to Robert Gwyn's harsh judgement of Welsh gentry for their lack of commitment to their native culture. Gwyn's words are continually hard-hitting, comparing their contribution to guiding and educating their dependants unfavourably with their English counterparts:

---

[74] Ibid., CCLVII, p.331.
[75] J. G. Jones, 'Bishop William Morgan's dispute with John Wynn of Gwydir in 1603-04', *JHSCW*, XXII, 1972, 49-78.

Mae r Bonheddigion ar hai Cyfoethoccaf heb feddwl am phydd yn y byd, heb fod na thwymyn nag oer...Ond yn lloegr mae r gwyr Bonheddigion yn amal yn dda, ag yn rhoi sampl mywn phydd a buchedd dda ir Cyphredin: Ar Cymry Bonheddigion yn rhoi sampal ir tylodion cyphredin, i fod heb na Phydd na Chydwybod.[76]

[The gentlemen and the wealthiest do not think about faith in the world, and are neither warm nor cold...But in England gentlemen are often good, and give an example in faith and good conduct to the common folk. And the Welsh gentlemen give example to the common poor to be without faith or conscience.]

These words bear a double-edged meaning. While Gwyn deplores the lethargy of the gentry in not attending to the needs of their dependants in secular life they are also brought to book for not giving them proper spiritual instruction according to the tenets of the old faith. Similarly, but in far less uncompromising terms, Rhosier Smyth, Roman Catholic priest and translator, besides dealing with the human condition, the abhorrence of the human body and the dignity of the soul, refers in his translation of Boaistuau's work to the need for leaders in society to instil the true faith in their fellow Welshmen:

> *Antur naws dolur nes du i'm gan amrant am gymru*, gan obeithio drwy hyn, annos a chyphroi y pendefigion a'r penaethiaid, i garu i gwlad, ag i'm gleddu i aith a hefyd y gwyr dyscedig hybarchys i y scrifenu rhyw beth tyladwy er mwyn budd a lles iw gwlad...[77]

[I have made this [translation] out of love of my country, hoping that I can inspire other members of the gentry and the leaders to love their country and succour the language, and other revered and learned men to write something worthy for the benefit and good of their country...]

He followed the same trail as Smyth but is less prepared to upset those whom he intends to address. His mentor, Gruffydd Robert, however, while issuing a stern riposte to those gentry who despised their native tongue because of 'either true boldness or conceited arrogance and utter vanity' ('...naill ai o wir pholder, yntau o goeg falchder a gorwagrwydd'),

---

[76] *Rhagymadroddion*, p.52.
[77] Rhosier Smyth, *Theater du Mond* (*Gorsedd y Byd*), ed. T. Parry (Cardiff. 1930), p.222.

continued to receive Sir William Herbert, earl of Pembroke's patronage.[78] His *Gramadeg Cymraeg* (1567) was dedicated to him. At that time Herbert was 'a pure opportunist' in religious matters, and his main ambition was to increase his estates and hold high office, becoming Lord-President of the Council in the Marches on two occasions (1550, 1555-8).[79] Under Mary he declared his support for the Spanish match, led forces which suppressed Wyatt's rebellion (1554) and served as diplomat and as governor of Calais (1556). Despite his busy official life doubtless it was his support for the Welsh language (his mother tongue), more than his religious fervour, that appealed to Gruffydd Robert in his first preface in which the language addresses Herbert:

> ... gan fod yn eglur, nid o feun loegr yn unig, eithr ymhob mann y mae son am dani, nad oes dim a phruyth yndo yn perthynu at stad y deyrnas meun heduch, a rhyfel, ond a luniuyd truy'ch cyngor, ag a unaethbuyd truych grym a'ch cymorth, a'ch anorphuys lafur. Am hynny mae gennyf obaith yrouron y byduch ymy yn argluyd da, i 'mdiphyn rhag argoued, a drug, ac im helpu urth geisio ymossod ala' i dangos f'uyneb ymysc yr ieithoed erail nid ydynt uel i braint no minnau; ond cael o honynt imgeled, ai mourhau gan bennaduriaid, a bonedigion i gulad ag urthynny gadel lauer arnafi, a fum cyd heb nag ymgeled, na mourhaad. [80]

[...by being clear, not within England only, but everywhere there is mention of it, where there is nothing with fruit in it related to the state of the realm in peace, and war, but was formed by means of your counsel, and accomplished by your means, aid and indefatigable labour. For that I have hope now that you may be my Good Lord, to defend me from crisis and evil and to help me as I attempt to move out and to show my face among other languages which are not better privileged than me; but to obtain from them succour and bounty from chieftains, gentlemen of the country and by that learn much of me who has been so long without succour or greatness.]

Owing to his successful public career Herbert appealed greatly to the Roman Catholic scholar. In his mind he was just the person to nourish

---

78   *Rhagymadroddion*, p.47.
79   P. Williams, *Council in the Marches*, pp.36-8, 234-6.
80   Gruffydd Robert, *Gramadeg Cymraeg*, ed. G. J. Williams (Cardiff, 1939): Address to William Herbert, earl of Pembroke [unpaginated].

interest in the Welsh language and its literature. In his view Herbert was a model of cultural rectitude rather than a spearhead of the new faith. Gruffydd Robert was firm in his support of Morus Clynnog's *Athravaeth Gristnogawl* (1568) which he published in Milan and, in a letter to Clynnog from there in that year, he drew attention to the propaganda value of the work:

> Gobeithio pan ddelo i ddwylaw y crefyddgar Gymry, y gwna lawer o les iddynt trwy eu hwylio i baradwys a'u troi o ffordd uffernawl...Gwyn eu byd trwy Gymru pe parent ymhob eglwys wrth aros y gwasanaeth neu ar osteg offeren, gartref ymysg tylwyth y tŷ i ddifyrru'r amser, ac ymhob cynulleidfa i ddiddanu'r bobl, ddarllen hwn neu'r cyfryw ymadroddion, a gadael i ffordd henchwedlau coegion, a chywyddau gwenieithus celwyddog.[81]

[It is hoped when it comes to the hands of the religious Welsh people that it will do them much good by facilitating their move to paradise and turn them away from the road to hell...Blessed be they throughout Wales if they can cause in each church, while waiting for the service or when celebrating the mass, to pass the time at home among the house's family, and in all congregations to console the people, that this or the like phrases are read, and the road of vain old legends and false and flattering odes in strict metre abandoned.]

Robert saw the work as a means of reconverting the people to the old faith for he considered it to be a treasure in the Welsh language and a directive to introduce the ways of Christ among them, whom he regarded as 'children crying for bread... and no one there to break it for them and give it to them without poisoning it' ('plant yn crio am fara...heb fod neb a'i tyr iddynt ac a'i rhydd heb ei wenwyno').[82]

Protestant apologists described the old faith as the remnant of antiquated religious customs adhered to particularly in rural areas. Constant references to the persistent hold which superstitious practices had on the peasantry caused Protestant commentators to ridicule a faith which reflected the 'tyme of blyndness'[83] which revealed a bewildering devotion

---

81   H. Lewis (ed.), *Hen Gyflwyniadau*, pp.5-6.
82   Ibid., p.5.
83   G. Owen, *Penbrokshire*, III, p.57.

to relics and images which could hardly be regarded as being compatible with a rational faith. The letters of Dr Ellis Price of Plas Iolyn to Thomas Cromwell, following his visitation of Llandderfel in Merioneth, described the attraction which the imposing image of Derfel Gadarn had for the common folk and he entirely disapproved.[84] So also did William Herbert in his comments on the shrine at Pen-rhys.[85] Indeed, pilgrimages to such well-known shrines was a lucrative business. Bishop Robinson of Bangor informed Sir William Cecil about the 'lewd and indecent vigils and watches obtained, much pilgrimage-going... countries full of beads and knots', all of which revealed a dire situation which underlined a serious 'wante of knowledge'.[86] Robinson considered that assistance by the agencies of law and order in the region, together with his own efforts, would improve spiritual life in Gwynedd. The words of Sir Richard Pryse of Brecon are similar in tone: He was particularly concerned about the lack of good preachers in his shire to undertake the task of improving the ways of common people described as 'so rude and ignorant in the most necessary points of the Christian faith [and who] ...live in contempt both of the laws of God and man.'[87] The most graphic descriptions of the 'gross idolatrie' practised in Wales, which caused the author much irritation, were given by Dr Ellis Price in 1589:

> ...I have harde by dyvers of great & abhominable Idolatries comited in ye countrey, as yn the people went one pylgrymages to offer unto idoles farre & neare, yea, and that they do offer in these dayes not onely monye, and that librallye, but also bullocks unto Idolles... Also the people do carye beades openlye and make suche clappinge with them in ye churche, as yf a man can hardly here the minister read for the noise therof, alledging that they can read upon their beades as well as others can upon their bookes.[88]

Price blamed secular authorities for their lack of insight and diligence when inquiring into such matters and warned that God's wrath might descend upon the nation. Other similar reports dwell upon the religious

---

84 E. Breese, 'Dervel Gadarn', AC, V (4th ser.), 1874, 152-4; W. G. Evans, 'Derfel Gadarn – A celebrated victim of the Reformation', *JMHRS*, XI, 1990-93, 137-51.
85 *Letters and Papers Foreign and Domestic*, XIII (Pt. 2), no. 34 (14 September 1538), p.134.
86 D. Mathew, 'Some Elizabethan documents', 78.
87 *Original Letters Illustrative of English History*, ed. H. Ellis, III (2nd ser, London, 1827), p.44.
88 *Cal. State Papers Dom.*, 1581-1590, CCXXIV, no.74, p.603.

inadequacies of Wales, all of which dealt principally with the external manifestations of superstitious practices instead of tackling the basic reason for their persistence, namely the social structure of Wales which hindered the spiritual rehabilitation of the Welsh people. William Salesbury was even more forthright in his comments, for his agenda included broader scholastic considerations as well as the advancement of Protestantism. The punitive tone of his words in *Oll Synnwyr Pen...* (1547), his publication of Welsh proverbs collected in manuscript by the chief bard Gruffudd Hiraethog, makes the point patently clear:

> A ny vynwch ymado yn dalgrwn dec a fydd Christ, a ny vynwch yn lan syth na bo ywch ddim a wneloch ac ef, ac any vynnwch tros gofi ac ebryfygy i ewyllys ef y gyd achlan, mynwch yr yscrythur lan yn ych iaith, mal ac y bu hi y gan ych dedwydd henafieit yr hen Uryttanneit.[89]

[Unless you wish utterly to depart from the faith of Christ, unless you wish to have nothing at all to do with Him, unless you wish entirely to forget His will, obtain the holy scripture in your tongue as your fortunate ancestors, the ancient British had it.]

He issued a stern warning because he saw that in the Wales of his time there was great danger that not only the Welsh language would suffer and be denied a status equal to that of Greek and Latin but also that Protestantism would lose its momentum. In fact, prominent laymen were as ardent, if not more so than higher clergy, to advance the Protestant faith. As mentioned above, Robert Llwyd, vicar of Chirk, praised Rowland Vaughan for translating Lewis Bayly's *The Practice of Piety* in 1630. Vaughan apparently knew Robert Llwyd, calling him his 'dear teacher' ('am hanwyl athro') which may imply that Vaughan had learnt the linguistic techniques employed by Llwyd in his notable translation which appeared a short time before *Yr Ymarfer o Dduwioldeb*.[90] There is no firm evidence, however, to prove what the literary connections were between both, except that Llwyd was aware of the fact that Vaughan's translation was in the press.

---

89 *Rhagymadroddion*, p.11.
90 Ibid., p.130.

If the younger generation of gentry applied themselves to godly and spiritually profitable occupations, Llwyd continued, ill-government and worldly avarice would not be accorded so much pomp. Michael Roberts, Fellow of Jesus College, Oxford (and later principal of the college), to whom is ascribed the preface to the small Bible (1630), lavishly praised the two sponsors, Rowland Heylin and Sir Thomas Middleton, as true representatives of the enlightened commercial middle class which

Title-page of 'Y Beibl Bach', 1630

assumed a significant role in promoting Puritan propaganda in the seventeenth century.[91] He combined his testimony to the excellence of this edition with the need to appreciate the peace and security enjoyed in Charles I's reign, a blessed state which served to enhance godliness and integrity:

> Ac yma y mae'n rhaid i ti gydnabod yn ddiolchgar fawr ofal a chost rhyw dduwiol ac vrddasol ddinasyddion a marsiandwyr o Lundain...Duw o'i ddaioni a'u cofio hwy, a phawb eraill mewn Symlrwydd calonnau ffyddlon dda ydynt yn ewyllysio ac yn gwneuthr daioni iw Sion ef. Dy ddled a'th ofal di a ddylai fod yn gyntaf mawrygu a chlodfori Duw am y dedwyddwch a'r rhyddid yr ydym ni o'r deirnas hon...yn ei fwynhau tan adn a chyscod ein grasusaf Arglwydd Frenhin CHARLES, tan yr hwn y gallwn ni fyw yn llonydd ac yn heddychlawn mewn pob Duwioldeb ac honestrwydd...[92]

[And here you must acknowledge thankfully the great care and expense of some godly and dignified London citizens and merchants...God of his goodness remembers them, and all others in the simplicity of faithful hearts who will and do good to his Zion. Your debt and care should be first to magnify and praise God for the bliss and freedom that we in this kingdom enjoy under the wing and in the shadow of our most gracious Lord King CHARLES, under whom we can live quietly and peacefully in all Godliness and honesty...]

He desired the reader to adopt a social as well as a religious conscience. The connection forged between Protestantism and religious developments in the apostolic age, he maintained, had raised the prestige which the faith achieved in Elizabeth I's and James I's reigns. He expressed reservations, however, because he did not consider that the scriptures had had the desired effect –'nid ydoedd na'r lles, nar arfer o air Duw mor gyhoedd ac mor gyffredin, ac y chwenychai lawer o Gristnogion bucheddol' ('the welfare nor the habit of the Word of God were not as public and as common as many devout Christians had hoped for').[93] He was aware that the first edition of the Bible needed to be placed securely in parish churches and other religious centres since it was an essential part of the church's liturgy and service. He added, however, that

---

[91]   Ibid., pp.124-5; R. G. Gruffydd, 'Michael Roberts o Fôn a Beibl Bach 1630', *TAAS*, 1989, 35-6..
[92]   *Rhagymadroddion*, pp.124-5.
[93]   Ibid., p.123.

the deepening of Protestant convictions within family circles demanded that it be available for household and private consumption. He cited the saint and theologian John Chrysostom (347-407 A. D.), who called on laymen and other ranks of men to supply Bibles since St Paul himself had commanded that the Word of God should dwell in the heart of the individual. You need to consult the scriptures on a regular basis, he continued, and not every week or every month, as and when you attend church:

> Yn awr, gan fod yn ceisio gennym chwilio a darllain yr Scrythyrau yn neilltuol gartref, heb law yr ydys yn ei wneuthr yn gyhoedd ac ar osteg yn yr Eglwys...Ac lle y dylai yn bendifaddeu breswylio yn y galon, yr hon yw dodrefnyn pennaf yr enaid, Etto mae'n angenrhaid iddo hefyd breswylio yn y ty. Ni wasanaetha yn vnic ei adel ef yn yr Eglwys, fel gwr dieuthr, ond mae'n rhaid iddo drigo yn dy stafell di, tan dy gronglwyd dy hun.[94]

[And now, since we are searching and reading the scriptures, particularly at home, apart from doing so publicly and quietly in the Church...And where it should verily reside in the heart, which is the chief furnishing of the soul, Yet it is essential for it to reside in the house. It does no service to leave it in the Church only, as a strange man, but it must dwell in your room, under your own roof.]

Together with the new Bible appeared, under the same covers, the Book of Common Prayer and the metrical Psalms of Edmwnd Prys, the aim being to improve Christian conduct 'according to God's word' ('yn ôl gair Duw').[95] Prys rejected the idea of setting the Psalms to strict metres because he feared that, by doing so, he might lose the meaning of the original. The psalms were to be available for participation by a congregation and it was hoped that they might appeal to the lower clergy and their parishioners:

> Ac o achos bôd yn berthynol i bob Christion wybod ewyllys Duw, a'i foliannu ef, mi a ymadewais â'r gelfyddyd, er mwyn bod pawb yn rhwymedic i wario ei dalent at y gorau.[96]

---

94 Ibid., pp.123-4.
95 Ibid., p.124; J. Ballinger, *The Bible in Welsh* (London, 1906), p.28.
96 E. Prys, *Llyfr y Psalmau, wedi ev cyfiaethv, a'i cyfansoddi ar fesvr cerdd yn Gymraeg* (London, 1621), A2.

[And because it is relevant for each Christian to know the will of God and to praise him I abandoned the craft, in order that everyone will be bound to spend his talent to the best (of his ability].

The motive for the publication of the 1630 Bible is similar to that which initiated Dr John Davies of Mallwyd's *Llyfr y Resolusion* (1632), a Protestant adaptation in Welsh of the Jesuit Robert Persons's *The First Booke of the Christian Exercise Appertayning to Resolution* (1582) by Edmund Bunny, Anglican Puritan and canon in the cathedral church of York. His aim was clearly explained:

> So the substance of the booke is such, as that a minde that is wel disposed, may with one, and the selfesame labor, gather out of it, both lessons of godliness unto it selfe...which wil yeeld us this fruit that we shal addresse our selues to do, in som good measure, our service to God...[97]

Priority was accorded to the exercise of piety and a Calvinist interpretation of Persons's Catholicism gave Bunny's work a new approach. Llwyd added that the purpose was to set 'our whole desires and our thoughts on being true Christians, that is abandoning our evil life and turning towards goodness and godliness.' ('...rhoi cwbl o'n bryd a'n meddwl ar fod yn wir Gristianogion, hyny ydyw ar ymadel an drwg fuchedd a throi ar ddaioni a duwioldeb').[98] What appeared as Protestant literature in the years following the publication of the small Bible was not only what has been called part of the 'Middleton-Heylin movement'. Of greater significance is that, despite social limitations, so much literature did appear in so short a time, such as Vaughan's *Yr Ymarfer o Dduwioldeb*, Llwyd's *Llwybr hyffordd yn cyfarwyddo yr anghyfarwydd i'r nefoedd* (1630) and Oliver Thomas's *Car-wr y Cymru* (1631).[99] All these works were based on theological and devotional meditations and were propaganda pieces aimed at influencing the intelligentsia of Wales.

---

97   E. Bunny, *Christian exercise appertaininge to resolvtion*...(London, 1584), preface to the reader; Davies, C. John Davies o Fallwyd pp.87-93.

98   *Y Traddodiad Rhyddiaith*, p.187; J. Davies, *Llyfr y Resolusion neu Hollawl Ymroad* (Caernarfon, 1885), pp.8-9.

99   *Y Traddodiad Rhyddiaith*, pp.191-2.

Oliver Thomas, author of *Car-wr y Cymru*, made the point quite clearly in his Epistle Dedicatory to 'True-hearted Well-willers and furtherers of the spiritual weale of Wales':

> May it please you therefore...to vouchsafe the acceptance thereof [of the Bible], and as you haue beene lately pleased, after your great care...in procuring the printing of the *Welsh Bible*, to send it abroad into the country of *Wales*, so be pleased to send this *Welsh* booke after it, which may happily ouertake it, spurre it forward, yea, goe before it as an Harbinger into many houses and families, to prepare a roome for it, in the houses and in their hearts...[100]

Robert Llwyd, in translating *The Plaine Man's Pathway to Heaven* (*Llwybr hyffordd...*) insisted that the aim was to bring spiritual benefits and to console the soul ('wneuthur i ti lesâd, a dwyn diddanwch i'th enaid').[101] The role of the Protestant leader in his community, and especially in his household, is fundamental to extending the appeal, understanding and acceptance of the faith. The translated work, therefore, was primarily an instrument to enrich spirituality within the nuclear family:

> Oni wnei ddaioni i dylwth dy dŷ, na wna gam a hwynt am ymborth eu heneidiau...Canys er porthi o honot gyrph dy blant, a'th deulu, a gadel ar hynny heb ymorol a'm eu heneidiau, beth yr wyt ti yn ei wneuthur iddynt chwaneg, nac a wnei i'th farch, i'th ŷch, ie i'th gî? Darllein hwn gan hynny, i'th wraig, ac i'th blant.[102]

[If you do no good to the family of your household, do not do them injustice concerning their souls' sustenance ... Because, although you feed your children's and your family's bodies, and leave it at that without caring for their souls, what are you doing more to them than you do to your horse, your ox, yes your dog. Read this, therefore, to your wife and children.]

This preface is directed towards the *paterfamilias* whose role was considered essential to maintaining the spiritual well-being of his

---

100   M. Morgan (ed.), *Gweithiau Oliver Thomas ac Evan Roberts* (Cardiff, 1981), p.[26].
101   *Rhagymadroddion*, p.126.
102   Ibid., p.127.

household. It was regarded as a part of the state, a central cog in a well-ordered regional community. 'The family', it is said, 'was the nursery and fort of spiritual life',[103] and its head, being a 'governor', would act as a spiritual and moral guide, a counsellor to improve standards, and a justice to maintain good conduct and impose order and discipline. It was Lewis Bayly who came nearest to identifying the essence of this godly disposition in *The Practice of Piety*:

> If thou be called to the government of a Family, thou must not hold it sufficient to serve God, & live uprightly in thine *owne* person, unles thou cause all under thy *charge* to do the same with thee...And God himselfe gives a special charge to all Housholders that they doe instruct their Family in his *Word*, and traine them up in his feare and service...If every *housholder* were thus carefull, according to his *duty*, to bring up his Children and Family in the *service & feare* of God in his owne house, then the house of *God* should be better filled...and the Pastors *publike* preaching and labour, would take *more* effect than it doth...call every morning *all* thy *family* to some *convenient* roome; and first, either reade thy selfe unto them a Chapter in the Word of God...[104]

Devout action by the householder not only spreads the gospel among his immediate family but, through them, to the neighbourhood and further afield. The message was universal and it is in that setting that Bayly interpreted it. No wonder that Rowland Vaughan made such an appeal in his preface to the reader in the Welsh edition:

> Am y llyfr hwn, a sail yr athrawiaeth sydd ynddo, nid yw ond golau canwyll yngoleuni yr Haul i mi ei glodfori... Edrych a ddichon y llyfr hwn roddi meddyginiaeth i'th enaid, neu lyfrau eraill oi gyffelyb: megis y llyfr odiaethol a gyfenwir *llwybr hyffordd i'r nefoedd* o gyfieithiad y llên dyscedig, am hanwyl athro Mr Ro. lloyd Ficar y waen, neu bregeth am edifeirwch o waith yr vnrhyw gymreugydd rhagorol: ac oni ddichon hynny beri i ti wellhau dy fuchedd, ni byddit ti ddim gwell *pe cyfodai vn oddiwrth y meirw* i'th athrawiaethu.[105]

---

103 J. G. Williams, 'Rhai agweddau ar y gymdeithas Gymreig yn yr ail ganrif ar bymtheg', *Efrydiau Athronyddol*, XXX, 1968, 45.
104 L. Bayly, *The Practice of Piety* (London, 1640 ed.), pp.289, 290, 291, 294.
105 *Rhagymadroddion*, pp.118, 120-1.

[And with regard to this book, and the foundation of the doctrine in it, it is but lighting a candle in the light of the sun for me to praise it...See if this book can give physick to your soul, or other books similar to it: such as the exquisite book entitled *Llwybr Hyffordd i'r Nefoedd*, translated by the learned clergyman and my dear teacher Mr Robert Lloyd, vicar of Chirk, or the sermon on repentence by the same excellent writer of Welsh: and if that does not make you improve your life, you would be no better if one arose from the dead to instruct you.]

The emphasis is on fostering 'buchedd' (Christian conduct) and obtaining 'meddyginiaeth i'th enaid' ('physick for your soul'), a theme which is featured prominently in all religious manuals in the Reformation period. More often than not Rowland Vaughan's propaganda emerges in the light of his ardent royalism. All his translations, such as *Eikon Basilike* (c. 1650 – written by William Gauden c.1648-9), *Prifannau Sanctaidd neu Lawlyfr o Weddïau* (1658 – a translation of William Brough, dean of Gloucester's *Sacred Principles, Services and Soliloquies* (1649)), and *Prifannau Crefydd Gristnogawl* (1658 – a translation of Bishop James Ussher's *The Principles of the Christian Religion* (1644)) all reveal his strong attachment to the Stuart Crown and the Anglican Church. Vaughan saw himself as a lay translator who abhorred unordained preachers and dissociated himself entirely from them. He presented his translation of *Eikon Basilike* to Sir John Owen, the royalist commander from Y Clenennau in Eifionydd, and drew attention to his Christian piety and unswerving loyalty to Charles I during the most troubled part of his reign.[106] Vaughan suffered many tribulations for his loyal support of the Crown and his rhetorical style reveals his attitude towards uncompromising Puritan preachers and their followers who opposed the Crown and the Anglican Church.

When discussing the imposition of authority in the state, the Church and the family household, one of the major concerns is the interplay of social relationships, and historians, such as Paul Griffiths, have devoted their researches in recent years to the 'age hierarchy' in early modern England.[107] One cultural phenomenon was possession and the role of

---

[106] NLW Brogyntyn MS. II.56; E. D. Jones, 'The Brogyntyn Welsh manuscripts', NLWJ, VII (3) 1952, 165-8, 192; M. Ellis, 'Cyflwyniad Rowland Vaughan, Caer-gai, i'w gyfieithiad o *Eikon Basilike*', ibid., 1, 1939-40, 143; J. G. Jones, 'Rowland Vaughan o Gaer-gai a'i gyfieithiad o *Eikon Basilike* (1650', *Y Traethodydd*, CLVI, 2000, 18-40; idem, 'Cyfieithiad Rowland Vaughan, Caer-gai, o *Eikon Basilike* (1650),' *Studia Celtica*, XXXVI, 2002, 99-138

[107] P. Griffiths, A. Fox and S. Hunter (eds.), *The Experience of Authority in Early Modern England* (Macmillan, 1996).

witchcraft in the lives and experiences of the younger generation, which involved what has been described as the 'disruption of the well-ordered household'. All aspects of misbehaviour were interpreted as signifying a rejection of religious discipline and a mockery of Christian beliefs. Charges of blasphemy and other forms of irregular behaviour were all challenges to orthodox religious practice and, in turn, to authority. Attached to this is the concept of the 'reformation of manners' which highlighted the need for personal morality, a feature that was to become patently clear in Anglican as well as Puritan writings.[108]

The role of the household in the religious sphere implied an attachment to social relationships. The church was but one agency of authority but it was crucial since it imposed punitive as well as reformatory measures and counselled as well as coerced. Society changed so quickly and methods of exercising control were periodically changed. In a secular context discipline in the state was maintained chiefly through its courts of law; that was the case also in the church courts but exhortation, counsel and moral directives also played a significant role. In his last years John Penry advised his wife to maintain good order in her household if he were put to death:

> Be much and often in prayer, day and night, in the reading and meditation of His word, and you shall find that He will grant you your hearts desire, according to His good pleasure and will Pray with your poor family and children, morning and evening, as you do. Instruct them and your maid in the good ways of God, so that no day may pass over your head wherein you have not taught them...some one principle of the truth.[109]

In a petition of his in 1592 seeking a pardon, he argued that he needed to control his household adding 'and what is youth without government?'[110]

---

[108] J. A. Sharpe, 'Disruption in the well-ordered household: age, authority and possessioned young Men', ibid., pp.187-209, M. Ingram, 'Reformation of manners in early modern England', ibid., pp.47-81. For witchcraft and anti-witchcraft propaganda see R. Holland, 'Ymddiddan Tudur a Gronwy' in T. Jones (ed.), *Rhyddiaith Gymraeg: Detholion o Lawysgrifau a Llyfrau Printiedig 1547-1618*, II (Cardiff, 1956), pp.161-73; G. Williams, *Wales and the Reformation*, pp.324-9; D. S. T. Clark and P. T. J. Morgan, 'Religion and magic in Elizabethan Wales', *JEH*, XXVII, 1976, 31-46; J. G. Jones, 'Y "tylwyth teg" yng Nghymru'r unfed ar ail ganrif ar bymtheg', *LlC*, VIII, 1964, 96-9.

[109] W. Pierce, *The Life and Times of John Penry* (London, 1923), pp.406, 418.

[110] Cited in J. G. Williams, 'Rhai agweddau ar y gymdeithas Gymreig', 46; J. G. Jones, 'John Penry: government, order and the "perishing souls" of Wales', *TCS*, 1993, pp.49-50.

He advised his four daughters to be obedient to their mother 'in word and in deed, and miss not to be the staff of her age, who is now the only stay and support that is left unto you in your youth and infancy.'[111] His own mother was his chief support during his undergraduate days, which suggests that she came from fairly substantial Brecknockshire freeholding stock.[112] Advocating discipline and control was meaningful only when it could be communicated effectively to the rank and file of the population through the appropriate channels. In that context the crucial factor accompanying literary activity emerging from religious propaganda and used to promote either Roman Catholicism or Protestantism was the nature of the audience for whom publications were intended. If the prefaces to such works were to have any impact then they had to emphasize the methods used by the author to promote his faith. Such prefaces, which varied in length, are essential to an understanding of the social and religious climate which motivated the author to publish his prose. Doubtless undertaking such a task, which often involved financial strains, incurred a serious risk, and one serious drawback was the small market for such works together with poor economic resources, inadequate patronage and the lack of institutions of higher education to foster high academic standards.[113] Moreover, widespread illiteracy was a debilitating factor, and references frequently appear in the prefaces to either illiteracy on a broad scale in Welsh communities or the withdrawal of gentry patronage, particularly among the younger generations, from Welsh culture generally. Prefaces are variously addressed to 'the reader' ('y darlleawdyr'), 'all the Welsh' ('ir Cembru oll'), 'the nobility, gentry, bards, Welsh authors and others of my dear ones in the Welsh nation' ('At Bendefigion, a Boneddigion, a Phrydyddion, a Chymreigyddion, ac at eraill om Annwylieid o Genedl Gymry...'), 'the benign Christian reader' ('yr howddgar ddarlleydd Cristnogawl'), priests ('periglorion') and even 'the monoglot Welshman' ('...y darllennudd o Gymro vniaith'). 'Sir' Thomas Wiliems, however, went further, and addressed 'the gracious commonalty of Wales' ('...hygar Gyphredin yn holl Gymru') as well as those of the privileged orders. Sir Glanmor Williams considered this issue of readership and came to the conclusion that prefaces reveal that a broad

---

111 W. Pierce, *Life and Times of John Penry*, p.418; J. G. Jones, 'John Penry: government, order and the "perishing souls" of Wales', loc. cit.
112 Ibid., p.419; J. Penry, *Three Treatises concerning Wales*, ix.
113 Williams, *The Welsh Church from Conquest to Reformation*, pp.522-6; idem, *Wales and the Reformation*, pp.,149-51, 290-1.

range among the social ranks had been given education and benefited immensely from the degree of literacy they achieved.[114] Propaganda in this context was expected to penetrate deeply in social circles which, excepting the lowest social orders, had some grasp of letters. How far that implied literacy in either English or Welsh or both is not easily answered but apologists on both sides of the religious divide seemed sufficiently confident that a sizeable number of prosewriters merited the publication of their religious and scholarly works.

Having said that, certain evidence suggests that literacy in the Welsh language was more prevalent in the sixteenth century than historians are prepared to acknowledge. In his preface to *Yny lhyvyr hwnn* Sir John Pryse, attempting to justify his inclusion of translations of short sections of scripture, states as follows:

> Am hynny gweddys yw rhoi yngymraec beth or yscrythur lan, oherwydd bod llawer o gymry a vedair darllein kymraeg, heb vedru darllein vn gair saesnec na lladin, ag yn enwedic y pynckeu y sy anghenrheydiol y bob rhyw gristion y gwybot dan berigyl y enaid...pechod mawr oedd ado yr sawl mil o enaideu y vyned ar gyfyrgoll rac eiseu gwybodaeth y fydd gatholic, ac y sydd heb wybod iaith yny byd onyd Kymraeg.[115]

[And for that it is fitting to put into Welsh some of the holy scriptures because many Welsh people can read Welsh but cannot read one word of English or Latin, and especially the tenets which are essential for every Christian to know for fear of his soul...it was a great sin to leave so many thousands of souls lost for want of knowledge of the catholic faith, and who do not know any language in the world except Welsh.]

This statement seems to clarify the point but the address to 'y darlleawdyr' ('the reader') can only refer to the literate members of Welsh society. Other writers, as noted above, salute all those expected to have some reading knowledge in their own tongue. Sir Glanmor Williams maintains that literacy was not confined necessarily to the upper reaches

---

[114] G. Williams, 'Religion and Welsh literature in the age of the Reformation', *The Welsh and their Religion*, 166-8.; idem, *Grym Tafodau Tân: Ysgrifau Hanesyddol ar Grefydd a Chymdeithas* (Llandysul, 1984), pp.75-7; L. Stone, 'The educational revolution in England', 1560-1640', *Past & Present*, 18, 1964, 41-8.
[115] *Rhagymadroddion*, pp.3-4.

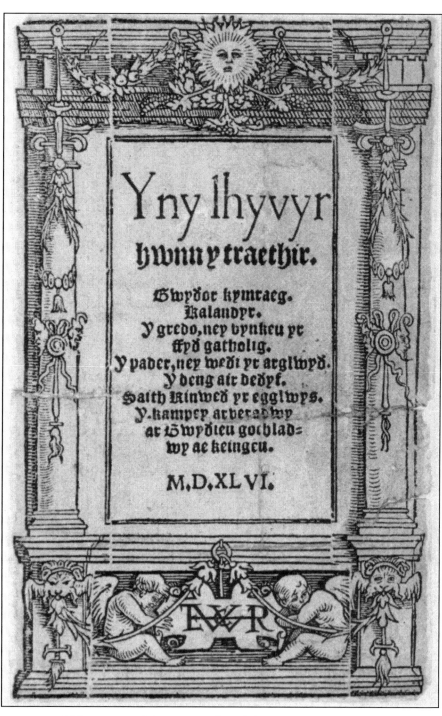

Title-page and first page of Sir John Pryse's preface to
Yny lhyvyr hwnn...(1546)

of society but probably extended lower down the social ranks to the parish gentry, yeomen and freeholders,[116] and Humphrey Lhuyd, writing in 1572, described a transformation in Welsh society in his generation and addressed the matter of literacy:

> Howbeit also, of late they haue very commendably begun to inhabite Townes, to learne occupations, to exercise merchandise, to till the grounde well, and to doo all other kindes of publique, and necessary functions, as wel as Englishmen. And in this one thing surpassyng them, there is no man so poore, but for some space he setteth forth his children to Schole, and such as profitte in studie sendeth them vnto the Universities, where, for the most part, they enforce them to studie the Ciuile law...And you shall finde but few of the ruder sorte, whiche cannot reade, and write their owne name...[117]

Having said that, the situation seems not to be as clear as it might be. Sir John Pryse accused the priesthood of being either reluctant or unable to instruct their parishioners in matters which priests were expected to know and which their flocks should be made aware of. In *A Treatise containing the Aequity of an Humble Supplication* (1587) John Penry, eager to propagate Puritan views, testified to the inability of priests to communicate the faith effectively to their parishioners. He proceeded to supply an answer, that is, that they should make use of the vast vocabulary that is available in the Welsh language. In due course those words would become familiar to the clergy and to their congregations:

> But why can we not haue preaching in our owne toung? Because the minister is not able to vtter his mind in welsh. He maie. For we haue as manie words as in any vulgar toung whatsoeuer and we might borrow from the latine etc. The straunge words would become familiar thorough custom.[118]

A revival of Welsh learning in print and its availability among the gentry and clergy, William Salesbury maintained, would enable the Welsh people to understand the preacher more easily and to assist him in expounding

---

116 G. Williams, *Grym Tafodau Tân*, pp.75-7.
117 Translated by Thomas Twyne, *The Breuiarie of Britayne* (London, 1573), Fo. 60b-61a.
118 J. Penry, *Three Treatises concerning Wales*, p.37.

the Word more meaningfully. Salesbury's *Dictionary in Englyshe and Welshe* (1547) was intended to teach the unlearned the English tongue and not those familiar with it. He added that the standard of spoken Welsh among the clergy was hardly commendable and maintained that if the Welsh language was to attain the standard worthy of the new Learning then it had to be of better quality than the spoken tongue:

> A ydych chwi yn tybieit nat rait amgenach eirieu, na mwy amryw ar amadroddion y draythy dysceidaeth...nag sydd genwch chwi yn arveredic wrth siarad beunydd yn pryny a gwerthy a bwyta ac yfed? Ac od ych chwi yn tybyeit hynny voch tuyller.[119]

[Do yo consider that better quality words are not needed and no variety of phrases to expound learning...than you customarily have when speaking daily buying and selling and eating and drinking? And if you consider that to be so you are deceived.]

Salesbury accepted that dialect was indispensable but, at the same time, totally unworthy of being considered part of a learned language. Renaissance scholars continually insisted that the gentry should set an example for they were largely responsible for the poor quality of the spiritual life of the peasantry. This was forcefully expressed by Robert Gwyn in his preface to *Y Drych Cristianogawl*:

> Py baei r bonheddigion Cymreig yn ymroi i ddarllen ag i scrifennu eu hiaith, hynny a wnaei ir cyphredin hefyd fawrhau a hophi r iaith...er mwyn denu r cyphredin i ddarllain ag i wrando ar hyn o gyngor, nhwy a wnant yn dda gar bron Duw, a daioni yw Gwlad, os darllennant hefyd y llyfr yma, er mwyn rhoi sampl ir cyphredin i fod yn chwannoccach yw ddarllein ai glywed.[120]

[If the Welsh gentlemen were to set about reading and writing their language that would make the common people to exalt and like the language...in order that the common people can read and listen to this advice they would do well before God and the good of their country if they also read this book in order to give an example to the common people to be more eager to read and hear it.]

---

119 *Rhagymadroddion*, p.10.
120 Ibid., pp.53, 54.

How many would respond favourably to his plea that people should peruse a heavy Roman Catholic theological work in an age of severe persecution is beside the point; the relevant fact is that the onus lay on the natural leaders of society to improve the rate of literacy among their dependants. Gwyn was aware that words easily understood in both north and south-Wallian dialects had to be used to ensure that the commonalty might be able to follow the text. He feared greatly that linguistic purists would blame him for not translating sections of the scriptures and works of the saints into literary Welsh but advanced what he considered to be a valid explanation for that:

> Ond pan fytho vn yn pregethu i ddynion cyphredin ag ychydig ddeallt ganthynt, yna y dychon gyfieithu r geirieu yn y modd goreu ag y gallo r cyphredin bobl y ddyall...Ag am fy mod i yma yn ceisio dyscu r cyphredin gymry, rhaid i mi droi r geirieu yn egluraf a goleuaf y gallwyf, i gaphel o honynt eu deallt hwy yn ddibetrus...[121]

[But when one preaches to common people which have little understanding, then it is possible to translate the words in the best manner so that the common people can understand them...And since I am here trying to teach the common Welsh people, I must make the words most clearly and most succinctly as I can so that they can understand them without delay.]

Hugh Lewis, later to become rector of Llanddeiniolen, in his censorious comments in the preface to *Perl Mewn Adfyd* (1595), made some scathing remarks about illiteracy in the Wales of his day. He was aware that the Bible and Book of Common Prayer – both of which he applauded – were unavailable except in parish churches so that they were beyond the reach of peasant folk wishing to understand and practice Christian conduct. It is impossible, he stated, for the ignorant to obtain that knowledge so as to satisfy and comfort themselves. He praised the book translated by him for setting out in orderly concise fashion what is contained in the Bible, but the poor quality of the clergy created many serious problems which led to men in their sixties and beyond being totally illiterate:

> ...mal y digwydd yn fynych, fod mewn amryw o leoedd, henafgwyr briglwydion, trigeinmlwydd oed, ne fwy, mor ddeillion, ac mor anyscedic,

---

[121] Ibid., p.61.

ac na fedrant roi cyfri o bynciau yr ffydd, a'r crefydd Cristnogaidd, mwy na phlant bychain newydd eni.[122]

[...as happens so often that in many places hoary-headed old men, sixty years of age and more, so blind and so unlearned that they cannot account for the tenets of the faith and the Christian religion more than little children newly-born.]

A harsh but meaningful comment. In addition to the underlying religious motives here there were also equally compelling social and political implications. It was considered essential that heads of families should be well-versed in the Protestant faith so as to maintain unity and uniformity in the state. Richard Hooker had drawn attention to the pivotal position held by the master of the household in religious affairs:

> To fathers within their private families Nature hath given a supreme power; for which cause we see throughout the world even from the foundation thereof, all men have ever been taken as lords and lawful kings in their own houses.[123]

This emphasis on order and authority within the basic familial unit represented what might be regarded as the microcosm of monarchical authority exercised within the state. The hearth of the *paterfamilias* and pulpit were indispensable to achieve religious unity, hence the desire among Protestant apologists to see the lower orders in society acquiring education, not only to better themselves socially but also to attach themselves more firmly to the faith. It is in the preface to *Yr Ymarfer o Dduwioldeb* that Rowland Vaughan draws attention to the vital needs of the heads of households. He is concerned that children are not taught to read:

> ...ac ni cheir yn lloegr nemmawr o eurych, neu scubwr simneiau na fedro ddarllain, ac na byddo a'i lyfr tan ei gessel yn yr Eglwys, neu yn ei ddarllain pan fyddo'r achos.[124]

---

122 Ibid., p.101.
123 Hooker, *Of the Laws of Ecclesiastical Polity*, p.191.
124 *Rhagymadroddion*, p.119.

[...and there is not in England hardly any goldsmith or chimney sweep who cannot read, and without his book under his armpit in Church or reading it when it was appropriate.]

Since Welsh people were eager to emulate their English neighbours in all other things, Vaughan continued, why didn't they follow their example in creating a literate society? 'If you or anyone else in your household cannot read Welsh', Robert Llwyd wrote, '...only God can help you' ('Ai ni fedri di ddarllain Cymraeg, na neb o'th dy chwaith...ond Duw a'th helpio druan').[125] He urged heads of families to learn to read or employ someone else in the household to learn to read so that many others can learn from him. Llwyd was himself prepared to instruct for a week if that was deemed necessary so that one member of the household could master the written word – 'i ddyfod i ddarllain o honaw ei hun yn adrybelydr...' ('to be able to read proficiently himself...').

Where does all this evidence leave the social historian who attempts to gauge the extent of literacy in early modern Wales? The evidence is at best unclear and, in places, somewhat contradictory.[126] There are indications that most gentryfolk had a good grasp of both English and Welsh, a significant proportion of them having obtained a degree of education at home, in local schools, universities and inns of court. This evidence is forthcoming mainly in a large corpus of legal, administrative and educational records, private correspondence and literary sources. It is well nigh impossible to know how many in Wales had a grasp of the Bible soon after it had appeared, but indications reveal that keeping it in the parish churches was a serious disadvantage. Religious propagandists, of course, followed their own agenda when they repeatedly denigrated the lower orders for their illiteracy and their superiors for neglecting them. It is not surprising to find that members of landed and professional families, who had benefited from formal education, were fully literate, but it is difficult to measure how many of their dependants could read. This skill among lower gentry, yeomen and freeholders, as Humphrey Lhuyd and George Owen and their kind testify, should not be wholly underestimated.[127] Indeed, building up private libraries and other

---

[125] Ibid., p.129.
[126] D. Cressy, *Literacy and the Social Order: Reading and Writing in Tudor and Stuart England* (Cambridge, 1980), pp.42-61.
[127] G. Owen, *Penbrokeshire*, III, pp.56-7.

repositories by the most opulent had increasingly become a flourishing occupation. Evidence of literacy among the peasantry, however, is distinctly unclear. Despite Bishop Robinson's despair at seeing 'ye dregges of superstition' and other signs of ignorance in his see and aged priests who could no longer benefit by being 'put to schole', he does compliment the Welsh people who were 'not obstinate to heare, nor dull to understand' but who had suffered from 'want of knowledge'.[128] Sir John Pryse made similar comments in his preface to *Yny lhyvyr hwnn*, and Richard Davies in his epistle prefacing the New Testament in Welsh. He exhorted the Welsh people to proceed to read it:

> Am hynny dos rhagot a darllain. Llyfr yw hwn y bowyt tragwyddol...Rhoddet Duw yt wyllys da: can ys yma i cei ymborth yr enait, a chanwyll i ddangos y llwybyr ath ddwg i wlat teyrnas nef.[129]

[Therefore go forward and read. This is the book of the eternal life...God grant thee good-will: for here thou wilt obtain food for the soul, and a candle to show the path which will bring thee to the country of the kingdom of Heaven.]

It is hardly conceivable that this exhortation would have had an immediate impact on the bulk of the Welsh people. Apart from the gentry and clergy, ordinary parishioners would not even have seen it sufficiently to read it! What Davies had in mind was that parish clergy should use the New Testament and Book of Common Prayer to instruct them in the precepts of the faith, which was considered to be the essential need. Grasping the letters might come in due course but, to what extent, it is difficult to estimate.

Despite the ambiguities that arise it is important not to underestimate the degree of literacy that might have existed in the latter half of the sixteenth-century in Wales. While propagandists rightly pressed the dire need for better instruction their presuppositions might need some re-examination. The salutations of 'Sir' Thomas Wiliems, Robert Gwyn and others cannot be ignored for it is not impossible that the lower orders had a grasp particularly of English in the border areas and their own mother

---

128 D. Mathew, 'Some Elizabethan documents', 78.
129 *Rhagymadroddion*, pp.42-3.

tongue elsewhere, as John Penry testified when advocating the need for Welsh-speaking preachers to spread the gospel:

> There is neuer a market towne in Wales where English is not as rife as welsh. From Cheapstow to Westchester [city of Chester][130] (the whole compasse of our land) on the Seaside they all vnderstand English. Where Munmoth & Radnock shiers border vppon the marches, they all speake English. In Penbrok shier no great store of Welsh. Co'sider Anglisey, *Mamgymrû Caernarûon*, & see if all these people must dwel vpon mount Gerizzin and be subiect to the curse, because they vnderstand not the English toung.[131]

In 1630 Robert Llwyd addressed the monoglot Welshman ('At y darllennudd o Gymro vniaith') and urged him to read *Llwybr hyffordd yn cyfarwyddo yr anghyfarwydd i'r nefoedd* to his family. Can it be assumed that his words would have fallen on deaf ears? The evidence both ways is unclear but it is a fact that Evan Roberts included an alphabet in his *Sail Crefydd Gristnogawl* (1649) for the use of those who had become more acquainted with English through constant intercourse with communities over Offa's Dyke.[132] His colleague, Oliver Thomas, in his preface to *Car-wr y Cymru* (1631), urged churchmen ('Eglwys-wyr') to ensure that those in their care should purchase the small Bible (1630) and meditate upon it with their families, a means of propagating popular piety by means of popular literacy.

> ...ag attolwg i chwi er mwyn Crist Iesu, er mwyn eneidiau eich praidd, ac er eich mwyn eich hûn fod yn eiriol ar eich plwyfolion, ar iddynt brynu Biblau bychain y rhai sy yr awr'hon drwy râs Duw a'i ragorol ymgeledd tu ag attom ... ac yn hawdd i'r tlawd eu cael, fel y gallo pob dyn anyscedig â dim athrylith dduwiol ynddo, o medr ddarllein ei iaith ei hûn ...gan fanwl chwilio Gair Duw, a bod yn hyspys ynddo...Oherwydd chwi â wyddoch mai hynny yw ei ewyllys ef, sef fôd i bawb o'i bobl tan eich gofal chwi fynych gyrchu at ei Air ef; myfyrio yn ei gyfraith ef ddyd[d] a nôs, fel y

---

130 D. A. Thomas (ed.), *The Welsh Elizabethan Catholic Martyrs*, pp.93, 309.
131 J. Penry, *Three Treatises concerning Wales*, p.37.
132 M. Morgan (ed.), *Gweithiau Oliver Thomas ac Evan Roberts*, p.6. See W. P. Griffith, 'Humanist learning, education and the Welsh language, 1536-1660' in G. H. Jenkins (ed.), *The Welsh Language before the Industrial Revolution*, pp.293-6.

byddo iddynt yn gannwyll i'w traed, ac yn llewyrch i'w llwybr; ac i chwithau fynegu hyn, au ddwyn ar góf iddynt beunydd, heb attal dim buddiol oddi-wrthynt..[133]

[and prithee, for Christ Jesus, for the sake of your flock's souls, and for your own sake intercede on behalf of your parishioners so that they purchase small Bibles which are [available] at this time through God's grace and his excellent care for us...and it is easy for the poor to obtain them, so that every uneducated man with no godly talent in him, if he can read in his own language... [may] closely search the Word of God and be familiar with it...Because you know that this is his will, that all his people in your care should approach his Word frequently and meditate in his commandments day and night, so that it will be a candle to their feet and light to their path, and for you to indicate this, and make them mindful of it daily, not withholding anything beneficial from them...]

Reading material in this context illustrates how scanty the evidence is with regard to the extent of literacy among the lower orders in the Wales of the Reformation period. What is evident is the degree of responsibility placed on the clergy and privileged orders to impart the truths of the gospel orally, thereby acquainting their inferiors with words which they, through hearing them continuously, might in due course learn and become literate. According to the eccentric William Vaughan, a scion of a junior branch of the Vaughans of Golden Grove, Carmarthenshire, that would never be achieved because, as he stated in 1630, neglect of preaching and pastoral work and absence from divine service were constant abuses:

> ...now that thousands within our country of Wales resort not to Church above once a yeare, I could likewise produce many parishes which were not partakers of sermons in any man's memory, no nor...their Curates never graced them with one poor Homily or catechisme.[134]

On what evidence Vaughan could pronounce so firmly on Wales generally it is difficult to say, but it is conceivable that he might have been referring here to hardened recusants. The basic fact, however, remains a solemn

---

[133] M. Morgan (ed.), *Gweithiau Oliver Thomas ac Evan Roberts*, [A3b-A4], pp.4-5.
[134] W. Vaughan, *The Arraignment of Slander Perivry Blasphemy and other malicious sinnes* (London, 1630), p.94.

reminder that the Church had lagged behind in its attempts to improve the spiritual condition of the lower orders.

The emphasis placed on the disabilities of the majority of the population gave Protestant and Roman Catholic propagandists the opportunity to press the basic needs and to seek the most expeditious way forward in achieving them, principally through preaching and the use of the vernacular press. Thus Christian piety and conduct were enhanced. Nevertheless, measures of literacy pose more questions than answers, 'Although we would like to know how many people read their Bibles and what proportion of the population could follow religious tracts', David Cressy states, when referring to literacy in England during the period: '...Unfortunately reading leaves no record, so some of the most tantalizing and important questions about literacy...will remain unanswered.'[135] That statement could equally be applied to the state of affairs in Wales.

---

[135] D. Cressy, *Literacy and the Social Order*, p.53.

CHAPTER III

Religion and the Community in Wales:
Bardic Responses, c.1536-1640

In 1546, at a time when he was busily occupied pursuing his public offices, Sir John Pryse, as a member of a substantial Brecknockshire family, decided to publish a Welsh translation of short, but well known, sections of the scriptures in a small commonplace book. In his preamble he states that it was appropriate that parts of the holy scriptures should be translated into Welsh because there were many Welshmen who could read Welsh but who were unable to read one word of English or Latin, particularly those sections essential for each Welshman to know for the good of his soul. Of interest in this respect is Pryse's suggestion that illiteracy among the Welsh in his age was more evident in languages other than in the mother tongue and that they were able to read their language if only they were given instruction by the clergy. Pryse proceeded to note that the 'precepts of the Catholic faith' [1] were those translated by him, and since the printing press had become commonly used in England and the continent, he believed that these sections of the scriptures should be made available in print in Welsh. Without faith, he added, God's will could not be obeyed ('Canys heb ffydd ni ellir rhyngu bodd Duw') and the Welsh could not be raised from their spiritual malaise. In order that they might taste God's sweet will and save their souls ('er dangos blas iddynt o felysber ewyllys Duw ac er cadw eu heneidiau') he set about to accomplish the task.[2] The translations appeared at the end of *Yny lhyvyr hwnn* (1546), the first Welsh book to be printed.

Pryse was well aware of the religious problems of Wales in the early years of the Protestant Reformation. Since he was no mean scholar and a staunch Protestant as well as being one of the Crown's chief administrators in Wales and the Marches, with close connections with the

---

[1] In a Protestant context meaning the true pristine Apostolic church. G. Williams, 'Some Protestant views of early British Church history', in *Welsh Reformation Essays*, pp.208-9.

[2] J. H. Davies (ed.), *Yny lhyvyr hwnn* (Bangor, 1902), tt.xii-xxx; *Rhagymadroddion*, tt.3-4. See also G. Williams, 'Cymru a'r Diwygiad Protestannaidd' and 'Dadeni, Diwygiad a Diwylliant Cymru', in *Grym Tafodau Tân*, pp.63-86. The orthography here has been modernized as in several other quoted sources.

royal court and legal institutions, he firmly believed that the New Faith should be promoted among poor ill-endowed parishioners who, for want of better instruction, continued to uphold the traditions and superstitions of the Roman Catholic Church.[3] He was equally aware of the difficulties, particularly the strong bonds between the people of Wales and the Church, their illiteracy and superstitions as well as the serious shortcomings of the parish clergy. Pryse knew of the permission granted by Henry VIII for the Church to use the new translation of the Bible in English.[4] 'There is nothing more acceptable to his grace our dignified King', he maintained, 'than to see that God's Word and his gospel is being extended generally among his people' (...[nid] oes dim hoffach gan ras ein brenin urddasol ni na gweled bod fersiwn Duw o'i efengyl yn cerdded yn gyffredinol ymysg ei bobl ef']. In these words he referred to the appearance of the Great English Bible (1539), the work of William Tyndale, Miles Coverdale, John Rogers and others. Thomas Cromwell, chief secretary of the king and his deputy in church matters, and Thomas Cranmer, archbishop of Canterbury, were supporters of the policy to promote the use and acceptance of the Bible in church services in England. They argued that to obtain one official version of the complete Bible was better than having to make do with other versions which were regarded as heretical, such as Tyndale's own translation. One authorized version, it was considered, would serve to strengthen the loyalty of the kingdom to Henry VIII soon after he had taken the major step of rejecting the power and jurisdiction of the papacy and acknowledging himself as supreme head of the Church within his dominions.[5]

When Sir John Pryse published *Yny lhyvyr hwnn* at the end of Henry VIII's reign the religious situation and the doctrines of the Church were not altogether clear despite the emphasis which that king placed on orthodox Catholicism. From the Welsh angle the country had been assimilated legally with England some years previously and it was

---

3   R. G. Gruffydd, 'Yny lhyvyr hwnn (1546): the earliest Welsh printed book', *BBCS*, XXIII, 1968-70, 106-16; N. R. Ker, 'Sir John Prise', *The Library*, 5th ser., X, 1955, 1-4; G. Williams, 'Religion and Welsh literature in the age of the Reformation', *Proceedings of the British Academy*, LXIX, 1983, 371-6; idem, 'Unity of religion or unity of language', in G. H. Jenkins (ed.), *The Welsh Language before the Industrial Revolution* (Cardiff, 1997), pp.208, 210, 215; idem, 'Sir John Pryse of Brecon', *Brycheiniog*, XXXI, 1998-9, 57-8.

4   A. G. Dickens, *Thomas Cromwell and the English Reformation* (London, 1959), p.40 et seq.

5   G. R. Elton, *England under the Tudors* (London, 1974 ed.), pp.130-7, 165-75; C. S. L. Davies, *Peace, Print and Protestantism, 1450-1558* (London, 1984), pp.195-210.

expected that Henry's religious policies would be enforced in the four Welsh dioceses as elsewhere. The Crown's new position was based on a legal footing: the Pope, it was declared, had no power any more to legislate on spiritual matters in what was considered to be a nascent national sovereign state which emerged from statutory changes that were legislated in parliament during the 1530s.[6] Henry's intention was to 'nationalize' the Church to the degree that he, and he alone, would act as its executive head under God, with the highest authority to judge and to govern it and safeguard its interests. An arrogant statement of this kind, however, did not enable him to maintain his power without constant supervision by his ministers. Henry was no Protestant, unlike Cromwell, who followed Luther, and he did not doubt, as did Thomas Cranmer, the truths and values of the central beliefs of the Roman Catholic Church. On his death he left a divided kingdom in religion and a kingdom which was, on the accession of a young and weak king to the throne, politically subject to the power of faction in the King's Council.

Owing to the doctrinal confusion the Church did not function as effectively as it might have done and certainly the spiritual condition of the local priesthood or the peasant folk did not ease the situation in England and Wales. Under governmental policy to defend the traditions and beliefs of the Old Faith, in the face of stout Protestant opposition which was gradually increasing its hold, the clergy and lower orders were deprived of leadership. In addition, they were restricted by limitations imposed by the social and economic circumstances and age-old traditions were still cherished, pilgrimages being the most popular custom.[7] Over the generations bards of all grades, particularly those who composed in free metres, gave expression to the feelings and loyalties of peasant folk. Many of them also sang the praises of the Old Faith, emphasizing chiefly its external and most appealing features. Bards, such as Llywelyn ap Hywel ap Ieuan ap Goronwy (fl. 1460-70), Gwilym Tew (fl. 1470-80) and the most famous of them, Lewys Morgannwg (fl.1520-35), paid homage to the popular shrine of the Virgin Mary at Pen-rhys in Glamorgan and other

---

6   G. R. Elton, op. cit., pp.130-5, 420-5; A. G. Dickens, *The English Reformation* (London, 1964), pp.105-13; G. Williams, *The Welsh Church from Conquest to Reformation* (Cardiff, 1962), pp.521-40.

7   G. Williams, *Welsh Reformation Essays*, pp.11-21; idem, *Welsh Church*, Chap. XIV, pp.521-58.

similar venues. They could not but express amazement at the sanctity of the place of pilgrimage, as expressed by Lewys Morgannwg.

> mae dynion yma dynnir
> Mair oth wyrth hyd mor a thir
> yna i daüthost vendithfawr
> ir lle hwnn or nef ir llawr
> dy ddelw bob dydd a welynt
> yn vyw a gad o nef gynt
> mawr yw Rif mewn ysgriven
> mwy Rif dy wrthav Mair wenn [8]

[There are men here who are drawn by your miracle, Mary, over land and sea. There you have come as a great blessing to this place, from heaven to earth. They see your image every day which came hither alive from heaven. The number in writing is great; the number of your miracles is greater, venerable Mary.]

This kind of poetry characterized several other bards who cherished the main tenets and practices of the Old Faith, and the miraculous virtues associated with ceremonial, relics and pilgrimages were continually revered. In this kind of poetry one major aspect of the office and craft of the Christian bard in the Middle Ages was truly exemplified, and appeals were made to the deepest feelings of the individual Christian believer in his relation to the faith of his forefathers and the universal Church. By the early years of the sixteenth century the problems of the Church increased and the bitter attacks on it by humanist scholars in England and on the continent exposed its vulnerability in a period of changing cultural values.[9] Nevertheless, these scholars had hardly any impact on the religious life of Wales, chiefly because the dioceses were so poor, remote and far-flung, and despite the revival which occurred in the external and internal appearance of churches very few changes, and very little desire for change, were evident in the pattern of imagery and worship

---

8 Cardiff City Library, MS.5.44 (Llyfr Hir Llanharan), 20b-21b; T. Charles-Edwards, 'Pen-rhys: y cefndir hanesyddol, 1179-1538', *Efrydiau Catholig*, V, 1951, 43-5; C. W. Lewis, 'The literary tradition of Glamorgan down to the middle of the sixteenth century', in T, B, Pugh (ed.), *Glamorgan County History*, III, *Medieval Glamorgan* (Cardiff, 1971), pp.523-35. See also the *cywydd* to the shrine by Rhisiart ap Rhys (NLW Llanstephan MS.164,157-9).

9 J. K. McConica, *English Humanists and Reformation Politics* (Oxford, 1965), pp.76-149; C. S. L. Davies, *Peace, Print and Protestantism*, pp.134-55.

throughout most of the century which preceded the dissolution of the monasteries and the destruction of shrines and relics.[10] It was revealed how popular image-worshipping was among the people. 'The innocente people', Dr Ellis Price of Plas Iolyn maintained in his letter to Thomas Cromwell in 1536, when referring to the respect accorded to the famous idol Derfel Gadarn at Llandderfel, 'hathe ben soe aluryd and entisid to worshipe the saide image, inso muche that there is a commyn sayinge as yet amongist them whosoever will offer aniethinge to the saide image...he hathe power to fatche hym or them that so offers oute of hell when they be dampned.'[11] Price's vivid description of the image and its properties and the threat posed by survivals of popular culture to the leaders of the Protestant faith arose from the persistence of conservative practices in backward rural communities. It is hardly surprising that the destruction of such an attractive and venerated image should be recorded in Edward Hall's *Chronicle* and John Foxe's *Book of Martyrs*. The following rhyme reveals the superstitious hold which the image had on ordinary folk:

> David Darvell Gatheren,
> As saith the Welshmen,
> Fetched outlaws out of Hell
> Now is he come with spere and shilde
> In harness to burn in Smithfeilde,
> For in Wales he may not dwell.[12]

In view of this impoverished state, the inability of ordinary folk to understand the central tenets of the faith, together with the ineffectiveness of the clergy, there was no substantial improvement in the quality of the spiritual life of the Welsh people and that dire situation, in addition to the fact that the Bible was available in English, was the reason why Sir John Pryse proceeded to accomplish his task. He was not the only one who deplored the spiritual malaise among his people and who

---

10 G. Williams, *Welsh Church*, chaps. XII and XIII.
11 T. Wright (ed.), *Three Chapters of Letters relating to the Suppression of the Monasteries* (London, 1843), XCV, p.191.
12 E. Breese, 'Dervel Gadarn', *AC*, V (4th ser.), 1874, 154; W. G. Evans, 'Derfel Gadarn – a celebrated victim of the Reformation', *JMHRS*, XI, 1990-3, 147; E. Hall, *Chronicle, containing the History of England...*(1548) (London, 1809 ed.), p.826; S. R. Catley (ed.), *The Acts and Monuments of John Fox*, V (London, 1838), p.180.

attempted to improve their moral condition. William Salesbury of Llansannan also, in the same period, had stressed the need for the translation of the scriptures into Welsh. 'Make a barefooted pilgrimage to the king's grace and his Council', he appealed to his fellow countrymen in 1547, 'to implore him to obtain the Holy Scripture in your tongue'. ('Pererindotwch yn droed noeth at ras y brenin a'i Gyngor i ddeysyf cael cennad i gael yr Ysgrythur Lan yn eich iaith').[13] In view of all the dismal circumstances, he perceived that such an appeal could be the only way forward to instruct the people in the principles of the Christian faith. Despite the zeal shown by Bishop William Barlow of St. David's in preaching the gospel in his diocese in 1536, he soon discovered how difficult his task really was and he complained to Thomas Cromwell about the serious weaknesses in the religious life in the diocese as he conceived them. He referred to 'the hungry famyne of heryng the worde of God and desolate scarcete of true prechers', and despondently added:

> I have endeveryd my selfe with no smalle bodely daunger agenst Antichrist, and all his confederat adherentes, sincerely to preche the Gospel of Christ, whose verite as hit is invincible so is hit incessantly assautyd of faythles false perverters.[14]

Since Barlow was an Englishman, it was in his language that he endeavoured to accomplish the immense task. In view of the background and character of that bold prelate too much credence perhaps should not be given to his words, but he certainly drew attention to a crucial aspect of spiritual *malaise* in the Wales of his day, especially ignorance of the Word.[15]

Little direct information exists to illustrate the condition of the priesthood in Wales on the threshold of the Protestant Reformation but some official sources, such as the *Valor Ecclesiasticus* (1535) and other documents, give the impression that they were deprived of the qualities needed to serve their parishioners and instruct them in the faith.[16] In earlier years bards

---

13 *Rhagymadroddion*, p.12.
14 T. Wright (ed.), *Three Chapters of Letters...*, XXXIV, p.77.
15 For the background see G. Williams, 'The Protestant experiment in the diocese of St. David's, 1534-55', in *Welsh Reformation Essays*, pp.111-24.
16 G. Williams, *Renewal and Reformation: Wales c.1415-1642* (Oxford, 1993), pp.283-93.

like Guto'r Glyn, Hywel Swrdwal and Tudur Aled sang ecstatically to the virtues of individual heads of religious houses and the shrines which the bards visited.[17] In that rich corpus of strict-metre poetry they testified to the lavish hospitality and the role of some of the secular clergy in maintaining standards in the parishes. During the unstable years between c.1536 and 1600, however, bards like Siôn Brwynog, Wiliam Cynwal, Wiliam Llŷn and Simwnt Fychan often sang on religious themes but it was the eulogistic tradition, to all intents and purposes, which chiefly highlighted the structure and quality of the poetry. Little was composed reflecting on the disappearance of the monasteries and priories in 1536 and what does survive affords only slight information. Siôn ap Rhisiart Lewys, in two stanzas, deplored the destruction and the compelling of 'Jesus's churchmen' to retreat from their houses. Another anonymous bard reacted similarly when describing the priory which had become a farmhouse and 'God's close' converted into a 'cattleyard'.[18]

The content of poems to individual clergy in the early period of religious change emphasized their place in society as well as their spiritual powers and worldly interests. Sir Rhys Wynn ap John Fychan, vicar of Nannerch in Flintshire, was described by Ifan ap Hwlcyn Llwyd, for example, as a versatile and athletic person and a master of the twenty-four feats:

> Mae yn ei gorff mwy no gŵr
> Grym deugain gramadegwr,
> Dysg Awstin o'i fin a fydd,
> Sain Bened ei swn beunydd.
> Dysg Padrig a Sain Grigor,
> Eu swn, a'u gwaith, sy'n ei gôr.[19]

[There is in his body, which is greater than that of a hero, the power of forty grammarians. Augustine's learning comes from his lips, the talk of St. Benedict is his talk every day; the learning of Patrick and St. Gregory, their discourse and work are in his chancel.]

---

17 C. T. B. Davies, 'Y cerddi i'r tai crefydd fel ffynhonnell hanesyddol', *NLWJ*, XVIII, 1973-4, 268-86, 345-73.
18 NLW Peniarth MS. 313,18; D. J. Bowen, 'Detholiad o englynion hiraeth am yr hen ffydd', *Efrydiau Catholig*, VI, 1954, 11-12. See also Peniarth MS.313,98.
19 E. D. Jones, 'The Brogyntyn Welsh manuscripts', *NLWJ*, VI, 1949-50, 243; D.R. Thomas, *History of the Diocese of St. Asaph* (Oswestry, 1908) II, p.421.

Prominent abbots, renowned for their learning and hospitality in the last years of the monasteries, were applauded for their spiritual gifts and erudition, such as Dafydd ab Owain, successively abbot of Strata Florida, Strata Marcella and Aberconwy and the famous Lleision Thomas of Neath, to whom Ieuan Deulwyn and Lewys Morgannwg, among others, sang.[20] Lleision Thomas was particularly renowned for his erudition and for creating Neath abbey a reputable centre of learning:

> Unifersi Nedd, llyna fowrson Lloegr,
> Llugorn Ffrainc a'r Werddon...
> Ysgol hygyrch ysgolheigion...
> Ac organau i'r Gwyr Gwynion,
> A mawr foliant ymrafaelion,
> Arithmetic, Music, Grymyson, Sophistr,
> Rhetrig, Syfyl a Chanon [21]

[The University of Neath, how much talked of in England! The lamp of France and Ireland! A school much resorted to by scholars...With its organs for the White Monks, and the great praise of disputants, Arithmetic, Music, Grammar, Philosophy, Rhetoric, Civil and Canon (law).]

Not all abbots, however, were so well received and generally their circumstances were extremely poor although the aspect was not given much attention in strict-metre poetry. In the early days of the Protestant Reformation free-metre poetry was more overtly prepared to reveal the major features of the Catholic faith, such as praise to God the Creator, the Virgin Mary, the saints and the angels, the day of judgement, death and the grave, the Crucifixion, the Creed and the Ten Commandments, together with many other themes in the tradition of Siôn Cent, dealing with the sins of humanity, the brevity of life, death, mortality and the conduct of life, and divine judgement on the world. William Salesbury referred to deficiencies in Roman Catholic interpretations of the essential

---

20 I. Williams (ed.), *Casgliad o Waith Ieuan Deulwyn* (Bangor, 1909), pp.58-9; NLW Peniarth MS. 100, 456; BL.MS. 15003,82a; G. Williams, *Welsh Church*, pp.384-5; C. T. B. Davies, 'Cerddi'r tai crefydd' (unpublished University of Wales M. A. dissertation. 1972), I, pp. 49-84, 206; idem, 'Y cerddi i'r tai crefydd...', *NLWJ*, 280-2, 359-60; D. H. Williams, 'Fasti Cistercienses Cambrenses', *BBCS*, XXIV, 1971, 194.

21 G. Williams, *Welsh Church*, pp.393-4 (English translation cited therein); idem, '*The dissolution of the monasteries in Glamorgan*', in *Welsh Reformation Essays*, pp.91, 995-6; C. T. B. Davies, 'Y cerddi i'r tai crefydd', I, pp.184-8, esp. 186-7.

truths of the gospel when he gave his reasons for publishing *Kynniver llith a ban* in 1551. Sir John Pryse, however, also expressed his firm opinion when noting what he regarded as the deceptions of the faith and the needs of the people:

> Ac am hynny gyt a gwelet vot rhan vawr om kenedyl gymry mewn tywyllwch afriuaid o eisieu gwybodaeth duw ae orchymineu ac o herwydd hynny y digwyddon mewn dyfynder pechodeu a gwydyeu yn rhagorach na chenhedloedd eraill, ac am synyeid y bod a donyeu da o synwyr a deall gwedy y dduw y rhoi yddynt, val y gobeithiwn y bai hawdd gentyn wellau eu drycarveron onyd discu yr iawn fordd yddyn, mi a veddyliais er kariad vyngwlad roi yddyn y pynkeu hyn ynghymraeg er dangos blas yddyn o velysper ewyllus duw ac er kadw eu henaidieu ...[22]

[Therefore, because I see a great number of my countrymen in extreme darkness for want of knowledge of God and His Commandments, and that because of this they fall into depths of sin and vice to a greater extent than other nations, and because I believe that they have ample gifts of wit and understanding which God has given to them, so that I would hope it were not difficult for them to improve upon their bad habits should they be taught the right way, I have decided, because of the love I have for my country, to convey these matters to them in Welsh in order to give them a taste for the sweet and pure will of God and for the salvation of their souls ...]

This reference reveals that, in Pryse's opinion, the priests were largely to blame and that their deficiencies, together with the superstitious beliefs of the Old Faith, were responsible for the condition of religion and the spiritual oppression which the Welsh people endured.
For the ordinary Welshman, in the latter years of Henry VIII's reign and subsequently, the Roman Catholic faith was the only religious institution which had any spiritual consolation to offer. Diocesan records from that period onwards reflect the strength of loyalties, and it did not appear that any official edict or enactment in Edward VI's reign impaired Welsh loyalties to the Old Faith. It took considerable time for the force of law to take effect in the parishes for it was no easy task to enforce the new dispensation on the clergy and to ensure its acceptance among peasant communities.

---

22   G. Williams, *Welsh Church*, pp.415-28, 464-5; *Rhagymadroddion*, p.4

In 1549 the first official version of the Book of Common Prayer in English by Archbishop Thomas Cranmer appeared. That was a firm and significant move forward in the development of the Protestant faith.[23] It was issued following the Act of Uniformity of that year and, although that version was considered to be too moderate for many Protestant leaders because it maintained several Catholic forms of worship, it revealed the path which the government intended to follow in religious matters. Neither the first version nor the revised one, which appeared three years later and which introduced changes concerning the Eucharist and the Forty-two Articles which followed (1553) denoting a compromise between Lutheran and Zwinglian creeds, made hardly any impact at all on the monoglot Welsh. From the point of view of establishing the new Protestant faith, William Salesbury discovered the root of the problem and accordingly proceeded to publish his translation of the gospels and epistles. In his letter of address to the bishops of Wales he constrained them to consider means of 'combating the uncompromising oppression of the Bishop of Rome, of banishing that oppression from among His Highness's subjects, and dissolving it' ('llwyr danseilio gormes digmrodedd Esgob Rhufain, alltudio'r gormes hwnnw o blith deiliaid Ei Fawrhydi, a'i ddiddymu').[24] His solution at the time was to prepare a translation of the gospels and epistles for their use, in the hope that the bishops would recommend them and use them in their services.

At the end of his address he emphasized the deficiencies to which other commentators, including the bards, had drawn attention at the time:

> ...os oeddwn am deimlo unrhyw dosturi tuag at y rhai a aned yn yr un wlad ac o'r un genedl â mi – pobl, er eu bod yn anhyddysg mewn gwybodaeth sanctaidd, a fyddai heb amheuaeth yn fwyaf eiddgar o bawb am Dduw, pe dywedwn wrthynt fy mod wedi bod yn rhyw ystyried geiriau'r Apostol... 'Ac os cuddiedig yw ein hefengyl ni, yn y rhai colledig y mae yn guddiedig' — ymddangosai i mi...fod yr amser yn addas i geisio gweld a allwn ddod o hyd i ryw ffordd i fedru gwrthwynebu'r gormes hwn ac yn y diwedd ei droi ymaith.[25]

---

23 G. R. Elton, pp.202-14.
24 C. Davies (ed.), *Rhagymadroddion a Chyflwyniadau Lladin, 1551-1632*, p.18.
25 Ibid., p.19.

[...if I were to feel any pity towards those born in the same country, and same nation as myself – people, although they are unfamiliar in holy knowledge, who would without hesitation be more eager than anyone for God, if I were to tell them that I have been considering the Apostle's words...'And if our gospel is hidden, it is lost in those who are damned' – it appears to me that the time is appropriate to see whether I can find any way to oppose this oppression and in the end to defeat it.]

Salesbury expressed hope that key sections of the scriptures would appear in print and be disseminated publicly 'so that the Word of God can freely travel through our localities and so that less people would be offended by it' ('fel y gall Gair Duw dramwyo'n rhydd drwy ein hardaloedd, ac fel y bo llai o bobl yn tramgwyddo wrtho'). He and Sir John Pryse realized how wretched the situation was in the early years of reform and emphasized that the main weakness, as in England, was the universally blind devotion to the Old Faith and serious lack of education. 'The inveterate superstition of Wales 'with horrible blasphemy of God and His verity', Barlow had maintained in his letter to Cromwell in 1536, 'has been supported in St David's...what Bethel and Dan were in Israel'.[26] 'The clergy is unlearned and the people ignorant', he continued, 'and the English tongue nothing preferred after the Act of Parliament'.[27] Consequently, owing to the remoteness of the cathedral church, he wished it to be moved to the more accessibly placed Carmarthen for 'the bishops nor residentiaries there, though they would, hav little profit for th'institution, reformation, oversight, keeping of hospitality, or any other commodity unto the diocese'. Such a response is an example of the appeal on the part of Welsh bishops for the government to realise the nature and immensity of the dire circumstances which faced them. The constant despoliation of church property and buildings had a serious effect on the standards of religious provision offered to parishioners. In the diocese of Llandaff, for example, where it was formally complained to Stephen Gardiner, the lord chancellor, in 1558, that local gentry were dispossessing the church of its meagre resources, references were made to the impoverished state of the cathedral church. There was no vicar there at the time, 'no mass by note nor any sang this three or four years

---

26 *Letters and Papers, Foreign and Domestic*, XI, 1536, pp.570-1.
27 For a similar response to the isolation of St. Davids 'lurkynge in a desolate corner' see T. Wright, (ed.), *Three Chapters of letters ...*, CXIII, p.184.

scarcely one low mass a day and that not very certain'. The canons of the church were regarded as being among the most avaricious and assertive: 'they have let out the most part of the farms of the said church to their friends', it was said, 'and have diminished the rents'. It was further recorded how poor the circumstances of the cathedral were, and it was suggested strongly that it was the religious climate of the day and the continual adaptation to new conditions of religious practice and belief that, in part, accounted for such deprivation.[28] Many examples could be given to reveal how unsatisfactory religious conditions were or, at least, to state that the mechanism of the Church was not functioning well. There was no firm or dedicated leadership offered by foreign bishops who were, for the most part, absentee, grasping and deficient in their administration.

The changes in the liturgy of the church in 1549 and 1552 had considerable effects on the future form of religious worship in England but, in Wales, developments were very slow to follow, principally for social and linguistic reasons. Significant changes were introduced in the reign of Edward VI, largely because of the influx of Protestant theologians from the continent – Lutherans, Zwinglians and Calvinists – and strong leaders, such as Peter Martyr in Oxford, Martin Bucer in Cambridge and John à Lasco in London, all of whom were critical of the state of religion, rose to some prominence. Theological matters were discussed, chiefly the doctrine of grace, the holy communion and transubstantiation. They were all given freedom to voice their opinions which created a period of intense debate and controversy. The government, however, proceeded to introduce radical change. Chantries were abolished in 1547 as well as the urban guilds, and their endowments were seized because they were regarded as centres of superstition.[29] Moreover, idols were destroyed and churches desecrated on a large scale. It was the impact of this activity on ordinary parishioners which caused anxiety among the bards who composed their free-metre *cwndidau* (popular religious verses) and carols in which they expressed their concerns in verse.

---

[28] J. H. Matthews (ed.), *Cardiff Records* (Cardiff, 1898), I, pp.377, 386; H. M. Isaac, 'The ecclesiastical and religious position in the diocese of Llandaff in the reign of Elizabeth' (unpublished University of Wales M. A. dissertation, 1928), pp.45-7.

[29] G. R. Elton, pp.206-14; W. K. Jordan, *Edward VI; the Young King* (London, 1968), pp.310-23; J. Ridley, *Thomas Cranmer* (Oxford, 1962), pp.272-90.

The second Book of Common Prayer (1552) strengthened the Protestants' hold over the religious life of the kingdom. Among other changes Roman Catholic belief in transubstantiation was rejected, as were the mass vestments, and a wooden table replaced the stone altar. Following the Act of Uniformity bishops and priests were expected to enforce these changes among the laity on pain of excommunication and that caused additional tension in the relations between individuals and the government. These were the first of a number of changes enforced by the government to establish conformity and adopt the Protestant faith. Some priests complained – Thomas Cranmer among them – that such a policy, whereby one religious order was to be imposed, was unacceptable. Martin Bucer informed the king that the people needed instruction to ensure that they would understand the faith and, in due course, accept it. He saw great danger in 'taking away by force false worship from your people without sufficient preliminary instruction'. That also was the opinion of William Salesbury in 1547 when he referred to the need for instruction in the Welsh language. 'And it would be easier for the Welshman', he declared, 'to understand the preacher while he preached God's Word. And much easier for the preacher to declare God's Word intelligently' ('Ac fe fyddai'n haws i Gymro ddeall y pregethwr wrth bregethu Gair Duw; fe fyddai'n haws o lawer i'r pregethwr draethu Gair Duw yn ddeallus'). If the power and influence of the papacy were to be rejected, it was said, then the tenets of the Protestant faith would have to be introduced to the people in their own tongue. That was the only way in which religious policy, in his view, could make an effective breakthrough in the Welsh rural hinterland.

The rebels, led by Robert Ket in Norfolk in 1549, expressed fierce opposition to Edward VI's policies as did those in Devon and Cornwall in the Western Rebellion of the same year. In Cornwall the first Book of Common Prayer was rejected because English was not the language of the inhabitants there and, because Cornish was the mother tongue, it was demanded that the Old Faith be restored because English services were as strange to them as Latin.[30] The Common Prayer was called 'a Christmas game': it was meaningless compared to the mass, the Six Articles and the monasteries. By then, however, three formative developments had taken place which were to have a lasting impact on the progress of

---

[30]   J. Cornwall, *Revolt of the Peasantry, 1549* (London, 1977), pp.56-61.

Protestantism from then onwards, namely the destruction of images to simplify the order of service, allowing priests to marry and administering the cup to laity in the Eucharist. That enabled the New Faith to consolidate its hold on the Church and, despite Mary I's short period on the throne, there was no reversion to old methods of worship.

Amidst all the religious fervour in the middle years of the sixteenth century some bards, composing in free and strict metres, referred to different aspects of religious practice and expressed their opinion, some quite explicitly, revealing their support for one form of worship or the other. Such literary declaimers, however, were inconsistent in their views; that ardent Roman Catholic bard Siôn Brwynog of Anglesey, for example, sang an ode (awdl) praising Henry VIII for his achievements, his main theme being the success with which the king had resisted papal power and had imposed his supremacy within his own realm.[31] Likewise, Lewys Morgannwg, another Catholic bard, responded in similar fashion, elevating Henry's status and applauding him for dealing with the bishop of Rome in as firm and resolute a manner as he did his secular enemies on the continent:

> Llywiawdr ymddiffyniawdr ffydd
> Penn dan grist penna dan gred...[32]

[The guide and defender of faith; a head under Christ, supreme in Christendom.]

And in his awdl to the king he praised him for establishing his supremacy:

> Pennaf dan Dduw nef pand da ymddyrchefaist
> Penn eglwys d'ynys pinagl ystynnaist
> Penn ffydd a ffaunydd yr amddiffynnaist
> Penn wyt an llywiawdr pand da y llywiaist...

[The highest under God of heaven, is it not good that you have exalted yourself; head of the church in your island, you have reached the pinnacle; head of the

---

[31]   NLW Llanstephan MS.133.82.
[32]   E. J. Saunders, 'Gweithiau Lewys Morgannwg' (unpublished University of Wales M. A. dissertation, 1922), I, XVII. XIX.

faith, and daily you have defended it; you are our head and guide, is it not well that you have governed.]

Bardic convention was chiefly responsible for this kind of magniloquent expression of eulogy, but it appears that there were other reasons for the bard's eloquent outburst. He sang often to Henry Somerset, Earl of Worcester, and to other members of that family which ruled Glamorgan in Henry VIII's time.[33] In some of his poems he responded very differently and according to his Catholic conscience. He sang, for example, to the shrine at Pen-rhys but, in another poem, praised those who were responsible for delivering the idol of the Virgin Mary to London in 1538.[34] Two years later he accorded praise to Henry VIII for closing the religious houses:

> ffalswyr krefyddwyr ai kor a veyddaist
> Am dwyll a phechod yr llawr i dodaist
> Y traha ai balchedd da i diweddaist.[35]

[You destroyed false men of religion in their choir [and] for their deceit and sin you cast them down; well did you put an end to their arrogance and pride.]

This kind of reaction was not wholly unexpected because it was the rigidity of bardic convention, once more, which largely accounted for the manner in which the strict-metre bards expressed their emotions. An acknowledged bard, who had been fully trained in the bardic schools and who practised his craft by eulogising in verse, reflects the achievements or feats of the patron addressed. In this context the supremacy of one of the strongest of Tudur monarchs is given prominence, and the heroic ideal is revealed by portraying the majesty and sublimity of the virtuous chieftain, in this case the supreme head of the realm. It was considered that unity and order among governors and heads of state were essential, which was a consistent theme in the works of the bards throughout the sixteenth century. In Lewys Morgannwg's poem, however, the emphasis is placed almost exclusively on the military might of Henry on the fields of battle in France and Scotland, and it appears that the poem was

---

[33] NLW Llanstephan MS.164,123.
[34] G. J. Williams, *Traddodiad Llenyddol Morgannwg* (Cardiff, 1948), p.67.
[35] Ibid., p.68; E. J. Saunders, 'Gweithiau Lewys Morgannwg', I, XIX, p.206.

composed shortly before the king's death in 1547. Once again, a bard emerges who stoically keeps to convention, elevating the recipient of eulogy and attributing to him a high moral status in accordance with the canons of the bardic craft.

Altogether only a few poems survive to express opposition to the dissolution of the religious houses, which is especially remarkable since those institutions appealed to bards in the fifteenth century.[36] They were considered to be true representations of an exclusive tradition known for its hospitality, purity of faith, artistry and scholarship. Two stanzas (*englynion*) by Siôn ap Rhisiart Lewys censured the English for destroying the monasteries and sending 'Jesus's religious men cautiously from their houses' ('a gyrru krefyddwyr Iessu ar wagel oi dai'), and the anonymous poem 'to the priory which was turned into a farmhouse when the religious houses were destroyed in the time of henry 8' ('ir priordy a droespwyd yn amaerdy pann dynwyd i lawr y tai krefydd yn amser hari 8').[37] There are no specific references in either poem to the houses as such, attention is given rather to 'flattery' ('(g)weniaith') and 'plunder' ('herwa') which were responsible for the sad destruction. The four lines of verse are scathing in their contempt:

> Y llys a welais garllaw
> kor wendec a chwyr yndaw
> ef aeth yn vuarth i wartheg
> klos duw a vu n eglwys deg.[38]

[The court I saw nearby, with its fair holy choir with wax in it; it became a cattle yard, God's close which had been a fair church.]

Margam abbey had been an important and busy Cistercian centre in its day and Lleision Cradoc expressed his sadness that a wilderness had completely extinguished 'the garden of faith' ('Diffodd gardd y ffydd i gyd'). The virtues of learning obtained there were emphasized:

---

36 Davies, 'Cerddi i'r tai crefydd', 268-86, 345-73.
37 D. J. Bowen, 'Detholiad o englynion...', 10-11.
38 Ibid. 11.

I ble 'dd â bardd hardd ei hirddysg – bellach?
E ballawdd nawdd i'n mysg.
Trwm ar ein iaith yw'r trymysg—
Trais rhyfedd a diwedd dysg[39]

[Where will a handsomely well-educated bard go from now on? Patronage has ceased in our midst; this confusion lies heavily on our language – a strange violation and the end of learning.]

The poem refers to Margam as a most splendid centre of learning and offers an exaggerated description of the abbey, in view of the degree to which such houses had declined by that time.[40] By then also a great change had occurred in the attitude of some professional bards who had a more worldly motive for composing so ecstatically to these shrines, idols and crosses because they would have been of material advantage to them, and also, before the dissolution, to those who resided in religious houses. Little was composed on this theme from the days of Henry VIII until about 1549, and from then onwards some of the bards, especially those who sang in free metres, voiced the popular opinion among peasant folk, reviling the rapid religious changes which came in Edward VI's reign. Gruffudd ap Ieuan ap Llywelyn Fychan composed verses in honour of several relics in north-east Wales, but after the dissolution he changed his view and began to despise them: 'Thus in true belief we were enticed from a rigid world' ('Felly, mewn pur grediniaeth, fe'n hudid cwyn o fyd caeth').[41] It is assumed that religious change to about 1549 had little meaning to simple peasants in the Welsh hinterland, and it was from then on that the power of Protestantism was felt at a more local level. It is probably the poem of Thomas ab Ieuan ap Rhys, the eloquent *cwndidwr* of Llangynwyd in Glamorgan, which represents popular opinion at its best. He felt the heavy loss 'pan drosbwyd Rhufain heibo' ('When Rome was cast aside') and saw religion languishing without any meaning when so many values had been lost:

---

39 Ibid.; R. O. F. Wynne, 'Y Cymry a'r Diwygiad Protestannaidd', *Efrydiau Catholig*, VI, 1954, 18.
40 G. Williams, 'The dissolution of the monasteries in Glamorgan', in *Welsh Reformation Essays*, pp.91-107.
41 J. C. Morrice (ed.), *Detholiad o Waith Gruffudd ab Ieuan ap Llewelyn Vychan* (Bangor, 1910), XII. p.31.

Nac un crefyddwr yn bod
Na bai wraig briod iddo.
Felly 'dd aeth Ynys Brydain
Pan drosbwyd Rhufain heibo,
Heb na gweddi nac ympryd,
Na phenyd nac ynseilio,
Na chyffes nac anghenu,
Na chladdu na bedyddio,
Na sens na chwyr bendigaid
Na phacs, nid oedd raid wrtho.[42]

[Nor one priest exists who has no wife; that's how the isle of Britain became when Rome was cast aside, with no prayer or fast, no penance or absolution, no confession or the ministering of the last rites, no burial nor baptism, no incense nor holy candles, no kiss of peace, there was no need for it.]

This poem was composed during the great despoliation and the upsurge of new teachings which had arrived from the continent. The views of simple parishioners were also publicised in another poem by the same bard, entitled significantly 'Residing stupidly in three minds' ('Trigo yn ddwl mewn Tri Meddwl'). In this poem there are specific references to the bard's confused state of mind as to which beliefs he should accept. Some (Papists) say, he stated, that God 'was corporately in the people' ('yn gorfforol yn y bobl'); others believe 'that there is nothing but the spirit in the world' ('nad oes yn y byd ond yr ysbryd'). And thirdly he maintains that 'God is one and complete everywhere' ('un a chyfan yw Duw ymhob man'). What is certain in his mind is that the devil had been responsible for destroying the unity and integrity of the Church:

Rhows y kythrel y lawn afel
Ar yr eglwys ynte ay espeiliws
Venny fryntyn blasoedd meinin
Ve yrws ty dduw yn wak ty.[43]

---

42 L. J. Hopkin-James and T. C. Evans (eds.), *Hen Gwndidau, Carolau a Chywyddau* (Bangor, 1910). XXVI, p.32. For the social background to the free verse and an interpretation of its importance see G. Williams. Yr hanesyddol a'r canu rhydd', in *Grym Tafodau Tân*, pp.145-59. See also C. W. Lewis, *Glamorgan County History*, III, p.531.

43 L. J. Hopkin-James and T. C. Evans (eds.), *Hen Gwndidau*, XXVII, p.33; J. G. Jones, 'Rhai agweddau ar y consept o uchelwriaeth yn nheuluoedd bonheddig Cymru yn yr unfed a'r ail ganrif ar bymtheg', in J. E. Caerwyn Williams (ed.), *Ysgrifau Beirniadol*, XII, (Denbigh, 1982), pp.216-20.

[The devil took hold of the church and despoiled it...stone mansions contain the knave, he has made the house of God to be uninhabited.]

Following the arrival of the Book of Common Prayer this new teaching was called 'the faith of the English' ('ffydd Saeson') which, it was believed, had been imposed stealthily on the descendants of the ancient Britons. There were references to that belief which Richard Davies and his fellow Protestant humanists wished to discard in Elizabeth's reign:

> Y Saeson meinion, fal moch – ewch ymaith,
> > Eich amod chi a'i cawsoch;
> A thair gwaith o'r iaith yr aethoch,
> A chloi'r pyrth ar aberth a chloch.[44]

[You lean English, like pigs take flight; your fate has been sealed; and three times you departed from the language (of the Latin mass) and locked the door on sacrifice and bell.]

Moreover, Ieuan ab Wiliam ap Siôn, in his stanzas composed 'to the old and new faiths and to the sacrifice' ('ir hen ffydd ar ffydd newydd ag ir aberth'), emphasized the foreign element in reforming circles:

> Grym ydiw Aberth gramadeg – naws gwell
> > Nis gellir yn Saesneg
> Gwir vwch vngair ychwaneg
> A wnaeth Dvw n iaith deg.[45]

[Powerful is the Sacrifice brought about by grammar (i.e. the Latin) – no better can be achieved in English; the truth in addition to the one word created by God by means of a fair language]

Siôn Brwynog's response was similar. He was one of the most ardent among strict-metre bards of the mid-sixteenth century who demonstrated their loyalty to the Old Faith and he referred to 'the opulent and unclean English – unrooted' ('y breision Saeson yn serth – heb wreiddyn'), and

---

44 NLW Mostyn MS. 131.827.
45 Ibid., 92; *Efrydiau Catholig*, VI, 1954, 11.

140

'the race of Rhonwen' ('hil Rhonwen')[46] Siôn's lines imply that parishioners were not able to accustom themselves to the language of religion nor to the mannerisms of new ministers, and many poems by 'Sir' Thomas ap Maredudd, Raff ap Robert and Edward ap Ieuan ab Ithel, among others, scorned what was taking place in the order and quality of religious services. Siôn Brwynog again emphasized the features of the new ritual when the communion was adminstered by the pastor at the table:

> Wrth y bwrdd o nerth ei ben
> A bregetha brygawthen...
> On'd oedd dost, un dydd a dau,
> I'r llawr fwrw'r allorau?[47]

[By the table in full voice he preaches in jabbering sort...was it not a bitter blow to have cast down the altars to the ground within a day or two?]

These are couplets from his famous ode 'To the two Faiths' ('I'r Ddwy Ffydd'), and in it he dwelt vividly on the chief features of both faiths in administering religious worship. After weighing both carefully in the balance, the bard, with a degree of mischievous malice, supported the Old Faith:

> Cyffeswn, neswn i'r nod –
> Duw a wrendy – ar Drindod.
> Iddo, fal Pedr, y medrwn
> Ufuddhau, fo faddau hwn.
> Awn i'w nawdd yn un weddi –
> Ymprydiwn, penydiwn ni.
> Ar hwn, er mwyn grwn y Grog,
> I nawdd, wiwgrair, yn ddagrog.
> Iawn obaith un a wybydd
> Orchmynnau a phynciau'r ffydd.[48]

---

[46] R. M. Kerr, 'Cywyddau Siôn Brwynog' (unpublished University of Wales M. A. dissertation, 1960), LXI, pp.133-4 and Appendix XIV, p.186.
[47] Ibid., LXI, p.133; G. Williams, *Welsh Reformation Essays*, p.49; DWB, pp.912-3.
[48] Kerr, loc. cit.

[Let us confess, let us come closer to the aim, God will listen, and the Trinity. We, like Peter, can obey him, he will forgive. Let us put ourselves under His protection with one prayer. Let us fast and make penance before Him for his protection for the sake of the land of the Cross, fair relic, tearfully; the true hope of one who knows the commandments and articles of faith.]

The bard's description of the pastor and his practices is pure satire, and he reveals how rapid changes had led to divisions between and among families and to confusion and hatred that could arise from differences of opinion on religious dogma. In a day and age when so much emphasis was placed on the organic unity of the family and the concept of hierarchy, religious change often served only to destroy the bonds which had kept families together. Now they were in danger of loosening and, among other factors, becoming the means of social disintegration:

> Y brawd a ddwg, gwg a gwall,
> Obry dir y brawd arall.[49]

[The brother steals, wrongfully and with a scowl, on earth, the land of the other brother.]

This is yet a further reference to the plundering of lands by those who saw material benefits accruing from the acceptance of the New Faith. Although many still clung to the Catholic tradition it was increasingly considered that Protestantism had as many secular as spiritual blessings to offer: 'In every head there is an opinion' ('Ym mhob pen y mae piniwn'), the bard maintained, and the differences of opinion, in his view, were detrimental to the survival of the Old Faith.[50] The response of 'Sir' Owain ap Gwilym, vicar of Tal-y-llyn in Merioneth, to Roman Catholicism was similar, and he satirized women for expecting to deepen their profession of faith and divinity since they claimed to know 'the will and estate of God' ('Ewyllys Duw a'i stad')! In their minds, he added, young girls measure the law of Moses ('A phob rhyw eneth o'i phen /Yn mesur cyfraith Moesen').[51] In a period when education was increasing among the laity, who were busily clawing their way up the social ladder

49 Kerr, loc. cit.; L. Stone, *The Family, Sex and Marriage in England, 1500-1800* (Oxford, 1977), pp.154-9.
50 Cardiff MS. 63.279.
51 D. G. Williams, 'Syr Owain ap Gwilym', *LlC*, VI, 1960-1, 184.

in rural and urban areas alike, and when gentlemen were benefiting from private education, it is not surprising that matters of faith appealed to them.[52]

Siôn Brwynog complained that priests, after the Act of 1549, were taking wives, a practice, he considered, that was not becoming of their profession.[53] At the same time he appealed to supporters of the Old Faith to repent and relinquish their customary beliefs. No one can embrace the true faith, he maintained, who is not completely certain in himself that it is the correct one. That reflected a degree of uncertainty which was expressed in the works of some bards, and contained in the *englyn* by Hityn Grydd, an obscure rhymster:

> Duw, dy gyngor, pa un ore – o'r ddwyffordd
> Sy i 'mddiffyn eneidie?
> Duw deg, pa un a'm dyge,
> Ai'r Hen Ffydd ai'r Newydd, i'r Ne?[54]

[God, your counsel, which is the better of the two roads, with which to defend our souls? Fair God, which of the two will guide me to Heaven, the Old Faith or the New?]

Confusion made some bards express doubt as to the genuineness of the Roman faith. That could imply that the power of the Protestant mission was growing, that individuals were more prepared to weigh and analyse the basic tenets of faith, and that Roman Catholicism, faced by heated scholarly controversies and threats to its survival in the realm, would hasten its own decline under immense pressure.

Despite the uncertainty, strict-metre bards sang using traditional conventions in the years before Elizabeth I's accession. That implied avoiding burning issues of the day and concentrating on divine praise and its attendant idealism. Siôn Brwynog sang, for example, to Dr Ellis Price of Plas Iolyn, a bold and assertive squire and one of the chief

---

52 W. K. Jordan, *Edward VI: the Young King*, pp.309-10.
53 St. Edward VI c.12; *Statutes of the Realm*, IV (Pt. i), 1547-1585, pp.146-7.
54 NLW Mostyn MS. 131.93-4, From the series of englynion 'i'r Hen Ffydd a'r Ffydd Newydd ac i'r Aberth' ('to the Old Faith and New Faith and to the Sacrifice'); Jones, 'Rhai agweddau ar y consept…', p.218.

representatives of the Tudor state in his native Denbighshire and adjoining shires of north Wales. He was a man of law, having obtained his doctorate in civil law in 1534, and served as a commissioner who, along with others, was responsible for visiting religious houses and recommending their dissolution.[55] In 1538 he was appointed general deputy of the diocese of St Asaph by Thomas Cromwell and served as member of parliament for Merioneth between 1555 and 1558. At different times he also acted as sheriff of four shires in north Wales and, as a reward for his constant plundering of the Church and discovering concealed lands of the Crown in those shires on behalf of Robert Dudley, earl of Leicester, he was given the lands of the Knights of St. John at Ysbyty Ifan.[56] He became prominent in public affairs long before Protestantism was officially established and Siôn Brwynog addressed him with great applause.

The bard praised his legal learning and linguistic skills but significantly desisted from referring to his religious loyalties:

> ...Sifil o'i ben sy fel bwyd;
> Doctor, uwch y côr y'ch caid:
> Dy act ar y doctoriaid.[57]

[...Civil law from his head is like sustenance; Doctor, your prowess in dispute exceeded that of the doctors.]

The bards adopted a similar attitude towards William Herbert, earl of Pembroke and lord president of the Council in the Marches at Ludlow from 1550 to 1553 and 1555 to 1558.[58] He was an influential officer of law and government in royal service over many years, a member of the Privy Council, a 'chief gentleman of the privy Chamber' and, through royal favour, he also received many lands, including Wilton Abbey in Wiltshire.[59] Although he supported the duke of Northumberland and

---

55 NLW Brogyntyn MS. 6.139; *DWB*, pp.805-6. See Sister M. Consiglio (R. M., Kerr), 'Siôn Brwynog – un o feirdd cyfnod y Diwygiad Protestannaidd', *Ysgrifau Catholig*, II, 1963, 28-30.
56 E. Roberts, 'Teulu Plas Iolyn', *TDHS*, XIII, 1964, 70-81; J. G. Jones, 'Gentry in action: the Plas Iolyn experience, c.1500-1600', in *Conflict, Continuity and Change in Wales c.1500-1603: Essays and Studies* (Aberystwyth, 1999), pp.65-79.
57 NLW Brogyntyn MS.6.139.
58 BL MS.31056.181a.
59 *DWB*, p.350; G. Williams (ed.), *Glamorgan County History*, IV (Cardiff, 1974), pp.162-3, 219-20.

Lady Jane Grey on Edward VI's death in 1553, this bard sang enthusiastically to his greatness and to his contribution to the welfare of the Tudor state. He was flexible enough to overcome personal difficulties on the accession of Mary I to the throne on the death of her half-brother and he gained favour throughout her short reign because he supported her marriage to Philip II of Spain. The bard addressed him entirely because of his praiseworthy service to the government and his noble Welsh virtues. He was a favoured Welshman, Siôn Brwynog declared, who deserved to be adored ('Cymro rhag cam ydoedd...ei addoli a ddylid').[60] The same bard also sang to Thomas Bulkeley, who possessed the living of Llangefni from 1543 to 1570 and, according to convention, he referred to his learning and generosity but included nothing about his spiritual values.[61]

Men of this kind were middle of the road adventurers who were elevated by virtue of their lineage, their hospitality and their skills in public administration. Such hyperbole revealed that too much credence cannot be placed on the poems of strict-metre bards, particularly with regard to expressing firm opinion on religious or political issues. The bards were often wary in such matters because they feared that the patronage which they enjoyed would be damaged and because they did not consider such matters to be entirely relevant to their craft or their duties. Gruffudd Hiraethog's response was similar in an ode to Sir John Pryse. In it he sang as follows:

> Ceidwad twysowglys cadarn,
> Cymro ar fainc am roi'r farn...
> Ym mraich y Cwrt marchog gwych
> Ard fâr Edward fry ydych.
> Synnwyr yn pasio ynys
> Sy ras ein Prins, Syr Siôn Prys...
> Brycheiniog berchenogaeth,
> Henffordd yr unffordd yr aeth.[62]

---

60 BL MS.31056.181a.
61 NLW Peniarth MS.61.33. See also Peniarth MS.197.90.
62 D. J. Bowen (ed.), *Gwaith Gruffudd Hiraethog* (Cardiff, 1990), XIX, pp.71-2.

[A strong guardian with a princely court, a Welshman on the bench to dispense justice...In the arms of the Court a splendid knight, as your judge Edward you are exalted. Wise beyond anyone of our nation, he is at the disposal of our prince's grace, Sir John Pryse, ...the possessor of Brycheiniog and also Hereford.]

There are no religious references in these lines either. What is given attention is the public offices and authority which Pryse enjoyed because of his loyalty to Henry VIII and his son in Brecknockshire and Herefordshire. He also served as a member of the chantry commissions for north Wales in 1546 and commissioner of vessels and church property in Hereford. He also owned Brecon priory in 1537 and the priory of St Guthlac in Hereford where he resided. His office as secretary for royal affairs in Wales and the borderland from 1540 to his death in 1555 was of great benefit to him in pursuing his aim to increase his public authority.[63] References appear to all these honours which he received, and which are referred to in these lines, but there are no references to his religious affinities. They are merely suggested in view of the tremendous power which men of Protestant leanings wielded in his generation.

The sharpest reaction to new religious changes as they affected the peasant folk came from among the *cwndidwyr* and *carolwyr* (rhymesters) who sang frequently to the shrine of the Virgin Mary, the Paternoster, the Creed and the Ten Commandments as well as to other revered relics and practices in the Church. Among strict-metre bards most of the opposition to the Protestant faith appears in the works of Siôn Brwynog. There is a stridency combined with a marked sincerity about his style. The following lines indicate how the bard felt when a new religious order, led by the Protestant minister, replaced the old Catholic rites:

> Oerder yn yn amser ni,
> Yr iâ glas yw'r eglwysi...
> Côr ni bydd cŵyr yn y byd
> Na channwyll yn iach ennyd.

---

63   *DWB*, pp.786-7. For the background to Welsh humanist activity see B. Jarvis, 'Welsh humanist learning', in R. G. Gruffydd (ed.), *A Guide to Welsh Literature, c. 1530-1700* (Cardiff,1997), pp.128-53; R. G. Gruffydd, 'The Renaissance and Welsh literature', in G. Williams and R. O. Jones (eds.), *The Celts and the Renaissance: Tradition and Innovation* (Cardiff, 1990), pp.17-39.

Yr eglwys a'i haroglau
Yn wych oedd ein hiachau.
Yr oedd gynt arwydd a gaid
Olew yn eli enaid.[64]

[There is coldness in our times, the churches are as cold as ice...There is no wax nor a single candle for a moment in the chancel of any church; the church that with its incense well healed us. There was once oil as a symbol of balm for the soul.]

Siôn Brwynog also composed a series of twelve stanzas 'to queen Mary, daughter of King Henry the eighth and to the earl of Warwick and the old masses' ('ir vrenhines mari verch y brenin harri wythfed ag I iarll warwig ag ir hen offrenneu').[65] The bard revived the memory of an incident at Beaumaris when Sir Richard Bulkeley proclaimed Lady Jane Grey queen immediately after the death of Edward VI and then, in his perplexity, changed his attitude altogether towards her when he heard that Mary had already been crowned. 'Queene Marie this day was proclaimed trateress at Bewmaris', he sternly declared, 'and the next day a lawfull Queene so also at Denbigh by Dr Ellis and old Jo(hn) Lloyd before noone a Traitress, and by the same men in the afternoone a Queene'.[66] This is the *englyn*:

Mari yn y Dvwmares – o gelwydd
    galwyd yn draetvres
    fo wnai wlad a fynnai les
    varnu honn yn vrenhines.

[Mary, at Beaumaris, was lyingly called a traitress. The country that desires its own well-being will judge her to be a queen.]

The bard continued to praise her because of her lineage descending from the Tudors of Anglesey, especially Owen Tudor. He blamed the duke of Northumberland, formerly earl of Warwick, for the poverty of the church, making it 'empty-handed' ('yn waglaw') and giving the traditional faith a warm-hearted welcome:

---

64 G. Williams, *Welsh Reformation Essays*, p.49; D. J. Bowen, 'Y gymdeithas Gymreig yn niwedd yr Oesoedd Canol fel yr adlewyrchir hi yn y farddoniaeth uchelwrol' (unpublished University of Wales M. A. dissertation, 1951), pp.101-2.
65 NLW Mostyn MS. 131.152; D. J. Bowen, 'Detholiad o englynion', 6-7.
66 Bodleian Library, Oxford, Jesus MS. 18.51.

Wele vraint y saint yn nessav – eilwaith
Wele hen offrennav
Wele Ddvw ai law ddeav
Yn gallv oll yn gwellav.[67]

[Behold once more the privilege of the saints drawing near, behold the old masses; behold God making us all whole with his right hand.]

These stanzas reveal the bard's attitude towards belief and teaching at the time. Of considerable interest in this respect is the series of *englynion* which 'Sir' Dafydd Llwyd, the scholar-clergyman of Brecon, sang to Gruffudd Dwnn, Ystradmerthyr, Cydweli, a patron of bards, copyist and collector of manuscripts, expressing his longing for the Old Faith. He is addressed as a 'man of wisdom, well-graded, the possessor of learning and wealth' ('gŵr doeth a graddawl, Perchen dysg a chyfoeth'),[68] and, although not specifically stated, the purpose of these poems probably was to appeal for patronage and sustenance. The *englynion* were composed in 1551 and, because of his attachment to Roman Catholicism, he could not obtain a priesthood in Edward VI's time without declaring his loyalty to the young king:

Oherwydd fy ffydd ffi ffi – iradwch
yr ydwyf ar grwydri
Ni chaf gyflog o'm crogi
Na braint gan lawer na bri.[69]

[Because of my faith, fie fie, wretched me, I am made a vagabond; I shall have no wage even if I were hanged; no privilege nor distinction from many.]

His intention was to 'recite prayers'('arddywedyd paderau'), and he gives a very interesting view of the attitudes of contemporary scholars and priests towards the Roman Catholic faith and the problems which beset it:

---

[67] D. J. Bowen, 'Detholiad o englynion', 7; G. Williams, *Welsh Reformation Essays*, p.51.
[68] NLW Llanstephan MS. 133,303v.
[69] D. J. Bowen, 'Detholiad o englynion', 5-6.

148

Pawb o'r gwyr llen [sic] a'u henwi – sy barchus
berchen rhent Eglwysi
A'u ffydd hwy sy dda trwyddi
A ffiaidd yw fy ffydd i.

[All of the named men of letters respectfully possess church livings; their faith is good throughout, and my faith is repugnant.]

It is uncertain to what degree priests were dismissed from office in Wales after the new religious order was imposed but it seems that most of them clung to their livings, often in difficult conditions.[70] New beliefs and practices took a very long time to have any effect on remote parishes, and it was no easy task for uneducated and lethargic clergy to promote the Protestant faith. In another series of *englynion* sorrow was expressed following the desecration of local churches, and these poems are remarkable for their disconsolate mood when declaring their sense of loss:

Heb laswyr heb gŵyr heb gweirio – y marw
heb ymorol am sensio
Heb ganv knvl heb gwyno
Heb anrrydedd ar i fedd fo.[71]

[Without Psalter, without wax, without the laying out of a corpse, without troubling to incense...without the knell toll, without grief...without honour on his grave.]

The bard proceeds to express his personal loss with the abandonment of the confessional, charity, the ashes, the idol, the cross, the organ and the sacrifice:

Heb eglwys heb gynnwys gweiniaid – heb dda
heb weddi heb enaid
Ai on kof eilwaith in kaid
Awn [n]i fal anifeiliaid.[72]

---

70   Ibid., 5.
71   NLW Mostyn MS. 131.93.
72   D. J. Bowen. 'Detholiad o englynion', 10.

[Without a church welcoming the weak, without goodness, without prayer, without a soul; have we again been found to have gone mad, we shall become animals.]

In another context, the words of William Salesbury are recalled concerning the lack of education and the state of ignorance which arose from it. The bard found the Church languishing following the fierce attack upon it; for him, Protestantism was synonymous with a state of dissipation and spiritual vacuum.

Edward VI died suddenly on 6 July 1553 when only fifteen years old and that placed the duke of Northumberland in a dangerous position as protector of the realm. According to Henry VIII's will, if Edward died without an heir then Mary and Elizabeth, in turn, were to succeed to the throne. In this crisis Northumberland persuaded the young king to proclaim his half-sisters illegitimate so that Lady Jane Grey, grand-daughter to Henry's sister Mary, wife of the duke of Suffolk, might accede to the throne. By such cunning he sought to maintain his authority and he arranged a marriage between his son, Lord Guildford Dudley, and Jane Grey. Soon after Edward's death, however, Mary Tudor, with the support of East Anglian Protestants, marched triumphantly into London. To save his own life Northumberland decided to proclaim Mary lawful queen and tried to persuade her that he was a sincere Roman Catholic, but his plot failed and he was executed. The rapid religious changes in 1553 revealed, more than all else, how strong support for the Tudors really was in the country. Rebellion might have caused disorder, but that was avoided, again because of strong allegiance to the Tudor family. It is not surprising that Siôn Brwynog sang effusively to Mary's coming on the throne –'The warm queen from the centre of Gwynedd with a fortuitous guise' ('Brenhines gynnes o ganol – Gwynedd; ag wyneb ffortuniol') because she restored the 'true faith' ('iawn ffydd'). In retrospect, he expressed his sadness in a series of *englynion* that the faith had been forsaken and neglected:

> Aeth y saint mawr y braint a bras – dros amser
> drwy symsan dvw a las
> a Mair i gyd mewn mawr gas
> a waharddwyd oi hvrddas[73]

---

[73]   Ibid., 7-8.

[The great and highly privileged saints, have gone over a period; through inconstancy God has been slain; and Mary, with great hatred, has been denied her dignity.]

He found hope in his belief that the faith would again be reinstated for he could not tolerate the dismal years of Edward's reign. ('blynyddoedd blin oddiaith').

With Mary Tudor's accession to the throne the Old Faith was restored only to the extent that circumstances would allow, for the changes that had already occurred in religion and politics under Edward could not be dismissed out of hand. Her main aim was to restore the medieval Church, an impossible task because, by her time, the concept of Christendom had lost much of its meaning. Changes introduced by her first parliament were at first very slow. Edward VI's religious legislation was abolished and the traditional liturgy installed. The Book of Common Prayer was abolished and the full Latin mass restored. In addition, imprisoned Catholic bishops were released and appointed. These measures were not extreme for, as the bards testified, there had been a desire to see the return of the mass, the sacraments and other ceremonies because they formed a central part of pastoral life in the country and were essential to maintain social harmony. However, there was some opposition to the restoration of papal power; many of the landed families and official classes, who were extreme in their religious beliefs, demanded that Mary should follow her father's policy, placing herself as supreme head of the national Catholic Church, but she refused.[74] Mary believed that she had a mission to accomplish, and to establish an independent secular state was not part of it. Parliament refused to meet her most extreme demands, such as restoring church property, declaring Henry VIII's marriage to Catherine of Aragon legal, abolishing Henry's and Edward's religious policies and prohibiting Elizabeth from acceding to the throne. In addition, there was stern opposition to Mary's marriage to Philip II of Spain because a strong wave of national spirit was nurtured at the time. From Mary's standpoint the marriage was a symbol of unity, to strengthen England's ties with Spain, and of her intention of re-entering the Roman Catholic Church.[75] Mary's unpopularity, however, reached

---

[74] D. M. Loades, *The Reign of Mary Tudor* (London, 1979), pp.332-9. For the Welsh background see G. Williams, 'Wales and the reign of queen Mary I', *WHR*, X, 1980-1, 350-60.

[75] D. J. Bowen,. 'Detholiad o englynion', 7-8.

new heights when the fierce persecution of Protestants occurred in 1555-6, when Catholic orthodoxy was defined formally and when about three hundred Protestant zealots were burnt at the stake for rejecting the queen's religious policy. These burnings were recorded for posterity in John Foxe's *The Book of Martyrs*, one of the most famous Protestant works ever published. Mary's policy, however, served only to intensify Protestant feeling, and the fires of Smithfield and elsewhere did more than any of Mary's actions to foster the growth of the New Faith.

On Mary's death Elizabeth, daughter of the Protestant Anne Boleyn, succeeded to the throne. She possessed a different temperament from her half-sister and it was in her first year as queen that her first parliament tackled the problem of religion. The settlement that ensued placed the Church under secular control and it formed one of the major bastions which created unity in the kingdom. It was the state's responsibility to impose order in religious matters, to maintain the policy of establishing the Church by statute law and to secure the loyalties of the majority of the queen's subjects.[76] Church leaders headed by Matthew Parker, archbishop of Canterbury, established a framework for the national Church. Parker sought to root the Church in a new Protestant tradition. The new Church was identified with stable government and a spirit of national independence. It was the government's will which imposed religious reform on the kingdom. Elizabeth, it was said, 'would not tolerate a Church independent from the state. Royal supremacy was at the very centre of both her political and religious ideals.'[77] The Welsh bards who sang to Elizabeth were constantly aware of her status as the new Protestant head of state and the traditions which maintained her position. In his ode to the Godhead Edwart ap Raff censured Roman Catholics and upheld the monarchy, as represented by the queen, for its one major gift to the Welsh nation:

> Gras Duw a ddoeth, gorau stôr,
> I'n mysg o iawn ymesgor,
> Elsbeth bu odieth ei bod
> Yn frenhines fry'n hynod...

---

[76] C. Cross, *Church and People, 1450-1660: the Triumph of the Laity in the English Church* (London, 1976), pp.124-52.

[77] N. L. Jones, *Faith by Statute:Parliament and the Settlement of Religion, 1559* (London, 1982), p.9.

Eisoes iddi'n y swyddau
Yn un prins inni'n parhau.[78]

[God's grace, the best store, came among us In the fullness of time; Elizabeth, worthily has she been a notable queen over us, a one ruler remaining for us in her dignities.]

In a kingdom which had experienced such rapid religious change, confused doctrines and uncertainties and prejudices it was not surprising that the new order created much anxiety and hesitation among the 'political nation' seeking to make religion a bastion of its material prosperity. Along with other government institutions, the Church was to be defended by local and regional administrators and legal officials whose allegiances to the Crown were strong. Religious diversity and the power of individual consciences could create doubts and animosities and, in certain respects, outright opposition to the establishment. Even the long-serving Anthony Kitchin of Llandaff, who was remarkably flexible in being able to cling on to his office as bishop of Llandaff from 1545 to his death in 1563, adapted himself to the demands of the new religious order by taking the oath of allegiance.

Elizabeth's succession, however, brought with it many problems, not least with regard to enforcing religious allegiance. The heightened tensions between Protestants and Roman Catholics were evident among members of many families whose consciences were not clear in the 1560s. In 1570 Pope Pius V excommunicated the queen by the bull *Regnans in Excelsis*.[79] Previous to that papal declaration loyalty to Rome was a matter of heresy but then, after it, it became treason to oppose the queen, and those who chose to defy allegiance to the queen were subject to severe penalties. In Wales, however, several bards sang praiseworthy odes to members of Catholic families who were intent on restoring the Old Faith, such as the Pughs of Penrhyn Creuddyn in Caernarfonshire.[80] Generations of that family remained faithful to Rome but, at the same time, managed to hold local office under the Crown. The first of the family to be called a recusant

---

[78] D. H. E. Roberts and R. A. Charles, 'Raff ap Robert ac Edwart ap Raff', *BBCS*, XXIV, 1970-2, 298.
[79] Ibid., pp.144-5.
[80] E. G. Jones, 'Robert Pugh of Penrhyn Creuddyn', *TCHS*, VII, 1946, 10-19.

was Robert Pugh, a lawyer and landowner. His grandson, Gwilym Pugh, in 1676, composed a long ode to him entitled 'Llwyrwys Penrhyn ai Mawl' which traced the family's long and stubborn opposition to Protestantism.[81] He wrote in a clear and unyielding manner with no intention of hiding his feelings. Although his grandfather was an expert lawyer, he maintained, he was stronger in his religious convictions.[82] Following the anti-recusant campaign mounted by Henry Herbert, earl of Pembroke and lord president of the Council in the Marches, in 1586 Robert Pugh was persecuted and forced to take refuge in Rhiwledyn cave on Y Gogarth Fach, Llandudno, where *Y Drych Cristianogawl* was printed about that time. This extraordinarily large theological work was compiled by the Jesuit priest, Robert Gwyn, and it was possibly William Davies, a Catholic missionary who came to Wales in 1585, who was responsible for bringing a manuscript of the work from the continent. References to this remarkable event appear in Gwilym Pugh's ode:

> Mewn ogo brudd o gil y brunn:
> Trech waith blin tri chwarter blwyddun...
> O fewn y Brunn heb fawr or braw
> Ar gwascprenn, y gwur sûn pruntiaw
> Y llufr mwyn, a llawer mawl
> Ar drwch cred Drûch christnog'awl.

[In a sombre cave in the corner of the hill the difficult work was accomplished in three-quarters of the year... Within the hill, without great fear, with their wooden press, men are printing, with much praise throughout Christendom, the fair work, the Christian Mirror.]

The bard describes vividly the persecution led in Wales by Pembroke and its effects on the Catholics of Penrhyn Creuddyn:

> Lledau'r llid o burth Llwydlaw:
> Fo daunau drô, i adennudd draw.
> Ir Creuddyn at criaidd ddynion...
> Gwilio brô a gwlâd a brynn:
> Chwalu pûrth a chwilio Penrhyn[83]

---

81   G. Bowen, 'Gwilym Pue, "Bardd Mair", a theulu'r Penrhyn', *Efrydiau Catholig*, II, 1947, 12.
82   Ibid.
83   E. G. Jones, *Cymru a'r Hen Ffydd* (Cardiff, 1951), p.20.

[The anger spread from the gateways of Ludlow and spread in time its wings yonder to Creuddyn to beloved men. Watching the neighbourhood, country and hill, demolishing porches and searching Penrhyn.]

An anonymous poet composed an elegy to Robert Pugh. Two similar poems were dedicated to the memory of his wife, Jane Bulkeley, daughter of Sir Richard Bulkeley of Beaumaris, by Huw Machno and Rhisiart Cynwal. Not surprisingly, in an age of persecution the three poems emphasized their lineage and the lavish patronage they dispensed rather than their religious affiliations.[84]

Although Pembroke persecuted Roman Catholics in 1586, many years previous to that their movements were closely monitered, especially from 1572 when John Whitgift was appointed deputy to Sir Henry Sidney at Ludlow.[85] Although recusancy was not considered a serious problem at the time, Whitgift decided to root out such activity in Llŷn and the Chirk area. When Sidney returned from Ireland the Privy Council urged the Council in the Marches to act and, in 1582, John Bennett, a Jesuit priest from Flintshire, was imprisoned along with Richard Gwyn (White), a schoolmaster from Llanidloes, noted for composing anti-Protestant verses. Gwyn had been reared a Protestant and was educated at St John's College, Cambridge, but, while keeping school at Overton near Wrexham, he was converted and forced to flee the authorities.[86] In five long satirical poems he attacked the New Faith and rejected Martin Luther's 'false' doctrines:

> Gochel hon a chais y ffydd
> Rrag bod dy ddydd yn agos
> I roi kyfri ar ben bryn
> A meddwl hyn ddechrevnos. [87]

[Avoid this and seek the faith in case your day is near to give account on a hilltop, and think of this as night falls.]

---

84   R. G. Gruffydd, 'Gwasg ddirgel yr ogof yn Rhiwledyn', *JWBS*, IX, 1958, 1-23; idem, *Argraffwyr Cyntaf Cymru: Gwasgau Dirgel y Catholigion adeg Elisabeth* (Cardiff, 1972), pp.1-23.
85   P. Williams, *The Council in the Marches of Wales under Elizabeth I*, pp.42-9.
86   T. P. Ellis, *The Catholic Martyrs of Wales* (London, 1933), pp.18-33; D. A. Thomas, *The Welsh Elizabethan Catholic Martyrs* (Cardiff, 1971), pp.22-56.
87   T. H. Parry-Williams (ed.), *Carolau Richard White* (Cardiff, 1931), I, p.21

He deplored the Calvinist church ('eglwys Calfin') which, in his view, divorced God from man ('sy'n ysgar Duw a dyn') and the English Bible which, he considered, was 'full of false imaginations' ('yn llawn o gau ddychmygion') and 'the greedy and sad minister who directs a lesson towards the laity' ('gweinidog chwannog chwith yn llywio llith i'r ll(e)ygion').[88]

This kind of poetry was not entirely new; the belief was well known that the 'faith of the English', as it was called, was not as commendable as the faith of the mass. Little attention was given in these poems to the Pope's authority and emphasis was placed on the essentials of faith and its visible symbols. The concept of royal supremacy was beyond the comprehension of ordinary rural folk, which accounted for the simple manner in which the bard appealed to them, referring to the extent to which services were affected and relics ignored. It is hardly surprising that Richard Gwyn emphasized the destructive emptiness that remained after their departure:

> Yn lle allor, trestyl trist
> Yn lle Krist mae bara;
> Yn lle 'ffeiriad kobler krin,
> Yn kamv'i vin yw fwyta.
>
> Yn lle yr kreiriwr, tinker tôst
> Yn gwnevthvr bôst oi gnafri ...[89]

[In place of an altar, a miserable trestle, In place of Christ, there's bread, In place of a priest, a miserly cobbler, twisting his mouth to eat it. In place of the pilgrim to a shrine, a harsh tinker, boasting of his rascality.]

His style is livelier and more direct than that of Siôn Brwynog and the *cwndidwyr* who sang years earlier, and the reason for that being, probably, that the Protestant faith had emerged and had gained ground, mainly through the policies of the queen's governments and the weakness of the Catholic mission in Wales. In his opinion Protestantism was despicable because it meant 'losing the virtue of Christ's sacrifice' ('colli

---

88   Ibid., III, p.32.
89   Ibid.

156

rhinwedd aberth Crist') and rejecting the miracles of the Lord's blood ('gwrthod gwyrthe gwaed yr oen'), abandoning the communion of all the saints ('colli cymun yr holl saint') and forsaking the privilege of authority ('colli braint awdurdod').[90] He mocked those who burnt effigies and desecrated saints and saw no virtue at all in a lay ministry replacing the priesthood, regarded as the chief symbol of communication between God and the sinner:

> Tinker pedler kobler krydd
> ar gwydd o ddiwrth i brwyde
> pibydd pobydd kigydd kog
> syn llowio llog pregethe.[91]

[Tinker, pedlar, cobbler, shoemaker, And a weaver from his looms. Piper, baker, butcher, cook, Are managing the profit of preaching.]

Richard Gwyn was imprisoned in 1580 and appeared before the Council in the Marches where an attempt was made to force him to give information about Father John Bennett, a priest trained at Douai who was active in Flintshire. All was in vain and Gwyn, after his long trial at the assizes, was cruelly executed at Wrexham in October 1584.[92] His poetry reflects his commitment at a time, in the 1580s, when recusancy posed grave difficulties to Elizabeth and her governments. Sir George Bromley, chief justice of Chester, who was involved in the proceedings against Gwyn, was eager to stamp out all sign of Catholic propaganda and activity.

Owing to the subversive activities of Richard Gwyn and others the government saw the need, from 1572 onwards to the 1590s, to consolidate the realm's unity, since it faced dangerous threats such as the treasonous designs of Mary Queen of Scots, Catholic factions at Court and the Catholic powers of Europe, all of which caused immesurable problems for Elizabeth. Moreover, anxiety was expressed regarding the succession since there was no direct male heir to the throne. Also, new economic factors were threatening, particularly financial inflation and increasing

---

[90]   Ibid., p.33.
[91]   Ibid., IV, p.39.
[92]   D. A. Thomas, *The Welsh Elizabethan Catholic Martyrs*, pp.58-63.

poverty among the lower orders. Recusancy was but one aspect of the political situation in Elizabeth's reign which, in the 1580s, created adverse pressures but it certainly was a distraction which the government could well do without. The need to strengthen the realm and maintain the monarchy intact was a dominant theme in many pro-royal and Protestant poems. Rhosier Kyffin, a royalist soldier, contrasted the favourable circumstances in Wales and England with the slaughter that occurred in the continental religious wars of the time, and he appealed to his fellow Welshmen and the English to beware of sin since it brought destruction in its train, as proven elsewhere:

> Mae tyrnasoedd yn y byd
> Yn rhy anhyfryd gower
> Gan ryfeloedd mawr a thrin,
> A bowyd blin bob amser.
>
> Chwithe a'r heddwch yn ych mysg,
> A dawn a dysg a chyfreth
> Yn cael bawb yr eiddo'i hun,
> On'd gwych yw'r llun ac odieth?[93]

[There are kingdoms in the world too unpleasantly affected by great wars and battles and a continuously tedious life. You who have peace amongst you and skill, learning and law; all of you possessing your own; is not the picture perfectly splendid?]

In a carol composed to kings, Elizabeth was praised as one who was supreme in her kingdom, a true heiress to Cadwaladr the Blessed, the last British king (d. 664 A.D.). He was the reputed leader of the British against the Saxons ('benna dros y tir; A gwir aeres…I Gadwaladr Fendigaid'). In a long poem composed in Elizabeth's honour entitled 'Sidanen' ('the silken one') she was described as a worthy descendant of the Brythons. She was the 'golden pillar and the ray and power of the kingdom' ('piler aur a'r paladr, a hefyd grym y deyrnas'), words which reveal the content and nature of the praise poetry in strict metre in which privileged nobility (uchelwriaeth) was idealized:

---

[93] D. Lloyd Jenkins (ed.), Cerddi Rhydd Cynnar (Llandysul, 1931), XXIII, p.41.

...A Duw a roes iddi dynged
I 'mgadw rhag ei gelynion,
Ac i heuddu [sic] gwisgo'r goron.[94]

[And God decreed her fate – to defend herself against her enemies and to deserve to wear the crown.]

The poet desires God to maintain and defend the monarchy. There is a hint as well of the divine-right of kings, but the main theme is the call for peace and unity within the isle of Britain to safeguard it from internal and external threats. That appeal formed a significant element in the political thought of Wales and England from the sixteenth century onwards. Strong zenophobic tendencies emerged, especially after the execution of Mary Queen of Scots in 1587, and during the early stages of the war with Spain two years previously.

This theme also emerged in the verse of Thomas Jones, vicar of Llandeilo Bertholau in the northern part of Gwent, and later rector of Llanfair Cilgedin near Llanofer. The title of his poem is 'Cân am y waredigaeth a gadd y Brytanieid o law y Spaeniaid cynhennys yn y flwyddyn 1588' (A poem about the deliverance of the Britains from the hand of the quarrelsome Spaniards in the year 1588').[95] Each of the twenty-nine verses ends with the word 'ynys' ('island') and with the following lines: 'Am gadw'n gwlad a'n hynys' ('For preserving our country and island'); 'Lle enillwyd clod i'n hynys' ('Where glory was won for our island'); 'Dros Eglwys Grist a'i ynys' ('For Christ's Church and his island'). This was a simple technique designed to emphasize the deepest needs of the sovereign state, namely to defend its unity and integrity based on a national Protestant monarchy. In the last verse the bard reached the climax of his accolade to the queen:

A'n brenhines brydnerth [sic] brydd
Dra doniog ddedwydd ddawnys
Duw rhoddo i hon enioes hir
I gadw tir ein hynys·[96]

---

94 Ibid., LXVIII, LXIX, p.124.
95 J. H. Davies (ed.), *Hen Gerddi Gwleidyddol, 1588-1660* (Cymdeithas Llên Cymru, Cardiff, 1901), I, pp.7-11.
96 Ibid., p.11.

[And our wise and comely queen, very talented, contented and able, may God give her a long life to maintain the land of our island.]

These would be verses easily learnt and memorized describing fully the manner in which England succeeded in defeating Spain. There are references to Philip II and his grandiose plan to invade England, and the bard compliments the contributions of many maritime commanders, including William Howard of Effingham, Lord High Admiral, and Sir Francis Drake, together with other wise advisers among the queen's counsellors, the local militias and the viccisitudes of the weather! They all, the bard declared, contributed significantly to England's victory. Above all, these factors symbolized the sustaining guidance of the Almighty, the fount of the Protestant state. The following two verses exemplify the bard's thoughts on this matter:

> Llawer blwyddyn cynllwyn blin
> Bu'r Pab a brenin Spaenys
> Yn dychymmyg gan eu pwyll
> Brad a thwyll i'n hynys...
>
> Pe tycciasai yn ddi-ffael
> I'r Spaniaid gael eu gwyllys
> Bysai ddynion yn llai rhif
> A gwaed yn llif yn yr ynys.[97]

[Many a year a grievous plan by the Pope and the king of Spain; contrived in their wisdom treason and deceit in our island. If it availed the Spaniards to succeed in their will men would be fewer in number and blood would flow in the island.]

These are not merely simple narrative rhymes for they reflect vital aspects of the way in which contemporaries would have interpreted a crucial episode in the history of Wales and England. It is in that context that Thomas Jones[98] viewed the victory over the Armada when, in free-metres, he thanked God for preserving the island from destruction:

---

[97] Ibid., pp.7, 10.
[98] *DWB*, p.513-4; *Glamorgan County History*, IV, pp.230, 231, 568, 571, 572; G. J. Williams, *Traddodiad Llenyddol Morgannwg*, p.129.

Ag am hyn Gristnogion glan
Rhowch glod ar gair diolchys
I yr unig Frenin nef
Am glywed llef ein hynys.[99]

[And for this, pure Christians, Give praise and a thankful word; to the one King of heaven for hearing the plea of our island.]

In this verse the bard combines the blessings which both God and the queen had given the realm in that crisis. In that context, Christianity is the faith introduced by the Elizabethan settlement. It is the unity and uniformity under a pious 'prince' which, in his view, enabled the 'island' (i.e. the state) to maintain its independence and sovereignty. The Protestant faith is innately incorporated in the joy expressed by the bard on the occasion. He refers to the fear which came as a result of such a direct threat, and embracing Roman Catholicism was considered to be tantamount to treason. In peacetime, war and rebellion were feared, and for several years after the first Armada the danger remained that Spain would again try to conquer England. The Old Faith, and the cause of religion generally, had become political questions for, if religious unity could not be achieved, the preservation of the country's welfare would be at stake. John Penry revealed the same kind of fears in his severe condemnation of the Church in 1587-8. He considered that Catholic threats were detrimental to the cause of religion and blamed the Crown, parliament and the prelacy for the failure to reform the situation.[100] Immediately after the victory in 1588 the government expressed anxiety about the increase in recusancy, especially in the borderlands, and it was that threat which caused anxiety among Welsh Protestant humanist scholars.

Another poem composed to commemorate 1588, this time by an unknown bard, emphasized the unifying features of monarchy in a period of dearth and oppression and its ability to discipline and maintain good order. References appear in it to God's omnipotence with the stern reminder that, despite the power of kingship ('trwy nerth a grym brenhiniaeth'), nothing could be accomplished without God's assistance.

---

[99]   J. H. Davies, *Hen Gerddi Gwleidyddol*, p.9.
[100]   J. Penry, *Three Treatises concerning Wales*, ed. D. Williams (Cardiff, 1960), pp.27-34.

161

Elizabeth was described as a Prince (a sovereign ruler applied here to a female), second to wise Judith ('Prins...ail i Siwdith ddoeth'); the duke of Parma, head of the Spanish army in the Netherlands, who was expected to assist the Armada, was cursed and prosperous people were advised to be generous to soldiers who had served in the army and defended the realm.[101] It is clearly a poem composed by a soldier – possibly Rhosier Kyffin – who desired to acknowledge his loyalty to the queen publicly and who was aware, on the one hand, of a prosperous and victorious country and, on the other, of a world of poverty and want which characterized soldiers returning from foreign campaigns. The poem also has a wider appeal and, like Kyffin's other poem, it reflects some of the dire economic straits in that period.[102]

Ieuan Llwyd Sieffre's poem to Robert Devereux, second earl of Essex ('Yr Hydd o Essex'), composed in 1599, also dwells on the need to protect the acknowledged secular order. He recorded the earl's feats in Ireland suppressing the earl of Tyrone's rebellion.[103] The poem also has its social dimension; apart from death there were two factors which shattered society, namely financial inflation ('drudaniaeth') and war ('rhyfel'). He referred to the dire straits ('cyfyngder'), famine ('newyn'), fatigue ('blinder') and the need to extend charity and hospitality to soldiers who successfully fought against the Spaniards and Irish. By then the kingdom was in the throes of a bitter economic crisis and pressures caused by Roman Catholic recusancy also created tensions. In Catholic Ireland, according to the bard, under Essex's leadership a notable victory was gained and he thanked divine intervention and protection, saving the realm from the oppression of foreign powers. He greeted what he described as 'the true British nation, the remainder of Troy's blood' ('Gwir genedyl Britannia gweddillion gwaed Troia'), allusions which have associations with ancient traditions. As worthy descendants of their forebears they possessed the duty and the privilege to preserve their patrimony from oppression and dissension under the united Crown of England:

---

[101] D. Lloyd Jenkins, *Cerddi Rhydd Cynnar*, LXVI, p.119.
[102] Ibid., XXIII, pp.40-2.
[103] T. H. Parry-Williams (ed.), *Canu Rhydd Cynnar* (Cardiff, 1932), XCIX, pp.390-3.

kyd genwch yn llafar gwrandewch yn wyllysgar
a rhowch yn feddylgar ych gweddi.

Ar adel or arglwydd j chwi yn dragowydd
Elizabeth pen llowydd goronog
rhoi gras yw chynghoried j swkrio i chowiried
gan gosbi Travtvriaid enwog.[104]

[Sing together loudly, listen willingly, and present thoughtfully your prayer that the Lord may permit you to have for ever Elizabeth, crowned sovereign, that he may give grace to her counsellors to succour her faithful subjects and to punish famous Traitors.]

The political element is emphasized yet again. No ruler has ever flourished nor overcome his enemies without first being able to establish a constitutional unity based on monarchy. Essex's efforts are magnified so as to undermine misgovernment and treason, and was a cause for celebration. Some free-metre poems were composed on that key theme, because it was among ordinary people that the severity of economic or political adversity was first felt. The queen's success was attributed to the discovery of the Babington Plot in 1586, hatched to assassinate Elizabeth and place Mary Queen of Scots on the throne. In lines which directly refer to Elizabeth there are no references to politics and religion but the bard depicts her as a symbol of order and unity. Widely acclaimed were her skills that had saved the realm from traitors and 'boorish devils' ('cythreiliaid caython'). One verse does draw attention by name to the main conspirators and is, in itself, a sound record of fact and detail:

Tra fo imi anadl chwyth am gweddi byth am cyffes
Mi folianna f'arglwydd Dduw am gadw'n fyw'r Frenhines
Llawer gwaith a llawer awr mewn perigl mawr y glowes…
O ddvw tan dy law fel llen ath fraych ywch ben ein dvwies
estyn cynnal maes i hon a chadw n llon Frenhines
Er maint cynllwyn dirgel frad drygowydd fwriad males
Tra fych iw chadw hi yn fwyn ni ellir dwyn brenhines

---

[104] Ibid., p.390.

Ar ai gwnaeth o daw gofyn Eglwysig ddyn ai canes

Sy yn brusur ddydd a nos ai weddi dros Frenhines.[105]

[While I still have breath and my prayer and confession I shall praise the Lord my God for keeping the Queen alive. I have heard that she has been many times and many an hour in great danger...Oh God, spread your hand and arm as a mantle over our goddess, extend your hand and keep her a contented Queen. Despite secret and treacherous plots of everlasting malicious intent, while you will to keep her safe the Queen cannot be taken away. He who made it, if any ask, it was a Churchman who sang it, who is busy day and night praying for the Queen.]

This laboriously verbose poem was probably composed by a priest, its main objective being to expose the evil deeds of Roman Catholics.

The years 1585-1603 were critical. A series of crises led to insecurity and instability. Only a few Catholic poems are known from the period after Richard Gwyn's execution. While it is true that the power of government agencies and royal policy was responsible for undermining recusant activity, adherence to the Old Faith, whose mission was not strong, was one significant factor which accounted for the failure of the Catholic Reformation in Wales. Sentiments expressed in poems dating from the 1540s and 1550s were still echoed in some compositions such as that entitled 'Dadl ynghylch yr Hen Ffydd' ('Debate concerning the Old Faith') in which there is an attempt by the Catholic participant to persuade its readers that Protestantism was a corrupted faith.[106] In arguing against the Protestant, the verses disclose strong Catholic feelings and a degree of intensity.

i maen groeso wrth y ffydd ar sawl y sydd yn kredv

ni welsom i rvn or wlad oddiwrthy pab yn medrv...

mae goriadav pyrth y nef gidag ef yn sikir

nid a yno ond afyno fenaid bydd di gowir...

[There's a welcome to the faith and to those who believe, we never saw anyone in the country who had come from the Pope who understands it ...

---

105 W. A. Bebb, *Cyfnod y Tuduriaid* (Wrexham, 1939), p.216.
106 B. Rees, *Dulliau'r Canu Rhydd, 1500-1650* (Cardiff, 1952), VII, pp.230-2.

He safely has the keys of the portals of heaven and no-one will go there unless he wish it; (therefore) my soul be true ...

The bard blamed economic instability on Protestantism. The country was 'in its heat' ('yni gwres'), he maintained, when queen Mary was on the throne and 'all the land full of corn prepared to believe' ('a ffob dayar yn llawn yd para bryd i kredi'). This is an important piece of propaganda composed, probably, during the years of adversity, possibly in the 1590s or even earlier. Towards the end of Mary's reign an English poem appeared, a version of part of it being available in Welsh, which gives priority to the Old Faith. In it the splendid history of the faith is recounted, extending back centuries, and the bard maintains that the doctrines of John Wycliffe and Martin Luther were false. This was originally a poem by George Marshall, written in 1554, and the intention behind its composition was to reveal where the first sacrifices and offerings were made, and where the altars and churches lay, and 'how Christ's faith began in England according to the learning of the English or Saeson' ('ple dechreawyd gynta aberthu ac offrymau ag am allorau ag eglwysey ac val y dechreuawdd fydd grist gynta yn lloyger y nysck [sic] yr Einglis ner Sayson').[107] The English version was composed in praise of Mary Tudor; it was translated into Welsh 'in affection for the same queen and to enlighten the Welshman who knows no English' ('er cariad ir vn frenhines ac er goleu o'r peth yr kymro na wyr Saesneg'). Although only a small part of the Welsh version has survived, the gist of Marshall's argument is what appears in the following verse in English:

> The Churche, the aulter & Gods sacred bodye
> They [namely the Protestants] robbed & spoiled and their faith did denie
> Lyke desperate wretches, thus played they their parte
> All was forlone, tyll good Queen Mary
> Restored them agayne to gods honor & glorye.[108]

In this verse the confused state of religion in the reign of Edward VI is compared to the joy expressed on the restoration of the faith under Mary.

In a kingdom where the religious climate was unclear and where there

---

107 Ibid., p.131.
108 B. G. Owens, 'Un o lawysgrifau Cymraeg y Diwygiad Catholig', *NLWJ*, I, 1939-40, 140.

was a legacy of conservatism, Elizabeth ascended the throne to establish a reformed Church based on a compromise. She failed to unite her subjects under the authority of one Church and religious loyalties remained divided. Protestant leaders considered her to be almost divine, hence the description of her as 'next to the Virgin Mary' ('yn nesa ar Fair Forwyn') – all damned heresy in the eyes of Catholics – and 'the white Sidanen of the maidens' ('Sidanen wen y morynion'):

> ... a gerdd ym mlaen dan i choron
> ac a gadw[o]dd ei chyrefydd
> gida dvw kadwedic fydd.[109]

[Whoever walks forward under her crown; whoever kept her religion; will be saved by God.]

The Protestant faith was described as simple and direct and an inextricable part of the Crown's authority. It was no easy task to establish the new order effectively because, in addition to the survival of Catholic practices, the standards of the clergy were deficient. Protestant bishops under Elizabeth were aware of the basic weaknesses although they themselves were unprepared, because of their own impoverished state, to refuse the temporalities of the Church. In some poems references appear to the role and condition of the clergy in exposed parishes:

> Ni fedr fe dduw Sul
> Ddarllen yr Epystyl,
> Ond fo a fedr yn rhugul
> Feddwi a rhegi.[110]

[On Sunday he cannot read the epistle, but he can swiftly get drunk and swear.]

Humanist scholars also referred to the inadequacies of the clergy in meeting required standards, and the bards commented bitterly on this deficiency:

---

[109] T. H. Parry-Williams (ed.), *Canu Rhydd Cynnar*, XCVI (iii), p.380.
[110] W. A. Bebb, p.140.

Ag o medre un ddarllen Saesneg,
Ef a fynnai urddau ar redeg,
Ag ai [sic] i gerdded y gwledydd
I ddoedyd efengyl newydd[111]

[If one is able to read English he desires ordination rapidly; and goes to walk the countries to speak of a new gospel.]

In these lines again the bard noticed tendencies among the most scholarly of priests to serve the Church in English livings in order to earn a higher income. They often blended their material needs with their spiritual obligations. Presumptuously, Siôn Tudur referred to such practices in his ode 'Bustl y Byd' ('The World's Choler'). He severely criticized the lust and desire of clergy for material gain and other worldly desires. He deplored the action of bishops in this context and bemoaned the lack of spiritual guidance. The bard's words on that theme echo what was said in other sources about the greed of prelates like the notorious pluralist, William Hughes of St Asaph:

Gwŷr yr eglwys lwys a lysir am chwant,
Arian a gadwant ac a'i gwedir.
Bugeiliaid enaid, ni 'stynnir rhoddion
Angylion, person tyn y pyrsir.
Curadiaid llawnaid llenwir yn ddiriaid,
Defaid buarthaid a ddrwg borthir.
A'r bugail di-sail dwys holir am hyn,
Eu cnu a ofyn ac a'i cneifir.[112]

[The men of the holy church are corrupted by lust, they keep silver and deny it. The shepherds of souls, they do not give gifts of angels, well does the parson fill his purse. Curates obtain their fill by deceit (while) a yardful of sheep are ill fed spiritually. And the shepherd without calling will be straitly examined about this. He will demand their fleece and will shear it.]

Only part of the poem refers to the abuses prevalent in Welsh society towards the end of the sixteenth century as Siôn Tudur interpreted them.

---

[111] Ibid., p.141.
[112] E. Roberts (ed.), *Gwaith Siôn Tudur* (Bangor, 1978), I, CXLVI, p.583.

Consequently, a new field was opened where greater emphasis was placed on the shortcomings of the Church rather than the inertia in attempting to restore the Old Faith.

That bard, however, underlined the deficiencies of the Catholic church. In an *englyn* he attacked it ferociously:

> Wyth diawl anneddfawl, naddfain – anneddfawr,
> Noddfa lleidr a phutain;
> Nythod i'r chwilod a'r chwain,
> Nid tre ofer ond Rhufain.[113]

[Eight ungodly devils, ... a great palace of dressed stone, the sanctuary of the thief and prostitute; nests for beetles and fleas, there is no dissolute town but Rome.]

His description of the glories of that ancient city was immensely different in his ode to William Parry, the papist conspirator from Flintshire, executed for treason in 1585. In that poem the bard offered a splendid portrayal of Rome, indicating that bards, when necessary, could easily adapt their own views to meet the needs of their own generation, especially if that meant enjoying patronage. To that extent, it is difficult to imagine the degree to which the products of contemporary bards are genuine sources to assess political and religious loyalties. Doubtless free-metre bards offer the best yardstick since they reflect the view of the lower orders who scratched a living from the soil rather than project images and concepts of gentility. The quality of the poems of *cwndidwyr* should not be undermined because most poets came from solid freeholding families. Some had good knowledge of Catholic belief and were able to defend it in metre. Hopcyn Tomas Phylip testified to the scriptural knowledge of the Catholic Thomas ap Ieuan ap Rhys early in the sixteenth century:

> Os sonnid am Ysgrythur,
> Ydd oedd e'n fyfyr yno,
> Ac fe wnâi i'r gwyr o ddysg,
> Pan fai'n eu mysg, ystwmlo.[114]

---

113 Ibid., CCXXXIX, p.937; C. W. Lewis. *Glamorgan County History*, III, pp.521-35; L. J. Hopkin-James and T. C. Evans (eds.), *Hen Gwndidau*, pp.31-50; T. Parry, *Hanes Llenyddiaeth Gymraeg* (Cardiff, 1953), pp.131-44.

114 E. Roberts (ed.), *Gwaith Siôn Tudur*, I, XL, pp.165-6. L. J. Hopkin James and T. C. Evans (eds.), *Hen Gwndidau*, XXXVI, p.50.

[If scripture were discussed, he would be learned in that place; and he would make men of learning stumble when in their midst.]

Free-metre bards were key agents in assessing the religious climate among peasant folk. They are perhaps the most important sources to measure the response of the peasantry to their new environment in a rapidly changing religious society. It was a matter of regret for such bards to witness the destruction of forms of worship which had won the allegiance of the people over the centuries, to be replaced by a sterner and more demanding faith. By emphasizing human feelings in their poems the bards gave expression to the essential features of the life of the 'common man', dominated by the lord and bailiff and administered to by the parish priest. The essence of rural life lay within the parish with the church providing spiritual sustenance. 'God reveals to the world', declared Thomas ap Ieuan ap Rhys, 'how to love the Church' ('Mae Duw yn dangos i'r byd sut i garu'r Eglwys'); that was accomplished through visual symbolism comprehensible to those affected by adverse economic conditions.

The new national Church progressed in unstable political circumstances in the latter half of the sixteenth century. It had inherited many of the weaknesses of the mother church in its order and ceremonial. It did not have a strong enough tradition to ensure the success of its mission. Allegiance to it often fluctuated and divisions appeared within it in matters of doctrine and practice. The majority of gentry clung to it mainly for their own benefit, but the transformation was slow and varied from region to region and from family to family. This feature was reflected in several strict and free metre poems in the middle decades of the sixteenth century. In the years 1518-26, for example, the Catholic Gruffudd ap Ieuan began to attack the symbolism of the Church, despised the influence which St. Winifred's Well had on pilgrims ('ffyniant Gwenffrewi ffynnon'), and deplored the cross at Chester ('Ar grog o Gaer') and 'the grease, the rosaries and the fragile wooden beads' ('Ar tyrs cwyr a'r llaswyrau, a gleiniau o brennau brau').[115] No golden-headed angel, the bard continued, nor a multitude of saints could do him good any longer

---

[115] W. A. Bebb, pp.90-1; *Detholiad o Waith Gruffudd ab Ieuan ap Llewelyn Vychan*, pp.31-2. For the background see J. G. Jones, 'Yr eglwys Anglicanaidd yn oes Elisabeth I: ei phwrpas, ei phryderon a'i pharhad', *Cristion* (September/October, 1988), 4-8.

('Ni all angel penfelyn, Na llu o saint ddim lles yn'). In the long and famous free-metre poem entitled 'Breuddwyd Thomas ap Llywelyn ap Dafydd ap Hywel', composed as a debate between the Church and the tavern, moderate Calvinist and Lutheran beliefs emerge. The Church addressed the tavern:

> ffrwythau ffydd gweithredoedd da
> i ddyn a dystiolaetha
> i ddyfod at ei geidwad
> drwy fôdd duw ei nefol dâd
> nid ydiw y saith pechod
> marwol baiedig hynod
> i neb yn tystiolaethu
> eu dyfodiad at jesu.

[The fruits of faith and good works testify that a man has come to his saviour through the will of God, his heavenly father. The seven deadly culpable, blatant sins do not bear witness of any that they have come to Jesus.]

The tavern responded positively casting doubts on the effectiveness of religious worship in the Protestant fashion and referring to the barren interior of the churches:

> nid oes ynod na thapreu
> na phax na phich na delweu
> na gwisgoedd gwych o sidan
> na chrwys o aur nag arian
> ond yn debyg i ysgubor
> heb lofft y grog nag allor.

There are in you no tapers, no kiss, no pyx or images nor any splendid rainment of silk, no gilded or silver crosses, but like a barn with no rood-loft or altar.]

This gives the church the opportunity to respond positively on behalf of Protestantism:

> mae'n erbyn y gorchmynion
> addoli delwau meirwon

a'r jdol ddoedd offeiriaid

yn twyllo pobloedd ffiliaid

i gael arian o'u pyrsau

dros ddywedyd offerennau.[116]

[It is against the commandments to worship dead images, and the priest was the idol deceiving foolish people in order to obtain silver from their purses by saying masses.]

The bard proceeds by stating that the human heart is 'a perfect and beneficial sacrifice' ('offrwm buddiol perffaith'). In this poem the responses of two specific aspects of spiritual life are revealed and expressed and the emphasis is placed increasingly on the superiority of the Protestant faith. The tavern is reviled as a haunt of sin and immorality, a fact which, in itself, reflects the problems of the lower orders – the growth in population, increasing unemployment and financial inflation. In a period of economic depression the situation was complicated by doctrinal uncertainty. One bard found it difficult to describe and explain the meaning of 'justification by faith' and others entered into debates about the nature of God's presence.[117] References are found to several free-metre poems of this kind which hint strongly at uncertainty and instability but, on the other hand, a firm opinion was expressed, as in the case of Llywelyn Siôn of Llangewydd, Trelales in Glamorgan.[118] He deplored the acceptance of Protestant doctrines by church leaders, and was sufficiently knowledgeable in them to be able to quote the names of some theologians on the continent. He had harsh words to say about John Calvin, Martin Luther, Theodore Beza and Ulrich Zwingli, all four expounding different doctrinal interpretations of the Eucharist. According to the bard, however, they had pretended to supplant the authority of the four evangelists by their devilish intentions. The evangelists, he declared, had been sent to propagate the Word of God in its purity, but by his age the holy practices of the mother church had been cast aside because Protestantism had too many followers.

---

[116] L. J. Hopkin-James and T. C. Evans (eds.), *Hen Gwndidau*, LV, pp.81-91 (here pp.85-7).

[117] See G. Williams, 'Breuddwyd Tomas Llywelyn ap Dafydd ap Hywel', in *Grym Tafodau Tân*, pp.164-79.

[118] L. J. Hopkin-James and T. C. Evans (eds.), *Hen Gwndidau*, LX. pp.98-9. See C. W. Lewis, *Glamorgan County History*, IV, pp.567-70.

In the following lines the bard reveals his unyielding allegiance to the Roman Cathlic faith:

Marc, Matho lân,   Luc a Ieuan
A ddodai sêl,   ar dy chweddel,
A'th ddisgyblion,   I gyd o'u bron
I'r byd a fu,   yn pregethu.
Fe fu'r ffydd hyn,   Iawer blwyddyn
A'r saint bob tro   yn cytuno.
Fe ddaeth heb gêl   gan y Cythrel
Bedwar 'n eu lle   o'i wŷr ynte,
Luther, Calfin,   Beza, Zwinglin,
Felly gelwir   y pedwargwyr,
Ac mae digon   o ddisgyblion
O'u dysgeidiaeth   hwy'n mynd waethwaeth.

[Mark, pure Matthew. Luke and John placed a seal on your story; and almost all your disciples preached in the world. This faith existed for many a year, and the saints always agreed. The devil openly brought four of his men in their place, Luther, Calvin, Beza and Zwingli. That is what the four men are called, and there are plenty of disciples who go from bad to worse as a result of their teaching.]

This poem cannot be accurately dated but it may have been composed in the early years of Elizabeth's reign in a period of intense doctrinal debate. Llywelyn Siôn was not the only one who expressed his views so intensely because Twm ab Ifan ap Rhys fiercely attacked the dissolution and plunder of the monasteries.[119]
He attributed the famine in 1547 to the religious changes, and poured his wrath on the 'faith of the English' ('ffydd Saeson'):

dwyn yth [sic] trysor briwo ych tai
bod ar fai ddigon
dwyn ych trwsiad gweddaydd glan
a diddan ych gweision…

briwor allore mawr y braint
ay troi yn ddifraint ddigon

---

119 L. Hopkin-James and T. C. Evans (eds.), *Hen Gwndidau*, XXXI, p.40; XXXIII, p.44.

gosod trestel yn ddiglod
vel gwarchiod [sic] gweddwon
gwedy esbeilio duw ay dy
pery yddy weision
gyddio y gorff e agalwr byd
y gymeryd briwsion.

[Stealing your treasure, injuring your houses, being greatly in the wrong, stealing your clean and seemly apparel and seducing your servants. Destroying great and privileged altars causing them to be truly unprivileged; placing a trestle completely without respect like widowed hags; after God's house has been despoiled causing his servants to hide His body and to summon the world to partake of crumbs.]

He tearfully complained about the depressed state of society around him, and the responses of ballad-singers in England were similar:

of preachers nowe adayes
be many fariseys,
that live the lordes layes
and preche their owne wayes.
My church ys yn derision
And almost in confusion,
My sacramentes sett at nawght
Presthoode ys dispisid
Tru fayght ys clene disgisid
And heresy sett a-lofte.[120]

The work of Meurig Dafydd also exposed his loathing in this context because of the boldness and arrogance of the 'antikristian' who had 'sown the seed among the pure wheat, a little and much weeds' ('hau ymlith, y pur wenith/ychydig ever [sic], a chwyn lawer'). A similar response appeared in the work of Gronw Wiliam and others.[121] 'Sir' Owain ap Gwilym, curate of Tal-y-llyn, Merioneth, echoed the same sentiments. In a series of *englynion* in 1560 he referred to the desecration of idols, and

---

[120] F. J. Furnivall, *Ballads from MSS. on the Condition of England in Henry VIII's and Edward VI's Reign* (Hertford, 1868), pp.226, 285; T. O. Phillips, 'Bywyd a gwaith Meurig Dafydd a Llywelyn Siôn' (unpublished University of Wales M. A. dissertation, 1937), I, pp.274-5.

[121] T. O. Phillips, pp.275-9; *Hen Gwndidau*, LVII, p.93.

his answer to that was that 'God in his own houses in bright heaven' ('Duw hoywnef o'i dai'i Hunan') had been expelled. He deeply resented Protestant teachings and disdainfully referred to the 'long treachery' ('brad hir') of those who adhered to that faith.[122]

In the latter half of the sixteenth century there was an increase in Protestant propaganda in the contents of formal eulogies to bishops and other churchmen as well as to Welsh gentry who were either for or against the New Faith. It appears that a fairly substantial number of modest gentry were conservative and clung to the faith although they increasingly held office locally. The corpus of strict-metre poetry provides evidence that efforts were made, through patrons, to 'sell' the new church. Having said that, it was no easy task to discover how many of them, except those who were staunchly Roman Catholic, fully accepted Protestantism. It appears that many lower gentry remained loyal to the mother church but others, particularly the more prominent, saw that their future lay with the new religious order. One who did well out of the Reformation was Sir William Herbert, 1st earl of Pembroke of the second creation, a peer of whom Wiliam Llŷn thought highly:

> Gwasnaethodd, treiodd bob trin,
> Duw freiniol, a dau frenin;
> A dwy frenhines yn deg,
> Heblaw Ffylib, lu Ffaleg,
> Ac ni chad, drwy fwriad draw,
> Afal teyrnas, flot arnaw.[123]

[He served and fought in every battle for God and two kings, and fairly for two queens besides Philip of splendid company, and he, the apple of a kingdom, was not blemished.]

He was described as 'a firm baron to the prince' ('farwn sad i'w Brins') who offered gracious counsel ('gyngor...gaing o ras'). He was 'the magnanimous backbone of justice' ('cefn dor fawr cyfiawnder'), 'a royal

---

122   D. H. Williams, 'Syr Owain ap Gwilym', 182-3.
123   R. Stephens, 'Gwaith Wiliam Llŷn' (unpublished University of Wales Ph.D. dissertation, 1983), II, CXVI, pp.398-9. For more information on Roman Catholic loyalties see J. J. Scarisbrick, *The Reformation and the English People* (London, 1984), pp.109-84.

baron of ancient lineage' ('barwn henwaed brenhinol') and 'a powerful hand in England' ('llaw gref o fewn Lloegr'). Herbert was also regarded as a judicious and gracious regional governor who offered the Tudors loyal service through the innate virtues which he was deemed to possess.

Another like him was Sir John Salusbury of Lleweni who also enjoyed high office, eventually being appointed chamberlain of north Wales. He remained loyal to the earl of Leicester during the controversy between the earl and a group of Llŷn freeholders and remained active in local government until his death in 1578.[124] Although known to be abrasive in his relations with others of his class he was regarded as a diligent governor of his region who steadfastly executed his duties and, for that reason, was highly acclaimed by Wiliam Cynwal:

> Gwasanaethodd ar far yr wythfed Harri,
> Gwasanaethodd Edwart, goedwart gwedi,
> Gwasanaethodd, mawr rodd, deyrnasiad Mari,
> Gwasanaethodd Elsbeth, aur lyweth loywi.[125]

[He served at the bar of Henry the eighth; he served Edward as his forester; he served, a great gift, in Mary's reign; and served Elizabeth with her sparkling golden ringlets.]

This 'man firm in his stand' ('gŵr gwastad ei stad') revealed his own skills in government in different directions and was able to adjust his conscience to suit his own needs. Although no references exist to his religious leanings it appears that he clung to the New Faith in return for material benefits. William Salesbury composed an *englyn* to Gruffudd Dwnn of Ystrad Merthyr, Cydweli, a prominent squire and copyist of manuscripts of high repute, while enjoying his hospitality in 1565 when translating the New Testament, and described him as a person 'sailing the true faith' ('hwylio yr jawnffydd'). In this context it appears that Dwnn supported the policy to translate the scriptures into Welsh.[126] Moreover,

---

124 Griffith, *Pedigrees*, p.222; *DWB*, pp.899-900.
125 J. Rowlands, 'A critical edition and study of the Welsh poems written in praise of the Salisburies of Llyweni' (unpublished University of Oxford D. Phil. dissertation, 1967), XXXII, p. 224.
126 G. H. Hughes, 'Y Dwniaid', *TCS*, 1941, p.144; *DWB*, p.175.

Siôn Phylip referred to Gruffydd Vaughan of Corsygedol in Merioneth as a humanitarian in his region, generous to the poor and benefiting churches ('…ac i lesiant eglwysau'), a reference, in part, to the chapel which he had built adjoining Llanddwywe church in 1615.[127]

In perusing the eulogistic poetry fewer references are found to religious allegiance, and the likelihood is that evidence of loyal service to the Crown was in itself sufficient to signify religious allegiance within the broader spectrum of national institutions, principally the monarchy, the law, parliament and the Elizabethan Church. More specific religious references are found in several poems composed to Welsh bishops and individual clergymen. The role of bishops propagating the Word of God, revealing their profound learning ('Dyfnder a Duwiolder dysg')[128] and their fervent belief in God's grace are amply illustrated in odes of this kind by Wiliam Llŷn and others, for example Thomas Davies, bishop of St. Asaph, his successor William Hughes and Richard Davies, bishop of St David's.[129] In a purely ecclesiastical setting the superior position of the Godhead and its role in entrusting the government of the church to able scholars and administrators is encapsulated in Siôn Phylip's elegiac lines to Bishop Nicholas Robinson:

> Troes Duw awr drom trist yw'r dreth
> Torri brigyn tw'r bregeth;
> Mae'r Eglwys lwys ei 'lusen
> A'r ffydd wedi torri ei phen.[130]

[God has turned on us a heavy hour, the onus is sad; the branch which sustained the sermon has been broken; the Church of beneficent alms and the faith have been decapitated.]

In such poems emphasis is placed on the integrity of the faith as well as that of the individual prelates. Thomas Davies, Wiliam Llŷn declared, kept the faith and promoted its progress:

---

127 A. Lloyd Hughes, 'Rhai o noddwyr y beirdd yn sir Feirionnydd', *LlC*, X, 1968-9, 137-205 (here 143).

128 E. Roberts (ed.), *Gwaith Siôn Tudur*, I, CXX, p.471; CXXVI.p.496.

129 R. Stephens, 'Gwaith Wiliam Llŷn', I, (II) pp.6-10, (IX), pp.37-40; (XXXIII) pp.142-4; (LXII),pp. 230-5.

130 Ca. MS.2.68.527.; A.O. Evans, 'Nicholas Robinson (1530?-1585)', *Y Cymmrodor*, XXXIX, 1928, 195

Goleuaist, rhyglyddaist glod,
Ordr o bwyll, air Duw i'r byd;
Salmon iaith gyfion y'th gad,
Sawdiwr Crist sy hyder Cred.[131]

[You did enlighten, meriting praise and according to the rule of wisdom you have shed light on the word of God, you have been found a Solomon of righteous language, a soldier of Christ, who is the encouragement of Christendom.]

This was probably a reference to the use made in 1561 by Davies of Salesbury's versions of parts of the scriptures in parish churches in the diocese on his appointment to St. Asaph.[132] He was primarily a church administrator, well-qualified in the law, having graduated Doctor of Laws at St John's College, Cambridge in 1548, and in 1558 became archdeacon of St Asaph.[133] His Welsh offices, before his elevation to the episcopal bench, revealed the high regard in which he was held.

This was reflected in the odes composed in his honour, for he was described as a bishop who was dedicated to his task of enrooting the Protestant faith in his diocese:

Swyddog dan Grist sy addas,
Swydd o Grist yw ansawdd gras...

Holl gred adwaened lle duna – gras Duw,
Gŵr o stad, fal Asa;
Dysgu enwog dasg yna,
A pheri'dd wyd gadw'r ffordd dda.

Duw a wna yd – nid ai'n is –
Ffynnu'n gryf, ffynnon y gras.[134]

[An officer under Christ is suitable; a Christian office is the quality of grace...Let all Christendom recognize where the grace of God binds together, you are a man of stature, like Asaph; you teach a notable lesson there and you cause the good

---

131 'Gwaith William Llŷn', p.7.
132 D. R. Thomas, *History of the Diocese of St. Asaph*, I, pp.89-90, 225; J. G. Jones, 'Thomas Davies and William Hughes: Two Reformation bishops of St. Asaph' *BBCS*, XXIX, 1980-2, 320-8.
133 Browne Willis, *A Survey St. Asaph* (London, 1723), I, p.81.
134 R. Stephens, 'Gwaith Wiliam Llŷn', I (II), pp.6-7.

way to be kept. God will cause you to prosper mightily – a fountain of grace, you shall not go lower.]

These lines testify to the central features of the New Faith as reflected in Thomas Davies's stand for the Church in the early years of the Elizabethan Settlement. Emphasis is placed on the sovereignty of God's grace, justification by faith and the final authority of God's Word. Despite his valuable services to the Church prior to Elizabeth's accession to the throne it was his role as bishop of St. Asaph between 1561 and 1573 which gave him that accolade as Protestant leader.

Richard Davies also received the same treatment by Wiliam Llŷn and other principal bards. He was famed as one who 'lived by the ways of Peter and Paul' ('byw drwy ffordd Bedr a Phawl'), and the references to his labours, with William Salesbury, in enlightening the nation by translating the New Testament and Book of Common Prayer into Welsh by 1567:[135]

> ... Deall Gair oedd dywyll gynt,
>
> ...A Gair Duw oedd o gred wan
> Yn gaead, bu, 'i rad yn brin
> Agoriad dysg aur wyt ym,
> Agoraist ffordd Grist o'i phen...
>
> ... Ynn nithiaist ffydd – can dydd daed –
> A throi y llyfrau wrth raid
> I Gymraeg, da Gymro wyd.

[In the past God's word was unclear to understand... and God's word, with its grace with-held, remained closed from its beginning. You are the key to golden learning, opening Christ's way, winnowing the faith for us, ... you, who are a good Welshman, and turning the books which were needful into Welsh.]

These lines again emphasize the importance of God's Word as a source of creed and conviction, and a similar response was obtained in 1588 and subsequently when the whole Bible appeared, including the Apocrypha.

---

[135]   Ibid., I (IX), pp.37-8.

In the strict-metre poetry at that time the contrast is revealed between the period of spiritual enlightenment, which came as a result of the translation, and the centuries of darkness and confusion that existed before that in Christendom. The most effective way used by the bards to glorify the scriptures was to highlight the value placed by them on the wealth of their contents compared to the negative faith of Rome. Richard Davies drew much attention to it in his Epistle to the Welsh people in 1567 when he described the pressures placed on the ancient Britons after the power of Rome had been imposed forcefully on them:

> O hyn allan leilai fu ey rhwysc, a mwyfwy eu gorthrymder ay caethiwet ym hob helhynt bydol.[136]

[From then onwards, their ostentation diminished, and their oppression and captivilty in all earthly tribulations increased.]

Siôn Tudur's response was similar in his *cywydd* to Dr William Morgan, seeking a copy of the Welsh Bible:

> Gloywddwys bryd gledd ysbrydawl,
> Gair Duw yw'r arf a darf diawl...
> Dwyn gras i bob dyn a gred,
> Dwyn geiriau Duw'n agored.[137]

[A spiritual sword of brightest appearance, the word of God is the weapon which strikes the devil...bringing grace to all believing men, bringing God's words into the open.]

The bard refers to the weariness ('blinder') of the Welsh people and the plundering of their souls. All Wales and its people, he added, were overcast with mist and deceptions blinded them:

> Niwl fu dros Gymru a'i gwŷr
> A'u dallu a wnâi dwyllwyr.

[Mist extended over Wales and its people, and deceivers blinded them]

---

136   *Rhagymadroddion*, p.23.
137   E. Roberts (ed.), *Gwaith Siôn Tudur*, I, XCV, p.374-5.

In such a critical situation one achievement, in his opinion, could solve the perplexing problems of Wales's spiritual condition, namely to spread the Word of God among the people in their own tongue. Accepting the Bible was not only a way in which the dignity of the nation and its language could be maintained but also a way, in the bard's opinion, which would improve the moral life of that nation. Ieuan Tew Ieuanc referred to Morgan's achievement as a crucial moment in the nation's history, when the faith was about to be extinguished ('ffydd ar ddiffoddi') and when light was brought to the people. The scriptures were a well which did not ebb ('Ffynnon heb na thro na thrai') and the sun which provides light ('haul yn rhoi'r goleuni').[138] In his poem of gratitude for the Bible Thomas Jones emphasized three basic features which it embraced, namely learning, language and faith. He regularly used images which highlighted the achievement: 'the shield' ('tarian'), 'stalwart faith' ('ffydd gref'), 'the spiritual sword' ('Cleddyf ysbryd'), 'living bread' ('bara bywiol'), 'sustenance' ('bwyd') and 'the great physician' ('meddyg mawr'):

> heb ddysk heb ddim heb ddoniay syw, heb lifr düw yn athro
> heb ddyscediaeth gwir gan neb, mawr oedd ddallineb kymro.
>
> o düw hir byr pabiaidd waith, mewn estron iaith ny dwyllo,
> drwy hydoliaeth blinaf blaid, yn dally llygaid kymro...
>
> ond yn awr mewn cryfder ffydd, y rwyf yn prydd obeithio,
> yn ol hyn o hydol haint, y ceifyd braint ar gymro.[139]

[Without learning and skills, without anything, without God's book to instruct; without true teaching from anyone: great was the Welshman's blindness; for a long time under papal rule God's word was presented in a foreign tongue; through seduction, blinding the Welshman's sight...but now in strong faith I hope, after this seductive contagion, that the Welshman will be privileged.]

Later, Edward Turberville, a fervent Roman Catholic from Coety in Glamorgan, responded fiercely and deplored his extreme religious views:

---

138 R. G. Gruffydd, *The Translating of the Bible into the Welsh Tongue by William Morgan in 1588* (London, 1988), V, pp.44, 46.
139 T.H. Parry-Williams (ed.),*Canu Rhydd Cynnar*, XCV, p.368

Gwae ni o'u codi, Liwtheriaid ceudon!
gwae ni o'u geni, Galfiniaid gweinion!
gwae ni oi gwegi, Swingliaid gweigion![140]

[Woe to us that they have risen, false Lutherans; woe to us that they have been born, weak Calvinists; woe to us because of their vanity, vain Zwinglians.]

In these lines there is a distinctly strong feeling of dissatisfaction with the Protestant fathers who were blamed for undermining religious moderation.

In a carol composed in 1597, the year of great scarcity ('drudaniaeth'), the Welsh Bible was again applauded for bringing God's commandments ('gorchmynion Duw') among the people in their own language.[141] It was a means, it was said, to lure people's minds away from the hollowness of the economic world and the misery it caused. It is interesting to note the dating of this carol, nine years after the publication of the scriptures. Was it at that time that they began to have their earliest impact on the Welsh people? Since it was locked up in church, Hugh Lewis, in 1595, did not consider that the Bible had any lasting impact on Wales, and he believed that his translations of Miles Coverdale's *A Spyrytuall and Most Precious Pearle* in that year best summarized the truth of God's Word for those deprived of Christian conduct ('yn amddifad o gyngor…a heb wybod pa wedd y mae ynddynt i ymddwyn eu hunain, yn eu hadfyd a'u cledi').[142] The carol's author, however, saw the advantage of having the scriptures in Welsh and attributed the achievement to the queen's magnanimity and benevolence towards her Welsh subjects:

Pob Cristion arbennig sy'n credu i Dduw'n unig,
Byddwch ostyngedig bawb i'w stad…

Gorchmynion Duw a ddoeth i'n mysg,
A gwŷr o ddysg i draethu'r rhain,
A fu'n dowyll yn hir faith,
A heddyw yn iaith yn hunain.

---

[140] E. D. Jones, 'The Brogyntyn Welsh manuscripts', *NLWJ*, VI, 1949-50, 233, 244.
[141] D. Lloyd Jenkins (ed.), *Cerddi Rhydd Cynnar*, XXII, p.39.
[142] *Rhagymadroddion*, p.100.

I'n brenhines moliant fo;
Hir y bo'n tyrnasu:
Teg yw'r heddwch sydd o'r gwaith,
A'n ffydd yn iaith y Cymry.[143]

[All Christians, who believe only in God, be humble according to your estate...God's commandments came amongst us along with learned men to expound them, which have been obscure for far too long, now in our own language; praise be to our queen, and long may she rule; fine is the peace which the work has brought, and our faith in the Welsh tongue.]

As noted above, Rhosier Kyffin's testimony is similar when comparing political and social stability in the realm and the situation on the European continent. An essential feature of that prosperity was religious unity which William Lambarde stressed in his charge to legal officials in Kent in 1595:

> And forasmuch as all the duties of all men, whether public or private, do concern us all either the service of God, the obedience of their prince, or the mutual life and conversation of themselves one with another, therefore also the laws of the realm have propounded unto us meet rules and directions, not only for the external worship of God by the free use of His Word and sacraments and for the lawful and loving obedience of the Queen's Majesty by a careful preservation of her person...but also for the tranquillity and good peace of ourselves.[144]

These words summarized the qualitative bases of public and private conduct revealed in service to God, loyalty and obedience to the Crown, and probity, which implied self-discipline and the exercise of steadfast control of one's activities. The ideal governor had gradually emerged by submitting to such gracious guidelines:

Gwladwr oedd, â'r glod yr aeth
Mal derwen am wladwriaeth.[145]

---

143 D. Lloyd Jenkins (ed.), *Cerddi Rhydd Cynnar*, pp.37, 39.

144 *William Lambarde and Local Government*, ed. Conyers Read (New York, 1962), p.117.

145 E. Roberts (ed.), *Gwaith Siôn Tudur*, I, L, p.207. For more information on this theme see R. Kelso, *The Doctrine of the English Gentleman in the Sixteenth Century* (Massachusetts, 1964), pp.20-60; J. G. Jones, *Concepts of Order and Gentility in Wales, 1540-1640: Bardic Imagery and Interpretations* (Llandysul ,1994), Chap. I, pp.1-41.

[He was a man of affairs and to him praise accord, as to an oak tree.]

This couplet by Siôn Tudur, describing one of his patrons, incorporates the concept of integrity in public service. The governor stood for the state's well-being, established on the balance of power apparent in secular and religious institutions. Likewise, Wiliam Llŷn sang to patrons whom he considered were paragons of civic authority and whom he linked to sound Christian doctrine and conduct.[146] In the Protestant context he placed God's omnipotence above all and, within the state, the spirit of the grandiose public servant appearing as a divine representative in secular society. He also drew attention to the belief that it was original sin in men that necessitated good government. Authority is defined as God's grace working in man, and the doctrine of predestination adhered to because of the unique position granted squire-gentlemen in his neighbourhood:

> A Duw wyn ai rhod yn rôdd
> Dwysog ef ai dewisodd
> Ni ddewis Duw ddewiswr
> Y fath yn iarll fyth yn ŵr.[147]

[And pure God selected him to a princely status; God does not select an earl ever to be a gentleman.]

The bard offers a view of society which had become more aware of its position in a Calvinist framework. He exalts heirarchical principles in the social order and the Protestant doctrine of God's supremacy. The gentleman, it is stated, is subordinate to the Almighty and His agent in all aspects of public service:

> Nid dyn byw, nid da na barn,
> A'th gododd, ŵr doeth gadarn;
> Duw Dad a'th gododd, di dwng,
> Dyna dyst n'all dyn d'ostwng;
> Duw a'th roes yn ail Moesen,
> Duw'n barch a'th adawo n ben.[148]

---

146 J. G. Jones, 'The Welsh poets and their patrons, c.1550-1640', *WHR*, IX, 1979, 263-9; Kelso, *The Doctrine of the English Gentleman*, pp.18-41, 70-110.

147 J. C. Morrice (ed.), *Barddoniaeth Wiliam Llŷn* (Bangor, 1908), LXXXII, p.225.

148 R. Stephens, 'Gwaith Wiliam Llŷn', I, XXXI, p.138;. See B. Jones, 'Beirdd yr uchelwyr a'r byd', in J. E. Caerwyn Williams (ed.), *Ysgrifau Beirniadol*, VIII (Denbigh, 1974), pp.29-42 (here pp.36-42).

[It is not a living man, or substance or judgement, which elevated you strong wise man; God the father raised you, who does not swear unto himself, and that is testimony that man cannot undermine you. God placed you as a second Moses, may God with respect permit you to be head.]

The Calvinist order is given prominence; if man is raised by God, then he possesses virtues and the necessary skills to serve his people within the local community and the state. The poems of Rhosier Kyffin do not have the same comprehensive or intellectual penetration but, in his carol which compares England favourably with the continent, he emphasizes the Bible as a source of salvation:

> Mae'r efengyl yn ych mysg,
> A gwŷr o ddysg i'w dreuthu [sic]:
> Gair Duw 'n berffaith i chwi i gyd
> I'ch dwyn i'r byd a bery.[149]

[The gospel is among you with learned men to expound it; God's word is given you all perfectly to lead you to the everlasting world.]

Siôn Tudur, in his eulogy to Queen Elizabeth, referred to her as the symbol of the protective and defensive monarchy – 'Your realm and land', the bard stated, 'are graced' ('Mae gras i'ch teyrnas a'ch tir'), thereby reflecting elements of the will of 'Gloriana'.[150]

> Wyd biler hyder yrhawg
> I'r Efengyl grafangawg.
> Caid enw cryf yn cadw'n crefydd,
> Ceidwad, amddiffyniad ffydd.[151]

[You are the sustainer of confidence at this time as regards the far-spreading gospel. You have obtained a strong reputation for maintaining our religion; keeper and defender of the faith']

Sections of Edwart ap Raff's eulogy to the queen also suggest the innate

---

149 D. Lloyd Jenkins (ed.), *Cerddi Rhydd Cynnar*, XXIII, p.41.
150 E. Roberts (ed.), *Gwaith Siôn Tudur*, I, XCVI, p.381.
151 Ibid., I, XCVI, p.380.

qualities of the Christian faith which were incorporated in her being:

> Mwy ogoniant mae gennym
> Ffydd Grist yn hoffaidd ei grym.
> A'r efengyl i filoedd
> O enau Crist, eu câr oedd...
> A Duw'n y blaen – dyna blaid –
> I'th goron a'th gywiriaid.[152]

[More glory, we have Christ's faith well-received in its power. From Christ's own words, our kinsman... And God is showing the way – that is support for the Crown and its faithful followers.]

According to these lines it is the Protestant faith which unites the sovereign and her loyal subjects, the most prominent among them recorded in these poems being her counsellors and regional governors. Politically Elizabeth's reign was not entirely successful because she faced many crises in her foreign and domestic policies, not least rebellions, the inflationary processes and the persistent threats of Roman Catholic recusancy and Puritanism. Yet, the bard interprets them against the background of what he regarded as the queen's illustrious lineage and Welsh family connections. She is recognised as the custodian and leader of her people in a peaceful and independent kingdom. An English verse expresses similar sentiments in a Biblical context:

> Jabin, of Canaan king, had long, by force of arms,
> Oppressed the Israelites; which for God's people went:
> But God minding, at last, for to redress their harms;
> The worthy DEBORAH, as judge among them sent.[153]

This feeling was interpreted in a Welsh secular and religious context. George Owen of Henllys gave expression to the euphoria when he referred to the 'great metamorphosis'[154] that had taken place in Wales since the accession of Henry VII, and Richard Davies considered the

---

[152] D. H. E. Roberts and R. A. Charles, 'Raff ap Robert ac Edwart ap Raff', 298-9.
[153] Quoted in J. Guy, 'The Tudor age 1485-1603', in K. O. Morgan (ed.), *Illustrated History of Britain 1485-1789* (London, 1985), p.48.
[154] G. Owen, *The Description of Penbrokshire*, ed. H. Owen (London, 1906), III, p.57.

Protestant Reformation, nurtured by the Tudors, to be the restoration of the old faith of the Britons in Wales.[155] Huw Machno's opening section of a *cywydd* touched upon the same theme and offered lavish praise to Henry Tudor:

> O bu i Gymru i gyd,
> Drwy anap, flinder ennyd,
> A'i rhoi yn gaeth, waethwaeth oedd,
> A'i thai araul a'i thiroedd...
> Yn rhydd o hyn i'n rhyddhau,
> Yn frenin iawnfawr rannau,
> Iesu erom roes Harri
> Seithfed yn nodded i ni.[156]

[If Wales, owing to bad fortune, became troubled and was enslaved, losing its houses and lands...Jesus gave us Henry the seventh, a noble and illustrious king, to emancipate us and give us refuge.]

Once the new religious order had been established it was considered to be one of the foundation stones of the political structure of the realm. A philosophical framework was provided for it in the work of John Jewel, bishop of Salisbury, in *Apologia Ecclesiae Anglicanae* (1562), and *Of The laws of Ecclesiastical Polity* (1593-1600), Richard Hooker's magisterial definition of the church, an ardent plea for religious unity as well as a bold declaration of the medieval belief in church and state as one conjoined entity.

It was a Church established by secular law and regarded as a stronghold against disorder at home and abroad. Siôn Tudur dexterously wove his thoughts into this context:

> O chymraist Loegr a Chymru,
> Elsbeth, d'etifeddiaeth fu...
> Iti rhoed caniatáu'r hedd...
> Iti rhannwyd tair rhinwedd—
> Doethineb, cywirdeb coeth,
> Pryd iwch hefyd, a chyfoeth.

---

155 *Rhagymadroddion*, p.37.
156 G. Davies, *Noddwyr Beirdd ym Meirion* (Dolgellau, 1974), pp.32-3.

... Troi'r cledd a'i rinwedd oedd raid
At herwyr neu draeturiaid,
Os bradwyr Ynys Brydain
Na bo rhwydd i neb o'r rhain.[157]

[Elizabeth, you possessed England and Wales, your inheritance ... you have been entrusted to maintain the peace...and you have been given three virtues, wisdom, justice and prosperity ... It was necessary to turn this virtuous sword on outlaws or heretics. Let it not be easy for any who are betrayers of the Isle of Britain.]

This is an unambiguous statement of the position assumed by the Elizabethan Church. Although it faced several threats during the early growth of Puritanism and Roman Catholic opposition, the bard attributed to it formal duties which would ensure its survival. It was necessary to turn the sword justly against outlaws or traitors ('Troi'r cledd a'i rinwedd oedd raid/At herwyr neu draeturiaid').[158] The Church would persecute heavily 'traitors to the Isle of Britain' ('bradwyr Ynys Brydain') and restrict their activities. It was not among recusants only that opposition and deceit were discovered because abuses were also rife among local government officials bent on enriching themselves by misusing their authority, profiting from false religious allegiance and corruptly using the power entrusted to them:

'Sgrythur lân lydan ni chofleidir hon...
Pregeth dda'i 'styriaeth a ddi'styrir.
Llygrwyd ein crefydd, llygrir yn wastad,
Llygriad hwyr fendiad o'r Rhufeindir.[159]

[The holy scriptures are not cherished... a well considered sermon is despised. Our faith has been corrupted, is always corrupted, a corruption occasioned by the late reform which comes from Rome.]

These shortcomings in public office were attributed largely to the influence of the Roman Catholic faith on men who had not the power nor desire to withstand its repulsive influences. The impression given is that

---

[157] E. Roberts (ed.), *Gwaith Siôn Tudur*, I, XCVI, pp.379, 380, 381.
[158] Ibid., p.381.
[159] Ibid., CXLVI, p.584.

sincerity in the conduct of religion was lacking because of deceit and private ambition. The consequence of bad government, it was said, was social disorder, and it is evident that Siôn Tudur found corruption and a marked decline among men in public life. He pronounced that law was flouted because religion was undermined. It was under a divinely-appointed monarchy alone that good government could be established:

> A theg rym Elsbeth a'i gras
> Ydyw eurnerth y deyrnas.
> Grasol, Duw o'i hir groesi,
> Y gwnaeth gyfraith i'n iaith ni.[160]

[And Elizabeth's fair power and grace are the kingdom's gilded succour; God blessing her long, graciously did she legislate for our language.]

In most religious verse bards concentrated on some central aspects of the Protestant faith, its creed and doctrines. References were made to the Ten Commandments, the Lord's Prayer, the Three Enemies of the Soul, the Seven Deadly Sins, the Seven Words of Mercy, the Seven Virtuous Acts, faith, hope and charity and so on. Sins such as gluttony, covetousness, infidelity, miserliness, oppression and corruption, together with many other moral lapses, were also given attention. Free and strict metre poetry is full of moral themes, and after the appearance of the Bible more positive references were made to scriptural citations, drawing from them the principles of the Christian faith. Greater emphasis was placed on the execrable void in secular life in the tradition of the early fifteenth-century bard Siôn Cent whose compositions foretold the fate of mankind. It is in lines like the following that Wiliam Llŷn sang to such themes:

> Y byd hwn a'r bywyd teg
> Yw yr hudol yn rhedeg;
> I fewn golau fo'n gelwir
> O'r hudol hwn i'r hoedl hir.[161]

[This world and the fair life are enchantments; in His light he calls us from this enchantment to the long life.]

---

[160] Ibid., CL, p.602.
[161] J. C. Morrice (ed.), *Barddoniaeth Wiliam Llŷn*, xxxviii, XVII, p.41; 'Gwaith William Llŷn,' II, CIX, p.379.

The occasional bard could be very precise in defining the central matters of the faith, and couplets and epigramatic or expository stanzas began to appear:

> ffydd yw sywrder, or pethau pêr
> a obeithir, er nas gwelir.[162]

[Faith is the certainty of delicious things hoped for but not seen:]

> Duw'r Tad, Duw'r Mab rhad, priodol – dwysbr[yd],
> Duw Ysbryd sancteiddiol;
> Duw Tri'n Un nis detry'n ôl,
> Duw yw Hwn diwahanol.[163]

[God the Father, God's appropriate free gift of a blessed Son – of sober mien; God the holy spirit; God three in one, He will not be separated again, He is the inseparable God.]

To what extent verses of this kind were understood in the rural hinterland of Wales it is impossible to say but it is certain that the outlines of the faith would, in the course of time, become familiar to the majority through the services of the priesthood. What is clear is that the bards used their craft to express the truths of the Christian faith and that a proportion of them, especially free-metre bards, were more prepared to express their feelings on faith and doctrinal matters. It cannot be accepted that the Protestant faith was firmly entrenched in Wales and England by the close of Elizabeth's reign. The faith's progress was very slow and protracted among peasant folk and modest parish priests. Many cherished the Old Faith, Siôn Tudur maintained, and others the new ('Llawer o'r Hen Ffydd/ Ac eraill o'r Ffydd Newydd') when he referred to the conservative nature of community life in his day.[164] William Evans, chancellor and treasurer of Llandaff and a staunch patron of bards, was accused of being a papist but he kept his offices and became a prominent figure in diocesan administration. In verse composed in his honour no references appear to

---

[162] L. J. Hopkin-James and T. C. Evans (eds.), *Hen Gwndidau*, LVII, p.95.
[163] E. Roberts (ed.), *Gwaith Siôn Tudur*, I, CCCXXII, p.1012. See G. Williams, 'Crefydd a llenyddiaeth Gymraeg yn oes y Diwygiad Protestannaidd', in G. H. Jenkins (ed.), *Cof Cenedl: Ysgrifau ar Hanes Cymru*, I (Llandysul, 1986), pp.51-6.
[164] E. Roberts (ed.), *Gwaith Siôn Tudur*, I, CCIII, p.833.

his religious leanings, greater stress being placed on his efficiency in office.[165] According to Llywelyn Siôn he was the wise, dignified and well-endowed person ('graddol, doeth, duwiol diwall'), a bountiful gentleman to the poor and needy.[166] Siôn Tudur sang to William Parry, the most remarkable member of a Llaneurgain, Flintshire family, and a member also of the cadet family of Coedymynydd, who became a papist while spying on the continent on behalf of the English government in the years 1579-80. Clearly the bard in that age was not opposed to the Old Faith, for at Rome Parry adopted 'the church and candle, the Old Faith, the fine shepherd and his crook or crozier' ('llan a channwyll... yr Hen Ffydd... a'i bugail gwych, baglog iôn'):

> A thrwy fawrserch ei berchi,
> Duw a saint eu braint a'u bri.
> A beddau y saint buddiawl,
> A'u creiriau, a'u mannau mawl;
> A'u holl barchusfodd noddfa,
> A'u stasiwn, defosiwn da.[167]

[By his great love for God, the saints, their privilege and esteem, and the graves of saints, their relics and places of worship as well as all their sanctuaries and their station, the basis of good devotion.]

He sang as ardently also to Thomas Goldwell, the last Roman Catholic bishop of St. Asaph and 'the saintly disciple of Christ' ('Disgybl Crist yn santaidd'). In stanzas composed to him in 1556, however, there is no reference to his religious convictions.[168] Goldwell refused to accept Henry VIII's changes; he served Cardinal Pole, took steps to try to restore Rome's jurisdiction in his diocese and, in 1558, fled to the continent.

Siôn Brwynog could sing as ardently to Henry VIII and William Herbert, earl of Pembroke, as he could to the presence of the flesh and blood of Christ in the Catholic communion.[169] In one of 'Sir' Owain ap Gwilym's

---

165 G. J. Williams, *Traddodiad Llenyddol Morgannwg*, pp.88-90; L. Thomas, *The Reformation in the Old Diocese of Llandaff* (Cardiff, 1930), p.xix; C. W. Lewis, *Glamorgan County History*, IV, pp.546-8, 549.
166 T. O. Phillips, XXXI, p.566.
167 E. Roberts (ed.), *Gwaith Siôn Tudur*, I, XL, p.166.
168 Ibid., CCXXXIII, p.932.
169 NLW Llanstephan MSS. 123.626; 133.82.

odes an attempt is made to criticise those who clung to the middle way between the two faiths, and although he pleaded the Pope's cause in some stanzas, in this ode he expounded Luther's belief in justification by faith:

> Credwn i Dduw cariadol,
> Caru dwy ffydd yw cred ffôl.
> Duw o nef, da iawn ei waith,
> A brynodd bawb ar unwaith.
> Nid gweithredoedd, salmoedd sail,
> Yw'n ceidwad a'n cu adail.
> Unig ffydd, enwog o'i phen,
> A geidw pawb, ac adwen.[170]

[We believe in a loving God; to cherish two faiths is foolish; God in heaven redeemed all altogether. Our guardian is not works; the only faith all maintain and know it.]

Many other bards also sang to men whose allegiance to the Protestant faith was rather ambivalent, but the rigidity of bardic conventions prevented them from commenting on matters other than those authorized by their schools. The occasional poem, however, does supply some incisive comment as, for example, in the *cywydd* by Wiliam Cynwal to the palace of Dr Edmund Meyricke, archdeacon of Bangor and brother of Rowland Meyricke, bishop of the see. He refers to the declining state of the priesthood and to the effects on standards of patronage enjoyed by the bards:

> Bu gymwys gwŷr eglwys gynt,
> Brig ieithiau a bregethynt.
> Wedi hyn, hud a honnir,
> O chwant da, uchenaid hir,
> Gwŷr yr eglwys, grair oglyd,
> Sumier bai, a somai'r byd.
> Yr awron, drwy greulon gri,
> Yr oedd ffydd ar ddiffoddi.[171]

---

[170] D. G. Williams 'Syr Owain ap Gwilym', 183.
[171] Rh. Williams, 'Wiliam Cynwal', *LIC*, VIII, 1964-5, 197-213 (here 211).

[Churchmen in the past were suitable who preached in chief languages. After this, palpable enchantment was professed, which brought a long sigh. Churchmen, putting their faith in a relic, let this be accounted a fault, brought disappointment to the world. Now, faith was about to be extinguished.]

It is no easy task to assess the quality of the Welsh clergy on the threshold of the seventeenth century, but there is evidence which reveals that educational provision had led to higher standards and better opportunities in the Church, although hospitality was gradually on the decline.[172] Siôn Tudur sang to Hugh Evans, dean of St. Asaph (1560-87), a pluralist and prominent official in local government who was also described as a man 'for the faith' ('am y ffydd'), He had been well-educated at Oxford ('Di-chwyn ddysg Rhydychen dda'), and the bard proceeded to praise his virtues:

> Dydi a wnaeth dy dai'n wych,
> Dyma ddawn da y'i meddiennych.
> Mwya' saig, fal y mae sôn,
> Wisgi daw saig y deon.[173]

[You made your houses splendid. This is an attribute, may you possess it well. However great the dish, as it is said, briskly comes the dean's dish.]

Thomas Banks, Evans's young successor in that office, was praised by the same bard for his material prowess because he constantly sought religious preferment. He was a 'learned and great preacher' ('Praff addysg pregethwr'), a 'font of learning' ('sylfaen dysgeidiaeth') and a priest 'profound in godly learning' ('Cryfder a duwiolder dysg'). The bard also praised his householdership:

---

172 G. Williams, *Welsh Reformation Essays*, pp.22-7; idem, 'Education and culture down to the sixteenth century', in J. L. Williams and G. R. Hughes (eds.), *The History of Education in Wales*, I (Swansea, 1978), pp.17-27; L. S. Knight, *Welsh Independent Grammar Schools to 1600* (Newtown, 1926); P. Heath, *The English Parish Clergy on the Eve of the Reformation* (London,. 1969), pp.82-134, 187-96.
173 E. Roberts (ed.), *Gwaith Siôn Tudur*, I, CXXII, p.478.

Hygar iaith lafar i'th lys,
Yn ddiddan iawn ddydd a nos;
Hyddgarw ffraeth, hawddgar, ffres,
Hardd i'n gwlad, hir ddoniog les.[174]

[Courteous conversation is made in your court, most entertainingly day and night; eloquent, amiable, witty and fresh, handsome for our country, a many-faceted asset.]

In such poems to prelates and higher clergy the bards eulogized the intelligentsia in the Welsh Church of their day, praising their halls and mansions, their patronage, their lavish hospitality and their standing in their community. Regardless of the hyperbolic style, doubtless the man of God, whatever his rank, deserved praise by virtue of his status in the Church. Despite references to his material interests a clergyman was primarily eulogized because of his spiritual rather than secular qualities. Rhisiart Cynwal praised Dr John Davies of Mallwyd, the famous late Renaissance scholar, for his preferments, not because of any worldly desire for advancement on his part, but because he wished to maintain his reputation as a man of God in his locality:

Mae iti renti drwy ras
Mab ddewrddoeth, mwy bo d'urddas.
Mallwyd sydd am wellad sant
A Mawddwy yn eich meddiant.
A Llanfawr, blaenfawr heb ludd,
Llawn afael a Llanefydd.[175]

[You have, by grace, church livings, may your dignity increase. Mallwyd is, for the benefit of the saint, and Mawddwy also in your possession, as well as Llanfawr, foremost without doubt, in your full grasp and also Llanefydd.]

Huw Pennant went a step further in a *cywydd* to Robert Madrun, seeking the gift of a sword, on behalf of Henry Rowlands, bishop of Bangor. He explained that it was by preaching the Word, and by the power of the

---

174 Ibid., CXXVI, pp.494-6. See J. Peter and R. J. Pryse (eds.), *Enwogion y Ffydd* (London, 1880), I, p.142.
175 NLW MS 5269,414

193

sword that the Protestant faith would be promoted. This was a growing concept which the bards used increasingly to promote the faith:

> Un ei draethu drwy ieithoedd,
> Da yw'r gwaith, Air Duw ar goedd;
> Er dwyn oll i gredu'n iawn
> Y ffieiddlu anffyddlawn,
> A'r ail o rym gwroledd
> Wrth ei glauddewr nerth a'i gledd.[176]

[One who expounds in languages; the work is good, God's Word declared publicly to bring all, who were the unfaithful band, to believe rightly; and the second does so by valour and the power of the sword.]

It is religious conviction, however, and not the use of violence, the bard declares, that will improve moral standards in the realm, and he proceeds to describe the bishop as a humanitarian and defender of the faith, the two qualities which he considered to be uppermost in his character. Sir John Wynn of Gwydir also referred to his provident governorship of the Church, a quality endorsed by the bard on this occasion. Rowlands's predecessor and kinsman Richard Vaughan was similarly praised for possessing qualities enabling him to be a zealous defender of 'the pure and sure faith' ('ffydd lân ffyddlon'). As archdeacon of Middlesex (1596) Siôn Phylip sang to Vaughan seeking, again on behalf of Robert Madrun, copies of the three books needed in the parish church of Llandudwen, Llŷn, namely the Bible, the Sacrament Book and John Foxe's *The Book of Martyrs*.[177] Since Richard Vaughan was a favoured son of that region and regarded as a scholar of repute it is hardly surprising that he was considered the most appropriate person to supply them with these books. In an area where Roman Catholic recusancy was quite strong Foxe's work reminded them of the martyrdoms which their faith had produced and urged them to defend it. What is also particularly interesting about this request is that although the poet was, early in his career, fully committed to propagating the faith, he was primarily interested in obtaining a just reward for his services.

---

[176] NLW MS.16129.17
[177] Ibid., 86.

By the early decades of the seventeenth century the Elizabethan Church had gradually grown in confidence and had become closely linked with most of the governing families in Wales. Under John Whitgift's leadership, guidance had been offered by most of the Welsh bishops and the Church had deepened its roots. Although Roman Catholic recusancy continued to threaten, particularly on the Welsh borderland, and some of its leaders were involved in plots hatched early in James I's reign, adherents of the Old Faith, while being able to maintain their numbers in most parts of Wales, failed to have a lasting impact. 'Sir' Huw Roberts Llên composed a *cywydd* to commemorate the king's victory over his Catholic conspirators in the Gunpowder Plot of 1605,[178] and an anonymous free-metre poem triumphantly recorded the disastrous failure of the plot and deplored the traitorous intentions of the conspirators, described as 'excommunicate knaves' ('knafys yskymyn').

Consequently, the poem took the form of an eulogy of King James, concentrating on the peace and good order he had established following his accession to the throne:

> Rhai or papists oedd valevsic
> rhwng kalangaia ar Nodolic
> oni chadwan ffydd ar brenin
> rhowch nwy o hyd ar vache heyrn.[179]

[Some of the papists were malicious between Allhallowtide and Christmas. If they do not maintain the faith may the king place them continually in iron clasps.]

The poet-soldier Richard Hughes of Cefnllanfair, Llŷn, composed a series of six *englynion* on that occasion and adopted a similar viewpoint, praising James for his firm faith, adding that if all bishops had been as steadfast in their faith recusancy would not have posed such a serious threat. The monarchy's will in maintaining the religious order is exemplified in the first two stanzas:

> Ffydd Rhufain filain ffydd i foli – 'r Pab
>   Ffydd mam pob drygioni;
> Ffydd waedlyd hefyd yw hi,
> Ffydd ddwl hen ffei ddiawl honi.

---

[178] Ca. MS.3.68,221.
[179] B. Rees *Dulliau'r Canu Rhydd*, p.242.

Ffei o ffydd a rydd ryddid – eneidiawl
    Dan wadu yffern-lid.
    I wŷr i ladd o wir lid,
    Deyrnas a'i holl gadernid.[180]

[The faith of vicious Rome, a faith which worships the Pope, a faith which is the mother of all evil; it is also a bloody faith, a worn, stupid faith, fie to the devil because of it.
Fie to the faith which gives absolution, denying the wrath of hell, to men whose intent is to slay out of pure anger a kingdom and all its strength.

Some bards deplored the guile and deceit of recusants. Dafydd Benwyn composed a long *cywydd* 'against idolatry' ('yn erbyn delwaddoliaeth'), and severely attacked its popularity among the peasant population. Like others of his generation he addressed gentry who had adopted the Protestant faith by the close of Elizabeth's reign, urging them to destroy all relics and vestiges of 'false beliefs' ('ffug goelion'):

    delwe a phob hydoliaeth
    dig iawn wedd an dyg yn waeth
    Iawn ddüw awnaüthon yn ddig
    a chary koed a cherig
    a delwau a swynau son...
    y rhain kredasson nin hawdd
    hwyntaü ollawl an twyllawdd.[181]

[Idols and all magic makes us worse. We made the true God angry by worshipping trees and stones and idols...these we readily believed and they all deceived us.]

The same bard sang to squire-gentlemen such as Thomas and Edward Lewis of Y Fan, Caerffili, William Evans, chancellor of Llandaff, and Sir Thomas Stradling, all of them, although they held public offices under the queen, privately remaining loyal to the Old Faith.[182] Early in the seventeenth century, however, with some notable exceptions, the Welsh

---

180 Nesta Lloyd (ed.), *Ffwtman Hoff* (Abertawe, 1998), p.37.
181 L. J. Hopkin-James and T. C. Evans (eds.), *Hen Gwndidau*, XCV, p.162.
182 Ca. MS. 2.277.16, 108, 164, 219, 383, 463; NLW Llanstephan MS.164.23.

gentry were increasingly being portrayed as being loyal to church and state.[183] Because of the belief among scholars and antiquaries in the Galfridian myth concerning the ancient lineage and claims of the British people to the isle of Britain, James's claims to be 'King of Great Britain' assisted in strengthening gentry ties with the Crown. Moreover, with the growth of a Puritan tradition inside and outside the Church, the concept of the devout *paterfamilias* in his household became more prominent, thus placing greater emphasis on piety and godliness within the family unit.[184] Thus sang Huw Machno to a patron:

> Gwaedol a chefnog ydoedd,
> Gwarant iawn i'w geraint oedd;
> Cynghorwr, ymg'leddwr gwlad,
> Clau hyd elor, clo dwywlad.[185]

[He was of good lineage and substantial; a full warranty to his kindred; a counsellor and guardian of his country; upright until death, the key to two regions.]

Sentiments of this kind can easily be identified with the religious context because the gentry highly regarded their alliance with the monarchy and its institutions. Gruffudd Phylip of Ardudwy echoed such feelings:

> Gwrda gwych, caredig iawn...
> Yn siampler i'w amser oedd;
> Sant a llwyddiant oll iddo,
> Siampler o'i gyfiawnder fo;
> Bucheddol rasol erioed,
> Buchedd rinwedd i'r henoed.[186]

[A splendid and very generous nobleman...he was an example to his generation; a saint who obtained success, which is an example of his justice; ever pious and gracious, a virtuous life into old age.]

---

183 T. Jones Pierce (ed.), *Clenennau Letters and Papers in the Brogyntyn Collection* (NLW Jnl. Supp. 1947), no.204, p.61; A. H. Dodd, 'The pattern of politics in Stuart Wales', *TCS*, 1948, 9-23; J. G. Jones, 'The Welsh poets and their patrons, 1550-1640', 248-53.
184 A. H. Dodd, 'Pattern of politics', loc..cit.; G. D. Owen, *Wales in the Reign of James I* (London, 1988), pp.45-8; J. G. Jones, 'Cyfraith a threfn yn sir Gaernarfon c. 1600-1640', *TCHS*, XLVII, 1986, 25-70.
185 G. Davies, *Noddwyr Beirdd ym Meirion*, p.175.
186 Ibid., pp.107,159.

The religious gentleman here is characterized by his probity and piety, an example to his household and the wider community, and a person of *gravitas*. In a similar context Wiliam Phylip of Hendre Fechan, again in Merioneth, described his father, Phylip ap Siôn, in the following words:

> I Dduw byw gweddïo bu
> Am ras ac ymroi i Iesu.[187]

[He prayed to the living God for grace and devotion to Jesus.]

In the ecclesiastical world there were also men of high repute, a good number of them ranking below the upper clergy. Erudite scholars were accorded well deserved accolades, often for their contribution to their community as well as for their religious duties and contribution to scholarship. Thus emerged individuals such as Dr David Powel, vicar of Rhiwabon, Dr Edmund Meyricke, archdeacon of Bangor, Dr John Davies, rector of Mallwyd, Edmwnd Prys, archdeacon of Merioneth and 'Sir' Wmffre Dafis, vicar of Darowen in Montgomeryshire, a remarkable copyist of manuscripts, whose expertise was described as follows:

> Ficar, a rwydda'r addysg,
> Darowen, dad dwyran dysg,
> Syr Wmffre, dwys rym ffrwd iaith,
> Dafydd dda, burffydd berffaith.[188]

[A vicar of Darowen, well educated, the father of both parts of learning; 'Sir' Humphrey Davies, of pure and perfect faith.]

By virtue of his immense scholarship Dr John Davies of Mallwyd was saluted by several bards, especially in his capacity as the reviser of Morgan's Bible (1620) and the Book of Common Prayer (1621). Here are Gruffudd Phylip's lines in his honour:

---

187 Ibid., p.113.
188 Ibid., p.15.

Perffeithiaist, nithiaist yn well
Y Beibl oll i'r bobl wellwell.
Yn oes dyn trefnaist yna
Y llyfrau gweddïau'n dda.[189]

[You perfected and winnowed well all the Bible and improved it for the people. Within a man's lifespan you organized the prayer books well.]

Bards sang profusely to the availability of the scriptures, and William Morgan was widely acclaimed for his achievement, Rhys Cain being as enthusiastic as any in his accolade:

Dy araith gall draw o'th gôr,
A'th bregeth, biau rhagor...
Doctor, pen cyngor cangell,
Wyd yn ail Dewi neu well;
Aaron gryf fu'r un grefydd,
Ail wyd ffyrf aelod y ffydd.[190]

[Your sensible speech yonder from your chancel, and your sermon, even better...a Doctor, chief counsellor of the chancel, a second David or better; you are second to Aaron of the one religion, a sturdy adherent of the faith.]

References of this kind could be multiplied. Some bards praised his defence of the Church and his preaching skills, and Huw Machno, like Morgan a native of Nanconwy, expressed delight in the outcome of his labours. The bard also made a pertinent comment on the impact of the queen's act of parliament in 1563 to grant the Welsh people the scriptures in their own language:

Rhoes inni o'i gras uniawn
Ffydd dda i'n mysg, dysg a dawn;
Ordeiniodd wŷr da enwawg,
Gwaith rhwydd, i bregethu rhawg...[191]

---

[189] NLW MS.5269B.428b; Rhiannon Ff. Roberts, 'Dr John Davies o Fallwyd', *LlC*, II, 1952-3, 35, 97-110.
[190] R. G. Gruffydd, *The Translation of the Bible...*, I, p.32.
[191] Ibid.. VII, p.51.

[She gave among us of her just grace a good faith, learning and skill; she ordained good and famous men to preach fluently for a long time to come.]

The insistence on preaching the Word based on scripture became a more prominent feature in eulogies of the clergy.

When Wiliam Cynwal, in his famous bardic debate with Edmwnd Prys, inquired of him what authority he wished to follow, the firm reply was:

> Llyfr ffydd Duw, llywydd i'm llaw.
> Llawn faethrâd, llyna f'athraw.[192]

[God's book of faith, a guide in my hand. Full of blessed nourishment, behold my teacher.]

He interpreted the Bible as the chief foundation of poetry as well as faith. Rhys Prichard ('the old vicar') of Llanymddyfri followed the same trail when he composed a large number of carols to welcome and promote the 1630 Bible.[193] He saw it as a glowing candle, a guiding light and a treasure more essential than a father's patrimony to save the individual sinner. Prichard used his verses to extend propaganda on three different levels – to promote the Bible and the Word as a spiritual guide, to elevate the sinner to a position which made him aware of the need for personal salvation and to familiarize his parishioners with the concept of the Trinity:

> Y Gair yw'r gannwyll a'th oleua,
> Y Gair yw'r gennad a'th gyf'rwydda;
> Y Gair a'th arwain i baradwys,
> Y Gair a'th ddwg i'r nef yn gymwys.
>
> Heb y Gair ni ellir 'nabod
> Duw, na'i natur na'i lân hanfod,
> Na'i Fab Crist, na'r sanctaidd Ysbryd,
> Na rhinweddau'r drindod hyfryd.[194]

---

192 G. A. Williams (ed.), *Ymryson Edmwnd Prys a Wiliam Cynwal* (Cardiff, 1986), XXV, p.114; D. G. Jones, *Y Ficer Prichard a 'Canwyll y Cymry'* (Caernarfon, 1946), p.39.
193 *DWB*, pp.795-6; N. Lloyd (ed.), *Cerddi'r Ficer: Detholiad o Gerddi Rhys Prichard* (Cyhoeddiadau Barddas, 1994), intro., xi-xv.
194 N. Lloyd (ed.), *Cerddi'r Ficer*, pp.55,56.

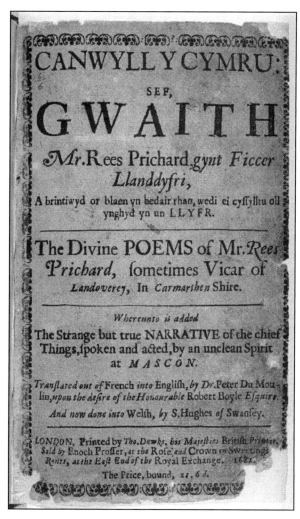

Title-page of *Canwyll y Cymry* (1672)

[The Word's a candle which gives you light. The Word's the messenger who will guide you, The Word will lead you to paradise, The Word will bring you directly to heaven.

Without the word God cannot be known, Neither His nature nor His holy essence, Nor His Son Christ, nor the Holy Spirit, Nor the virtues of the benificent Trinity.]

Prichard promoted the moral welfare of his parishioners by urging them to purchase the portable Bible which was published in 1630. He gave the head of the household advice how to read it and meditate upon it:

N'âd ei drigo yn yr Eglwys
Gyd â'r 'ffeiriad 'r hwn a'i traethwys,
Dwg ef adref yn dy galon,
Ail fynega rhwng dy ddynion.[195]

[Do not let it remain in the church with the priest who proclaims it; bring it home in your heart, and repeat it among your people.]

The vicar constantly reminded his flock of the main obligation of the head of the household, primarily to promote discipline and Christian conduct:

Planna gyfraith Dduw'n wastadol
Y 'nghalonnau pawb o'th bobol;
Sonia amdanynt hwyr a bore
I mewn, i maes, wrth rodio ac eiste'.[196]

[Plant God's law constantly in the hearts of all your people; talk about it to them evening and morning, inside, outside, when walking and sitting.]

The bard's Puritan sentiments became abundantly clear when he advised that control and discipline were imperative in the well-governed household:

Bydd reolwr, bydd offeiriad,
Bydd gynghorwr, bydd yn ynad
Ar dy dŷ ac ar dy bobl,
I reoli pawb wrth reol.

Gwna di gyfraith gyfiawn, gymwys,
I reoli'th dŷ a'th eglwys;
Pâr i'th bobol yn ddiragrith
Fyw yn gymwys wrth y gyfraith.

---

[195] R. Rees (ed.), *Y Seren Foreu neu Ganwyll y Cymry* (Wrexham, 1897), II (59), p.20.
[196] N. Lloyd (ed.), *Cerddi'r Ficer*, p.101.

A'r fath drefen sy'n yr eglwys
Yn rheoli pawb yn gymwys
Ddyle fod yn nhŷ pob Cristion
I reoli'r tŷ a'r dynion.[197]

[Be a ruler, a priest, a counsellor and a magistrate over your house and people,
ruling them all according to rule.
Institute a just and proper order to govern your house and your church. Make your
people, without guile, to live strictly according to the law.
And that order which in the church governs all strictly should also be in the house
of every Christian, governing the household and the people.]

Doubtless he was the most forthright commentator on the 'evils' of
illiteracy, his comments being aimed exclusively at the gentry and their
relations with their dependants:

Mae'r cobleriaid a'u morwynion
A rhai gwaetha' 'mysg y Saeson,
Bob yr un a'r Bibl ganthynt,
Dydd a nos yn darllain ynddynt.

Pob merch tincer gyda'r Saeson
Feidir ddarllain llyfrau mawrion;
Ni ŵyr merched llawer sgwiar
Gyda ninne, ddarllain pader.

Gw'radwydd tost sydd i'r Brutaniaid
Fod mewn crefydd mor ddieithriaid
Ag na ŵyr y canfed ddarllain
Llyfyr Duw'n eu 'iaith eu hunain.[198]

[The cobblers and their maids and the worst among the English, each have a Bible
which they read day and night. Each tinker's daughter among the English is able
to read big books; with us the daughters of many an esquire cannot read as much
as the Lord's Prayer. It is a foul disgrace for the Britons to be such strangers to
religion that not a hundredth part of them can read the Book of God in their own
tongue.]

---

197 Ibid., pp.102, 107.
198 Ibid., p.64.

Rhys Prichard often emphasized the need to be able to read the scriptures:

> Darllain bennod o'r 'Sgrythurau
> I'th holl dylwyth, nos a borau;
> Pâr i bawb repeto' allont
> A byw'n ôl y wers a ddysgont.[199]

[Read a chapter of scripture to all your family, morning and evening; make them all repeat what they can and live according to the lesson they learn.]

In another context Rhisiart Cynwal pressed John Hanmer, bishop of St Asaph, born just over the border in Shropshire, to preach in Welsh.[200] It was he who encouraged Robert Llwyd, vicar of Chirk, to exercise his literary skills to advance the Protestant faith. Hanmer's dedicated service to promote piety and learning among his clergy and parishioners had probably impressed Robert Llwyd very much, and it is unfortunate that correspondence between the two some time before Hanmer's death concerning Llwyd's translation of *Llwybr Hyffordd yn cyfarwyddo yr anghyfarwydd i'r nefoedd* has not survived. Doubtless it would have highlighted some of the motives which moved Protestant clergy to promote the Church by preaching and publication.

The vast corpus of poetry in the period c.1540-1640 which depicts aspects of religious life, its vicissitudes and progress in times of dire social and economic conditions, has a fundamental role to play in any examination of society in early modern Wales, and deserves close attention. The poetry does not dwell on the demands of successive governments to use religious doctrine and practice to serve the needs of the state, nor does it have a political agenda to follow, but free-metre compositions do offer reflections on the attitudes of society at grass root level towards religious change. Likewise, the more formal strict-metre eulogies, restricted though their authors were to the rules of the bardic order, have much to contribute when addressing men of affairs involved in establishing public order with regard to the standards they were expected to respect and to practise. The defence of the social and political order invariably involved the

---

[199] Ibid., p.102.
[200] E. D. Jones, 'The Brogyntyn Welsh manuscripts', *NLWJ*, V, 1949-50, 29.

preservation of moral and spiritual values. Aristotelian though the virtues all appeared to be, with the emphasis principally on justice, magnanimity and goodness, they were enhanced and enriched by the introduction of the formative Christian values of charity, faith, humility and piety. Such qualities were regarded as the essence of the gentry's 'rule of life',[201] which became more evident in the first half of the sixteenth century and which revealed the contribution of poetry to measuring the depth of loyalties and affinities in an age of profound religious transformation.

---

[201] Kelso, pp.70-6.

CHAPTER IV

The Welsh Bishops, 1603-1640

The problems which beset the Elizabethan bishops of Wales continued to cause much anxiety for their early Stuart successors. Despite the challenges faced by the Elizabethan Settlement (1559) by the end of the queen's reign it had formally been imposed on the realm and the structure of the new Church enforced in the parishes.[1] However, early Stuart bishops who attended to the serious problems which beset its progress were made increasingly aware that the Protestant faith *per se* had still not made the desired impact on the mass of a monoglot Welsh population. The deep-seated consequences of pluralism and impropriation of tithes and properties seriously limited clerical efficiency. Even the Welsh Bible had its limitations in terms of appealing to the Welsh, a hindrance which was echoed in the writings of Hugh Lewis, vicar of Llanddeiniolen,[2] and Michael Roberts, to whom is attributed the preface to the first cheap Welsh Bible (*y Beibl Bach*) in 1630. Roberts's words point directly to the confined use made of the first and second editions of the Bible. Despite these achievements he saw the need for a portable Bible:

> Etto nid ydoedd na'r lles, nar arfer o air Duw mor gyhoedd ac mor gyffredin, ac y chwenychai lawer o Gristnogion bucheddol. Cans (ac yntef wedi ei brintio a'i rwymmo mewn Folum fawr o bris vchel) ni ellid cen hawsed na'i ddanfon ar led, na'i gywain i dai a dwylaw neilltuol, eithr yr oedd efe gan mwyaf yn hollawl yn perthyn i Liturgi a gwasanaeth yr Eglwys, fel yr oeddyd hefyd wedi ei amcanu ef yn bennaf ar y cyntaf.[3]

[Yet neither the good nor the custom of seeing God's word were made public and generally used as many pious Christians would desire. Because (and it printed and bound in a large volume for a high price) it was not easily taken abroad or to

---

1   G. Williams, *Renewal and Reformation: Wales c.1415-1640*, pp.330-1; idem, *Welsh Reformation Essays*, pp.26-7; idem 'Landlords in Wales: The Church', in J. Thirsk (ed.), *The Agrarian History of England and Wales*, IV, *1500-1640*, pp.388-9; A. H. Dodd, 'Wales and the Scottish succession, 1570-1605', *TCS*, 1937, 201-5.
2   *Rhagymadroddion*, pp.100-1.
3   Ibid., p.123. For further discussion of Roberts's career see R. G. Gruffydd, 'Michael Roberts o Fôn a Beibl Bach 1630', *TAAS*, 1989, 25-41.

abodes and particular hands, for it was chiefly attached wholly to the liturgy and the service of the Church, as it was also intended in the first place.]

Illiteracy also was a marked feature, and although the quality of parish clergy showed signs of improvement in the latter decades of the sixteenth century, the Church still needed further reform in personnel and administration. There were serious problems associated with recruitment and the secularisation of Church property, the continued threat of Roman Catholic recusancy and burning issues related to clerical poverty in each of the Welsh dioceses. Responsibilities to strengthen the Protestant Church's reputation lay primarily on the new body of prelates installed in office, some of them continuing their service from the latter years of Elizabeth's reign and having the experience of attempting to exert stricter control over diocesan government and administration.[4]

The survival of the Elizabethan Church depended as much on the strength of leadership provided and on a resident prelacy as it did on the role of the clerical hierarchy generally in the dioceses. One factor complimented the other, and although John Penry harshly censured episcopacy and recommended its total abolition, it still maintained its status in the first half of the seventeenth century. The position accorded to individual Welsh bishops could not have been maintained if they themselves had not addressed the major problems affecting creed, organisation and discipline. The Elizabethan Church bequeathed as many frustrating problems to their Stuart successors as it did a uniform institution strongly allied to the monarchy and its form of government. Some of these problems were revealed in the controversy between William Morgan at St Asaph and his former mentor Sir John Wynn of Gwydir.[5] Morgan's determination to protect the welfare of the Church at the expense of his own private interests says much about the nature of episcopal power on the eve of James I's accession to the English throne. He was convinced that God's protection would enable him to defend the integrity of the

---

4   F. Heal, *Of Prelates and Princes: A Study of the Economic and Social Position of the Tudor Episcopate* (1980); K. Fincham, *Prelate as Pastor: The Episcopate of James I* (Oxford, 1990); idem (ed.), *The Early Stuart Church, 1603-1642* (Macmillan, 1993), esp. 'Episcopal Government, 1603-1640', pp.71-92; F. Heal and R. O'Day (eds.), *Church and Society in England: Henry VIII to James I* (Basingstoke, 1977), esp. R. A., Houlbrooke, 'The Elizabethan Episcopate', pp.95-8.
5   *Letters of Bishops Morgan and Parry* (privately printed, 1905); J. G. Jones, 'Bishop William Morgan's Dispute with John Wynn of Gwydir in 1603-04', *JHSCW*, XXII, 1972, 49-78; idem, 'Bishop William Morgan—Defender of Church and Faith', *JWEH*, V, 1988, 21-30.

Church against those, like Wynn, set to undermine it. Morgan took a hard line on ecclesiastical properties, firmly resisting the ambitions of David Holland of Teirdan in Llaneilian-yn-Rhos over the tithes of the parish of Abergele,[6] and Sir John Wynn. '...I assure youe', he steadfastly declared during his dispute with the squire of Gwydir, *'in verbo sacerdotis* that I think in my hearte that I weare better robb by the hygh waye syde then do that which he requeasteth'.[7] In the diocesan synod in October 1601, according to the Book of First Fruits, he tightened regulations regarding taxation on benefices and emphasized the need for preaching and complying with the injunctions of the previous general synod.[8] Rectors and vicars were to preach in their parishes at least once in every three months and conduct services at matins and vespers on Sundays and Festivals and at other times. His defence for translating the scriptures was in line with his adopted policy which sought to promote preaching and attend to the spiritual needs of a monoglot peasantry. It is in that mood that he formally defended his task in translating the scriptures:

> Besides, to prefer unity to piety, expediency to religion, and a kind of external concord among men, to that heavenly peace which the Word of God impresses on men's souls, shows but little piety.[9]

Morgan's weakness at St Asaph was his increasing ill-health and the fact that he remained there for so short a time, a mere three years. Doubtless, as his mentor John Whitgift wrote about him, he was 'a man of integrity, gravity and great learning...the most sufficient man...both for his learning, government and honesty of life'.[10] Likewise Dr Gabriel Goodman, dean of Westminster and Morgan's friend, gave him equally warm praise on his coming to St Asaph in 1601.[11] Had he survived a few more years he might well have produced an earlier version of the 1620 Bible, given the fact that he had already completed his revision of the New Testament before moving to St Asaph and that Dr John Davies, later

---

6   J. G. Jones, 'Bishop William Morgan's Dispute', 51-2, 72; Browne Willis, *Survey of St Asaph* (London, 1721), 107; D. R. Thomas, *History of St Asaph*, I, p.226; P. Yorke, *The Royal Tribes of Wales* (Liverpool, 1887 ed.), pp.137-8, 140.

7   J. G. Jones, 'Bishop William Morgan's Dispute', 75.

8   D. R. Thomas, *History of St Asaph*, I, pp.101-2.

9   W. Hughes, *Life and Times of Bishop William Morgan* (1891), p.127; C. Davies (ed.), *Rhagymadroddion a Chyflwyniadau Lladin*, p.64.

10 HMC *Salisbury MSS* (Hatfield House), V (London, 1894), XIV, p.144.

11 Ibid., XIV, p.144.

rector of Mallwyd, had been his chaplain at Llandaff.[12] Morgan was a worthy preacher, 'the gateway and head of Faith's pure language' ('Porth a phen puriaith y Ffydd'), according to the poet Owain Gwynedd,[13] and a stalwart defender of the Church, whose aspirations were shared by the best of his contemporaries in the Welsh sees.

Other bishops, similarly motivated but not as passionately perhaps, were aware of the devastating effect external forces had on the Church, and were continually alert to the need to rectify the wrongs which it had suffered. In the four Welsh dioceses a total of nineteen bishops served between 1598 and 1642. There were five at Bangor, five at St David's, five at Llandaff and four at St Asaph. Of these, nine bishops were born in Wales although not all were necessarily of Welsh ancestry, and, of the nineteen, eleven served in one diocese only during their careers. All Welsh bishops obtained their first bishoprics in Wales and five only were translated elsewhere, namely Richard Milbourne (to Carlisle), William Laud (to Bath and Wells), Francis Godwin (to Hereford), George Carleton (to Chichester) and Theophilus Field (to Hereford). Needless to say, in each case they moved to more lucrative dioceses. Two bishops were translated to other Welsh sees, namely Theophilus Field (from Llandaff to St David's) and William Morgan (from Llandaff to St Asaph). The Scotsman, William Murray, was the only bishop to be appointed from outside England, from Kilfenora in Ireland to Llandaff. John Owen of St Asaph was the longest serving bishop (22 years), closely followed by Anthony Rudd (21 years), Richard Parry (19 years) and Henry Rowlands (18 years). William Roberts of Bangor was initially in the see for nine years (1637-46), was deprived of his see in 1646 and returned for five years at the Restoration (1660).[14] Two bishops, John Hanmer[15] and John Owen,[16] although having Welsh connections, were born outside Wales, the one at Selatyn in Salop and the other at Burton-Latimer in Northamptonshire, his father, a native of Llŷn, being rector there. Four of the bishops were,

---

12 *Rhagymadroddion a Chyflwyniadau Lladin*, p.127; Rh. F. Roberts, 'Y Dr John Davies o Fallwyd', *LlC*, III, 1952, 19-35 (esp. 278); R. Williams, *The Cambrian Journal* (1863), p.159.

13 R. G. Gruffydd, *The Translating of the Bible into the Welsh Tongue...*, p.64.

14 For lists of bishops in Welsh dioceses see F. M. Powicke and E. B. Fryde (eds.), *Handbook of British Chronology* (London, 1961), pp.275, 277-80.

15 *DNB*, VIII, pp.1178-9; Browne Willis, *Survey of St. Asaph*, pp.285-6.

16 D. R. Thomas, *History of the Diocese of St Asaph*, I, pp.; Browne Willis, *Survey of Bangor* (London, 1721), pp.24, 109, 323.

in varying degrees, associated with the Welsh cultural activity of their generation, namely Henry Rowlands, Lewis Bayly, William Morgan and Richard Parry. Of these, William Morgan doubtless was the most prominent as the translator of the scriptures into Welsh and the best represented among patrons of professional poets.

All Welsh bishops were acknowledged scholars and were for the most part resident. Despite their shortcomings most of them also attended to their diocesan duties, some being regular preachers. They observed canons 36 and 37 of the December 1604 canons announced by Archbishop Bancroft, whereby all candidates for ordination and licences to preach or serve cures were to subscribe to the Three Articles of 1583, to declare their loyalty to the crown, to use the Prayer Book and to accept the three orders of ministry and articles of religion. Although all of them, like their predecessors, were pluralists, they were well aware of the needs of the Church at a time when poverty, ignorance and Roman Catholic recusancy caused serious threats to its well being. During James I's reign six of them had had experience of chaplaincy, namely Bayly, Milbourne, Hanmer, Carleton, Field and William Laud. Of the five bishops appointed to Llandaff in this period Morgan Owen, a native of Myddfai in Carmarthenshire and allegedly a descendant of the famous 'Meddygon Myddfai', was the only one with Welsh connections. He was patronised perhaps by the earl of Pembroke, became Laud's chaplain and was a staunch supporter of his policies in the 1630s.[17]

Most Welsh bishops were actively engaged in exercising control over their dioceses. They tackled the problems relating to their sees, particularly the problems caused by Roman Catholic recusants, the constant threat from the laity and the difficulty of maintaining order and discipline among parochial clergy. Considering their means and the amount of time they spent in the Welsh dioceses, it is safe to say that the majority of Welsh bishops in the first half century of Stuart rule were reasonably efficient. If diligence is increased with residence then it is correct to assume that the Welsh bishops were commendable.

The first task was to strengthen the ministry. Elizabethan bishops had

---

[17]   DNB, XIV, pp.1326-7; W. P. Griffith, *Learning, Law and Religion*, p.305 (and n. 99); K. Fincham, *Prelate as Pastor*, pp. 305-6.

already stressed the need for an educated clergy and had indeed produced some remarkable for their scholarship, particularly Richard Davies, William Bleddyn, William Hughes and William Morgan. Owing to the need to promote the faith, bishops, as well as the clergy, gave much-needed assistance in strengthening the ministry and maintaining discipline. Bishop William Roberts of Bangor had less faith in his better quality clergy than others for he complained that 'all clergymen of hope and worth seek preferment elsewhere'.[18] He also expressed grave concern about the standards of the clergy and, being aware of the pressures imposed by Laud on the Church during his period at St David's, called for more preachers. Prospects were very poor, particularly in the remoter areas of the Welsh dioceses. Theophilus Field at St David's described himself as an impoverished clergyman for, in a letter to Endymion Porter, groom of the bedchamber, he complained of his poor health and destitution and of his need for 'means of recovery in that desolate place'. He found travelling to London to transact his business difficult, 'the ways at all times steep, craggy and Welshy tedious...deep and dangerous'.[19] In another communication to the duke of Buckingham he desired 'to be translated to another Bishoprick, either Ely or Wells',[20] and later considered Hereford to be more suitable, 'alledging his Poverty, his wife, and six children'.[21]

The Hampton Court Conference (1604), which was held primarily to discuss disputes between Puritans and Anglicans concerning ceremonial, aimed to advance the preaching of the gospel, and its decisions were reinforced by further directives in 1605 and 1610.[22] A proclamation issued in July 1604 emphasized royal authority in matters ecclesiastical and declared that conformity according to the discipline of the Church of England should be enforced. Archbishop Bancroft, a stern opponent of Puritans, demanded of the clergy an oath acknowledging that the book of Common Prayer was not contrary to the Word of God.[23] This led to a rift

---

18   Lambeth Palace MS. 943, p.285. Cited in B. Williams, 'The Welsh clergy' (published Open University Ph.D. dissertation, 1998), I, p.71.
19   *Cal. State Papers Dom.*, 1628-29, CL, no.110, p.84.
20   *Glamorgan County History*, IV, p.241.
21   B. Williams, 'The Welsh clergy', I, pp.129-30.
22   K. Fincham, *Prelate as Pastor*, p.291.
23   K. C. Fincham, 'Ramifications of the Hampton Court Conference in the dioceses, 1603-1609', *JEH*, XXXVI, 1985, 216-8; J. K. Larkin and P. L. Hughes (eds.), *Stuart Royal Proclamations*, I (Oxford, 1973), pp.87-90.

between the king and the Puritans and between 73 and 83 clergy were deprived of their livings at a critical juncture in church-state relations.[24] The bishops, who were eager to strengthen their position *vis-à-vis* the monarchy, were equally aware of the need to reform their own office as well as the clergy, and their reports, as Godwin's Injunctions in 1603 revealed, continually played on the inadequacies and impoverished status of their dioceses.[25] Richard Parry at St Asaph and Francis Godwin at Llandaff (though called 'a very great simoniac' by Browne Willis)[26] were amongst the most ardent to see reform within their respective dioceses and they were not backward in deploring the spiritual poverty of their clergy. Godwin, in 1603, in reply to Archbishop John Whitgift's request, admitted that he had only 55 preachers to serve 177 parishes and 15 chapels of ease.[27] In his injunctions, issued probably to lessen criticism of the Church on the eve of the Hampton Court Conference, he expressed his concern to defend his clergy:

> Whereas many outrages are daily committed against preachers and ministers of God's Word, not only in reproachfull and Contemptuous speeches, but in laying violent hands upon them.[28]

Church lands were also subject to attack, and he recorded that new incumbents should record details of glebe lands so as to prevent land from being 'dayly imbeziled' from the Church.[29] Indeed, the situation had become so serious in 1609 that Godwin was obliged to allow laymen to officiate at church services, and planned to support the ministry of six with the fines paid by recusants.[30] What became of the project is not clear, but it is evident that the bishop, pressurized by the growing number of

24   K. Fincham, *Prelate as Pastor*, pp.212-3.
25   R. G. Gruffydd, 'Bishop Francis Godwin's injunctions for the diocese of Llandaff, 1603', *JHSCW*, IV, 1954, 19.
26   *DNB*, VIII, p.57; Browne Willis, *Survey of the Cathedrals of York, Durham, Carlisle...Hereford...* etc. (London, 1727), p.525; B. Williams, 'The Welsh Clergy', I, p.57.
27   Ibid.; K. C. Fincham (ed.), *Visitation Articles and Injunctions of the early Stuart Church* (Boydell Press, 1998), I, p.2.
28   *Visitation Articles*, loc. cit.
29   *Visitation Articles*, I, p.2. Griffith Lewis, dean of Gloucester, a native of St Asaph diocese, had hoped to become bishop on William Hughes's death (1600) but failed; he then hoped to be appointed bishop of Llandaff and drew attention to that diocese's poverty in 1600: HMC *Salisbury MSS*, XI, pp.20-1. See also XVI, p.227; *Cal. State Papers Dom., 1603-1610*, XLVIII, no.121, p.552.
30   *Cal. State Papers Dom., 1603-1610*, XLVIII, no.121, p.552.

recusants in Monmouthshire, considered that extreme measures were necessary at the time to combat the situation.

The Puritan preacher Walter Stephens, rector of Bishop's Castle, Shropshire from 1580 onwards, complained of the lack of a preaching ministry in Wales and the border. 'When he preached in his younger days', it was said, 'for a great space, there was never a preacher between him and the sea, one way, and none near him the other, but one in Shrewsbury.'[31] This general malaise led Richard Parry in 1611 to desire better conditions in St Asaph while Godwin formulated injunctions at the beginning of his time at Llandaff in 1603. He was aware of 'certaine notorious abuses...not reformable by ordinary courses...'[32] and was thereby obliged to take stringent measures to reform diocesan administration. The condition of cathedral churches, which were after all the centres of episcopal authority, caused grave concern, and Francis Godwin made it a matter of inquiry in his injunctions:

> Whereas the cathedrall church of this diocese, not having to the value of 10*l*...is now fallen into such decay, as 500 markes will not repaire the same, so that it must needs in short time fall to the ground without some extraordinary reliefe.[33]

He exhorted the clergy to remind parishioners, when making their wills, 'to put them in minde of the necessity of the said church' and 'to contribute towards the sustentation of this house', the names of such benefactors to be recorded in a register compiled for that purpose.[34]

Similarly at Bangor the eccentric and reputably 'very unworthy' Lewis Bayly was deeply concerned about the condition of his clergy and the cathedral church. His early career had been supported by the Jones family of Abermarlais, which secured for him the living of Shipston-on-Stour (1597), and the earl of Pembroke obtained Evesham (1601), for him, and it was there that he was appointed headmaster of the school. His sinecures

---

31 R. G, Gruffydd, 'In that Gentile Country...': the Beginnings of Puritan Nonconformity in Wales (Bridgend, 1975), p.7. idem, 'Bishop Godwin's injunctions', 17; Visitation Articles, I, p.1; E. J. Newell, Llandaff (London, 1902), p.155.
32 Cal. State Papers Dom., 1611-1618, LXI, no.10, p.2.
33 Visitation Articles, I, p.2.
34 Ibid.

were many and he was appointed Treasurer of St. Paul's (1610-16).[35] His coming to Bangor in 1616 made him tread very warily at first, but soon, irritated by circumstances, he began to show his true colours. In 1630 he admitted how impoverished his clergy were. 'I was sometimes compelled', he declared, 'to make some fewe ministers that were butt countrey schollers to serve poore Welshe chappells where the stipend is not sufficient to maintain a university man'.[36] His visitation in 1626 revealed some interesting facts about conditions in the diocese, particularly failure on the part of some clergy to hold services, negligence in relieving the poor, in administering the sacrament at marriages and in visiting the sick and needy in their parishes. Three parishes – Penmon, Llangwyllog and Dolwyddelan – had not had any preacher for a year and fewer sermons had been delivered than expected in several other churches.[37] Bayly clearly regarded these deficiencies to be more worthy of attention than the persistent abuses of non-residence, simony and pluralism. In 1638 William Roberts at Bangor was concerned about two 'considerable things': first that livings had been let for lives by each of his predecessors 'to the very mill that grinds his corn';[38] second, that owing to the general poverty of the diocese all 'clergymen of hopes and worth seek preferment elsewhere [and]…some weak scholars must be ordained, or else some cures must be left altogether unsupplied.'[39] Between 1617 and 1625 only 45% of ordinands in Bangor were graduates.[40] Theophilus Field, after he had moved to Hereford in 1635, bemoaned the condition of his previous diocese of St David's, reporting 'that there are few ministers in those poor and remote places that are able to preach and instruct the people.' [41] He, like other bishops in their visitation articles, inquired concerning the conduct of services in parish churches; to what extent did the clergy preach and catechise, or read homilies and pray regularly on Sundays and holy days and at other times?

---

35 Browne Willis, *Survey of Bangor*, pp.110-11; *Fasti Ecclesiae Anglicanae*, ed. J. Le Neve (London, 1854), I, p.592; II, pp.346, 357.
36 K. Fincham, *Prelate as Pastor*, pp.181-2; *Cal. State Papers Dom., 1611-1618*, XCIV, no.38, p.500.
37 *AC*, (3rd Series), IX, 1863, .283-5; A. I. Pryce, *The Diocese of Bangor during Three Centuries* (Cardiff, 1929), xvi-xvii.
38 Lambeth Palace MS. 943, p.285. Cited in Williams, 'The Welsh clergy', I, p.71.
39 Ibid.
40 K. Fincham, *Prelate as Pastor*, pp.182-3.
41 W. Laud, *Works*, V (ii), pp.335-6; J. M. Jones, 'Walter Cradoc a'i gyfoeswyr', *Y Cofiadur*, XV, 1938, 30.

Moreover, in a letter to Sir John Wynn in 1626 Lewis Bayly lamented the poor condition of the church of Bangor; 'the rainly weather, for want of a better mantle, weepeth' so much so, he maintained further, that 'it makes my heart bleed to see her.'[42] He was particularly eager to repair the steeple and the roof over the chancel and he exhorted Sir John Wynn to follow the example of his ancestors who had been charitable in supporting the church and to give what resources he had at his disposal to renovate it. He added a caution that Roman Catholics might 'revile' it by deploring the lack of attention given the edifice. He had communicated with other major gentry seeking the same support with the assurance that their illustrious reputation would be perpetuated:

> ...remember the pietie of yo'r worthie ancestors who did not only help to repaire their cathedrall church in their lives, but also at their blessed deathes could bestowe some part of what god gave them to the repaire of their mother church of Bangor w'ch godlie devotion in this frozen age is growne so small that the most legacie of that kinde amountes not to above a groate. And of all the goodlie landes wherw'th this eminent church was endowed, there is not now one close of land nor pennie of rent lefte for the repa'con of the fabricke thereof.[43]

Doubtless, despite his alleged incompetence, Bayly, in this respect, was among the most honest of prelates in his day, for his plea showed a strong desire to improve spiritual standards by restoring the cathedral to a state befitting the house of God. He revealed a mild Puritanism and tried to apply his piety to the needs of the impoverished:

> But if thou meetest one that asketh an Almes for Jesus sake and knowest him not to be unworthy, deny him not; for it is better to give unto ten counterfeits than to suffer Christ to goe in one poore Saint, unrelieved.[44]

Whether he endeavoured to emulate his predecessor Henry Rowlands in this respect, it is hard to tell but doubtless Rowlands's attitude was echoed by Bayly's sentiments later:

---

[42] NLW MS. 9061E. 1440.
[43] Ibid, 1445.
[44] *The Practice of Piety*, p.438; A. H. Dodd, 'Bishop Lewes Bayly, c.1575-1631', *TCHS*, XXVIII, 1967, 17-18.

What care I took for this temple whiles I was Bishop, and in what estate I found it, others do know, and though I leave it in far better estate than it was, yet God he knows it had need to be daily looked into having no other maintenance but the bishop's benevolence and his clergy from time to time.[45]

On another occasion his defence of the Church typified the stand made by William Morgan:

Neither horse nor mare shall choke me to betraye the church; I have vowed the fidelitye of my services that way to the church against kinrede fleshe and bloode.[46]

Rowlands had role models to follow in Nicholas Robinson and Richard Vaughan and built upon their work in propagating the Protestant faith. His successor Bayly, however, did not follow his example and had obviously allowed the cathedral to fall into disrepair, and it is in his latter years that he sought to make amends for that. The situation was not good elsewhere either, and early seventeenth-century bishops, such as William Morgan and Henry Rowlands, also attended to the task of renovation. Indeed, many of the Church's problems had been inherited from previous generations, not least the corrupt practices which tainted clergy high and low as well as powerful laity.

The income of Welsh bishops left much to be desired. They came from the lower middle ranks in the social order and, excepting Anthony Rudd, bishop of St David's, and Henry Rowlands, bishop of Bangor, they had little private means. Rudd was a thrifty prelate and managed to build for himself 'a hansom seat' for his family at Llangathen, thus laying the foundations of a small gentry family of some repute in Carmarthenshire.[47] Conversely, William Morgan was described on his death as 'a poor man',[48] and George Carleton, of a Northumberland Puritan family, who served in the prince of Wales's household and who distinguished himself

---

[45] J. Morgan, *Coffadwriaeth am y Gwir Barchedig Henry Rowlands, D.D., Arglwydd Esgob Bangor* (Bangor, 1910).p.58.

[46] NLW MS. 9052E.265.

[47] E. Yardley (ed.), *Menevia Sacra, AC Supplement 1927*, 103-4; Browne Willis, *Survey of St David's*, pp.124-5.

[48] J. Wynn, *History of the Gwydir Family and Memoirs*, p.63.

at the Synod of Dort (1618) as a defender of the episcopal system, confirmed that his elevation to the 'poor bishopric' of Llandaff by the king and prince of Wales, had pleased him because 'the favours of the princes are not to be rejected'. He did not consider, however, that he could do much good 'from ignorance of the language and opposition of great persons who hate the truth'.[49] Godwin ordered the clergy of Llandaff to repair their churches because he had heard complaints that 'many churches & chauncells lye vnrepaired'.[50]

A survey of higher clergy in Welsh dioceses in this period reveals how prepared they were to use the Church and take advantage of what resources it had to enrich themselves. At Bangor, of the fifty prebendaries appointed between 1560 and 1642, five became deans of Bangor and subsequently bishops, namely Hugh Bellot, Henry Rowlands, Edmund Griffith, Richard Parry and Griffith Williams (appointed bishop of Ossory in Ireland in 1641).[51] At Llandaff the inexperienced George Carleton, who was not an active preacher, and of whom more is known at Chichester (where he was translated) than at St David's, was appointed prebendary of St Dubricius in 1618.[52] Morgan Owen became rector of Port Eynon[53] and, in the diocese of Bangor, Henry Rowlands obtained the living of Trefdraeth *in commendam* (1601-06).[54] William Murray became rector of Shirenewton (1634-40) and vicar of Caerwent (1639-40)[55] and Morgan Owen was appointed rector of Shirenewton (1640).[56] Llandaff was the only diocese where distribution of patronage was equally divided between the bishop and the laity. In the other three dioceses the bishop had almost a monopoly of patronage.

The impoverished state of the Church was reflected in the failure of the bishops to maintain a standard of hospitality worthy of a prelate. On coming to Llandaff in 1595 William Morgan declared that the 'revenue is very small and the charge very great' and was doubtless already aware of

---

49   R. G. Gruffydd, 'Bishop Francis Godwin's injunctions', 19.
50   Ibid.
51   Griffith Williams, a native of Trefan near Caernarfon, served as dean of Bangor (1634-72); J. Wynn, *History of the Gwydir Family and Memoirs*, p.73; Williams, 'The Welsh clergy', II, p.13.
52   B. Williams, 'The Welsh clergy', II, p.24.
53   Ibid., p.255.
54   Ibid., p.143.
55   Ibid., pp.176, 182.
56   Ibid., p.182.

the poor condition of the cathedral church.[57] In 1576 the antiquary Rhys ap Meurig of Y Cotrel, in the vale of Glamorgan, took a dismal view of the situation:

> ...but now it [i.e. the city of Llandaff] is in ruin, which the rather came to pass...by the absence of the bishops dwelling at Mathern, and the canons or prebendaries sometime having fair houses and dwelling there, became non-resident and their houses almost in utter decay.[58]

Whatever reforms William Bleddyn tried to introduce in the following decades, little in fact was achieved for Godwin, who followed Morgan in 1601, maintained that the fabric of the cathedral 'had fallen into such decay...so that it must needs in short time fall to the ground without some extraordinary relief'.[59] Godwin was a scholar of considerable repute, the author of *Catalogue of the Bishops of England* (1601) and various other original and antiquarian works.[60] Anthony Rudd, referring to the bishop's residences in the diocese of St David's, declared that they were 'so ruinated and decayed for want of reparation' that they were unfit for any man, especially a bishop, to reside in and keep hospitality. These buildings were the bishop's house at St David's, the college at Brecon, the castle at Llawhaden and the palace at Abergwili.[61] In a case brought before the consistory court in 1615 Bishop Milbourne sought to make Rudd's executors responsible for renovating the buildings to his satisfaction.[62] Marmaduke Middleton, who was deprived of his see in 1590, was blamed by the respondents in the case because he had left his residences 'and dwelt in or about London, or some other place in England or out of the said Bishopric of St David's'.[63] It was stated that the see's poverty did not justify the maintenance of all these residences, the bishopric not being valued at more than £400 a year and the cost of living had increased considerably.[64] It was further declared that Rudd had done what he could to make Abergwili a fit place in which to reside, having spent £666 13s. 4d. on it during his time at St David's.[65] Added expenditure was used to

---

57   HMC, *Salisbury MSS.*, V (London, 1894), pp.290-1.
58   Rice Merrick, *Morganiae Archaiographia*, ed. B. Ll. James (Cardiff, 1983), p.94.
59   R. G. Gruffydd, 'Bishop Francis Godwin's injunctions', 19.
60   W. M. Merchant, 'Bishop Francis Godwin, historian and novelist', *JHSCW*, V, 1955, 45-51.
61   K. Fincham, *Prelate as Pastor*, p.52; W. T. Morgan, 'The cases concerning dilapidations to episcopal property in the diocese of St David's', *NLWJ*, VII, 1951-2, 149-50.
62   W. T. Morgan. loc. cit.
63   Ibid.
64   Ibid.

improve the other buildings. Consequently this burden, as well as episcopal taxations, meant that his income was seriously reduced, which sorely affected his ability to offer hospitality. Successive archbishops placed great emphasis on the need to maintain hospitality and, in Thomas Davies's case at St Asaph in 1561, Matthew Parker, according to John Strype, allowed him to keep preferments *in commendam* for 'the better keeping up of the post of Bishop…[so] that Hospitality and the Credit and esteem of the clergy should [not] be lost'.[66] Sir John Wynn regarded Henry Rowlands 'in housekeeping and hospitality, both to rich and poor, the greatest that has been in our time'.[67] His social connections in Llŷn and alliance with the Wynns accounted for his attendance at the feast at Gwydir to celebrate the marriage of Wynn's daughter Elizabeth to John Bodfel of Llŷn in September 1608.[68] By virtue of his office Rowlands was also a justice of the peace but, as he admitted (according to Sir John Wynn), got no joy out of it because he wished to devote his time to episcopal duties:

> And though he was in the commission of the peace continually and in other commissions that came into the country, yet he would put them off as much as in him lay, having no will to deal but in his own element.[69]

Rowlands's kinsman Richard Vaughan, bishop of Bangor before he moved to Chester in 1597, was also described as 'a worthy housekeeper and a liberal minded man'.[70] In an ode of praise to William Morgan, Rhys Cain included a concise reference to his hospitality at St Asaph:

> D'aur a renni drwy'r ynys,
> D'arian, dy wledd, draw'n dy lys.[71]

[Your gold you share throughout the island; your silver and your feast, are to be had in your court yonder.]

---

65   Ibid.
66   J. Strype, *The Life and Acts of Matthew Parker* (London, 1711), pp.147-8.
67   *History of the Gwydir Family and Memoirs*, ed. J. G. Jones (Llandysul, 1990), p.59.
68   NLW MS.9053E.484.
69   J. Wynn, *History of the Gwydir Family and Memoirs*, p.59.
70   Ibid., p.60
71   R. G. Gruffydd, *The Translating of the Bible into the Welsh Tongue…*, p.69

A survey of the contribution of bishops to the promotion of Protestantism in the early seventeenth century reveals that they devoted themselves as diligently as they could to their tasks. Episcopal negligence seemed not to have been a marked feature in the early Stuart Church although Lewis Bayly, more than any other colleague of his, was accused of committing several misdemeanours. Archbishop Abbot did not support him; for he leaned towards Puritans and probably had another candidate in mind.[72] It was the duke of Buckingham who sponsored his elevation to Bangor, for which favour, it was rumoured, Bayly paid him £600.[73] As a pastor he had weaknesses, although he himself put up a stern, if somewhat fallacious, defence. He rejected canon 36 of those drawn up by Archbishop Bancroft in 1604 to impose uniformity, which ordered that subscription be made during ordination.[74] In succession Bayly quarrelled with his dean, Edmund Griffith, the Wynns of Gwydir and the Griffith family of Cefnamwlch, of which the dean was a member. The conflict with the dean led to a suit in 1622 in the court of Chancery concerning a dispute over payments of £100 made to maintain four scholars or choristers in Bangor cathedral.[75] A suit in Star Chamber in 1626, this time against Griffith and his supporters, resulted in Bayly being successful, to his great relief.[76]

In the 1620 Caernarfonshire county election he ardently supported the Wynns of Gwydir against the Cefnamwlch faction whom he regarded as 'baboons' who spent 'no toil to credit their own'.[77] Complaints were voiced against him in the parliaments of the 1620s and 1630 when he was accused of a variety of offences including extortion, nepotism, slander and other more lurid offences which earned him the nickname 'bishop of Bangoore'![78] He blamed his chaplains for conducting improper ordinations.[79] In 1623 a curate, Thomas Edwards, was reported more than

---

72 N. E. McClure (ed.), *Letters of John Chamberlain* (Philadelphia, 1939), II, p.29; *Clenennau Letters and Papers*, no.326; A. H. Dodd, 'Bishop Lewes Bayly c.1575-1631, *TCHS*, XXVIII, 1967, 19-20. See *Notes and Queries: A Medium of Intercommunication for Literary Men, General Readers etc.*, 5th Ser., vol. V, January-June, 1876, p.47.
73 NLW MS. 9057E.999; K. Fincham, *Prelate as Pastor*, pp.23-4.
74 C. Cross, *Church and People, 1450-1660: The Triumph of the Laity in the English Church* (London, 1987 ed.), p.164; R. Ashton, *Reformation and Revolution 1558-1660* (London, 1985), pp.213-4.
75 NLW MSS. 9057E.934, 9058E.1040.
76 NLW MSS. 9060E.1410, 1414-7, 1420, 1425.
77 NLW MS. 9060E.1331.
78 NLW MS. 9061E.1415; K. Fincham, *Prelate as Pastor*, pp.32, 81-2.
79 *Cal. State Papers Dom., 1629-1630*, CLXIV, no. 23, p.230; K Fincham, *Prelate as Pastor*, p.221.

once for failing to read the service properly, brawling with parishioners, haunting alehouses, neglecting the homilies and preaching only three times in the previous year.[80] His personal ingenuity, as well as his contacts with some families of repute, enabled him to endure the opposition, particularly from the Llŷn political faction based at Cefnamwlch, and he remained in his see until his death in 1631. Bayly declared that he had spent £600 in repairing the cathedral, had 'planted grave and learned preachers over all my diocese, three or foure for one preachinge minister I found there', had allowed reputable priests who conformed only to preach, had confirmed laity during visitations and had delegated the examination of ordinands to his chaplains. He alleged that he catechized regularly, preached every Sunday, for which he was well known, kept hospitality above his means and governed his see well.[81]

When the early Stuart Welsh episcopacy is considered it appears that honest attempts were made to strengthen their ministry, maintain hospitality, improve educational standards, promote preaching, stifle Roman Catholic recusancy and foster close contacts with the Welsh and broader cultural worlds. Theophilus Field petitioned Charles I requesting the grant of temporalities from his previous diocese 'in regard the revenues of the...bishoprick are small'. He sought 'better supportacon of hospitalitie and other incident charges', which enabled him to hold 'some spirituall livings not exceeding 100 *li p. annum* on the fruits'.[82] Devotion to duty, however, did not necessarily imply complete success in achieving all their aims. Attention has already been drawn to the stringent material constraints placed upon them but attempts were made to manifest their native loyalties. This was expected of bishops in small as well as large dioceses, and in Wales a more intimate atmosphere was created in which a warm reception was given to litterateurs and to professional bards on their itinerancies. Such benevolence arose from the bishop's role as benign householder and literary mentor.[83] The most famous in this context was William Morgan to whom a total of fifteen odes in strict-metres were composed during his career as priest and bishop, most of them

---

[80]   Ibid., pp.273-4l "Llanllyfni Papers', *AC* (3rd series), IX, 1863, 283-4.
[81]   K. Fincham, *Prelate as Pastor*, pp.195, 273.
[82]   *Cal. State Papers Dom. 1627-1628*, LXXIV, no.42, p.302.
[83]   R. A. Houlbrooke, 'The Elizabethan episcopate' in F. Heal and R. O'Day (eds.), *Church and Society in England*, pp. 55-8; F. Heal, *Of Prelates and Princes: A Study of the economic and Social Position of the Tudor Episcopate* (Cambridge, 1980), pp.6-8, 76-8, 83-5.

celebrating his achievement in translating the scriptures into Welsh.[84] Among other Welsh bishops, Henry Rowlands, Richard Parry, John Hanmer and John Owen were patrons of prominent bards such as Huw Llŷn, Sir Huw Roberts Llên, Huw Pennant, Elis ap Siôn ap Morus, Huw Machno and Rhisiart Cynwal.[85] These bishops followed the same course as their predecessors, particularly Richard Davies, Thomas Davies and William Hughes. It is an interesting feature that most bardic patrons among bishops came from the two north Wales dioceses where the native traditions still remained strong in the early decades of the seventeenth century. The southern bishops, excepting Morgan, were non-Welsh and did not share in this cultural activity and, with the exception of Richard Davies and William Bleddyn, the situation was similar in Elizabethan days.

According to existing sources the most beneficent bishop was Henry Rowlands, a native of Mellteyrn in Llŷn, who climbed up the ecclesiastical ladder quite adeptly. Doubtless he was the best that the early Stuart church had to offer, and contemporary opinion regarded him as 'a good and provident governor of his church and diocese'.[86] He was regarded by one of his successors, Humphrey Humphreys, as a good preacher, 'a most excellent good man, very charitable and conscientious, and much more careful of his see and successors than any that ever sat there'.[87] His almshouses at Bangor, his school founded at Botwnnog and his constant support of a learned ministry made Rowlands a respected prelate among his clergy for he carefully distributed his patronage to the best clerics he could find, some of them serving for a considerable period in their living.[88] The poet Huw Pennant accorded him the highest accolade that any of his bardic *confrères* could offer:

> Di gefaist ddwy rodd gyfa,
> Gras a ffortiwn fel dyn da.
> Uchelfron ffynnon y ffydd –

84 R. G. Gruffydd, *The Translating of the Bible into the Welsh Tongue*, pp.31-83 (Welsh section)
85 NLW Mostyn MS.145,487; Llanstephan MS.125,560; Add. MS.16129,17; MS.841,5; Cardiff MS.84,493; UCNW Bangor Mostyn MS.9,104r-104v.
86 *History of the Gwydir Family and Memoirs*, p.59.
87 A. Wood, *Athenae Oxonienses*, ed. P. Bliss (1813-20), II, p.856; A. H. Dodd, *A History of Caernarvonshire, 1284-1900* (Denbigh, 1968), pp.85-6.
88 J. G. Jones, 'Henry Rowlands, Bishop of Bangor, 1598-1616', *JHSCW*, XXVI, 1977-8, 34-45.

Duw doniodd Dad enaid y gwledydd;
Enaid Llŷn ag Eifionydd
O ryw a gwaed rowiog Nydd...[89]

[You obtained two full gifts, grace and fortune as a good man. Highest well of the faith, God endowed the Father of the nation's soul; the soul of Llŷn and Eifionydd of the race and blood of genial Nudd.]

Among long-serving clergy, of the kind that Henry Rowlands considered worthy to promote the faith in the diocese of Bangor, were Edmwnd Prys, rector of Ffestiniog and Maentwrog (1572-1623), later archdeacon of Merioneth,[90] Griffith Williams of Llanaber (1569-1628)[91] and Edward Jones of Dwygyfylchi (1574-1632).[92]

It is evident that episcopal lifestyle in Wales was far less sumptuous than in England, but their relations with the clergy were generally satisfactory, due in part to the fact that patronage was mostly in the hands of bishops who were resident. Efforts were made to ease the burdens of the lower clergy with a view to safeguarding their livings. Henry Rowlands and Richard Parry did their best to prevent the granting of presentative benefices which was a growing concern. Parry was particularly anxious about the condition of St Asaph diocese in which, in 1604, there were only 41 preachers in a total of 121 parishes. His letter to Robert Cecil in 1611 related the sad condition of his clergy and deplored the extent of impropriations, admitting that the diocese was unable to support a powerful preaching ministry because stipends were inadequate to maintain a learned and dedicated clergy.[93] The value of his bishopric was £187,[94] the archdeaconry of St Asaph being better endowed. To obtain a reasonable income he possessed several benefices, including the archdeaconry, and because the livings of Welsh bishops had not kept pace

---

89 NLW Add. MS 16129,17.
90 B. Williams, 'The Welsh clergy', II, p.130; A. O Evans, 'Edmund Prys, archdeacon of Merioneth, priest, preacher, poet', TCS, 1922-3 pp.112-68
91 B. Williams, 'The Welsh clergy', II, p.130.
92 Ibid., p.117.
93 Cal. State Papers Dom., 1611-1618, LXI, no.10, p..2; J. G. Jones, 'Richard Parry, Bishop of St. Asaph: some aspects of his career', BBCS, XXVI (ii), 1975, 178; G. D. Owen, Wales in the Reign of James I (London,1988), p.93.
94 D.R.Thomas, History of St Asaph, I, 87-9; J. E. C. Hill, Economic Problems of the Church from Archbishop Whitgift and the Long Parliament (London, 1956), p.26.

with the rise in prices Parry found it necessary to lease episcopal lands to powerful lay proprietors.[95] He also drew Cecil's attention to the fact that of the 104 incumbents in the diocese, 57 of them were vicars and 4 vicars choral. To ease the situation he suggested that 28 vicarages could be joined with neighbouring ones. If that took place and if suitable candidates could be found then the diocese, he considered, would benefit by £1,000. Richard Parry endeavoured to maintain the Church's hold on the rectory of Llanuwchllyn and prevent the vicarage of Henllan from being annexed to its rectory. Installing a resident preaching ministry to replace the inadequate curate there, who lacked 'expository skills', would serve to counteract the influence of recusants. Moreover, in a petition to Bancroft in 1609 he deplored the 'ungodly manner of ye carriage of that sacrilegeous attempt to carry away a benefice from the church' and he expressed concern about the living standards of his clergy. 'If againe the consent of byshop deane and chapter may lawfullie consolidate these unto impropriate rectories', he declared, 'I have little hope but that w'thin short time manie resident and painefull vicars shalbe turned to gaddinge and beggerlie curates'.[96] In 1609, Francis Godwin admitted that he had been forced to appoint laymen to several cures 'as a minister will not accept thereof, as not being able to live by it'.[97] The poverty of livings was an underlying problem and it was obvious that glebe terriers were safeguards against lay encroachment. According to Robert Llwyd, vicar of Chirk, in his preface to his translation of Arthur Dent's *The Plaine Man's Pathway to Heaven* (*Llwybr hyffordd yn cyfarwyddo yr anghyfarwydd i'r nefoedd…*) in 1630, a devotional and argumentative work, dedicated to Bishop Owen of St Asaph, he dwells on these reputedly amicable relationships:

> …chwi a gewch weled yno lawer o'ch tan-fugeiliaid yn trin ac yn areilio eu praidd yn ofalus, yn daclus, yn drwyadl…Ac eraill yn rhagorol eu dysg a'u dawn yn dwyn i adeiladaeth Eglwys Crist roddion gorchestol o bur athrawiaeth, ffraethineb ymadrodd, a hyfedr i guro i lawr bechod a drygioni…Eto, er hyn I gyd, y mae yn hyderus gennyf na bydd anghymeradwy gan eich Arglwyddiaeth chwi weled eraill, eiddilach eu

---

95 J. E. C. Hill, *Economic Problems of the Church*, Chap. VI, pp.132-67; Jones, 'Richard Parry, bishop of St Asaph', 179.

96 *Cal. State Papers Dom, 1603-1610*, XLV, no.2, XLVIII, no.III, pp.507, 551; 'Richard Parry: bishop of St Asaph, 178-9.

97 *Cal. State Papers Dom. 1603-1610*, XLVIII, no.121, p.552.

grym a gwannach eu nerth, yn dwyn pwys y dydd a'r gwres, yn ôl eu gallu, drwy wneuthur cydwybod o drin yn ofalus ac yn ffyddlon y talentau bychain a distadl yr ymddiriedwyd iddynt amdanynt.[98]

[...you shall see there many of your under-shepherds training and guiding their flocks carefully, orderly and thoroughly...And others excellent in learning and skill bringing to the structure of Christ's Church, masterly gifts of pure doctrine, eloquence of speech and expertise to beat down sin and iniquity...Yet again, despite this, I am confident that it will not be unacceptable to you to see others, less their power and weaker their strength, bearing the day's pressure and warmth, according to their ability, through being conscientious in treating carefully and faithfully the small humble talents which were entrusted to them.]

Such passages, however, need to be treated with some caution since it was Llwyd's intention to please his patron and he did so in the most expeditious manner. It was Hanmer, and not his successor Owen, who originally commissioned the work, and he, like Godwin, was an acquaintance of William Camden and in his religious duties an ardent reformer of his clergy, as Llwyd explains in the opening section of his dedication to Owen:

> ...er mwyn cael o'r gwerin-Gymry cartrefol, yn enwedig o'i esgobaeth ei hun, drwy ymarfer a darllain y llyfr hwn, fodd cymwys i chwanegu eu gwybodaeth yn y wir ffydd, ac i'w cymell i fyned rhagddynt yn gyfarwydd ac yn hyfedr ar hyd iawnffordd iechydwriaeth.[99]

[...in order that the homely Welsh peasant folk, especially in his own diocese, by being used to reading this book, can in an appropriate way add to their knowledge of the true faith, and to induce them to go forward familiar and expert along the proper road of salvation.]

Such a motive identified Hanmer as a prelate who possessed philanthropic as well as pietistical tendencies. He held firm Calvinist views as his will of 30 November 1628 reveals, in which reference is made to 'the eternal glorie which [Jesus Christ] hath deerely purchased for all

---

98   H. Lewis (ed.), *Hen Gyflwyniadau* (Cardiff, 1948), p.16. See G. T. Clark, *Cartae et Alia Munimenta*, IV, 1215-1689 (Cardiff, 1893), pp. 555-6.
99   H. Lewis (ed.), *Hen Gyflwyniadau*, p.14.

the Elect children of God, of which number I assume myself one'.[100] His eagerness to see Dent's work translated into Welsh also emphasized his religious beliefs, the author of *The Plaine Man's Pathway to Heaven* being the ardent Puritan vicar of Shoebury in Essex[101] and although Llwyd's style was far too rhetorical his aim was to draw attention to the true vocation of bishops. Hanmer was eager to promote both Llwyd's career and the Puritan thought contained in his translation, and in his ode of

Portrait of John Hanmer, Bishop of St Asaph (1624-29)
NLW Carreglwyd Ms. 25

---

[100] PRO Prob. 11/156, sig. 83. I am indebted to Dr Vivienne Larminie, *New Dictionary of National Biography*, Oxford, for this reference.

[101] Llwyd also published a sermon entitled *Pregeth ynghylch Edifeirwch*, a translation of one of Dent's sermons.

praise to the bishop, Rhisiart Cynwal urged him to use his preaching power to evangelise throughout the whole of Wales:

Dod rannau a phynciau'r ffydd,
Dawn Duw lwyd, yn dy wledydd.
Cymro wyt, cymer rydyd
I bregethu i Gymru gyd.[102]

[Place the parts and points of the faith, the Holy God's gift, in your countries; You are a Welshman, take liberty to preach to the whole of Wales.]

John Owen also had similar intentions for he provided Welsh sermons in parish churches in the diocese on the first Sunday of the month, a venture that was funded by the revenues of parish tithes. His diocese harboured small pockets of Puritan activity in the 1630s and 1640s, particularly in the Wrexham area, and it was at Llanyblodwel, in Shropshire, that one of the earliest dissenting conventicles was set up in the diocese.[103] Owen also wished to publish a treatise on the Ten Commandments, and although he petitioned the king for permission to do so the work did not appear, probably because of the upheavals of the 1640s.[104] Owen was a prelate with good intentions. Griffith Williams thought highly of him, and in his dedication of *VII Golden Candlesticks holding the Seven greatest lights of Christian Religion* (1635) to him he expressed his joy in him as a man 'of true piety' who, in his opposition to Puritanism, would 'be an heavenly shining light and President unto all other circumstant and succeeding Bishops'.[105]

Early Welsh Stuart bishops should not necessarily be regarded as strong advocates of Puritanism in the Church but the literary pursuits of some among them do reveal a grave concern for the condition of the human soul and a deep spirituality. Lewis Bayly at Bangor, a staunch Protestant who opposed James I's *Book of Sports* (1618) and the Spanish marriage proposals (1621-3), is doubtless the most conspicuous among them

---

[102] NLW Brogyntyn MS.3,241; E. D. Jones, 'The Brogyntyn Welsh manuscripts', *NLWJ*, VI, 1949, 29, 41.
[103] *Cal. State Papers Dom., 1639-1640*, CCCCXXX, no.18, pp.7-8.
[104] Ibid., *1640-1641*, CCCCLXXIV, no.64, p.346.
[105] G. Williams, *VII: Golden Candlesticks holding the Seven greatest lights of Christian Religion* (London, 1635), Epistle Dedicatory [ii].

because of his *The Practice of Piety*. It has been described as his 'lasting memorial' which, next to the Bible and Book of Common Prayer, became the most popular religious manual of its day and was republished many times over in different languages, including Welsh, in subsequent generations. This work has also been called 'a classic of Calvinist piety' which reached its 25th edition in English in 1630.[106] It was intended primarily to assist the *paterfamilias* in conducting private and domestic devotions. The work had deeply influenced Sir John Wynn of Gwydir who, in 1620, approaching old age sent a copy of *The Practice of Piety* among other similar works to his puritanically-inclined son Maurice, an apprentice merchant in Hamburg, urging him to meditate upon it.[107] In his *Epistle Dedicatory* to Charles, prince of Wales, he divulged his reason for publishing the work:

> But without Piety there is no internall comfort be found in Conscience, nor externall peace to be looked for in the World, nor any internall happinesse to be hoped for in heaven.[108]

Puritan piety is the dominant feature, a factor which Rowland Vaughan, in the preface to his translation of the work made abundantly clear when addressing the heads of households, urging them to follow the moral instruction offered in the work:

> Am y llyfr hwn, a sail yr athrawiaeth sydd ynddo, nid yw ond golau canwyll yngoleuni yr Haul i mi ei glodfori.. Edrych a ddichon y llyfr hwn roddi meddyginiaeth i'th enaid...ac oni ddichon hynny beri i ti wellhau dy fuchedd, ni byddit ti ddim gwell *pe cyfodai vn oddiwrth y meirw* i'th athrawiaethu.[109]

[Concerning this book, and the foundation of the doctrine contained in it, it is but a candle light in the light of the Sun for me to praise it...See if this book can give medicine for our soul...and if that does not cause you to improve your conduct, you will be no better *if one rose from the dead* to instruct you.

---

106   A. H. Dodd, 'Bishop Lewes Bayly, c.1575-1631', *TCHS.*, XXVIII, 1967, 14-16, 36; B. Williams, 'The Welsh Clergy', I, p.67.
107   NLW MS. 9056E.896.
108   L. Bayly, *The Practice of Piety* (London, 1630), A5v.
109   *Rhagymadroddion*, pp.118, 120-1.

Vaughan hints at apathy that might have existed among some heads of families who cared little for the moral welfare of their dependants, hence his ardent plea to them to attend to such matters now that Bayly's work was available in their own language.

Later in his episcopacy Bayly became increasingly aware of the need to instruct his clergy in the Welsh language and to consider the means of doing so. Thus he, together with Sir John Wynn, promoted Dr John Davies's *Dictionarium Duplex*, the massive Latin-Welsh and Welsh-Latin dictionary published in 1632. He urged John Beale, of Aldersgate St., London, to print it for a good reason:

> ...a worthy and necessarie piece of work which all our Welsh preachers do much need...I do much desire to see it printed, and if you will undertake the worke I am perswaded it will sell very well for it is a worke that hath been long desired...[110]

Doubtless Bayly was conscious of the underlying shortcomings in the Church and of the inability of many clergymen to impart the tenets of the faith to monoglot parishioners. In 1624 Theophilus Field of St David's, a Londoner who had a Puritan background, published his *A Christian preparation to the Lord's Supper* and several occasional sermons, but what impact that had it is difficult to gauge. However, he was equally concerned that 'there [were] few ministers in thos poor and remote parts that [were] able to preach and instruct the people.'[111]

At St Asaph, Richard Parry was involved in the production of a much more imposing project, namely the first revised edition of Morgan's Bible in 1620. It is interesting that it was decided at the Hampton Court Conference (1604) that an authorized version of the scriptures should be published based on William Tyndale's and Miles Coverdale's translations of 1525 and 1535 respectively. This version appeared in 1611 but it does not appear that this decision had any effect on the work undertaken in Welsh some years later. It was not Parry but his brother-in-law, Dr John Davies, rector of Mallwyd, reputedly the greatest of late Renaissance

---

[110] Ca. MS 2.365; *Calendar of the Wynn of Gwydir Papers*, no.1542
[111] Yardley, *Menevia Sacra*, 108-9.

Welsh scholars, who carried out the work of revision.[112] Not that Parry had but little to do with the work itself; in fact, it was he presumably who dealt with the business side of the venture. He considered himself to be the main participant in executing this important task, and publicly declared it in his preface:

> ...necnon pio Reuerendorum praecessorum exemplo adductus, viz. Richardi Dauies, primo Asaphensis, postea Meneuensis Episcopi, qui axiliante Guilielmo Salesburio Nouum Testamentum; & Guilielmi Morgani Asaphensis nuper Episcopi, qui Sacra Biblia Sermone Br. in lucem edidit; ad illorum translationes, nouisimam praesertim, manus moui, atq, vbi opus videbatur, tanquam vetus aedificium, nouâ curâ instaurare caepi...similiter ego certe, quaedam cum praecessoris laude retinui, quaedam in Dei Nomine mutaui, atq; sic compegi, vt & hîc sit ἀμφιδοξουμενον παραδειγμα & dictu sit difficile, num vetus an noua, Morgani an mea, dicenda sit versio.[113]

[...and also, having been attracted by the godly example of my reverend predecessors – Richard Davies, Bishop of St Asaph to begin with, and then St David's, who brought the New Testament in the British language to light of day with William Salesbury assisting him; and William Morgan, former Bishop of St Asaph, who translated all of the Holy Scriptures into the British language — I turned my hand to their translations, especially the last, and where it appeared necessary, I undertook to repair the old edifice, as it were, with care anew...so precisely I have also, highly praising my predecessor, kept some things and, in God's name, have changed other things, and have bound all together in such a way that there is also a fair example which admits of various opinions, and that it is difficult to tell whether it should be considered that the old version that is found here, or a new one, is it Morgan's or is it mine.]

---

[112] R. G. Gruffydd, 'Richard Parry a John Davies', in G. Bowen (ed.), *Y Traddodiad Rhyddiaith* (Llandysul, 1970), pp.179-83; idem (ed.), *A Guide to Welsh Literature*, III, pp.171-3; R.F.Roberts, 'Y Dr. John Davies o Fallwyd', *LlC*, II, 1952, 19-35, 97-110; C. Davies, *John Davies o Fallwyd* (Caernarfon, 2001) pp.72-86; idem, *Latin Writers of the Renaissance* (Cardiff, 1981); idem, *Welsh Literature and the Classical Tradition* (Cardiff, 1995).

[113] *Y Bibl Cyssegrlan, sef yr Hen Destament a'r Newydd* (London, 1620), Preface, no page. Parry cites Plutarch, Theseus, 23. I wish to thank Mr Tom Dawkes for his assistance in interpreting this Greek phrase.

The presumption on his part may well have been a reflection on his character and possibly his zeal in promoting the use of the scriptures in the vernacular. Indeed, Michael Roberts in his preface to the new edition of the Bible in 1630, mentions only Richard Parry as the reviser[114] while both Rowland Vaughan, in his preface to his translation of Bayly's *The Practice of Piety* (1629)[115] and the cleric David Rowlands, in his foreword to his translation into Welsh of Christopher Sutton's *Disce Mori, Learne to Die* (1633), praised 'the worshipful litterateur' John Davies for accomplishing the task.[116] Doubtless Parry also was a good scholar and

Title-page of the Welsh Bible, 1620

---

114 *Rhagymadroddion*, pp.123.
115 Ibid., p.120.
116 Ibid., pp.132-3.

eager to see published a translation of the Psalms into Welsh for the use of parishioners.[117] The fifty Psalms translated by Edward Kyffin, entitled *Rhann o Psalmae Dafydd Brophwyd Ivv Canu ar ol y don arferedig yn Eglwys Loegr* were published posthumously in 1603 and the edition of metrical Psalms in Welsh by Wiliam Midleton of Llansannan, which also appeared in 1603, was considered unsuitable for use in parish churches.[118] It was through the intervention of the London-based printer Thomas Salisbury, originally of Clocaenog, who was eager to see a complete edition of the metrical Psalms in Welsh, that Parry met Sir John Wynn of Gwydir in 1610 to facilitate the work which was eventually completed by Edmwnd Prys, archdeacon of Merioneth, in 1621. It was probably Parry who included Prys's Psalms in the same binding as the new edition of the Book of Common Prayer in that year, edited by him and Dr John Davies.[119]

Owing to the personal problems experienced by bishops of Godwin's and Bayly's calibre in their dioceses urgent matters in the early seventeenth-century Welsh church were not dealt with as effectively as they should have been. The Church found it increasingly difficult to defend its position against growing opposition, particularly among recusants and Protestant separatists, but in the 1630s William Laud, pursuing his policy of 'thorough', introduced controversial reforms aimed at introducing high-church principles into the episcopal church,[120] which were ardently supported at Llandaff by bishop William Murray and his successor Morgan Owen. He emphasized the need for uniformity and conformity and his anti-Puritan policy was reinforced by a determination to increase ceremonial. The influence of Bishop Lancelot Andrewes's writings was extensive among Laudian bishops. He reflected Hooker's views and emphasized the need to preach sermons on worship as well as ritual

---

[117] 'Richard Parry a John Davies', pp.177-8, 182.

[118] 'Richard Parry: bishop of St Asaph', 187.

[119] NLW MS.9054E.543. See also 538; J. Ballinger, *The Bible in Wales* (Cardiff, 1906), p.23; 'Richard Parry: bishop of St Asaph', 187; D. R. Griffiths, 'Four centuries of the Welsh prayer book'. *TCS*, 1975, pp.163-5; G. Williams, 'Unity of religion or unity of language? Protestants, Catholics and the Welsh language, 1536-1660', in G. H. Jenkins (ed.), *The Welsh Language before the Industrial Revolution* (Cardiff, 1997), pp.218-21.

[120] I am indebted to Lloyd Bowen for some material contained in the following paragraphs. See his 'Wales in British politics, c.1603-42' (unpublished University of Wales Ph.D. dissertation, 1999), pp.377-408; P. Lake, 'The Laudian style: order, uniformity and the pursuit of the beauty of holiness in the 1630s', in *The Early Stuart Church*, pp.161-85. See also Yardley, *Menevia Sacra*, 105-8.

ceremonies, episcopacy, frequent communion, regular prayer and sacramental confession.[121] Laud's central belief was that the moveable communion table should be reverently placed and railed off at the east end of the Church. He wished to make church building revered by all, laying the main emphasis on the 'beauty of holiness'. He was convinced that 'the inward worship of the heart is the true service of God, and no service acceptable without it; but the external worship of God in His Church is the great witness to the world that our heart stands right in that service of God...Ceremonies are the hedges that fence the substance of religion from all the indignities which profaneness and sacrilege too commonly put upon it.'[122] His Arminian policy, which led him to emphasize ceremonial grandeur as the true way to approach God, wrongly aroused suspicions that he was a papal agent. In fact, he considered that a united church was the best defence against Rome, hence his stress on the dignity of the Church centred upon the Prayer Book. The authority of bishops, church courts and the clergy was to be fully restored and lay encroachments on church properties and lay control of tithes and clerical appointments restricted. In Laud's view, salvation could be achieved, not by constant preaching but by a priesthood administering the sacraments.

How successful, therefore, was Laud's policy in Wales? It can be argued that too great an emphasis has been placed on the growth of dissent in Wales and too little on the role of the Anglican church and on the impact of Laudianism which was more evident than historians have been prepared to accept. Having experienced a term of office as bishop of St David's, Laud had some knowledge of religious life in Wales and the need to reform it. The Church's problems can be traced to Elizabeth's reign when the Crown, despite its wish to defend it and its hierarchy, did little to prevent the laity from impoverishing it. Commissions of concealment enabled aggressive gentry and higher clergy to discover ecclesiastical possessions which they manipulated to their own use. They entered into leases of episcopal and capitular property, thus depriving bishops of the proceeds and other benefits which accrued from them. They amply provided for themselves and obtained substantial returns from high entry

---

121 *Prelate as Pastor*, pp.232-8, 279-88. For the influence that Andrewes's sermons had on Sir Owen Wyn, 3rd baronet of Gwydir, see NLW MS.9064E.1934, Add. MS. 469E.2249.
122 J. Bliss and W. Scott (eds.), *The Works of William Laud*, III (Oxford, 1853), pp.407-8.

fines while reducing expenditure to the minimum.[123]

Despite the Church's impoverished state Laud sought to maintain its integrity. He was aware that the office of bishop was under fire in Puritan circles but was equally determined to defend it:

> Our main concern is…that we are bishops…And a great trouble tis to them [the Puritans] that we maintain that our calling of bishops is *jure divino*, of divine right.[124]

The chapter of Llandaff in 1626 refused to renew the lease of the rectory of Eglwysilan and decided to convert 'the entire profits and annual rent…to the best use and most valuable advantage' of the Cathedral Church.[125] It also declined to accept rent from the earl of Worcester, and royal letters forbade leases from being granted for terms of lives. As in the past, bishops were given properties *in commendam* to supplement meagre incomes – John Owen at St Asaph in 1633 and Roger Mainwaring at St David's in 1637, for example – to strengthen the role of the Church 'if the authoritie of bishops bee not supported as it ought', as Charles I maintained.[126] In 1629 Charles I instructed all bishops not to negotiate leases for a term of lives but for 21 years instead, and they were prohibited from offering any leases in Laud's absence.[127] At Bangor, as noted above, 'everything was let for lives, down to the very mill that grinds his corn', a practice which caused the bishop, William Roberts, some concern in 1638.[128] This was part of the policy to restore diocesan revenues and Laud, following upon a policy embarked upon by Rowlands, Bayly and others, ensured that church buildings were repaired or rebuilt. Priority was given by John Owen to renovations at St Asaph and Wrexham, the latter causing some bad feeling between him and the parishioners. His predecessor, John Hanmer, had neglected it and 'that goodly fabric, the fairest within my diocese', in Owen's opinion, needed reparation and more financial help to restore it, half the parishioners refusing to yield a sum of £100 imposed on them from 'Llanelwy, among

---

123   G. Williams, 'Landlords in Wales: the church', pp.389-93.
124   W. Laud, *Works*, VI, pp.42-3.
125   NLW Llandaff Cathedral, Chapter Act Book, 4, p.106.
126   *Cal. State Papers Dom.*, 1637, CCCLXIII, no. 80, p.299.
127   NLW St David's Cathedral, Chapter Act Book, 4, 1621-1660, p.63; NLW Llandaff Chapter Act Book, 4, pp.126-8. Cited in Lloyd Bowen, pp.385-6.
128   W. Laud, *Works*, V, p.359.

the Welsh Alps'. Writing to the Court of Arches on 24 January 1635, he meant business:

> If the repairing thereof must be left to their courtesy or (if they had rather term it so) charity, surely it will be repaired (as may build castles) in the air of empty words and promises.[129]

The chapter at Llandaff in 1638 paid a local glazier to 'sufficiently glasse and afterwards keepe and maintayne for one whole yeare...all the windows...and all other places fitt for to be glased...of the whole Cathedrall'.[130] Laud's visitation articles of 1636 to Bangor, St Asaph and Llandaff inquired whether or not the cathedral churches were 'sufficiently repaired both in the body chauncels and all other iles and places belonging to the church?'[131] In his visitation articles of 1637, John Owen inquired about the interior arrangements of parish churches in his diocese:

> Is your communion table fairely railed about with joyners worke, your chancell and church paved, all seats within the seven foot within your chancell removed, the seats in the church made uniforme, and all other things performed according to an order delivered to the churchwardens of your parish in the metropoliticall visitation...of William (Laud).[132]

These articles were laid out in orderly fashion under different headings including public prayers and administration of the sacraments and church ornaments and other possessions.

In June 1634 the chapter of Llandaff gave 20 marks towards the repair of St Paul's church in London.[133] Laud, when bishop of St David's, built a chapel at Abergwili and adorned it as a symbol of his 'ecclesiological and aesthetic tastes' and, in line with his policies, placed the communion table in the east end and supplied the church with 'rich furniture and costly utensils...for the service of God'.[134] Laud, therefore, before his translation to London, had already put into practice his high-church principles. Indeed, several churches were renovated or refurbished, such as at

---

[129] Cal. State Papers Dom., 1634-1635, CCLXXXII, no.84, p.473.
[130] NLW Llandaff Cathedral/Chapter Book of Acts, 4, p.134.
[131] K. C. Fincham (ed.), Visitation Articles, II, pp.110-11; W. Laud, Works, V, p.467.
[132] K. C.Fincham (ed.), Visitation Articles, II, p.174.
[133] NLW Llandaff Cathedral Chapter, Act Book, 4, p.123.
[134] Lloyd Bowen, pp.395, 396-7.

Llanrhychwyn, Llangelynnin, Hawarden, St. Mary's Haverfordwest and Cadoxton-juxta-Barry. John Owen of St Asaph, a fervent Laudian, in his visitation articles of 1637, inquired whether the priest

> doth administer the hol communion every moneth, or thrice in the yeare at least...Doth he use and never omit the sign of the crosse in baptisme; or doth he ever baptize in any bason or other thing but the usuall form? Doth he marry without a ring...?[135]

Benefactions of church plate and communion vessels were made. In 1637 Sir Thomas Aubrey of Llantrithyd gave a silver standing cup to the parish church with the words 'drinke ye my bluid' engraved on it.[136] William Roberts of Bangor informed Laud that his parishioners had given 'testimony of their piety' by 'bestowing a couple of faire chalices of good valew vpon ye poore cathedrall' and he himself had given a 'fine service of plate' to it in 1637.[137] John Owen installed a new organ at St Asaph[138] and Morgan Owen, Laud's chaplain, erected a statue of the Virgin Mary and Child in the porch of St Mary's church at Oxford.[139] A deputation to the Court of Arches from the parish of Bangor in 1637 complained that the bishop, dean and chapter had forced them to pay for the repair of the cathedral church and to provide books or ornaments.[140] These were only some of the blemishes on Owen's character, but his short time at Bangor coincided with increasing tensions caused by Laudian policy which created deep resentment towards the Church. In 1634-5 the Court of Arches upheld his action in suspending the vicar of Aber-erch for a year for committing some misdemeanour[141] and another example of the spirit of Laud's policy of recuperating church property is found in the king's letter of 1637 to Bishop Mainwaring, another strong Laudian supporter, who was advised to retain the rectories in demesne of Ceri, Montgomery and Glascomb in Radnorshire after their expiry and the policy is clearly exposed:

---

135 Ibid., p.403; K. C. Fincham (ed.), *Visitation Articles*, II, p.175
136 Glamorganshire Record Office, P/38/cw/1, f.54, cited in Lloyd Bowen,, loc. cit.
137 *Cal. State Papers Dom.*, 1639-1640, CCCCXXXI, no.69, pp.58-9.
138 D. R. Thomas, *History of the Diocese of St Asaph*, I, p.161; Browne Willis, *Survey of St. Asaph*, p.87.
139 A. Wood, *Athenae Oxonienses*, IV, col. 804.
140 *Cal. State Papers Dom.*, 1636-1637, CCCXLIV. No.47, p.375; Lloyd Bowen, p.391.
141 *Cal. State Papers Dom.*, 1634-1635, CCLXXXII, no.54, p.465.

Among the cares that attend the princely office, that of the church has ever had the first place, whereupon we, well weighing what havoc have been made of it...and what great inconveniencies must arise...if the authority of bishop be not supported as it ought, which cannot be if their means of livelihood be taken away.[142]

It is clearly the case that Laudianism had some impact on Wales which is revealed, not only in church ceremonies but also in the private religious practices of heads of gentry houses. In 1637, for example, Rug chapel of the Holy Trinity, near Corwen, was built by Colonel William Salesbury, a staunch royalist during the Civil Wars and an Anglican with Puritan leanings. This squire copied Rhys Prichard's carols in 1637,[143] the same year when the chapel was erected. He was also a collector of free metre verses, some of them devotional (1655).[144] His appointed curate was required 'to read and celebrate divine service and other holy exercises therein in the native and vulgarly known tongue there...'. Decorations and Latin and Welsh inscriptions, painted in Gothic or Roman lettering taken from the 1588 or 1620 version of the Bible and 1621 edition of the Book of Common Prayer, adorned the chapel and are still to be seen. The altar was moved back to the east end of the chancell and fenced with altar rails complete with candles, reredos and screen.[145] Rowland Vaughan referred to this chapel in the dedication of *Prifannav Sanctaidd* (1658) to '[yr] ardderchog hen Frytwn Wiliam Salesbury o Fachymbyd' ['the excellent old Briton William Salesbury of Bachymbyd'], and he continued:

Ar eich deisyfiad chwi, ach trael yn bennaf, y cyfieithwyd ac yr Arhraphwyd y llyfr yna, y mae adgyweirio Ecclwysi ac adeiladu Ty ir goruchaf, sef capel y Drindod yn Edeirnion, ar cyflog ir llên a'i gwasanaetho, yn ffrwythau canmoladwy och ffydd, onid wyf fi yn camgymeryd; chwi a wyddoch *fides sola justificat non solum*...[146]

---

142 *Cal. State Papers Dom.*, 1637, CCCLXIII, no.80, p.299.
143 NLW Llanstephan MS. 37.
144 Ibid., MS.170; T. H. Parry-Williams (ed.), *Canu Rhydd Cynnar*, xliv,
145 D. B. Hague, 'Rug chapel, Corwen', *JMHRS*, III, 1957-60, 178; W. N. Yates, *Rug Chapel, Llangar Church, Gwydir Uchaf Chapel* (London, 1993), pp.12, 19, 20-1.
146 NLW Llanstephan MS.170,86; B. F. Roberts, 'Defosiynau Cymraeg', in T.Jones (ed.), *Astudiaethau Amrywiol* (Cardiff, 1968), p.108; *Prifannav Sanctaidd neu Lawlyfr o Weddïau a wnaethbwyd, yn dair rhan...*(London, 1658), A4; A. Ll. Hughes, 'Rhai o noddwyr y beirdd yn sir Feirionnydd', *LlC*, X, 1968-9, 177.

[At your request, and at your expence, mainly, this book was translated and printed, the repair of churches and building of a House to the highest, namely the Trinity chapel in Edeirnion, and employing the priest who serves in it, are praiseworthy fruits of your faith, if I am not mistaken; you know that faith alone does not justify.]

This private place of worship was similar to the chapel erected by Gruffudd Vaughan II of Corsygedol in 1615 as an addition to Llanddwywe parish church, and in it the altar was placed against the east wall and railed on three sides, a classic example of 'high-church' adornment.[147]

A succession of Welsh bishops, however, left much to be desired with regard to providing the stimulation needed for reform. At Bangor, Bayly was followed by David Dolben who, learned though he was, stayed a mere two years in the see and who was dogged by persistent poor health ('crazy and sickly' as he was called).[148] He was succeeded by his own nominee, Edmund Griffith, a scion of Cefnamwlch and Bayly's enemy, who served for three years only. Griffith doubtless was a more robust fellow but his career at Bangor was also marred by controversy, arising out of his strained relations as dean of Bangor with Bayly and others, his quarrels concerning the administration of Friars' School, Bangor, and the accusations brought against him for allegedly appointing corrupt churchwardens.[149] Moreover, in 1636, Beddgelert parishioners attacked him for appointing a non-preaching and non-Welsh-speaking curate. They declared that Hugh Jenkins was not a preaching minister because of his youth and lack of proficiency in the Welsh language.[150]

The visitation articles of Edmund Griffith and William Roberts of Bangor in 1634 and 1640 respectively and of John Owen at St Asaph in 1637 noted the need to cater for monoglot Welsh-speaking congregations in almost all parts of their dioceses. Prefacing these articles is the oath for

---

147 *Royal Commission on the Ancient and Historical Monuments...in Wales and Monmouthshire: Inventory*, VI, *County of Merioneth* (Cardiff, 1921), p.76. This chapel was not designed by Inigo Jones as once supposed. *Bye-gones*, 1901-02, pp.452-3.
148 *Cal. State Papers Dom.*, 1633-1634, CCXLI, no. 44 pp.110-1.
149 J. Wynn, *History of the Gwydir Family and Memoirs*,. P.73; R. Williams, *A Biographical Dictionary of Eminent Welshmen* (Llandovery, 1852), p. 180-1; Browne Willis, *Survey of Bangor*, pp.112-13; NLW Additional MS. 466E.568; MS. 9059E.1166; A. H. Dodd, 'Bishop Lewes Bayly', 23-4; *Dominican*, 1957, 41-4, cited in A. H. Dodd, 24 (n. 53).
150 NLW MS. 9062E.1592.

churchwardens in Welsh as well as English.[151] In 1634 articles inquired whether or not the Book of Common Prayer was available in both languages together with the *Book of Homilies* and service books and the 'large Bible of the last edition' in English and Welsh (1611 and 1620 respectively).[152]

The situation at St David's reveals interesting parallels. Anthony Rudd was not unlike his contemporary Rowlands for he also was highly regarded as a preacher, a firm governor of his diocese and a thrifty prelate. He showed concern for the needs of the Church and, in view of his fear that losing clergymen would be detrimental to the Church's reputation, initiated a policy of enforcing subscription to the Book of Common Prayer and Thirty-nine Articles.[153] His status in the diocese was far more auspicious than that of his successor, Richard Milbourne, whose six years there were singularly undistinguished despite his triennial visitation of the chapter in 1621.[154] William Laud, Milbourne's successor in that year, only spent two periods of residence in five years, and although he defended his diocese against recusants and Puritans alike and showed some pastoral care for the lower clergy, his impact on the see was unimpressive and underlying problems were left unreformed.[155] Theophilus Field, who was transferred from Llandaff to St David's in 1627 and who remained there for eight years, took a very dim view of the condition of his diocese regarding it as 'a desolate place...where there is not so much as a leach to cure a sick horse'.[156] His visitation of the chapter in 1630 confirming acts and statutes, like that of his predecessor, left no deep impression, nor did the stay of Roger Mainwaring, a renowned scholar, in the see from 1636 to the end of the Commonwealth in 1653. He was described as 'an excellent critick in ye Greek tongue' and he expressed three major aims of his, namely to record the details of his life, to deal with the public affairs of the Church and to recount 'ye remarkable passages of Providence that happened in the World'.[157] Although his

---

151 K. C. Fincham (ed.), *Visitation Articles*, II, p.118.
152 Ibid., p.118.
153 K. Fincham, 'Episcopal government, 1603-1640', in K. Fincham (ed.), *The Early Stuart Church, 1603-1642*, p.75; Yardley, *Menevia Sacra*, 103.
154 Yardley, *Menevia Sacra*, pp.104-5.
155 In fact, the see was offered to Dr Owen Gwynn, 18th Master of St.John's College, Cambridge, a kinsman of the Wynns of Gwydir, but he refused it. NLW MS. 9057E.959.
156 *Cal. State Papers Dom.*, 1629, CL, no.110, p.84.
157 Yardley, *Menevia Sacra*, 109-12.

ambitions in this respect were not realised he cannot be regarded as being wholly ineffective. He was a staunch defender of the Church and monarchy and his sermons on 'religion' and 'allegiance' led him to being accused of trying 'to infuse into the conscience of the majority the persuasion of a power not binding itself with law'.[158] He faced a charge brought against him by John Pym, was imprisoned and fined £1,000 and suspended for three years for 'endeavouring to destroy the king and kingdom for his divinity'.[159] John Owen at St Asaph also faced adversities. He had served his diocese well; he was a shrewd observer of the needs of his clergy and, in 1634, declared that he was more concerned about external than internal factors which threatened the Church.[160] Browne Willis thought highly of him, describing him as a prelate who had 'incomparable skill in the Welsh language' and an impressive repairer of his church.[161] In the crucial years before the Civil Wars he became aware of the increasing attacks on Laud. In view of the anti-Laudian policy in parliament in 1641-2, although he added a question aimed against 'schismaticall conventicles', he left out controversial clauses from his visitation articles, such as the canonical requirements for parishioners to kneel at communion and ministers to baptise with the sign of the Cross.[162] He was impeached for high treason and, in 1641, imprisoned, his rectories sequestered, episcopal properties sold and residence destroyed.[163] Morgan Owen, likewise, was also imprisoned for proclaiming the laws agreed to by convocation and was imprisoned for signing the protest by twelve bishops which declared parliamentary proceedings to be illegal.[164] Despite the frustrations which early Welsh Stuart bishops endured it would be misleading to regard these prelates as unassertive and feeble when attempting to combat challenging situations. These had, for the most part, been inherited from their predecessors but became enmeshed in increasing tensions within the Church and the impending political crisis which sorely wounded its reputation.

---

[158] Ibid.

[159] *Cal. State Papers Dom., 1640*, CCCCL, no.108, p.47. See also NLW *Catalogue of Tracts of the Civil War and Commonwealth Period relating to Wales and the Border (Civil War Tracts)*, no.124 (28 June 1642), p.6.

[160] Ibid.

[161] Browne Willis, *Survey of St. Asaph*, pp.86-7; D. R. Thomas, *Hist. Diocese of St Asaph*, I, pp.106-7; B. Williams 'The Welsh Clergy', I, pp.65-6.

[162] K. C. Fincham (ed.), *Visitation Articles*, II, xxvii.

[163] D. R. Thomas, *Hist. Diocese of St Asaph*, I, pp.106-7, 228.

[164] *Glamorgan County Hist.*, IV, p.242.

Of all the problems which beset Welsh bishops in the early seventeenth century doubtless the survival of Roman Catholic recusancy was one of the most irritating. Families in areas of Wales still persisted in practising the faith and diocesan records refer continually to attempts to suppress it. The Catholic community, which did not increase substantially in the early part of the century but rather consistently maintained its numbers, expected much from James I but the penal laws were reinforced and two anti-Catholic statutes were added to them in 1606.[165] In 1603 it was stated that the recusant population in Wales was 808, most of them residing in the two easternmost dioceses of Llandaff (381) and St Asaph (250).[166] In 1601 the Council in the Marches was cautioned by the Privy Council to attend to the situation which was a cause of serious concern:

> ...there is great backsliding in religion in these parts, and especially in the confines of the shires between England and Wales, as Monmouthshire and the skirts of the shires of Wales bounding upon them, and many runners abroad and carriers of mass books, superaltars, all kind of massing apparel, singing bread, of wafers and all other things used at or in the saying of mass.[167]

The Welsh borderland, particularly Gwent, and the vale of Glamorgan, was well known for its recusant activity, families such as the Morgans of Llantarnam (Gwent), Turbervilles of Pen-llin, Llandudwg and Y Scer (Glamorgan), and the powerful earls of Worcester (Raglan castle) being the most prominent harbourers of Jesuit priests.[168] Flintshire and East Denbighshire, particularly Wrexham, were also centres of recusancy, the leading family being the Edwards's of Plas Newydd, Chirk, principally the two John Edwardses, father and son.[169] Richard Parry in January 1613 informed Archbishop Bancroft of the danger posed by John Edwards the younger, described by him as 'a very dangerous ffelowe...of as pestilent disposicon as eny in all our countrey' and proceeded to disarm papists

---

165 J. G. Jones, *Early Modern Wales*, pp.163-70; E. G. Jones, *Cymru a'r Hen Ffydd*, pp.43-6.
166 BL Harleian MS. 280, fo.162b-164; G. Williams, *Wales and the Reformation*, pp.374-5.
167 HMC *Salisbury MSS.*, XI, p.460; E. G. Jones, *Cymru a'r Hen Ffydd*, p.34. See also F. H. Pugh, 'Glamorgan recusants, 1577-1611', *South Wales and Monmouthshire Record Society Pubs*, no. III, 1954, 49-68; idem, 'Monmouthshire recusants in the reigns of Elizabeth I and James I', ibid., IV, 1957, 59-65.
168 *Cal. State Papers Dom., 1603-1610*, XLVIII, no.121, p.552.
169 E. G. Jones, *Cymru a'r Hen Ffydd*, pp.21, 25, 47, 49, 72, 82; idem, 'Catholic recusants in the counties of Denbigh, Flint and Montgomery, 1581-1625', *TCS*, 1945, pp.117-19.

and impose the Oath of Allegiance in his diocese.[170] His letter contained a caution which was intended to cause general alarm: 'if the church may receive so great damage in this poore corner what mischeefe may be done through the whole kingdome...'.[171] He had some ten years earlier, on coming to his see, declared that there was 'an unfortunate and ungodly increase of papists',[172] echoing the warning which his predecessor Morgan had issued following his visitation in 1602 that there were 140 known recusants, and in his time 400, whose suppression depended entirely on the severity of the law. 'With the increase in their number', he maintained, 'their courage is increased [and] they little fear the words, until they feel the smart of the laws'.[173] In the same year Robert Bennett, newly appointed bishop of Hereford, stated that in Herefordshire and its 'confines' towards Monmouthshire, recusants were 'rife' and 'growne to boldness to take up weapons'.[174] Other concerns were voiced by Sir Richard Lewkenor, justice of the Chester circuit,[175] and Lord Zouche, lord president of the Council at Ludlow.[176]

In the rural areas of north-west Wales recusancy was more sporadic and associated with a small but powerful group of leaders from local gentry, such as the Pughs of Penrhyn Creuddyn (Creuddyn), Owens of Plas Du (Llŷn), and Woods of Tal-y-llyn (Anglesey). Hugh Owen of Gwenynog, in the parish of Llanfflewyn in Anglesey, was an intriguing individual; he was brought up a Protestant, he held responsible office in his native shire and was overseer of the local estate of Bodeon but, in 1621, he abandoned his lands and offices and fled to join the recusant household of the earl of Worcester at Raglan where he spent most of his time thereafter.[177] In December 1625, Lewis Bayly informed Charles I of his mysterious reappearance and threat in Anglesey in that year – 'very gallant and full of gold' – and recalled his disappearance:

---

170 *Cal. State Papers Dom., 1611-1618*, LXXVI, no.3, p.220; J. G. Jones, 'Richard Parry, bishop of St. Asaph',187.
171 J. G. Jones, 'Richard Parry, bishop of St. Asaph', loc. cit.
172 HMC, *Salisbury MSS*, XVII, p.374.
173 Ibid.,
174 Ibid., pp.93, 216, 235, 258, 389.
175 Ibid., XI, p.460.
176 Ibid., pp.498-9.
177 E. G. Jones, 'Hugh Owen of Gwenynog', TAAS, 1938, 42-9.

A man that had been a Captain of that Ile, a most dangerous felowe, a Romishe recusant who about 3 yeares before had given over his place, disposed of his lands and converted his estate into money, and went out of his country and no man knew why.[178]

Bayly ended his letter by urging the government to reinforce the island's defences because he feared that further threats, led by Owen and his 'crew' might plan an invasion, possibly with aid from Catholic Ireland:

...the rest of that faction are heere so audacious that they never durst be so bold if they knew not of some invasion or conspiracie intended.[179]

Owen was no mean scholar, for he was a lawyer, a linguist and able translator of Thomas à Kempis's *De Imitatione Christi* as *Dilyniad Crist* (published in 1684). The preface to this translation contains the following appraisal of him:

Ac oherwydd ei ddealltwriaeth rhagorol a'i gywreinrwydd yn y cyfreithiau...ei gymdogion o bob parth a gyrchent ato, megis at y cyfreithiwr godidocaf i gael cyngor yn rhad, ac i gael tynnu a sgrifennu eu gweithredoedd yn ffyddlon. Nid oedd fawr leoedd cyfrifol y pryd hynny ym Môn, lle nid oeddid yn cadw ac yn prisio'n werthfawr waith ei ddwylo ef.[180]

[And because of his excellent understanding and skill in the laws...his neighbours from all parts came as if to the most renowned lawyer to obtain counsel freely, and to have their deeds drawn up and accurately recorded. There were very few places in Anglesey at this time where his work was not preserved and highly valued.]

It is hardly surprising that Bayly was extremely alarmed by his connections ('that faction'), including the Woods, in the island. It is regrettable that no further information is forthcoming in the bishop's letter about the main leaders of that dissident group.

---

178 *Cal. State Papers Dom., 1625-1626,* XI, no. 37, p.172; E. G. Jones, *Cymru a'r Hen Ffydd,* p.55
179 Ibid.
180 J. H., *Dilyniad Crist* (1684), in *Hen Gyflwyniadau,* p.52. See W. P. Griffith, 'Schooling and society', in J. G. Jones (ed.), *Class, Community and Culture in Tudor Wales* (Cardiff, 1989), pp.110, 119.

Concern was also expressed about activities in north-east Wales in 1617, when the Council in the Marches proceeded to suppress large congregations of recusants at St Winifred's Well at Holywell.[181] Despite the legislation of 1538 to suppress shrines and pilgrimages, Catholic practices still persisted. Daily prayers and services were held at Holywell as well as sermons on Sundays and on festival days. Moreover, in 1629 it was estimated that between 1,400 and 1,600 assembled there, which shows that the Council's endeavours had been unsuccessful to stem traditional pilgrimages which continued to attract common folk.[182] Those estimates may well have been exaggerated but, in 1633, Bishop John Owen of St Asaph also expressed similar concern about the 'boldness' of recusants who continued to visit the shrine.[183] In Carmarthenshire Anthony Rudd complained in 1611 that Robert Acton, a fervent Catholic from Worcestershire, had settled with his family in Llandeilo Fawr. His son had a part in the Gunpowder Plot of 1605 and other members of the family resided in the area. It was feared that other recusants might be attracted there. 'I am certain', Rudd declared, 'that such natives of this country as were formerly recusants are made more obstinate and have increased in number since the coming of the Actons'.[184] Similarly, in Pembrokeshire, Sir James Perrott of Haroldston in 1611 expressed concern about the influx of recusants from Herefordshire and adjacent shires into 'these remoter parts of Wales'.[185] He also considered that Jesuit priests were fostering relations between Pembrokeshire recusants and their *confrères* in the border country, all of which, he feared, would have a devastating impact on the fortunes of the Protestant faith in west Wales. In a letter to the Privy Council 1627, Perrott expressed further concern about the safety of Milford Haven, owing probably to its close proximity to Catholic Ireland:

> The dangers of Milford Haven I conceive is known to your honours, and it is the more dangerous by dwelling or resorting of recusants and evil affected persons unto those parts. For Pembrokeshire it hath not many recusants...but I suppose that divers do resort unto them and that they

---

[181] BL Royal MS. 18.13vii; C. A. J. Skeel, *The Council in the Marches of Wales* (London, 1904), p.150.

[182] *Cal. State Papers Dom., 1629-1631*, CLI, no.13, p.87.

[183] Lambeth Palace MS. 943, pp.249, 255; *Hist. Diocese of St. Asaph*, I, p.105; B. Williams, 'The Welsh Clergy', I, p.66.

[184] *Cal. State Papers Dom., 1611-1618*, LXVII, no. 1, p.84.

[185] Ibid., LXVIII, no. 75, p.123.

have intelligence with the recusants of Monmouthshire where there are many not only of the natives but of strangers coming out of other parts of Wales and England that reside there, and no doubt keep intercourse with them of Pembrokeshire and the adjoining counties.[186]

Although slight increases appeared in the numbers of Catholic recusants by the eve of the Civil Wars, mainly because of the emergence of new generations among them, the faith in Wales did not pose further threats. By then the Elizabethan Church had deepened its roots. Bishops were political as well as religious figures. They were expected to live like gentlemen, extending hospitality, keeping a respectable residence and spending some time in London, in the House of Lords or the royal court. Regardless of the impoverished state of the Welsh sees, bishops attempted to keep up appearances, and despite the difficulties caused by recusants it was abundantly clear that the Catholic reformation had failed to achieve what it had intended. It had miscalculated badly and it faced insurmountable problems, not least parliament's anti-Catholic policy, the inadequate number of priests, problems associated with the press and publication, widespread ignorance and illiteracy and the loyalties of the gentry to the political and religious settlements.[187] It can be argued that Protestantism succeeded in enrooting itself more because of the weakness of its Roman Catholic opponents than its own inherent strengths. It is true that Welsh language Catholic literature worthy of Renaissance learning was published but its circulation was at best restricted. Indeed the Old Faith depended for its survival in the Welsh hinterland, where traditional religious practices were still popular, more on the adherence of gentry families and their dependants than anything else. They weathered periodic persecution, became increasingly accustomed to their 'deprived status' and, by the eve of the Civil Wars in Wales, although they had lost much of their impetus, gave what support they could to Charles I.[188] Complex though the nature of loyalty was at the outset of the wars it appeared that Welsh Catholics were decidedly in favour of the monarchy.

---

186 Ibid., 1627, LXXXVIII, no.23, p.487; E. G. Jones, *Cymru a'r Hen Ffydd*, pp.59-60.
187 G. Williams, *Wales and the Reformation*, pp.270-9;
188 P. Gaunt, *A Nation under Siege: The Civil War in Wales, 1642-48* (London, 1991), pp.16-17, 20-22.

Other threats came to occupy bishops in the 1630s, namely Protestant dissenting activity which has been traced by historians to the early 1630s, chiefly in the Welsh borderlands. John Penry had no known followers in Wales and the sporadic traces of Puritan thought are found mainly in the attitudes and writings of bishops and clergy in the early decades of the seventeenth century. Anthony Rudd was reputed to be a good preacher. [189] Although he accepted canon 30 of 1604, concerning the use of the cross in baptism, he considered that it would not be acceptable to dissenters whom he wished to see reconciled to the Church. He did not favour full uniformity since he believed that ejecting dissenters would benefit the Catholic population. References have already been made to the published works of Lewis Bayly and Robert Llwyd and to the Puritan upbringing of Theophilus Field and George Carleton,[190] but, in addition, Puritan 'pedlars and tinkers…hot Puritans and full of the gospel' appeared in Wrexham in the 1580s, an area influenced by Cheshire Puritanism led by Christopher Goodman, dean of Chester.[191] Feoffees for Impropriation acquired advowsons to raise clerical standards and a 'lecture system' was established in 1620 and continued to 1636 which allowed unbeneficed men to 'teach, preach and catechise'.[192] Puritan tendencies among the preachers, however, led to restrictions being placed on them but John White, a member of a prominent merchant family in Tenby, and Rowland Heylin, the London-based Welsh entrepreneur, who shared the financing of the small Bible of 1630, served as two of the trustees.[193] Puritan 'lectureships' installed in towns such as Cardiff, Swansea, Haverfordwest and Wrexham had some impact but Laudian opposition brought the experiment to an end. A small group of Baptists, who moved into the Welsh borderland from the Olchon valley in western Herefordshire in the early 1630s, were described as extremists 'which schismatically preach dangerous errors, and stir up the people to follow them'.[194] When they heard of any inquiry concerning them they would then, it was reported, move conveniently into another diocese. Foremost Puritan preachers,

---

[189] T. Fuller, *The Church History of Britain*, ed. J. S. Brewer (6 vols. Oxford, 1845), V, pp, 69, 437.
[190] A. H. Dodd, 'Bishop Lewes Bayly', 14-16.
[191] R. G. Gruffydd, *'In that Gentile Country'*: the Beginnings of Puritan Nonconformity in Wales (Bridgend, 1975), p.6; D. A. Thomas (ed.), *The Welsh Elizabethan Catholic Martyrs* (Cardiff, 1971), p.93; G. H. Jenkins, *Protestant Dissenters in Wales, 1639-1689*, Chap. II, pp.9-16.
[192] H. Thomas, *A History of Wales, 1485-1660* (Cardiff, 1972), pp.117-8.
[193] *DWB*, pp.356, 1016; R. Williams, *Eminent Welshmen*, pp.219, 517.
[194] J. M. Jones, 'Walter Cradoc a'i gyfoeswyr', 32.

such as Rowland Puleston of Bersham, Walter Stephens, an active preacher on the Welsh border, Robert Powell, vicar of Cadoxton-juxta-Neath, Rhys Prichard, the celebrated vicar of Llanymddyfri, Stanley Gower, vicar of Brampton Bryan in Herefordshire and chaplain to the Puritan Sir Robert Harley, Marmaduke Matthews, vicar of Pen-main, Gower, and Oliver Thomas, Puritan minister based at Oswestry, had some influence in spreading the gospel but it is difficult to quantify.[195]

Griffith Williams, who at the time was dean of Bangor and newly-appointed royal chaplain, severely attacked Puritan activity. He abhored any attempt to undermine the unity of the Church and set out to preserve the integrity of that institution which was in grave danger of being pulled apart:

> *Schisme* creepes into the Church, and it begins to grow so grievous, that it grieves me to thinke of it...yet behold the *state* of our Church...for they [the Puritans] beate at the *leaves* and we [the Church] strike at the *root* and under the name of the Church we seeke the supplantation of the Church: ô let us take heed; least, you see Satan fight against us more and *more*, so we should grow *worse and worse*; for this contention is but a *bridge*, but a passage to a greater evill...[196]

This small Puritan element, however, which like Roman Catholic recusancy was concentrated mainly in 'hard-core' areas on the borders of Wales, was gradually to make itself felt and matters came to the fore in 1634-5 when William Wroth, William Erbery and Walter Cradock, described as 'a bold ignorant young fellow', were brought before the Court of High Commission charged with dissident and irregular preaching, Wroth 'leading away many simple people', and the other two 'preaching 'very schismatically and dangerously to the people'.[197] Cradock had caused some stir when, in a sermon, he 'used this base and

---

[195] For further reference to Puritan preachers see T. Richards, *The Puritan Movement in Wales*, Chap. 1, pp.1-21; R. G. Gruffydd, *'In that Gentile Country': The beginnings of Puritan Nonconformity in Wales*, pp.6-9; G. F. Nuttall, *The Welsh Saints, 1640-1660* (Cardiff, 1957), pp.3-17.

[196] G. Williams, *The Right Way to the Best Religion* (London, 1636), p.11; W. P. Griffith, 'Anglicaniaid a Phiwritaniaid: myfyrwyr a diwinyddion prifysgolion Lloegr, 1560-1640', *LlC*, XVI, 1989, 38-9.

[197] W. Laud, *Works*, V(ii), pp.329, 334-5; J. M. Jones, 'Walter Cradoc a'i gyfoeswyr', 30.

unchristian passage in the pulpit: "That God so loved the world that for it He sent his son to live like a slave and die like a beast".[198]

A year earlier William Murray declared that there was not 'one refractory non-conformist or schismatical' in the diocese of Llandaff.[199] He was a strong Laudian supporter, and two years later he deplored the activities of the 'two noted schismatics', Erbery, vicar of St Mary's, Cardiff,[200] and his curate Cradock. Erbery, who was accused of being involved in 'schuismacital concerns', resigned his living and Cradock fled to Wrexham, where he became curate to Robert Lloyd and converted Morgan Llwyd, and then to Brampton Bryan, the residence of Sir Robert Harley and his wife Brilliana.[201] William Wroth was the rector of Llanfaches in Gwent. As a 'conscientious objector' to the *Book of Sports* he refused to read its reissue in 1633 [202] and was described by Edmund Jones, the dissenting preacher from Pontypool, as 'in all respects a strong Christian, and a foundation stone in the great building of God in Wales'.[203] By reputation he was a powerful preacher and, in November 1939, assisted by Henry Jessey, the London independent minister, became the founder of the first independent church in Wales on the 'new England' pattern. It was Erbery who described it so when applauding Wroth's work in establishing that church:

> For though separated Churches were before in England, yet the first Independent Church (according to the New-England pattern) was set up in Wales...For I will speak the truth without partiality; there were not more spiritual and suffering Saints in any part of English ground, as were in Wales; so self-denying, and dying to the world, yea so wise-hearted and knowing Christians; let all the English Counties about them testifie, and will tell, how many Saints from Somerset, Gloucestershire, Hereford-shire, Radnor, Glamorgan-shire came in multitudes with delight to Lanvaghes.[204]

---

[198] Ibid.

[199] Ibid.; W. Laud, *Works*, V(ii), p.321.

[200] B. Ll. James, 'The evolution of a radical: the life and career of William Erbery (1604-54)', *JWEH*, III, 1986, 38.

[201] T. Richards, Puritan Movement, pp.25-30; R. G. Gruffydd, 'In that Gentile Country', pp.9-16; Glamorgan County Hist., IV, pp.252-6; G. F. Nuttall, *The Welsh Saints, 1640-1660: Walter Cradock, Vavasor Powell, Morgan Llwyd* (Cardiff, 1957), pp.18-36; G. H. Jenkins, *Protestant Dissenters*, pp.10-11, 73..

[202] This is Dr Thomas Richards's description of Wroth, *DWB*, p.1093.

[203] NLW MS. 128C, f.76 a-b, cited in G. H. Jenkins, *Protestant Dissenters in Wales*, p.73.

Wroth was a strong personality whose appeal to dissenters as well as Anglicans gave him the support he needed. Murray was confronted by a highly-respected cleric described as 'ye apostle' of his country whose church was regarded as 'the Antioch in that gentile country'.[205] In 1634 Theophilus Field suspended a lecturer (possibly Evan Roberts, an associate of Oliver Thomas and translator of William Perkins's *Foundation of the Christian Religion* in 1649) for 'inconformity',[206] and soon after discharged the same one and two others who had 'with their giddiness offered to distemper the people'.[207] Likewise in 1636 Field reported Marmaduke Matthews, vicar of Pen-main in Gower, for preaching 'against the keeping of all holy-days' [208] and in 1640 John Owen at St Asaph drew attention to 'a conventicle of mean persons', located 'in the skirts of this diocese in Shropshire', which was the gathering of dissenters at Llanyblodwel referred to above.[209] In the diocese of Bangor, Bishop William Roberts had achieved some success in reaching an agreement between himself and some 'ill-affected' (possibly puritanically inclined) ministers which led them to agree to give financial support to the royal cause on the outbreak of civil war in 1642.[210]

Any assessment of the early Welsh Stuart bishops needs of necessity to deal in generalities because of the lack of evidence to examine all aspects of their career in all four dioceses. Moreover, comparisons also need to be drawn with trends in the Anglican church in a broader context in the half-century or so before the Civil Wars. Recent research has tended to place greater emphasis on the differences between episcopal activity in the reigns of James I and Charles I. It is argued that generally there was a change from an extensive pastoral ministry to the need to establish discipline, obedience and conformity. Also, the task of preaching gave way to the need to protect and prevent the alienation of church lands and

---

[204] W. Erbery, *Apocrypha* (London, 1652), pp.7-8; Jenkins, *Protestant Dissenters in Wales*, p.74.

[205] NLW MS.128C, f.76 a-b, cited in G. H. Jenkins, *Protestant Dissenters in Wales*, p.73; J. M. Jones, 'Walter Cradoc a'i gyfoeswyr', 32; R. G. Gruffydd, 'In that Gentile Country', pp.14-15; T. Richards, 'Eglwys Llanfaches', *TCS*, 1941, p.150-84; R. T. Jones, *Hanes Annibynwyr Cymru*, pp.34-43.

[206] W. Laud, *Works*, V(ii), pp.328-9 (1634), 335 (1636); J. M. Jones, 'Walter Cradoc a'i gyfoeswyr', 29-30.

[207] W. Laud, *Works*, V(ii), p.329.;

[208] T. Shankland, 'Anghydffurfwyr cyntaf Cymru', *Y Cofiadur*, I, 1923, 37; *Glamorgan County Hist.*, IV, pp.255-6.

[209] *Cal. State Papers Dom.*, 1639-1640, CCCCXXX, no.18, pp.7-8.

[210] NLW *Catalogue of Tracts of the Civil War...*, (110), p.7.

revenues. The 'beauty of holiness', symbolised by order and reverent worship which characterised the 1630s, gradually took over from the ceremonial nonconformity characteristic of the earlier period.[211] Religious activity in Wales in the reign of James I was represented at its best by Henry Rowlands and Richard Parry and, in the seond quarter of the century, by Roger Mainwaring and Morgan Owen. The dividing line is very finely drawn, not always as clear as one would like it to be. John Owen of St Asaph, for example, had as strong inclinations to promote preaching and to establish order as he had towards the policies of Archbishop Laud, and Lewis Bayly, despite his occasional perverse actions, was as much a disciplinarian as he was an administrator. Several other bishops did not spend long enough periods in their dioceses to be able to have the impact that they might otherwise have had. The English connections of bishops such as Milbourne, Carleton and Field also created a dilemma which affected the relationships between them and their dioceses. Francis Godwin and Anthony Rudd, on the other hand, despite their close connections with English cultural centres, did identify and, in part, discharge their obligations in Llandaff and St David's respectively as an essential part of their spiritual mission. So did William Morgan who, like his contemporary Rowlands, was throughly Welsh in outlook despite the education which both had received at Cambridge and Oxford respectively. They felt a deep sense of moral commitment to the Church, as Morgan unequivocally showed in his correspondence with the squire of Gwydir shortly before his death. Even Bayly, when opposed by Sir John Bodfel, head of the powerful Llŷn family, in 1623 concerning a presentation to a cure, declared that the reason why he placed a young curate there was to 'catechise all Lent and make the children fitter for confirmation against the visitation'.[212] It seemed a matter of conscience for him and he further maintained: 'Bodvel's great peremptoriness in so small a matter showed more stoutness than wisdom...Though Bodfel has the nomination he may not place a curate without the diocesan's leave and approbation.' [213]

The Welsh prelates, in different degrees, had an impact on Welsh religious life and were obliged to attend to their duties in dioceses that

---

[211] K. Fincham, *Prelate as Pastor*, pp.300-2.
[212] Cardiff MS, 4.58, pp.53-4.
[213] Ibid.

were blighted by poverty. Regardless of the introduction of high church practices into the Church ceremonial and services, their attempt to rehabiliate the Church and restore its integrity was part of their central mission before and during the Laudian period. Welsh bishops were aware of widespread illiteracy and ignorance, particularly in isolated parishes, but their achievement in improving the moral fibre of the Welsh people was indeed remarkable, especially when the quality of the literary products of Morgan and Bayly are considered. The pastoral and benevolent work of Rowlands and John Owen, as well as the efforts of Rudd and Roberts to keep order in their dioceses, do bear some relevance to the situation. Despite the connections established between several of the bishops and the royal court and their dependence on its patronage, they were aware of a mission they were expected to fulfil. From a pastoral viewpoint they were aware how the condition of the Church affected their fortunes, some voicing their grievances in the most vociferous manner. Excepting Morgan and, to a lesser extent, Parry, his successor at St Asaph, and Lewis Bayly, the early Stuart bishops in Wales down to the Civil Wars have, as a group of church leaders, not received the attention they deserve. In specialist works on the seventeenth-century Anglican church little attention is paid them. They all received good education, had a close understanding of political and religious developments of their day and sought what patronage they could to promote their careers in Wales and elsewhere. Their shortcomings, most of which stemmed from the weaknesses of the Church in the age of Elizabeth, were only too evident, but they had certain qualities which enabled them to serve the Welsh Church in a period when its hold on the nation was deepening. Their educational achievements compared well with their counterparts elsewhere, and they conducted articulate communication with their clergy. Most of them displayed administrative skills, and a proportion published in the Welsh language and, in some instances, such as Godwin and Bayly, gave to the church in England some notable literary works.

The length of residence of bishops such as Rudd, Godwin, Morgan Owen and Roger Mainwaring gave them the opportunity to come to terms with diocesan problems. They experienced many pressures, particularly when combating the Catholic recusant community and, towards the end of the period, early Protestant nonconformity which, despite its sporadic nature, served in due course to instil a regeneration of spiritual life. Nevertheless, the early seventeenth century was a period of consolidation for the Church because the powers of recusancy and nonconformity were not strong enough to impair its claims to the loyalty of the Welsh people. The alliance between the gentry and the monarchy and the Church was reinforced, not only because of the transference of loyalties from one royal family to another, but, more significantly, because the governing order in Wales had, over half a century and more, associated itself with the institutions of government at central and at local levels and had acquired the influence and authority associated with the agencies of power. At the centre stood those institutions which formed the bulwark of order, one of them being the Protestant Church.

Generally, bishops in Wales were served by some well-meaning and dedicated clergy. The Church, however, was tainted by bad practices inherited from the past and, in addition to the traditional problems of non-residence, pluralism, simony and the secularisation of church properties, there continued to be apathy and ignorance which bishops were expected to combat in the early Stuart Church. They themselves were made aware of the need to keep up appearances and to express a degree of humility in periods when secular pressures bore upon them. During his dispute with the Bodfels in 1623 Bayly made his situation very clear:

> For myself, the world is so various and every man so uncertain to hold what he hath already, that no wise man will make any great ado for any greater preferment. God grant that with the peace of the Gospel we may hold what we have already.[214]

He and his fellow bishops were also eager to foster high standards of scholarship in their dioceses and several individual incumbents, such as Edmwnd Prys, Humphrey Davies, Edward James, Dr John Davies of Mallwyd and Henry Perri of Flintshire, contributed extensively to maintain the integrity of the Church and establish high standards in cultural affairs. Their literacy skills indicated that intellectually the Church was at least equipped with the capacity, if not the vigour, to resist subversive elements bent on destroying its unity. On balance, the Church in Wales, in this formative period in its development, revealed that it had the leadership which laid the basis of its power which, regardless of the

---

[214] NLW MS. 9058E.1145.

onslaughts upon it during the Civil Wars and the Puritan Interregnum, enabled it to assume its traditional role in 1660. Doubtless the Protestant faith had fortified its position by establishing a strong doctrinal as well as pastoral basis and the Welsh bishops aided in maintaining an institution which, despite its inherited weaknesses, consolidated the Anglican faith down to the years when civil strife and rebellion seriously threatened its standing and reputation.

CHAPTER V

Puritanism in Action:
Local Government in Caernarfonshire, c.1649-1660

The contribution of local government records to the historian's knowledge and understanding of society and community life is remarkable and surviving records reveal the penalties imposed on religious dissenters by county administrators. One particular source is the Caernarfonshire quarter sessions records which, unlike those of other Welsh counties, have survived from the inception of the courts in 1541 and reflect the role of magistrates in maintaining order in times of religious and political turbulence and instability. One particularly interesting aspect which is highlighted is the growth of dissenting activity during the Puritan regime (c.1649-60). What is remarkable is the fact that such a remote county, not renowned for its Puritan following in its early stages, reflects well-defined aspects of religious dissent which emerged among modestly - placed Puritan landed families in the Welsh hinterland. The researches of Dr Thomas Richards, A H. Dodd and W. Gilbert Williams, among others, have drawn attention to the role of such families in the growth of Puritanism in parts of Snowdonia and the degree to which the inhabitants of Caernarfonshire accepted the new administration.[1]

Significant questions arise from a study of Puritan dissent in this region, more particularly the manner in which Puritanism progressed in

---

[1] For general studies on religion and society in local government in this period see A. Fletcher, *Reform in the Provinces: The Government of Stuart England* (London, 1986); M. James, *Social Problems and Policy during the Puritan Revolution* (London, 1966). More studies relevant to Wales include T. Richards, *A History of the Puritan Movement in Wales, 1635-1653* (London, 1920); idem, *Religious Developments in Wales, 1654-1662* (London,1923); G. H. Jenkins, *The Foundations of Modern Wales, 1642-1780* (Oxford, 1993); A. M. Johnson, 'Politics and religion in Glamorgan during the *Interregnum* 1649-1660', in G. Williams (ed.), *Glamorgan County History*, IV, (Cardiff, 1974), pp.279-309; idem, 'Wales during the Commonwealth and Protectorate', in D. Pennington and K. Thomas (eds.), *Puritans and Revolutionaries: Essays in Seventeenth-Century History presented to Christopher Hill* (Oxford,1978), pp.233-56; A. H. Dodd, *Studies in Stuart Wales* (Cardiff, 1952), pp.110-76; 'Propagating the gospel', in H. E. Bell and R. L. Ollard (eds.), *Historical Essays, 1600-1750, Presented to David Ogg* (London, 1963) , pp.35-59. (See also C. Hill, 'Puritans and "the dark corners of the land"', *Transactions of the Royal Historical Society*, 5th ser., XIII, 1963, 72-102).

Caernarfonshire and the diligence of its adherents in ensuring the success of policies adopted by the Commonwealth and Protectorate governments. What the records show is the impact of the growth of small pockets of Puritanism in both sparsely-inhabited areas of the county and the towns. Although Puritans constituted but a small minority in the county there is ample evidence to prove that their leaders played a vital role in establishing a new religious tradition which laid the basis of future dissent in the region. It could be argued that the 1650s, more than the previous decade, saw the enrooting of Puritanism and the establishing of a small number of families as its mainstay in a region known for its unswerving loyalty to the monarchy. In a decade when the Anglican Church was at a low ebb, the degree to which Puritan beliefs and conduct were accepted by a largely illiterate and even hostile population needs to be investigated. Henry Vaughan (Silurist) gave expression to the feeling of despair felt among those who resented the new regime:

> The wayes of Zion do mourne, our beautiful gates are shut up, and the Comforter that should releeve our Souls is gone far from us. Thy Service and thy Sabbaths, thy own sacred Institutions and the pledges of thy love are denied unto us: Thy Ministers are trodden down, and the basest of the people are set up in thy holy place.[2]

The Welsh were traditionally firm in their allegiance to church and state, as their allegiance in the Civil Wars amply demonstrates, but a new view of the situation needs to be examined to assess the extent to which that allegiance was durable and a matter of conscience in parts of north-west Wales.

Among the Wynn of Gwydir papers for the year 1656 there appears a copy of a remarkable sermon which, according to tradition, was delivered originally by John Dod, the Puritan divine, in the neighbourhood of Preesall in Lancashire, reprimanding drunks and other dissolute persons because of their irregular ways.[3] The sermon appears as an acrostic, and it is possible that Maurice Wynn, younger son of Sir John Wynn, had

---

2   'A prayer in time of persecution and heresie', in *The Mount of Olives: or Solitary devotions* (1652). See L. C. Martin (ed.), *Henry Vaughan: Poetry and Select Prose* (London, 1963), 131; G. H. Jenkins, *Protestant Dissenters in Wales, 1639-1689* (Cardiff, 1992), 76, 80.
3   NLW MS. 9065E.2103; *DNB*, XV, pp.145-6 for further details on John Dod (c.1549-1645). For further evidence of Maurice Wynn's Puritan leanings see NLW MS.9056E. 896.

obtained a copy of it. He, it appears, had adopted Puritan tendencies during his period as a merchant in Hamburg. Then after he returned to his native region he served as a member of the local County Committee and as receiver-general of north Wales.[4] It seems that moralistic sermons of this kind appealed to him and, probably, is why a copy was found among the family papers. The sermon, copied in the Wynn Papers on 22 March 1655, describes the moral campaign in Maurice Wynn's age against alehouses and alcohol, as the following extract reveals:

> Certeine men of Prisiall returning from a merry meeting at a certeine Alehouse mett in the fields a certeine preacher who had lately made a sermon against drunkards, and amongst oprobrious words he calld them mault wormes; whereupon they agreed to take him & by violence to compell him to preach a sermon, & his text should be malt. The preacher thinkeing it better to yeild then to content in this case, begann his sermon as followeth. There is noe good preaching without diuision. And the text cannot well be deuided, because it is but one word not into any sillables; because it is but one sillable it must be therefore deuided into letters & they are found to be foure M A L T. These 4 letters represent 4 interpretacons w'ch devide thus:
>
> M: morall
> A: Allegoricall
> L: Literall
> T Typographicall ...
>
> The Typographicall interpretacon somewhat, yt now is, or hath beene or shall be hereafter in this world or in ye world to come, the thing yt now is, the effect yf ye wyle of malt procureth & worketh in some of you. M: murther, others of you A adulterye, in all L, loose liuing in many T. treason. And that w'ch hereafter followeth both in this world & in the world to come is M. misery, A. anguish, L. lamentacon, T. trouble... [5]

---

4   J. E. Griffith, *Pedigrees of Anglesey and Caernarvonshire Families* (Horncastle, 1914), p.281; NLW MS 9056E,865, 895-6. He served as sheriff of Merioneth in 1650 (MS. 9064E.1952, 1965; PRO *List of Sheriffs for England and Wales* (New York, 1963), p.261) and receiver in 1653 (MS.9064E.2032). See also B. E. Howells (ed.), *Calendar of Letters relating to North Wales, 1533-c.1700* (Cardiff, 1967), pp.137 (227), 138 (228-9), 205 (393).

5   See D. Jones, *Cydymaith Diddan* (Chester, 1766 ed.), pp.15-18 for a variation of the Welsh and English versions respectively of this sermon. Also *Calendar of Wynn of Gwydir Papers*, no.2103 (NLW MS.9065.2013).

This was not the kind of sermon that would appeal to peasant folk in the middle years of the seventeenth century, and certainly men of 'vain religion' and 'deceitful doctrine', as they were called, who would accept its contents, were not respected as they travelled around the countryside preaching such extreme views.[6] The Puritan authorities between 1649 and 1660 depended to a great extent on itinerant preachers to foster moral life and conduct among illiterate parishioners. In Caernarfonshire, for example, where the Puritan hold was not very strong, men such as Henry Maurice of Llannor, Llŷn, Gruffydd Roberts, Llanengan, Ellis Rowland of Clynnog and Llanwnda and John Williams of Castellmarch Uchaf, who were appointed by the Commissioners for Approbation of Public Preachers (known as the 'Triers') after 1654 to spread the Puritan message in remote areas and to an ignorant and illiterate peasantry, represented a zealous group of preachers and missionaries who sought to improve moral standards in Welsh communities so that they might aspire to the ideals 'of those who walk in the company of the gospel'.[7] Since their hold on Gwynedd generally was very weak it is difficult to decide what degree of influence they were able to exert, and it appears that they had very little indeed.[8] According to the Puritan viewpoint, preaching and educating were the prime methods of puritanizing the country – 'these darke places', as Major-General James Berry called them – but since the resources were scarce they depended often on administrative institutions, old and new, to be the backbone of the venture.[9] Without continued official assistance to promote their policies the efforts of the Commonwealth to achieve its goal would not have been successful.

One of the most remarkable features of the Puritan governments between 1649 and 1660 in England and Wales is the fact that they continued to use royal institutions to maintain peace and good order, one of the main ones being the court of quarter sessions, arguably the most popular and most

---

6   'Caniadau'r Gwrthryfel Mawr', *Cymru*, XXI, 1901, nos 124, 218, citing from Edward Dafydd of Margam's 'Ode to the Fanatics'. For further background discussion of propaganda poems see W. T. Pennar Davies, 'Baledi gwleidyddol yng nghyfnod y Chwyldro Piwritanaidd', *Y Cofiadur*, XXV, 1955, 3-22.

7   *DWB*, pp.622-3, 1047;T. Richards, *Religious Developments*, pp.21, 30; A. H. Dodd, *A History of Caernarvonshire, 1284-1900* (Wrexham, 1990 ed.), pp.141-3.

8   *Cymru*, no. 214. Citing Colonel John Jones of Maesygarnedd's letter to Captain Wray, custodian of Beaumaris castle, 28 April 1657.

9   J. Berry and S. G. Lee, *A Cromwellian Major-General: The Career of Colonel James Berry* (Oxford, 1938), p.139.

stable of legal establishments and a solid framework for efficient local government.[10] Puritan legislators depended largely on this court and others, such as the court of Great Sessions, together with sheriffs, justices of the peace, constables and churchwardens, to promote the success of Puritan policy which had been formed primarily to improve morality and the spiritual life of the nation. Down to the years of civil war the governing county hierarchy was strongly royalist and Anglican and a regional loyalty prevailed which had a deep impact on the composition of local community life.[11] Although the Welsh gentry had shown some opposition to royal policy in the 1630s, especially to its fiscal policy, most of them, in spirit or in practice, favoured Charles I's cause on the outbreak of war in 1642.[12] In their view to cast doubt on royal authority was equal to being violently opposed to state law and, in the last resort, it was regarded as an onslaught on the status and authority of the gentry in their respective communities.[13] 'Thus we have found', John Corbet, a parliamentary military captain in Gloucester, explained, 'that the common people addicted to the King's service have come out of blind Wales and other dark corners of the land'.[14] Doubtless, a description of this kind exaggerated the situation from the viewpoint of families who had either been loyal and courageous enough to enter the king's service on battlefields or had been wary enough not to intervene on either side. However, as far as it can be judged, the peasantry were yearning for the return of the local priest, inefficient though he may have been, to administer the sacraments in the parish church and they wished to be able

---

10 J. Hurstfield, 'County government c.1530-c.1660' in *Victoria County History* (Wiltshire), V, ed. R. B. Pugh and E. Crittal (Oxford, 1057), pp.106-110; D. Underdown, 'Settlement in the counties, 1653-1658', in G. E. Aylmer (ed.), *The Interregnum: The Quest for Settlement, 1646-1660* (London, 1972), pp.165-82; T. M. Bassett, 'A study of local government in Wales under the Commonwealth with especial reference to its relation with central authority' (unpublished University of Wales M. A. dissertation, 1941), pp.345-62.

11 There are many studies of different counties, especially in England, during the early Stuart period. See A Everitt, *Change in the Provinces: The Seventeenth Century* (Leicester, 1969) for a discussion of the role of local history in national affairs.

12 A.H. Dodd, 'The pattern of politics in Stuart Wales', *TCS*, 1948, pp.47-63; G. Williams (ed.), *Glamorgan County History*, IV, and the contributions by Penry Williams, pp.195-7 and C.M. Thomas, pp.257-60.

13 W. H. Greenleaf, *Order, Empiricism and Politics: The Traditions of English Political Thought, 1500-1700* (Oxford, 1964), pp.58-67; J. G. Williams, 'Rhai agweddau ar y gymdeithas Gymreig yn yr ail ganrif ar bymtheg', *Efrydiau Athronyddol*, XXXI, 1968, 43-9.

14 J. Corbett, *A True and Impartial History of the Military Government of the City of Gloucester, repr. in Bibliotheca Gloucestrensis*, I, p.10 See also D. Underdown, *Pride's Purge: Politics in the Puritan Revolution* (Oxford, 1971), pp.11-14; J. E. C. Hill, 'Puritans and "the dark corners of the land"', 100-102.

to enjoy the gatherings in the taverns and fairs in the small towns and communities in which they lived. The new ways of preaching, the use of laymen to spread the gospel and the stringent code of conduct imposed upon them created much resentment. The words of Rowland Vaughan of Caer-gai concisely summarise the feeling among royalists and Anglicans in his translation of one of Jasper Mayne's works:

> Canys yn Gyffredin yr Athrawon newydd yma yn erbyn yr Ecclwys, ydynt yn chwarae r *Siaplen*...Eu *Pulput* gan hynny ydyw'r *Bwrdd* a wasanaetha yn dalgrwn i *bregethu* ac i *fwyta* arno, ai canllynwyr (yn fynych yn dlodion) yn caru y cyfriw flasus ac iachus *Athrawiaeth*, ac ydynt yn hoffi y fath *brawfiadau* a *phyngciau* cyssurus...yno yn cydwledda yn eu pesci eu hunain yn ddiofn (er bod yn yr Ecclwys, oll ar *betrusder*).[15]

> [For generally these new teachers against the Church act the *Chaplain*...Their *Pulpit* therefore is the *Table* which serves completely to *preach* and to *eat* on it, and their followers (often poor) love the tasty and healthy *Doctrine*, and like such comforting *experiences* and *tenets*... there feasting together fattening themselves fearlessly (although in the Church all is *uncertain*).]

Conversely, Walter Cradock applauded the use of such preachers who enlightened the people and advanced the Word of God:

> And let us not be so curious, or scrupulous, as to hinder people that they should not preach the Gospel...And let us not think so hardly in these dayes, of those men that God hath raised to preach the Gospel...they are filled with good newes, and they goe and tell it to others.[16]

Forcing a new and stringent way of life upon them would have adverse effects on their culture, which normally entailed enjoying traditional rural customs which alleviated part of the daily drudge. Half a century earlier John Penry had recorded how superficial religious beliefs were in the Welsh hinterland: 'our people', he maintained, 'are either such as neuer think of anie religion true of false, plainly meere Atheists, or stark blinded

---

15 R. Vaughan, *Ymddiffyniad Rhag pla o Schism neu Swyn gyfaredd yn erbyn neulltuaethau yr Amseroedd* (London, 1658), pp.14-15.
16 W,. Cradock, *Glad Tydings from Heaven: To The Worst of Sinners on Earth* (London, 1648), pp.49-50; G. H. Jenkins, *Protestant Dissenters in Wales*, p.76,

with superstition'.[17] It took a long time even for the Anglican Church to root itself among the Welsh and consequently a new English movement would certainly not gain much success within a short period of ten years in such a conservative country.[18]

In the Puritan era the administrative system imposed on Wales proved to be an uneasy marriage between the traditional and revolutionary and between the permanent and temporary in many areas of the country, and that is best reflected in the way in which Caernarfonshire, like other counties, was administered.[19] Those gentry who opposed Charles I in the Civil Wars were prepared to support the new regime in the 1650s. Victorian historians believed that the Commonwealth was a short period of confusion and neglect and that there was little co-operation with the new political order among a large proportion of the old county administrators who had royalist connections.[20] Despite the serious problems encountered in that unstable period, however, such an opinion conceals the truth. The structure of local government reveals that plainly, because the magistracy continued to function although it was a royal creation which had, over four centuries, formed part of the legal and administrative machinery. It had also proved itself to be indispensable to the central and local governments.[21] From the Acts of Union onwards down to the Civil Wars justices of the peace and deputy-lieutenants had built up their power and authority and had extended their interests at the expense of the county sheriff who had lost much of his importance, especially in military affairs, but who continued to serve as an officer subordinate to the justices.[22]

It is not difficult to understand why the court of Quarter Sessions and local government officials continued to function during the *interregnum*. By the middle of the seventeenth century the administrative systems of the English and Welsh counties had established themselves firmly and

---

[17]   J. Penry, *Three Treatises concerning Wales*, ed. D. Williams (Cardiff, 1960), p.32.
[18]   G. Williams, *Welsh Reformation Essays* (Cardiff, 1967), pp.22-7.
[19]   J. Hurstfield, 'County government c 1530-c.1660', pp.106-10.
[20]   F. A. Inderwick, *The Interregnum (A.D. 1648-1660): Studies of the Commonwealth, Legislative, Social and Legal* (London, 1891), pp.174-6.
[21]   Aylmer, op. cit., pp.168-73.
[22]   G. Scott Thomson, 'The origins and growth of the office of deputy-lieutenant', *Trans. Royal Hist. Soc.*, V, 1922, 150-66; G. Williams (ed.), *Glamorgan County History*, IV, 1974, pp.169-72; G. E. Jones, *The Gentry and the Elizabethan State* (Swansea, 1977), pp.33-5, 61-3, 77 et seq.

had proved themselves to be essential to the smooth-running of local and regional affairs. The military aspect of government, entrusted to the lord-lieutenants, deputy-lieutenants, captains and muster masters, had increased and the relations between the gentry and the central government, down to the Civil Wars, revealed a distinct alliance which had been formed between the Crown and its governors in the rural areas. Although the authority of the Council in the Marches, in the decades before its abolition in 1641, had declined considerably, the membership of commissions of the peace had increased and their responsibilities multiplied and individual justices of the peace held immense power in the localities. On the threshold of the Commonwealth years these justices continued to be prominent administrators in county affairs, a fact that was clearly revealed when compared with the County Committees whose membership was similar to that of the local commission of the peace. It was much more convenient, and indeed necessary, for the Puritan authorities to employ the administrative mechanism that existed under royal government to avoid risking disorder in local government by introducing new methods of control, which might do more harm than good to them. After all, Oliver Cromwell sought to establish a firm alliance with regional administrators, his intention being to secure co-operation, where possible, with the conservative elements in the Welsh ruling families in order to woo royalists into forming as firm an alliance as possible with him.[23] That did not involve any radical transformation in the framework of local government. Cromwell saw himself as 'the good constable who attempted to appease his own parish' and did not believe that political power should be given to anyone except to members of the ruling landed families. By the mid-seventeenth century justices of the peace had formed a solid body of administrators assuming autonomous power and functioning as the vital link between the central authorities and the localities. It is true that war-time circumstances impeded them from performing their tasks effectively, and it is evident that they had lost much of their impact at that time. However, despite the weaknesses in the system, the legal and administrative framework provided a solid base upon which the new Puritan magistracy conducted their affairs.[24]

---

[23] A. H. Dodd, *History of Caernarvonshire*, p.137 et seq.; J. G. Jones, 'Caernarvonshire administration: the activities of the justices of the peace, 1603-1660', *WHR*, V, 1970, 130-63.

[24] J. G. Jones, 'Caernarvonshire justices of the peace', 147 et seq.; W. O. Williams, 'The county records', *TCHS*, X, 1949, 79 et seq.; A. C. Bassett, Chap. XII, p.329 et seq.

One vital aspect of the government's regional policy during the Civil Wars was to create County Committees and they functioned for a short period to 1650 when sequestration affairs were transferred to London. Consequently, local officials were but mere sub-commissioners, and their authority in the finance and military committees (which continued to function) far less imposing.[25] In most Welsh counties Puritan supporters were scarce and therefore they were often placed under the authority of English military figures and a core of Welsh local gentry which were either supporters of Puritan governments or were willing to co-operate with the authorities and who had sufficient experience of running local affairs. The functions of the County Committee were not intended to conflict with those of justices in courts of Quarter Sessions and they were not meant to oust them from their positions of power. However, justices and hundred and parish officials were expected to perform their numerous duties so as to fulfil the needs of Puritan rule and ensure its success. Although the County Committees and Quarter Sessions were similar, in that they served the Puritan regime on a regional basis and had the same personnel, they performed different functions. The County Committees, on the one hand, were formed essentially to serve the government in financial and military affairs and were regarded as institutions 'which rapidly became the universal and standard organ of local government during the Civil Wars and Puritan rule. The courts of Quarter Sessions, on the other hand, survived the upheaval and continued to practise common law, to maintain the peace and to deal with legal and administrative matters in the hundreds and parishes as in the past.[26]

Because of the slow development of Puritanism in most areas of Wales, the changes in the composition of the Caernarfonshire magistracy in 1650 were very few, and most of the commissioners were moderate in their religious and political beliefs. One remarkable fact is that most of the records of the court of Quarter Sessions have survived from the Acts of Union onwards and they are full of detailed information about the conduct of affairs during the Commonwealth and Protectorate periods

---

25 A. C. Bassett, Chaps II and IV, p.33 et seq.; A. H. Dodd, *Studies in Stuart Wales*, p.118 et seq. Cf. A. M. Johnson, 'Politics and religion in Glamorgan', pp.279-83.

26 Cf. D. H. Pennington and I. A. Roots (ed.), *The Committee at Stafford, 1643-1645: The Order Book of the Staffordshire County Committee* (Manchester, 1957), intro., xi-xlii, xlvi-lv; *Acts and Ordinances*, I, pp.978, 1113; J. Morrill, 'The Stuarts', in K. O. Morgan (ed.), *The Oxford History of Britain*, III (Oxford, 1992), p.117.

when there was a significant increase in the number of cases brought before the court. The policy of maintaining good order depended largely on the extent to which the leaders of Welsh communities were prepared to accept the new order and to co-operate with it. The only change in the personnel of the Caernarfonshire commission was the appearance of one military figure and one Puritan preacher on the bench although they were not natives of the county.[27]

It is true that county government was entrusted to a small, albeit dedicated, band of justices during the *Interregnum*. Many, first and foremost, intended to strengthen their own positions and power and to enhance the reputation of the new regime but it cannot be said that any of them cherished extreme Puritan views. Many of them were prepared to conform and co-operate only on condition that they were given opportunities to increase their own prestige within the aegis of a system which was not approved by a small proportion of them. The court's procedures continued much as in the past but the close superintending of the administration became more evident since they were expected to administer several ordinances issued by the central government as well as attend to routine matters. Although the numbers of functional justices varied from 18 in 1649 to 22 in 1656 only a handful, and not more than eight in each year, took upon themselves the heavy burdens in the 1650s.[28] In a county where opposition to Puritan government was widespread, it is not surprising that these governors were unpopular. In 1649 it was officially reported that Griffith Jones of Castellmarch in Llŷn, second son of Sir William Jones, Chief Justice of the King's Bench in Ireland and then in England, and one of the most ardent of Puritan administrators, had been taken captive by John Bartlett, the pirate, near St Tudwal's island on the Llŷn coastline. Assisted by twenty of his followers, Bartlett attacked Castellmarch and after they had plundered the house and had taken the gold and silver vessels, the clothes and cloths, Jones was also taken hostage to Wexford in Ireland.[29] It appears that this attack had been

---

27 J. R. S. Phillips (ed.), *The Justices of the Peace in Wales and Monmouthshire, 1541 to 1689* (Cardiff, 1975), pp.31-2; A. H. Dodd, *History of Caernarvonshire*, pp.135, 139.

28 J. R. S. Phillips, *Justices of the Peace*, pp.31-2; J. G. Jones, 'Caernarvonshire justices of the peace', 139-40, 157.

29 J. R. S. Phillips, *Justices of the Peace*, pp.31-2; B. Owen, 'Rhai agweddau ar hanes Annibynwyr sir Gaernarfon o'r dechrau hyd y flwyddyn 1776', *Y Cofiadur*, XX, 1950, 6-7; *Cal, State Papers Dom., 1649-1650*, I, p.30; A. Eames, 'Sea power and Caernarvonshire', *TCHS*, XVI, 1955, 42-3; B. E. Howells, 'The kidnapping of Griffith Jones of Castellmarch', *Trivium*, XV, 1980.

planned in revenge for the death penalty imposed on Sir John Owen of Y Clenennau for his part in the second Civil War. Owen was not executed and Griffith Jones, on being released, returned home to Llŷn prepared, as fervently as ever, to serve the new regime set up after Charles's execution. Although described as 'well-affected' towards parliament A. H. Dodd believed Jones not to be an extreme Puritan but rather, in fact, taken prisoner as a reprisal for the undeserved treatment Owen had received.[30]

Who, therefore, were the main justices of the peace in Caernarfonshire to whom the burdens of local government were entrusted at this time? Some names were familiar because they had close connections with families of repute in the county. Thomas Madrun, eldest son of Thomas Madrun of Llŷn, was one of the most prominent and one of the few nominated by the government to administer his county. He served as army colonel, sheriff of the county (1643, 1648-9), member of parliament (1654) and a permanent member of the County Committee.[31] Madrun was a cunning public figure, carefully protecting his own interests, either through the authority which he had established for himself in the locality or through his marital connections. He managed to keep his brother-in-law, John Gethin, in the living of Llangybi, Eifionydd, after he had been ejected from Cricieth under the Propagation Act.[32] Also, he enabled Evan Lloyd, rector of Rhoscolyn, another kinsman through his marriage into the Plas Llandegfan family of Anglesey, to maintain the living of Llanbeulan during that period.[33] Moreover, since episcopacy was abolished in 1646, the Chapter at Bangor was unable to sue defaulters at law and the headmaster of Friars' School, Thomas Meredith, with a letter of introduction signed by Thomas Madrun and other Puritan gentry of the county, went to London in 1647 to seek means of maintaining the school.[34] Madrun was a member of the committee in 1650 which audited the school's finances and, in 1650, he was ordered, among other commissioners, to examine the state of Puritan schools in Anglesey and Caernarfonshire.[35] Owing to their Anglican origins such educational

---

30 A. H. Dodd, *History of Caernarvonshire*, p.127.
31 *DWB*, p.609; J. R. S. Phillips, *Justices of the Peace*, pp.30-2; J. E. Griffith, *Pedigrees*, p.242; E. Breese, *Kalendars of Gwynedd* (London, 1873), p.55; W. R. Williams, *The Parliamentary History of the Principality of Wales, 1541-1895* (Brecknock, 1895), p.60.
32 J. E. Griffith, *Pedigrees*, p.242; T. Richards, *Puritan Movement in Wales*, p.116.
33 J. E. Griffith, *Pedigrees*, pp.85, 242; T. Richards, *Puritan Movement in Wales*, p.115.
34 H. Barber and H. Lewis, *The History of Friars School, Bangor* (Bangor, 1901), pp.34-7.
35 T. Richards, *Religious Developments in Wales*, p.64.

institutions caused general concern. The Civil Wars had made it difficult to collect rents, trustees were unable to maintain them and provide the standard of instruction required and the Puritans stricly supervised them. Henry Maurice of Methlan wished to see Botwnnog school, established by Bishop Henry Rowlands (c.1618), moved to Pwllheli in 1656 'where there are frequent meetings of godly persons who would have a good influence on the youth of the place'.[36]

Sir William Williams of Y Faenol and his brother Thomas Williams of Dinas were also powerful members of the justices' bench and they married two sisters, namely the co-heiresses of Griffith Jones, Castellmarch, who was also a justice of note.[37] Together with other officials who leaned towards Puritanism, such as Edmund Glynne of Yr Hendre, brother of Colonel Thomas Glynne of Glynllifon,[38] George Twistleton, Governor of Denbigh and a native of Yorkshire,[39] Sir Griffith Williams of Cochwillan (nephew of Archbishop John Williams),[40] and Maurice Wynn of Gwydir (younger son of Sir John Wynn),[41] the members of the bench of justices in Caernarfonshire zealously applied themselves to the needs of government and administered the county down to the Restoration.

In addition to some members of traditional landed families, other less prominent gentry became men of some influence and all of them, except Richard Edwards, the Puritan attorney of Nanhoron in Llŷn,[42] won favour and some prestige because they were prepared to conform to the new system. Among them were Huw Griffith of Cefnamwlch[43] and William

---

36   *Cal. State Papers Dom., 1655-1656*, CXXVI, no.II (13), p.252. See also CXXVI, nos111 (9), 112 (i), p.297; G. Parry, 'Hanes ysgol Botwnnog', *TCS*, 1957, pp.1-3.

37   J. E. Griffith, *Pedigrees*, p.190; J. R. S. Phillips, *Justices of the Peace*, pp.30-2.

38   J. E. Griffith, *Pedigrees*, pp.172-3, 206; W. G. Williams, *Arfon y Dyddiau Gynt* (Caernarfon, 1915), pp.111-3; G. Roberts, 'The Glynnes and Wynns of Glynllifon', *TCHS*, IX, 1948, 27-30; J. R. S. Phillips, *Justices of the Peace*, pp.31-2; B. Owen, 'Rhai agweddau...', 12.

39   J. E. Griffith, *Pedigrees*, p.270; J. R. S. Phillips, *Justices of the Peace*, 31-3.

40   J. E. Griffith, *Pedigrees*, p.186; J. R. S. Phillips, *Justices of the Peace*, p.31

41   J. E. Griffith, *Pedigrees*, p.281; J. R. S. Phillips, *Justices of the Peace*, pp.30-1; PRO C 193/12 (no. 3), 193/13 (no. 3); NLW MS. 9053E.1712, 1720, 1725; Brogyntyn MS. 530; Llanfair & Brynodol MS.,94; *List of Sheriffs*, p.261.

42   *DWB*, p.193-4; Griffith, *Pedigrees*, p.161; T. Richards, 'Richard Edwards of Nanhoron: A Restoration study', *TCHS*, VIII, 1947, 27-34; B. Owen, 'Rhai agweddau...', 12-15; W. G. Williams, *Y Genedl Gymreig*, 29 May – 26 June 1923.

43   J. E. Griffith, *Pedigrees*, p.169; J. R. S. Phillips, *Justices of the Peace*, pp.31-2.

Stodart of Conwy.[44] Stodart is an interesting example. His family had been well established in the borough of Conwy and in Deganwy nearby but his rise to power was quite remarkable. William Stodart was a bailiff in the borough who took advantage of his opportunity to establish his own authority. Jeffrey Parry of Rhydolion in the parish of Llanengan, however, like Richard Edwards, was an example of a more extreme Puritan who came originally from Montgomeryshire.[45] He served as an officer and preacher in Cromwell's army and his marital connections with the Cefnllanfair family in Llŷn gave him the opportunity to involve himself wholeheartedly in local government affairs. He became known as one of the most conscientious and severe of Puritan county sequestrators and magistrates, despite the fact that he had supported Vavasor Powell by signing the 'remonstrance' called *A Word for God*...(1655), denouncing the Protectorate. Regardless of his strong Puritan connections he became the founder of the Parry and Jones-Parry family of Madrun which was to assume a significant role in the local politics of Llŷn in future generations.[46]

Despite their local prominence these governors were not as widely known or powerful as say Colonel John Jones of Maesygarnedd in Ardudwy or Colonel Philip Jones of Fonmon in Glamorgan, both of whom, regardless of their Puritan pride and ambitions, built up their landed power and became squires of some repute, bolstering the regime on the one hand, and creating the semblance of a sturdy Puritan middle class on the other.[47] They were influenced by a deep-seated materialism based on their quest for office and power, on the one hand, and the desire for estate-building on the other, all of which reflected the traditional interest in 'consolidating and safeguarding their patrimonies'.[48] Each successive government in the 1650s depended entirely on families and individuals of the kind found at Castellmarch, Rhydolion and Madrun to implement its policies; they were prepared to compromise with the established order so that they might maintain their property and increase

44   Ibid.; A. Hadley (ed.), *The Registers of Conway* (London, 1900), p.145.
45   J. R. S. Phillips, *Justices of the Peace*, p.31; B. Owen, 'Rhai agweddau...', 9-11; A. H. Dodd, *History of Caernarvonshire*, pp.144, 146, 151-4, 160.
46   *DWB*, p.730. For more information on pioneering leaders among Caernarfonshire Puritans see B. Owen, 'Rhai agweddau...', 3-18.
47   S. Roberts, 'Welsh Puritans in the Interregnum', *History Today*, XLI, March 1991, pp.36-41.
48   Ibid., p.41.

their power. Mr Gilbert Williams believes that there were more modest gentry in Caernarfonshire who supported parliament than was once thought, for there is ample evidence that freeholders were prepared to serve on jury panels and as tax collectors, bailiffs and high and petty constables in the commotes and parishes respectively.[49] At the apex of society, however, stood the justices of the peace. In order to reinforce the new administration in 1649, Colonel John Carter, Governor of Conwy and a native of Buckinghamshire,[50] and George Twistleton, who had married into the Glynne family of Lleuar,[51] came into prominence, introducing a new military element into the commission by virtue of their office. It was they who, for the most part, informed the justices on policy matters and they sat on the bench with other magistrates to supervise their tactics and advise them how to proceed with their new and numerous duties.

Soon after the execution of Charles I it was legislated that all local government officials were to continue in their posts and to function as they had in the past according to directions given them.[52] Some formal changes were made to official documents, and every word or phrase which had royalist connections was to be deleted. For example, all legal decisions were from henceforth to be made in the name of the 'Custodians of the liberties of England by the authority of parliament'. Justices were expected to take an oath of loyalty to the new regime and 'to be true and faithful to the Commonwealth of England as established without king or House of Lords'.

Monarchy was abolished by ordinance on 17 March 1649,[53] the Commonwealth was established formally on 19 May 1649 and a Council of State was formed on 13 February 1650.[54] The kingdom was to be governed as a Commonwealth by the high authority of the nation represented in parliament. The commisioners of the peace were ordered to suppress blasphemy and all signs of treasonous activity and meetings

---

49   W. G. Williams, 'Hen deuluoedd Llanwnda', IV, 'Teulu'r Gadlys', *TCHS*, VII, 1946, 22-3.
50   N. Tucker, 'Civil War Colonel: Sir John Carter', *TCHS*, XIII, 1952, 1-8.
51   *DWB*, p.990; J. E. Griffith, *Pedigrees*, p.270; N. Tucker, *Denbighshire Officers in the Civil War* (Denbigh,), pp.145-6; *Cal. State Papers Dom., 1650*, IX, p.160.
52   *Acts and Ordinances*, II, pp.5-6.
53   Ibid., II, pp.18-20.
54   Ibid., II, pp.122, 335-8.

of disloyal persons[55] and in the court of Quarter Sessions they were expected to assume responsibility for matters of the peace and internal and external security and, to reinforce its authority further, the Rump Parliament legislated in 1650 that each person accused of treason was to be given a six-month prison sentence without any surety and to be exiled for a second similar offence.[56] Moreover, legislation enforced sabbatarianism, suppressed blasphemy, common swearing, fornication, brothel-keeping and adultery, severe penalties being imposed for each offence. These orders were pronounced by proclamation in the courts of Great and Quarter Sessions.

With this information in hand the Caernarfonshire magistracy proceeded to accomplish its duties, led by Colonel John Carter. How effective they were at the time it is difficult to tell, but the remark made by Lucy Stodart, a spinster from Caernarfon, when complaining in 1650 that she had not been properly treated by the court for an offence committed against her, is probably more important than it appears at first sight: 'Oni chaf gyfraith', she maintained, 'mi fynnaf gyfraith ar rai ohonynt a'm llaw fy hun' ('If I am not given justice, I shall demand justice of some of them by my own hand'.)[57] It may well be that this was a rash and impulsive statement made in a moment of anger; on the other hand, it could reflect her opposition to the new government and her discontent with the desultory and slow manner in which the legal mechanism in its early days had attempted to deal with her case.

William Hookes of Conwy in 1650 wrote to his fellow justice Edward Williams of Y Wig near Aber, possibly in response to a parliamentary order to reduce opposition to the government. He enclosed a copy of regulations which obliged local officials to seize arms and explosives in parts of the county.[58] Security was a priority if the Puritan government was to achieve any success and that is why Cromwell, in 1655, informed Sir William Williams of Y Faenol of the Penruddock rising, a royalist conspiracy, hatched in Wiltshire in March of that year.[59] He ordered that all officials were to suppress signs of disloyalty and carefully watch the

---

55   Ibid., II, pp.409-12.
56   Ibid, II, pp.407-8, 420.
57   GAS, X/QS 1650.
58   A. H. Dodd, *Studies*, pp.159-60; *Calendar of Wynn of Gwydir Papers*, no.1927.
59   *Cal. State Papers Dom.*, 1655, XCV, pp.93-4.

moves of foreigners and strangers in the county, especially 'those who come from abroad to kindle fires here', particularly near the coasts. All 'wasters' were to be disciplined and those who could not account for their movements imprisoned and punished. Cromwell was aware that justices of the peace were not at all times accomplishing their tasks as efficiently as they might in such matters, and he ended his letter on a hopeful note – 'if what by law ought to be done were done diligently', he stated, 'these designs would be frustrated in the birth'.[60] Two quite influential men, supportive of the monarchy in Caernarfonshire, were thought to be acting suspiciously, namely Edward Williams of Conwy and Thomas Davies of Caerhun, Arllechwedd Isaf, and both were brought before William Stodart. Williams was imprisoned although he denied any wrongdoing, and Davies was released on surety of £500 for his reappearance in court.[61] In 1652 Humphrey Orme, possibly a native of Peterborough and described as 'not a man of good conversation', refused to read the Instrument of Government publicly, and was taken into custody in Caernarfonshire for associating with royalists, for being drunk and an employer of two men who violently opposed the Puritan regime.[62]

In September 1643 the Long Parliament approved the Solemn League and Covenant with the intention, once the war was over, of introducing 'a reformation of religion...according to the Word of God and the example of the best reformed churches'.[63] In January 1644 the *Directory for the Publique Worship of God* was authorized and the Book of Common Prayer abolished.[64]

Soon after, in 1646, John Lewis of Glasgrug, Llanbadarn Fawr, in his Puritan tract in support of parliament, explained why the Prayer Book had been cast aside:

> ...the Common Prayer, though it was the publick service, yet they [i.e. the bishops] would permit the use of it in families, which rather then no serving of God at all, I held it allowable; but of preaching in families, you know how much they were against it...suppose the Common-Prayer book like the moon, which in its proper motions and seasons is a goodly

60 M. Ashley, *Cromwell's Generals* (London, 1954), pp.151-2.
61 GAS, X/QS 1650.
62 Ibid., 1652; *Cal. State Papers Dom.*, 1654, LXXIV, nos. 87-8, p.313.
63 *Acts and Ordinances*, I, pp.175-6.
64 Ibid., I, pp.582-607 (4 Jan. 1644), 755-7 (26 Aug. 1645).

beneficent creature; but if it interposes betwixt us and the sun, it becomes an opacous disastrous body. In the times of superstition, Common-Prayer book arising like the moon at a dark midnight, was comfortable; but now a sunshine of the Gospel breaking in upon us, think thou what thou pleasest of it.[65]

Lewis's main aim was to promote support for parliament among the Welsh people, but it is doubtful whether the vast majority of the population had ever seen the tract, and, if they had, they would not have been able to read it.

After the Civil Wars and the execution of Charles I the Anglican Church was abolished and the Rump of the Long Parliament proceeded to impose Puritanism on Wales by placing the country under the command of Major-General Thomas Harrison, a Staffordshire regicide and member of Cromwell's Council of State and 71 other commissioners. They were appointed, in an ordinance of 22 February 1650, to administer the Act for the Propagation of the Gospel in Wales, which was based on recommendations put forward by the Cornish Puritan Hugh Peter in *A Word for the Armie* (1647).[66] A total of 28 commissioners were appointed for north Wales and they ejected 46 clergy from their livings, mostly for pluralism.[67] Bishop William Roberts had been deprived of his office under the ordinance of 9 October 1646, which abolished episcopacy, and was heavily fined by the Puritan authorities.[68] Not one of those commissioners was a native of Caernarfonshire or Anglesey, and individuals such as John Carter and William Littleton, Justice of Great Sessions – men who had little if any family connections with those regions – administered Puritan policy in the short period to 1653 when the Act was abolished.[69] According to the evidence provided in a petition, signed by Sir Thomas Middleton of Chirk castle and Sir Owen Wynn of Gwydir on behalf of north Wales in July 1652, the effects of the Act were not beneficial in that region.[70] Depriving some clergy of their livings and the seizure of tithes

---

[65] J. Lewis, *The Parliament Explained to Wales* (Cymdeithas Llên Cymru, Cardiff, 1907), pp 29-30.
[66] Ibid., II, pp.342-8; H. Peter, *A Word for the Armie* (London, 1647).
[67] W.P. Griffith (ed.), *'Ysbryd Dealltwrus ac Enaid Anfarwol': Ysgrifau ar Hanes Crefydd yng Ngwynedd* (Bangor, 1999), pp.104-5.
[68] *Acts and Ordinances*, I, pp.879-83.
[69] Ibid., II, pp.342-8; T. Richards, *Puritan Movement in Wales*, pp.81-9; A. M. Johnson, 'Politics and religion in Glamorgan', pp.283-92.
[70] *Calendar of Wynn of Gwydir Papers*, no.1988 (NLW MS.9064E.1988).

had devastating effects on the quality of religious life generally:

> divers parishes have, for two years past, been left vacant on the Lord's day, without any minister to officiate and administer the sacraments of baptism and the Lord's Supper, or to marry or visit the sick, to the scandal and decay of religion.

It was their desire that the government would make proper account of tithes and provide able and godly ministers in parish churches, and the petitioners stated:

> the people are growing into a carelesse content of being without, methinks you might find some way...to send some able men into these partes. Many of the vacancies are elapsed into my Lords hand and the blame is much upon him that they are not supplied.[71]

The petition referred to the Lord Protector's possession of several livings, and the consequence was that many of them remained vacant, a problem which constantly occupied the Puritan authorities.

The whole question of tithes and tithe-collection in Wales during the short period when the Act for the Propagation was in existence, and for some years afterwards, has been thoroughly investigated by Dr Stephen Roberts in studies which cast a new light on its significance in the administrative and cultural as well as religious life of Wales. Under the aegis of the Puritan regime it helped to form a unity in Wales and created new relationships and an alliance between military leaders and civilians, and radicals and conservatives. It drew together Vavasor Powell, Walter Cradock and their followers with the intention of supplying a strong Puritan ministry to attend to 'the famine of the Word' in the Principality. One method used to maintain this ministry was the farming of parochial glebe lands and tithes in livings (known as 'letting the living') which had become vacant. A collective action was taken, the Act appealing to the middle orders in Welsh society. As Roberts maintains in his study of Glamorgan tithes, where it was viable 'godliness and good government coincided...the experiment was a progressive one because...it offered

---

[71] Ibid.; J. Berry and S. G. Lee, *Cromwellian Major-General*, p.163.

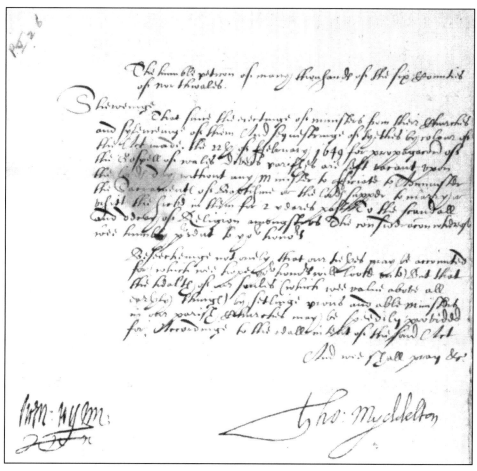

Petition from North Wales concerning the condition of religion, July 1652
(NLW MS.9064E.1988)

something to the ordinary parishioner, and especially to the godly one'.[72] The income generated by the scheme served to strengthen the economic base of the middle orders in some areas of Wales, for example in some parishes in the Vale of Glamorgan. It had the potential of increasing the preaching ministry and it introduced a degree of decentralization and 'community self-regulation'.[73] Although the tithe system was regulated by

[72] S. Roberts, ''Godliness and government in Glamorgan, 1647-1660', in C. Jones, M. Newitt and S. Roberts (eds.), *Politics and People in Revolutionary England* (London, 1986), p.250; idem, 'Deddf Taenu'r Efengyl yng Nghymru (1650) a diwylliant Cymru', in J. G. Jones (ed.), *Agweddau ar Dwf Piwritaniaeth yng Nghymru yn yr Ail Ganrif ar Bymtheg* (Lewiston, New York, 1992), pp.93-110.
[73] S. Roberts, 'Godliness and government', p.251.

William Erbery and his followers, it was in this manner that the Puritan commissioners reached the 'grass-roots' of society in Wales and the movement which they served narrowly achieved its goal.[74]

What impact this policy had on the less well-endowed areas of north-west Wales needs to be addressed further as the above-mentioned petition reveals. More research is required into this aspect of government but the hold which the traditional gentry still had on their communities in the more conservative areas must not be underestimated, as Major-General Berry found to his cost.[75] On 21 December 1655 he wrote anxiously to Cromwell expressing his deepest concern about the allegiances of gentry and freeholders in the counties of Gwynedd:

> ...there is hardly if at all, one man fitt for a Justice of the peace in those partes; truely my lord I am at a stand what to doe with Merioneth Anglesey and Carnarvon; honest men are hard to find, most of them even the justices and monethly assessors come before us as delinquents and there is little hopes of haveing it better at present...if you put in any gouvernour there let them be men of knowen integrity.

In Berry's view there were many Royalist delinquents but hardly any administrators whom he could trust among native gentry. On 12 May 1653, shortly after the Act for the Propagation had been abrogated, parliamentary commissioners ordered two unnamed persons in Caernarfonshire to keep tithes issuing from parishes which were void because of ejection, resignation or the death of an incumbent. Since the Act had expired no clear direction had been given as to the disposal of ecclesiastical profits.[76] This may have been an indication that the system already activated in some other parts of Wales needed to be continued for maintaining a preaching ministry. Thomas Richards calculates that there were 13 old ministers remaining in their livings in 1650, but that only 13 of a total of 63 preachers laboured in north Wales generally during the years 1650-3.[77] Moreover, it seemed that gentry still collected their tithes. In July 1651, for example, an examination was heard before Quarter

---

74 W. Erbery, *The Grand Oppressor, Or, The Terror of Tithes...*(1652), in *The Testimony of W. Erbery* (London, 1658), pp.50-1. See G. H. Jenkins, *Protestant Dissenters in Wales, 1639-1689*, p.81.
75 J. Berry and S. G. Lee, *Cromwellian Major-General*, p.144.
76 GAS, X/QS 1653.
77 T. Richards, *Puritan Movement in Wales*, pp.143-5, 148-50.

Sessions at Caernarfon concerning the detaining of tithes due in the parish of Llanddeiniolen to Sir William Williams of Y Faenol, an interesting glimpse, perhaps, of the manner in which lay landowners protected their interests.[78]

With regard to the employment of preachers in the county there was no increase in the number of new clergy acceptable to the government until the 'Triers' were installed after 'Barebones Parliament' was dissolved in December 1653. The experience of Robert Jones, rector of Llandwrog, is an excellent example of current practice for it is recorded that he paid a contribution of three shillings and eleven pence church rate in 1655. He had been ejected in 1652 by the Approvers but returned to his living within two months, possibly because he was related to Griffith Jones, Castellmarch, but more probably because there was no one competent to replace him.[79] Among the Triers appointed in the county were Ellis Rowland, vicar of Clynnog and Llanwnda (1657),[80] and Henry Maurice of Methlan in Llŷn, curate of Llannor and Deneio (1658).[81] Jeffrey Parry of Rhydolion,[82] a staunch Puritan preacher and administrator, and the Puritan squire and lawyer Richard Edwards of Nanhoron Uchaf, again in Llŷn, were equally ardent in their support of the new regime, although less is known of Edwards in the 1650s.[83] The last two among them were enthusiastic members of the commission of the peace and Jeffrey Parry took a prominent part in administration and, moreover, contributed to the advance of Puritanism in north-west Wales. For example, together with John Carter and Thomas Madrun, he arranged the implementation in the county of the 1653 act for conducting marriages by local justices outside the churches,[84] an arrangement that was not favourably accepted in a conservative community which, according to the old ballad, wished to see 'yr ystys a briodo' ('the justice who performs the marriage

78 GAS, X/QS 1651.
79 T. Richards, *Religious Developments*, pp.276-7.
80 *DWB*, pp.892-3; B. Owen, 'Some details about the Independents in Caernarvonshire', *TCHS*, VI, 1945, 39-41; idem, 'Rhai agweddau...', 22-3; T. Richards, *Religious Developments*, p.21.
81 *DWB*, pp.622-3; B. Owen, 'Rhai agweddau...', 5, 18-19; R. T. Jones and B. G. Owens, 'Anghydffurfwyr Cymru, 1660-1662', *Y Cofiadur*, , 1962, 57-8; T. Richards, 'Henry Maurice: Piwritan ac Annibynnwr', ibid., V-VI, 1928, 15-67;T. Richards, *Religious Developments*, p.21.
82 *DWB*, p.193; J. R. S. Phillips, *Justices of the Peace*, p.32.
83 *Acts and Ordinances*, II, p.856; T. Richards, *Religious Developments*, pp.3-4;J. R. S. Phillips, p.32.
84 *Acts and Ordinances*, II, p.715-18.

ceremony') dismissed, and similar methods of 'halogi'r gyffredin-wlad' ('polluting the country peasant folk').[85]

In an ordinance of 24 August 1653 Barebones Parliament legalized civil marriages and the registration of births, marriages and deaths.[86] According to the provisions, parties were to inform the parish registrar (appointed by parishioners) of their intention to marry within a period of twenty days. The marriage was announced in the church or market-place and the local justice of the peace would officiate. If any problem arose subsequent to the marriage the matter would be resolved in Quarter Sessions. There is no evidence to show that the justices of the peace had attempted to operate the ordinances harshly according to government guidelines but matters were taken in hand in an orderly fashion. At Conwy on 30 September John Carter and two other magistrates, in compliance with the ordinance, proceeded to appoint registrars in the parishes.[87] The new legislation, however, did not please the population generally and John Gruffydd, the bard of Llanddyfnan in Anglesey, for example, in an ode to the justices, expressed a firm opinion which he shared with his fellow-Welshmen, that the officials had degraded the sacrament of marriage when they administered the new ordinance:

> Rhyw ystys sydd ar osteg,
> Croywa dasg yn rhoi cri deg;
> Wrth y groes araith gresyn;
> Priodas ddiflas i ddyn.[88]

[Some justice proclaims, clearly he performs his task; by the cross he gives a pitiful speech, a wretched marriage for a man.]

Soon after the ordinance had been made law, John Carter kept a vigilant eye on similar matters at Conwy by consulting with Thomas Madrun and Jeffrey Parry concerning marriage registers, joining parishes together and preparing parties that were about to marry.[89] There is some evidence at Conwy of the administration of marriages, according to Puritan

---

85   J. H. Davies (ed.), *Hen Gerddi Gwleidyddol*, p.31.
86   *Acts and Ordinances*, II, pp.715-18.
87   GAS, X/QS 1653.
88   W. G. Williams, 'Dau gywydd o waith John Gruffydd, Llanddyfnan', *TAAS*, 1938, 53.
89   GAS, X/QS, 1653.

legislation, and in 1655, for example, it was said that a number of parties had been married lawfully at Llanbeblig but, at the same time, justices were informed that others had not been legally bound according to ordinance.[90]

On 12 May 1653 local commissioners were ordered to seize the tithes of vacant parishes because of the lack of a resident clergyman.[91] Previous incumbents had been ejected by the authorities and there was no one in those parishes to administer the profits of tithes. Records relating to business of this kind were kept in the court of Quarter Sessions because the commissioners were actively engaged on the bench, thus revealing close co-operation between officials in matters of administration and routine affairs conducted in the courts.

The increase in the workload of justices and the opposition which lower officials, such as constables in commotes and parishes, voiced to the arduous tasks they were expected to fulfil, together with the general ill-feeling among the populace towards the new regime, caused problems which the justices themselves had to resolve. Their responsibilities grew and they were overwhelmed by duties which constantly needed attention, such as the poor laws, maintaining highways and bridges and supervising weights and measures. They were also required to publish banns (previously administered by the church), solve matrimonial disputes, transfer cases of felony to Great Sessions, obey the proclamations and ordinances of the central government, administer civil marriages and ensure that the new ways of worshipping imposed by ordinance were practised in each parish church. To perform all these tasks justices depended on the co-operation of relucant constables in commotes, parishes and townships. Law and order became a major problem because taxes were collected normally in the townships and taxpayers did not take too kindly to the continual demands for money, especially by unpopular officials, A tax-collector was injured by a Faenol Bangor man in 1653, and in the same year some inhabitants of the parish of Caerhun, Arllechwedd Isaf, recovered goods which constables had seized for non-payment of the monthy tax.[92] Moreover, commissioners were libelled by two Eifionydd men who prevented them from assessing

---

90   Ibid., 1655; W. J. Hemp (ed.), 'Commonwealth marriages', *TCHS*, XI,1950, 103.
91   GAS, X/QS, 1653.
92   Ibid., 1657.

the county rate.[93] Major-General James Berry complained to the local magistrates in December 1655 that the accounts of the maimed-soldiers' mise[94] was in arrears and, in 1653, many Llanbedr-y-cennin parishioners refused to pay their tithes.[95] The Act for the Propagation of the Gospel stipulated that the wife and children of an ejected clergyman were to receive up to a fifth part of the living, a stipulation which, however, was not administered consistently as the wife of Hugh Robinson, rector of that parish, discovered when she complained that neither she nor her family had received any financial assistance.[96] These were not new problems because they reflected rural poverty and deprivation. County records reveal that part-payment of tax and default were common occurrences. Dire economic circumstances and rapid changes of government did not improve matters either because local officials were expected to adapt themselves to the demands of successive administrations. That implied that new methods of assessment were explored by the Puritans to strengthen their hold on the Welsh countryside.

Relative to these policies were the developments which followed the Instrument of Government in December 1653 when the office of Lord Protector was created, all legislative power given to parliament and executive power conferred on the Lord Protector and the Council of State.[97] Oliver Cromwell, as Lord Protector, was to govern by the advice of a Council, and legislative power was vested in a single-chambered parliament to be elected every three years on a property franchise. On attaining that office Cromwell set about governing with a firm hand and, following the royalist insurrection of 1655 in England, in April of that year, he issued a proclamation that the laws against Catholic recusants should be enforced. Local justices were to make search for them, imprison them and then force them to abandon their faith. If they refused they would forfeit two-thirds of their possessions.[98] Due to the lack of response to moral regeneration the country was divided into eleven districts, each under a Major-General who was given full administrative power within his region. By the end of October 1655 these officials were established and

---

93   Ibid.
94   Ibid., 1655.
95   Ibid., 1653.
96   Ibid.
97   *Acts and Ordinances*, II, p.825.
98   *Cal. State Papers Dom., 1655*, XCVI, pp.139-40.

had received their instructions to enforce 'reformation of manners' and mount a 'campaign of moral rearmament'.[99] They were required, among other things, to 'encourage and promote Godliness and Virtue, and Discourage and Discountenance all prophaneness and Ungodliness'.[100] Cromwell's policy combined a religious radicalism and social conservatism and upheld the hierarchical order. In his mind it was not society but rather ill-discipline within it that needed reformation.[101] Be that as it may, it is evident that the brief reign of the Major-Generals represented the climax of the 'godly reformation'.[102] Their main responsibilities were to assist justices of the peace to maintain peace and good order, to tax royalists heavily and to promote the cause of Puritan rule. These officials were far more than military figures because they were an essential part of the administrative machinery which was constantly increasing, and their brief was to establish effective central control, to administer a unifom policy and strengthen the Lord Protector's power. They were the links between the government and the local administrators and, like justices of the peace, they had to comply with stiff orders and instructions. This regional pattern of government suggested that the major-generals were required to support sheriffs and justices. In Wales and the counties of Worcester, Hereford and Monmouth this power was given to James Berry, a modest clerk in a Shropshire ironworks, who established his headquarters at Shrewsbury. Although his rule over his territory was harsh he did sympathize with the situation in Wales and criticized the social conditions which made them, in his opinion, poor and irreligious. His cry echoed that of John Penry in the 1580s:[103]

> ...onely one great evill I find here which I know not how to remedy, and that is the want of able preachers. Certainly if some course be not taken, these people will some of them become as heathens ....[104]

---

[99] M. Ashley, *Cromwell's Generals*, pp.121-45; *Cal. State Papers Dom., 1655*, C, p.275; *1655-1656*, CXXIV, p.175; CXXVI, p.275; D. W. Rannie, 'Cromwell's Major Generals', *English Historical Review*, X, 1895, 471-506; I. A. Roots, 'Swordsmen and decimators', in R. H. Parry (ed.), *The English Civil War and After, 1642-1658* (Basingstoke, 1970), pp.78-92; R. Ashton, *Reformation and Revolution, 1558-1660* (London, 1984), pp.410-12; C. Durston, *Cromwell's Major-Generals: Godly Government during the English Revolution* (Manchester, 2001).

[100] M. James and M. Weinstock (ed.), *England during the Interregnum* (London, 1935), p.144.

[101] J. Morrill, 'The Stuarts', in *Oxford History of Britain*, p.120.

[102] D. Underdown, *Revel, Riot and Rebellion: Popular Politics and Culture in England, 1603-1660* (Oxford, 1985), pp.241-2.

[103] J. Berry and S. G. Lee, *Cromwellian Major-General*, p.162 et seq.

[104] Ibid., p.163.

He often emphasized the need for more ministers and preachers in outlying parishes and he blamed ignorance mainly for the failure of Puritanism to make an effective breakthrough – 'they live farre off', he maintained, 'and want information and haveing got little prejudice stumble at every straw'.[105]

Berry wrote fearlessly to his co-officials and the chief governors in London complaining greatly about the problems he had to solve in Wales. On one occasion he described the ministers as being of poor quality, justices of the peace lethargic and all the people asleep.[106] In a letter from Monmouth to John Thurloe, Cromwell's secretary of State, he accused justices in the border market towns of being in deep sleep.[107] He deplored any sign of inefficiency, and in another letter, this time to Cromwell, in December 1655, he remarked that there was hardly one man competent to be a justice of the peace in north-west Wales.[108] He knew not how to deal with Merioneth, Anglesey and Caernarfonshire since it was so difficult to find honest men in those regions. Most of them, including justices of the peace and local assessors, were being brought before him as bankrupt royalists, and he saw no solution to the problem at that time. His words echoed the feelings of several lord chancellors, lord keepers and lord presidents of the Council in the Marches of the past who firmly believed that Welsh magistrates were inadequate because of their poverty. In his correspondence Berry draws attention to two grievances againt the justices. He accuses them of being too poor, too lazy and too unsympathetic to accomplish their task appropriately. In Caernarfonshire, like many other areas of Wales, the main deficiencies were material poverty and the lack of honest and discreet men, according to Puritan standards, prepared to uphold the government. Berry's views on sheriffs were similar. However, he did not complain only about the quality of administrators; the main consideration, in his view, was not only lack of co-operation and impoverishment but also their inability to pay taxes to maintain the military system, as well as their ignorance of Puritan rule in Wales. 'If you could send some of Cromwell's declarations into these dark places', he stated to Thurloe in December 1655, 'it would

---

105   Ibid., p.152.
106   Ibid., p.158.
107   Ibid.
108   Ibid., p.144.

do goode, this people extreamly want information'.[109] Later, he referred to the same deficiency which, in his opinion, had adverse effects on Wales during the *Interregnum*, namely their isolation and their ignorance of the new religious and political order.[110]

Despite all the difficulties Berry faced, his example and support in administrative and religious affairs were expected to stir justices, reluctant though they may have been, to adopt a healthier attitude towards maintaining the law and to impose it more firmly so as to ensure obedience. Some degree of compliance was seen in that respect when Berry was informed that Griffith Jones, Griffith Williams and Edmund Glynne had summoned many people before the court because they had not received the sacrament for a whole year.[111] Even that ardent magistrate, Griffith Jones, considered that the harsh tone of Cromwell's proclamation needed to be allayed,[112] and although that was done, according to a new letter and certificate given to the justices on 3 September 1655,[113] almost two years later he ordained that recusants were to be suppressed and the grand jury was ordered to make diligent inquiries among all those over sixteen years of age to see whether any could be bound by £100 to appear before the court.[114] This led to the appearance of a number of staunch recusants before the Caernarfonshire court, such as Griffith Wynn and his wife Dorothy of Penyberth, their son Charles and two daughters, together with Thomas Evans of Llwyndyrus, Aber-erch, and Evan Evans of Pwllheli and his wife.[115] Thomas Wynn, who was imprisoned at Caernarfon, was accused of being a Jesuit priest.[116] Again, in October 1657, Gwen Griffith, a spinster of Rhiw, was accused of being a papist together with five persons from Penyberth, one gentleman from Penrhos and a husband and wife from Pwllheli.[117]

Another aspect of legislation which placed a great burden on county magistrates was the imposition of the 'moral code'. Not that their duties

---

[109] Ibid., p.139.
[110] Ibid., p.145.
[111] *Cal. State Papers Dom., 1655-1656*, CII, pp.66-7.
[112] Ibid.
[113] NLW Chirk Castle MS. *Denbighshire Order Book*, 1655.
[114] *Acts and Ordinances*, II, p.1170; *Commons Journals*, VII, pp.561-2, 571.
[115] GAS, X/QS 1657; E. G. Jones, *Cymru a'r Hen Ffydd*, pp.66-9.
[116] GAS, X/QS 1655.
[117] Ibid.

in this respect were entirely new, for they had been responsible for maintaining public morality since their inception. The Puritan regime, however, introduced a stricter approach to these duties and greater pressure was placed on local officials to adhere to stringent demands with regard to morality. In May 1650, for example, they were ordered to suppress incest, adultery and prostitution and, judging by the amount of records on such matters and on drunkenness and destitution, it appears that the magistracy at Caernarfon accomplished their tasks, if not with complete efficiency, at least with some degree of thoroughness.[118] Berry, however, was not satisfied with the moral condition of the county, and the records for 1650 reflect the kind of moral latitude allowed in the town of Caernarfon itself. In 1655 he complained bitterly about the justices' remissness and ordered them to suppress all cases of blasphemy and immorality.[119] Furthermore, he appealed ardently to the justices to pursue their duties diligently. Since the government had placed so much trust in them they, in turn, should be more prepared to serve it loyally. He deplored the number of alehouses and the many cases of drunkenness. Indeed, he considered them, many of which were unlicensed, as an unnecesary burden in the country and believed that they increased poverty and destitution. Alehouses, he added, should only be used to serve the needs of travellers and soldiers, and drew his letter to a close by encouraging them to ensure that the law was strictly enforced and to act like 'leaven in the flour' for the well-being of the state.[120] Berry's relationship with the county magistracies in Wales and the border counties was not as satisfactory as it might be owing to lack of co-ordination in the adminstration of justice, and he often found it difficult to get them to carry out his orders. His rhetorical appeal to magistrates to suppress alehouses is a classic example of the Puritan 'moral code' in action:

> To see Townes abound w'th Alehouses, houses w'th drunkards, and the country w'th beggars is the reproach of our nation, and indeed Alehouses are become the pest of this Comonwealth, which infest all places and the contagion thereof spreads exceedingly. One Alehouse makes many poore ...and to what this mischeife will grow (yf not spedily prevented) the

---

[118] *Acts and Ordinances*, II, p.387; M. James, *Social Problems and Policy*, pp.12-13.
[119] GAS, X/QS 1655.
[120] Ibid.

Lord knowes. I beseech you gent thinke of itt and let some stop be put to this spreading Gangreene...I hope better things of you...that God will stirre up yo'r hartes to be zealouse for him, and to put on righteousnes and it will cloath you, and you shalbee a terrour to euill doers and like dew vpon the tender hearbe and a refreshinge shower vpon the new mowen grasse soe shall you be to those that feare God...[121]

Major-General Charles Worsley, whose district covered Cheshire, Lancashire and Staffordshire, made a similar plea for the justices to suppress sin and immorality and promote godliness.[122] The alehouse, he maintained, was 'the very bane of the countys...the very wombe that brings forth all manner of wickedness...' Justices were prohibited from licensing any alehousekeeper if he was unable to behave courteously, to command respect in his community and be able to provide suitable sustenance for at least two soldiers.

Alehouses caused many social problems as well, and long before this period legislation had been passed to try to control them. In 1622, for example, the Privy Council ordered that such establishments situated in remote and suspicious areas should be closed. Because of the high price of corn at the time alehouses which brewed ale of moderate quality were allowed to continue, in order to reduce the dire need for barley.[123] In 1636 it was estimated that between 25,000-26,000 alehouses existed in Wales and England outside London.[124] In a thinly-populated commote like Arllechwedd Isaf, for example, outside the borough of Conwy, it was claimed that there were at least eight alehouses in 1626.[125] In 1652, as a result of the detailed survey into the situation, six alehouses were closed in the commote of Nanconwy, five in the parish of Tryfan and 22 in the parishes of Pistyll, Clynnog, Aber-erch, Edern, Llaniestyn and Boduan, in the far-flung reaches of Llŷn and Eifionydd. Illegal alehouses could so easily sprout in remote areas unknown to the authorities.[126] In one day 17 such places were closed in the commote of Cymydmaen in the farthest reaches of Llŷn and 26 in Is-Gwyrfai[127] In 1655 it was stated that more

---

121 GAS, X/QS, 21 December 1655.
122 J. Berry and S. G. Lee, *Cromwellian Major-General*, p.160.
123 *Cal. State Papers Dom., 1622*, CXXXIII, no.52, p.455.
124 Ibid., *1635-1636*, CCCXXI, p.419.
125 GAS, X/QS 1626.
126 Ibid, 1652
127 Ibid.

entered two alehouses kept by William Griffith and Robert Williams at Llanwnda than attended the parish church and that a brawl had occurred there in the previous year on a Sunday.[128]

Berry and his associates considered alehouses not only to be the cause of social and economic deprivation but also of extreme hardship. In periods of need, as a result of bad harvests and plagues, the links between immorality and distress became clearer, and became a major consideration in the mainline legislation initiated by the Puritans. The fear of famine has haunted governments and communities over the centuries, and it was that fear which prompted legislation to suppress superfluous alehouses. From 1649 onwards they were controlled more firmly for two reasons. Firstly, the use of barley in brewing had harmful effects upon the price of food and secondly, from a different perspective, alehousekeepers gave shelter to suspicious wanderers who might incite local feeling against the government or become a burden on the parishes.[129] In 1656, three persons, including a pedlar, were accused of inviting others to their houses on a Sunday and other days to play illegal games.[130] In May of the following year William Stodart of Conwy collected fines in the county for illegal brewing and selling of ale.[131] Farmers had bitterly complained because of the severe drought in 1650-5 and, consequently, the price of corn and of cattle was lowered. In addition, in view of Berry's message, alehouses kept too many people from attending parish churches. That could cause practical problems since it was in local churches that public announcements and proclamations were made. It was there also that parochial dues were collected, such as the poor rate. It was also feared that the pleasures of tippling, especially on the sabbath, would degrade its sanctity, affect the quality of spiritual life among the peasantry, and urge people to neglect paying their dues to the government. In addition to moral and economic reasons given for the suppression of many alehouses and of pastimes such as dice, shuffleboard, cock-fights, race meetings, vigils and similar entertainments, the justices were aware that such activities could be breeding grounds of opposition and disaffection.

---

[128] Ibid., 1655; W. G. Williams, 'Llanwnda yn 1655', in *Moel Tryfan i'r Traeth: Erthyglau ar Hanes Plwyfi Llanwnda a Llandwrog* (Penygroes, 1983), pp.34-8.

[129] J. S. Morrill, *Cheshire, 1630-1660: The County Government and Society during the English Revolution* (Oxford, 1974), p.244 et seq.

[130] GAS, X/QS 1656.

[131] Ibid.

The harsh attitude towards them underlined the need to maintain public order as well as uphold public morality.[132]

Puritan leaders were very sensitive to the possibility that local unrest could obstruct their policies. Maintaining peace and good order was a prime target for the Major-Generals. Berry and his colleagues in other districts were eager to see a moral reformation which would encourage justices of the peace and urban corporations to take action.[133] Worsley, like Berry, aimed at making licensed alehouses centres of convivial conversation and hospitality and drew attention, as had been announced in a document issued in 1651, to the welfare of those sadly affected by their social conditions.[134] Justices of the peace were expected to make regular reports on their attempts to achieve what the authorities considered to be appropriate in a godly community. It may well have been that Berry's letter to the magistrates in December 1655 (cited above) had been written as a consequence of their lethargy and apathy.[135] Some officials, however, such as the petty constables of the parish of Clynnog in 1656, zealously executed their duties for they reported that they had visited many alehouses on the Sabbath and had found everything in order.[136] To what extent other constables acted in similar fashion it is difficult to tell, but it is a fact that lower officials of this kind were not, by reputation, known for their efficiency. One thing is clear, however, that the courts were regularly supervised by Puritan administrators who were often hindered by inefficiency within the administrative system.

The problems associated with wandering rogues, beggars, vagabonds and the movement of people generally were usually associated with poorly-controlled alehouses, and the county records reflect the miserable conditions of those who were brought before the courts. According to Puritan belief poverty was a basic deficiency in society, a condition to abhor and avoid on all counts.[137] In *The Scales of Commerce and Trade* (1659), the Puritan commentator Thomas Willsford maintained that

---

[132] R. Ashton, *Reformation and Revolution*, p.411.
[133] J. Berry and S. G. Lee, *Cromwellian Major-General*, p.160; J. Thurloe, *A Collection of State Papers* (London, 1742), IV, p.273; *Cal. State Papers Dom.*, XV, p.35.
[134] *Cal. State Papers Dom., 1651*, XV, p.35.
[135] GAS, X/QS 1655.
[136] Ibid., 1656.
[137] R. H. Tawney, *Religion and the Rise of Capitalism*, pp.263-4, 251-70; James, *Social Problems and Policy*, Chap. VI, pp.241-302, esp. p.272 et seq.

poverty made man evil and despised and that he needed to work to prevent him from committing offences because of his circumstances.[138] Puritan ideology underlined all the legislation readily provided to ease that problem, and poverty was increasingly being considered an offence in itself and a shameful condition. There was no doubt in Berry's mind that such dissoluteness was a stumbling block to the government and he reviled it in the same way as Leonard Lee in his petition in 1644-5 – 'Such persons as live idly out of any calling', he maintained, 'ulcers in a Commonwealth and oppressors and impovershers of a kingdome.'[139] To Puritans the greatest of sins was lethargy, and it was claimed that the condition of the poor was due, not to their wretched circumstances but their idleness and irregular behaviour. The plight of the wandering rogues was an old problem, much of it having been caused by the high prices and economic condition of the previous century. After 1646 bad harvests had a severe impact on rural areas and after the Civil Wars men returned from the battle sites with no employment and often injured and destitute. It is not easy to discover whether the justices of the peace differentiated between wandering rogues, able-bodied wanderers and beggars,[140] but the records suggest that they dealt with each category with equal severity. Acts and Ordinances were reinforced to try, unsuccessfully, to control vagabondage, and justices were directed to be heavy-handed on idle behaviour, immorality and theft. In the Puritan mind to suppress one of these offences would mean the suppression of many similar offences and would cleanse society of a necessary evil.

The Major-Generals were dismissed at Christmas 1656.[141] They had failed in their mission to impose moral regeneration. Rather they had become symbols of hatred because of their associations with the army and religious fanaticism. It was a tough task to quell unrest among recalcitrant royalists and to induce justices of the peace to enforce law and order. The Major-Generals have been compared to the *intendants* introduced by Cardinal Richelieu in France and recruited from the French middle class. Each was made responsible for governing a district, assessed and

---

138 Tawney, pp.263-4.

139 *The Releife of the Poor. Thomason Tracts. A Remonstrance by Leonard Lee.* E.273(8).

140 E. Trotter, *XVIIth Century Life in the Country Parish* (Cambridge, 1919), pp.171-3. According to this author justices differentiated between tramps who wandered and lawbreakers who did not necessarily wander.

141 T. Rutt (ed.), *The Parliamentary Diary of Thomas Burton*, 4 vols. (London, 1828), I, p.230.

collected taxes, imposed law and order and supervised the conduct of courts. Whereas the *intendants* served the French Crown, the Major-Generals were subject to the authority of the Lord Protector. These officials were to ensure that law and order was established in the provinces and they ruled with a heavy hand intending to convert the people to a godly way of life. The inadequate decimation tax, imposed on the property of royalist delinquents to maintain the system, was justifiably unpopular and discredited. Fundamentally, what made the Major-Generals unpopular was not merely the imposition of moral legislation aimed at undermining contemporary social values, but the 'inquisitorial' nature of their activities, the probing into private morals, the continued interference with local government agencies and their lowly, even inferior, social origins.[142]

Since the courts of Quarter Sessions dealt with so many aspects of local government an element of laxity often crept in which affected their efficiency, particularly in regulating the poor laws. The 1657 ordinance to control vagabondage was but one among many designed to ease a situation which caused justices much concern since offences arising out of poverty had multiplied.[143] In addition, many other policies were implemented, for example, Sabbath observance, which was the pivot of the Puritan 'moral code'. Their provisions were not entirely new since many acts of this nature had already been placed in the statute book. The justices had the burden of dealing with two legislative orders, royal and Puritan, each designed to preserve the Sabbath. In 1625, for example, it was commanded that no meetings or games and pastimes were to be held on Sundays.[144] In 1627 no person was to work or walk during the time of religious worship and butchers were not to kill on the Lord's Day.[145] As a reaction against Archbishop William Laud's policy it was further legislated, in 1642, against 'blasphemies, wicked prophanations, uncleanliness, luxury, excessive eating and drinking, vanity, pride and prodigality in apparel.'[146] In 1644 it was ordered that all in the kingdom

---

[142] R. Ashton, *Reformation and Revolution*, p.411.
[143] *Acts and Ordinances*, II, p.1098.
[144] St 1 Charles I, c.1, *Statutes of the Realm*, V (London, 1963 ed.), p.1; M. James, *Social Problems and Policy*, p.283 et seq.; J. E. C. Hill, *Society and Puritanism in Pre-Revolutionary England*, Chap. V, pp.145-218.
[145] St. 3 Charles I c.2. *Statutes of the Realm*, V, p.25.
[146] *Acts and Ordinances*, I, pp.80-2.

were to respect the sabbath 'by exercising themselves therrin in the duties of Piety and true religion, publickly and privatley'.[147]

Thus it is hardly surprising that stealing corn from a mill and salt from a neighbour on a Sunday together with allowing a feast of a patron saint (*gwylmabsant*) to be held at Llangwnadl on the Lord's Day were all frowned upon and the offenders punished.[148] How much of this legislation had any direct effect on rural districts in Wales it cannot be estimated. What can be said, however, is that the scarcity of preachers in remote areas impeded the success of Puritan policy generally, since so much depended on the eagerness and observations of constables in commotes and parishes and on the dedication of magistrates. They, in conjunction with other officials (including Major-Generals after 1655), had some hope of success, and according to the evidence uncovered in estreats of fines for 1650, rapid attempts were made to reduce the number of blasphemous and other serious offences in the county.[149] These records clearly reveal that people, particularly in the Pwllheli area, were unrepentant blasphemers,[150] and the attack on the justice Jeffrey Parry of Rhydolion in 1658 was made to look more serious because the assailants had cursed him four times![151] All those who ignored the law and who walked outside the church during divine service were guilty of defiling the Lord's Day. In 1653 the churchwardens of Llangwnadl were brought to book for not preventing a market being held on Sundays.[152] Also, Alis ferch Rhisiart in 1658 was accused of carrying a basketful of apples and nuts on the sabbath.[153] In the remoter parts of Eifionydd and Llŷn, as at Llangwnadl, 'publicke wakes' were held, 'tobacoe' was sold and alehouses were opened in 1653 and 1656 on Sundays.[154] Moreover, in 1659 several idle youths were brought to court for wandering around Aberdaron and refusing to attend church.[155]

---

[147] Ibid., p.420.
[148] GAS, X/QS 1655, 1656; 'Llanwnda yn 1655', pp.42-4.
[149] *Acts and Ordinances*, II, p.393.
[150] GAS, X/QS 1659.
[151] Ibid., 1658.
[152] Ibid., 1653.
[153] Ibid., 1658.
[154] Ibid., 1653, 1656.
[155] Ibid.

It is no easy task to measure the degree of success achieved by the Caernarfonshire justices of the peace during this crucial decade immediately following the execution of Charles I and the abolition of the monarchy. For each felon brought before the court, probably many more either escaped detection or, as Berry maintained, owing to the laxity in enforcing the strictest of Puritan ordinances, went unpunished. Some justices, of course, such as Griffith Jones, Thomas Madrun and Jeffrey Parry, were in the vanguard of officials desirous to please the authorities in the pursuance of public duty. The first two signed the declaration in 1658, made by the inhabitants of the county, welcoming Richard Cromwell as successor to his father as Lord Protector, urging him to pursue his father's policy by supporting the reformed religion.[156] Doubtless, not all their colleagues on the bench were endowed with such fervour on this occasion.

Thomas Willsford's comment in this respect, serves to describe attitudes in Caernarfonshire:

> Hardly the greatest part of magistrates could be got to execute such laws so that the legislators left in the power of any J.P. that has a sense of religion and his duty, to act in these things, that he might not be wind-bound by the vicious negligence of his bretheren.[157]

The most ardent of justices were in danger of being attacked, injured or threatened, as happened to Griffith Jones[158] and Jeffrey Parry. Parry was so unpopular that he was threatened in November 1659 by Robert Wynn of Pencaerau, Aberdaron, brandishing a gun.[159] Might he have been one of the sons of the recusants Griffith and Dorothy Wynn of Brynhunog, relatives of the Wynns of Penyberth, who were accused of brawling in Llannor churchyard in 1646?[160] When Parry attempted to placate him Wynn continued to challenge and threaten the justice, claiming that Parry could not punish him although he regarded himself to be a good and just person:

---

156 *Calendar of Wynn of Gwydir Papers*, no.2173 (NLW MS.9065E.2173).
157 T. Willsford, *The Scales of Commerce and Trade* (London, 1659), p.29.
158 *Cal. State Papers Dom., 1649-1650*, I, p.30.
159 GAS, X/QS 1659.
160 E. G. Jones, *Cymru a'r Hen Ffydd*, pp.67-9; N. Tucker, 'Wartime brawl in Llannor churchyard', *TCHS*, XXVI, 1965, 50-2.

Robert Wynn...threatened Jeffrey Parry...using divers opprobrious words...having a gun in his hands to strike him...and the said Jeffrey Parry reproved him...for swearing, nevertheless he multiplied the sayd oaths...did, three or four times swear in these words (*Myn Diawl*) and further sayd to...Jeffrey Parry that he could not punish him there (though he was never so great a man).

The outcome of this episode is unrecorded but it reflects the degree of resentment and hatred felt among the common folk for unpopular magistrates in the latter years of the Protectorate and a feeling that, as the Puritan government found maintaining its administration a strenuous task, its leaders in local communities were becoming more vulnerable to attack.

In this context it is fitting to examine how widespread was discontent with the Puritan regime. According to the evidence there were only a few signs in Caernarfonshire of open hostility which may signify that opposition among an ignorant and conservative peasantry was sparse and superficial. The attack on the bailiffs of Caernarfon during the parliamentary elections in January 1659, when Richard Cromwell restored a member for the borough, was caused partly by irregular election procedures and partly by Cromwell's ineffective rule.[161] Sir Griffith Williams of Cochwillan ordered an unruly crowd to keep the peace but he was ignored and 'five or six' swords were drawn on him by people unknown. This uproar near the County Hall led to one person commenting 'nad oes dim cyfraith rwan i'w gael' ('there is no justice to be had now'),[162] which may suggest strongly that opposition to the regime was reaching its climax in the county and that the government, although less extreme, was pressing more heavily than is usually thought on the shoulders of local governors and the governed in Gwynedd. To the vast majority of the population, however, the execution of the king in 1649 was the total suppression of justice, the end of divine monarchy and, as James Howell called it, 'that black tragedy'.[163] He declared that the dreaded event had 'fill'd most hearts among us with consternation and horror' and, in his experience, had shaken 'all the cells of my Brain'. Without the

---

[161] *Calendar of Wynn of Gwydir Papers*, no.2175 (NLW MS.9065E.2175).
[162] GAS, X/QS 1659.
[163] James Howell, *Epistolae Ho-elianae (The Familiar Letters of James Howell)*, ed. J. Jacobs (London, 1892),, II, XXIV, p.552.

monarchy justice could not be administered since the institution was the source of all law and justice. It was the symbol of unity, and its representative was regarded as the national *paterfamilias*.

The unknown ballad-singer expressed his anguish with what were the consequences and pleaded with God to deliver the nation from the Puritans:

> Rhag addysgy lladd brenhinoedd
> Rhag hyfforddi'r peth ar gyhoedd
> Rhag trais milwyr ai byddinoedd
> *Libera nos domine.*
>
> Rhag llywodraeth nerth y cleddau
> Rhag trethoedd gwragedd y tafarnau
> Rhag rhoi'r gyfreth oll yn ddarnau
> *Libera nos domine.*[164]

[From being taught to kill kings and proclaiming that publicly and from the violence of soldiers and their armies, Lord deliver us:

From government by the sword, from the taxes of tavern women, and from allowing the law to be broken in pieces, Lord deliver us.]

The lower orders resented seeing Puritan missionaries in church and court of law pronouncing on morality and prying into people's private lives. The church, alehouse, village and commote were, from time immemorial, regarded as social entities which were essential to maintain social harmony, and any attempt to disrupt that harmony was bound to create a rift between them and the authorites.

Examples of this tense atmosphere were occasionally highlighted in the county records as, for example, in the case of the Puritan preacher William Prytherch, a native of Llaneilian in Anglesey, who resided in Aber.[165] He was attacked by three young gentlemen, namely Richard

---

164 *Hen Gerddi Gwleidyddol*, pp.30. 32.
165 GAS, XQS 1652.; T. Richards, *Religious Developments*, p.21. Prytherch lost his living in 1660 but obtained the living of Llanllyfni in 1661. Ibid., pp.375, 458-9.

Thomas, Griffith Thomas (both of Aber) and Edward Williams of Y Wig nearby, near an alehouse at Aber on a Sunday evening in April 1652. Prytherch was on his way home 'from Llanvairvechan & Dwygyfylchye where he had beene to discharge his function in ye ministrye' and, having reprimanded them for their tippling on the Lord's day, he was set upon 'to the effusion of his bloud & bruising of his bodie'. This attack was not only a show of opposition to Puritan preaching but had deeper causes, for Richard and Griffith Thomas were two brothers and grandsons of Sir William Thomas of Aber and Coed Alun, Caernarfon, a prominent landowner and magistrate earlier in the century.[166] Both had serious grievances against the Puritan regime. Their father, second son of Sir William Thomas, had inherited family lands and had served as justice, sheriff and member of parliament for Caernarfon borough in the Long Parliament. In 1642, he joined the Crown and in 1644 was dismissed from parliament because of his royalist sympathies, and his property was confiscated. In 1651, however, he came to terms with the government, paid a fine of £780 rather than losing part of his lands, and, in 1654, died leaving his heir Richard Thomas in heavy debt. He also was forced to pay a heavy fine in 1651 because of his support for Charles I.[167] In the same year he married Dorothy, eldest daughter of Edward Williams of Y Wig, the man who assisted him to attack William Prytherch.[168] The attack therefore seemed to be a reprisal for what the family had suffered under Puritan rule.

Another example of opposition to Puritanism is Ellis Rowland's nasty experience in 1661.[169] He was vicar of Clynnog from 1657 to 1660 and was placed there by the Triers to preach the gospel. He was one of those who signed the declaration requesting Richard Cromwell to continue in his father's position.[170] He was prevented from entering his church at Clynnog by two of his parishioners, and this led to a scuffle by the church door because Rowland opposed the restored liturgy of the Anglican Church: 'ni a fynnwn weled llosgi y Bibles fydd heb y Common prayer ynddynt' ('we demand that the Bibles which do not contain the Common

---

[166] J. E. Griffith, *Pedigrees*, p.202.
[167] *DWB*, pp.935-6.
[168] J. E. Griffith, *Pedigrees*, p.194.
[169] *Calendar of Wynn of Gwydir Papers*, no. 2173; B. Owen, 'Some details', 38-43; idem, 'Rhai agweddau...', 22, 30-1.
[170] T. Richards, *Religious Developments*, pp.21, 137-8.

Prayer be burnt'), declared one witness who had attacked him, a clear indication of the tensions which surviving Puritan sympathies could create.[171] Moreover, on 18 May 1660 John Jones, rector of Llaniestyn and adjoining chapelries, was interrupted during his sermon in Deneio parish church by Frederick Wynn of Bodanwyddog, forcing him to end the service at that point. As he departed from the church he was set upon physically and verbally by Wynn in the churchyard.[172] This was a real grievance because the sacraments of baptism, marriage and burial could not be administered according to the rites of the Anglican Church. The *Directory for the Publique Worship of God*, which had replaced the Prayer Book and had imposed extempore prayers and preaching of the Word, was unpopular among the clergy generally, and several balladsingers criticized the new order and expressed their opposition to the 'letani newydd' ('new litany') used in public worship:

> Yr hen letani ni chawn beynydd
> Na llyfr gweddi'r Eglwysydd
> Heiddiw mynwn un o newydd
> *Libera nos domine.*[173]

[We shall not have the old litany daily nor the Prayer Book in churches; today we insist on having a new one; Lord deliver us.]

References were also made to the preacher 'gwaela i riw' ('worst of his kind'), with his 'gau athrawiaeth' ('false doctrine'), not knowing what he was saying ('beth i bo yn i ddoydyd').[174] It could be argued that political ballads of this kind, more than any source, reflected more the mood of peasant folk in rural Wales of the 1650s. The Puritan custom of sending 'a numskull to talk in the middle of the market' ('catffwl i shiarad ynghanol y farchnad')[175] or the 'false prophet' ('gau broffwyd') did not appeal to them.[176] The poetry constantly deplores the king's unjust execution, the oppression of soldiers and their armies, the instability of parliament, the power of the County Committee ('nerth y committee'), the plunder of

---

171 GAS, X/QS 1660. A copy of this documents appears in B. Owen, 'Some details...', 39-40.
172 GAS, X/QS 1660.
173 *Hen Gerddi Gwleidyddol*, pp.30, 33
174 Ibid., pp.27, 29.
175 Ibid., p.27.
176 Ibid., p.30.

church property, the heavy and frequent taxation and the refusal of church sacraments.[177]

The Restoration of monarchy in 1660 brought hope of a much brighter future, as signified in the petition sent by the gentry of north Wales to Charles II on that occasion. In addition to expressing their delight they also gave him advice – to punish harshly the rebel leaders and to monitor closely the movement of the moderates who, despite their previous loyalty to the Crown, had come to terms with the Puritans.[178] On the eve of the Restoration the desire to see monarchy reinstated was voiced vociferously in alehouses. In March 1660, 'the good people of this Commonwealth' were called 'knaves and asses',[179] and in a Caernarfon alehouse a sailor toasted 'King Charles his health', adding that he wished for 'shipps upon...to fetch over King Charles'.[180] Again, in Caernarfon, Edmund Brady of Llaniestyn, registrar of Dinllaen parish, was astonished to hear Thomas Hanson, a Llanllyfni kerver's comment that he would be glad to welcome the king and to 'wipe the kings brich'.[181]

All told the efforts of the radical Puritan government of the 1650s failed to settle the localities, and this was most clearly shown in north-west Wales. Even the most ardent of justices of the peace, such as Griffith Jones, Griffith Williams and Edmund Glynne, realized that policies were not succeeding as they were intended. In 1655, for example, it was reported that complaints had been made to the Council of State that Cromwell's officers were meddling with the lives of 'conscientious people' in Caernarfonshire in attempting, by proclamation, to suppress Jesuits and recusants.[182] They also tried to alleviate the severe policies entrusted to James Berry and his fellow Major-Generals, who found it altogether impossible to accomplish their tasks. What might be more easily enforced in urban areas was often considered to be impossible in exposed rural areas where population was scattered and where full co-operation by other officials was not forthcoming. Moreover, bad weather conditions, poor communications and language problems also added to a sense of

---

177 Ibid., p.29.
178 *Calendar of Wynn of Gwydir Papers*, no.2272 (NLW MS.9066E.2272).
179 GAS, X/QS 1660; W. O. Williams, 'The county records', 88.
180 GAS, X/QS 1660.
181 Ibid., 1659.
182 *Cal. State Papers Dom., 1655-1656*, CII, pp.66-7; T. Richards, *Religious Developments*, pp.149-50.

frustration and of ultimate failure. The economic climate also contributed immensely to any attempt to upset the traditional structure of rural society which was not sufficiently developed to absorb new methods of government, administration and religious practice. James Berry emphasized that he had not experienced any serious opposition to his rule in Wales: 'though Wales hath beene looked on as a disorderly place', he maintained, 'yet I find a very ready complyance with his highness orders'. 'I have not met with above one refractory person in all Wales', he continued, which made it clear that it was not opposition that concerned Berry in Wales but the ignorance, illiteracy and apathy among the population generally. In addition the number of Puritan governors was small and they were in power for far too short a time to have any long-term impact. Social conditions and customs cannot be changed overnight, thus the efforts to carry out revolutionary measures were almost totally ineffective and hardly touched the grass roots. Berry was well aware of his own failure. Apart from the fact that he was a stranger, his district, covering extensive parts of western England, was too large and far too unwieldy to govern effectively. He failed to come to terms with the Welsh people at gentry or at lower levels. Despite his good intentions he had very little, if any, experience of administration on a broad scale, and his unceasing travel, which was intended to meet with the efficiency expected of him, was often to no avail.[183] If a colleague, such as William Goffe, complained about his failures in Sussex and Thomas Kelsey, Edward Whalley and George Worsley felt exhausted in other districts, Berry's words expressing his exasperation with what had to be done in Gwynedd revealed a man of conviction if not of hope. 'I have little pleasure to stay in these parts', he remarked, 'but indeed here is muche worke to be done'.[184]

Following the dismissal of the Major-Generals in the early part of 1657 Cromwell recognized that yet another constitutional experiment of his was doomed to failure. He moved on to try to 'heal and settle' using other methods and, in local government affairs in Carnarfonshire, he was assisted by an emerging group of younger gentry, sons of old royalists, who had not been prevented, as were their fathers, from holding office.[185]

---

[183] Berry and Lee, p.134 et seq. esp. p.145.
[184] Ibid., pp.143-4.
[185] A. H. Dodd, *History of Caernarvonshire*, pp.147-9; idem, *Studies*, pp.159-62; J. G. Jones, 'Caernarvonshire justices of the peace', 139-41.

In the 1660 commission of the peace were added Robert, Viscount Bulkeley of Baron Hill, William and John Hookes of Conwy,[186] Griffith Bodwrda,[187] John Glynne (Cromwell's Chief Justice) of the Hawarden branch of the Glynnes,[188] Sir Roger Mostyn of Flintshire[189] and Maurice Wynn of Gwydir who was appointed receiver-general of north Wales.[190] William Hookes was a son-in-law of Sir Griffith Wiliams of Y Penrhyn, who earned praise for himself for disarming parliamentarians in the county in 1660. Men of this kind did not have sufficient zeal to be able to maintain the momentum needed to ensure that Puritan government was given added power. Indeed Cromwell, in his last year revealed a marked tendency to reach agreement with the more traditional elements in the localities. To weed the Caernarfonshire commission of undesirable justices was not a difficult task for their actions had spoken for them. It was also a time when wavering justices could, if they so wished, change allegiances purely for personal advancement. On the Restoration of monarchy, therefore, it is hardly surprising to see Griffith Jones and Thomas Madrun, among others, enthusiastically welcoming the new king to his throne, and they, like many others, were re-commissioned and served actively in local government for several years to come.[191]

Despite the revolution that occurred in the 1650s county communities still safeguarded the awareness of local and regional identity. In one of the old Welsh ballads the anger felt towards the Puritans is clearly revealed:

> Dymynwn na bytho yn troedio mor tir
> Un Rowndyn y Nghymru na Pharlamanttir.[192]

[I desire never to see walking the land one Roundhead or Parliamentarian in Wales.]

---

[186] J. R. S. Phillips, *Justices of the Peace*, pp.33-4; N. Tucker, 'The royalist Hookes of Conway', *TCHS*, XXV, 1964, 5-12.

[187] *DWB*, p.44.

[188] Ibid., p.281-2; J. E. Griffith, *Pedigrees*, p.261.

[189] J. E. Griffith, *Pedigrees*, p.pl.183.

[190] NLW MSS. 9063E.1846-51, 1857, 1860; 9064E. 1952, 2032; *Chirk Castle Accounts*, p.108; Llanfair and Brynodol MSS. 227-9; B. E. Howells (ed.), *Calendar of Letters relating to North Wales, 1533-c.1700*, pp.137 (227), 138 (228-9), 205 (393); *Acts and Ordinances*, I, pp.46-7, 313-4, 482-3, 679-80, 1335.PRO *List of Sheriffs*, p.261.

[191] J. R. S. Phillips, *Justices of the Peace*, pp.32-4.

[192] *Hen Gerddi Gwleidyddol*, p.36.

The 'Roundhead' was abhorred for what his close-cropped head stood for. The anonymous ballad to 'The Character of a Roundhead' revealed the contempt:

> What's he that doth the Bishops hate,
> And count their calling reprobate,
> Cause by the Pope propounded,
> And says a zealous cobbler's better,
> Then he that studieth every letter,
> Oh, such a knave's a Roundhead.[193]

Bards of this genre could not but draw attention satirically to 'the brother with the stiff ears' ('y brawd a'i glistiau sythion') and those who despoiled the countryside and destroyed the church:

> Lladd, lledratta, speilio'r gweinied
> Poini'r cyfion, perchi'r diried
> Llwyr ddychanu Duw drwy ddirmig
> Rhwygo'r Eglwys yn ddrylliedig.[194]

[Killing, stealing, despoiling the weak, perplexing the just, respecting rascals; satirizing God complelety by despising Him; rupturing and wrecking the Church.]

Their prime aim was to see the power of those who served the state 'by the power of the sword' ('...llywodraeth nerth y cleddau') being wholly destroyed.[195] It is hardly surprising, therefore, that those who remained loyal to the Commonwealth and Protectorate to the very end still considered the hinterland of Wales to be 'one of the dark corners of the land'.

---

193 T. Paulin (ed.), *The Faber Book of Political Verse* (London, 1986), p.87.
194 *Hen Gerddi Gwleidyddol*, pp.31, 33.
195 Ibid., p.32.

CONCLUSION

Early seventeenth-century Welsh bishops entered a difficult phase in the development of the Protestant Church. Not only were they expected to continue the arduous task of promoting the new faith established by law by Elizabeth I and to reform the ecclesiastical structure of the medieval church but they were also, in conjunction with the clergy and the mass of the peasant population, expected to make that Church an institution which, in the first instance, would achieve renown for its pastoral work and secondly for its role in maintaining the links between Church and state in the political arena in early Stuart Wales. The ground had been reasonably well prepared for them in the latter decades of the sixteenth century when a large proportion of Welsh bishops, several of them, unlike most of their predecessors, of Welsh origins, advanced the Protestant Reformation by adding personal attributes to foster good relations between the newly-established Church and the mainly rural communities which it served. Not that the rate of success was particularly remarkable. Much that was associated with the Old Faith continued to linger on and, despite the increasing attachment of gentry families to the Elizabethan Church, there were social and economic problems which hindered it from functioning as efficiently as it might for the benefit of the state and the religious communities alike.

These problems dogged the development of the Protestant Church in Wales. Efforts were made to counter the evil effects of medieval practices, most of which were remnants of Roman Catholic traditions and almost impossible to eradicate in the short term. Higher and lower clergy were equally hamstrung by poverty and the deficiences which made administering the church at parochial level an immensely difficult task. It does not appear that relations between Elizabethan bishops and their clergy were unduly strained. Occasions did arise when property, patronage and other allied matters did create tensions, but, since the condition of the church continued to be a cause of major concern, Welsh bishops did what they could to ensure that the new religious settlement was secure.

It is difficult to gauge the extent to which religious literature served to improve the quality of religious life in a country where illiteracy and ignorance were major social features. Not even the Bible would have had an immediate impact on a backward rural community and the works of Hugh Lewis and Maurice Kyffin, among others in the late sixteenth and early seventeenth centuries, worthy though they were in their own right as prose works, would hardly have had the effect their authors would have desired at grass-root level, and there is little evidence to show that even higher clergy made much use of such manuals. What is altogether surprising, however, is that no attempt was made to translate into Welsh Richard Hooker's famous work on the foundations of the Protestant church, advocating a balanced anglicanism, nor Matthew Parker's *Book of Advertisments* (1566), designed to establish uniformity in the order of service and the use of the surplice. In his later writings John Penry made no reference to the appearance of the Welsh Bible. He had sacrificed himself to the state before most of the Welsh religious works appeared, many of them as translations of eminent English manuals. Penry's intentions to chastise the Church in Wales seemed to have backfired because he achieved nothing by it. Had he lived longer he might well have realized that the propaganda used to promote that Church was sincere and aimed at reforming a system which other clerics as well as the layman Penry and his Puritan associates had considered to be a discredit to the true quality of religious life. What literary propaganda appeared in the reigns of Elizabeth and James I was disseminated usually by a small group of bishops and higher clergy, among whom Richard Davies, William Morgan, Edward James and Lewis Bayly were the most prominent. Their immediate appeal might well be questioned but their long-term effects doubtless were fundamentally important to ensure the success of the Protestant tradition. The laity also took a leading part in the campaign to give the newly-established Church a central role in community life. They were as ardent as the clergy, well-equipped in their knowledge of the tenets of the faith and eager to apply that faith in domestic surroundings as well as public services. In addition to the pietistic approach adopted by Lewis Bayly, Rhys Prichard and Robert Llwyd in the 1630s and 1640s laymen such as Maurice Kyffin and Rowland Vaughan stood alongside. The measure of their achievement in practical terms, however, needs careful reassessment for it is hardly conceiveable that the substantial works translated by Kyffin and Vaughan would have promoted the faith among the lower orders in Wales and it is doubtful whether the majority of parochial clergy would have regarded such works as a staple spiritual diet.

The condition of the church in the years between the accession of Elizabeth and the outbreak of Civil War in England and Wales is uniquely revealed in the rich corpus of bardic output, both in free and strict metres. This notable evidence tells as much about the religious propensities of the bards themselves as it does about those whom they intended to address. In this context religion, in its role as a social entity, emerges clearly for the intensity shown in the verses (*cwndidau*) of Thomas ap Ieuan ap Rhys and Siôn Brwynog, on the one hand, and Thomas ap Llywelyn ap Dafydd ap Hywel and Siôn Tudur on the other, indicates how ardent individual propagandists of this kind were in projecting their religious beliefs. Interwoven with this subject-matter was the position of the Protestant state in relation to uniformity in religious observance. This is revealed particularly in the strict-metre *awdlau* and *cywyddau* of prolific bards such as Edwart ap Raff, Rhisiart Cynwal, Siôn Phylip and Huw Machno. Their output is strongly worded for in their eulogies the public functions of the gentry in religious and secular matters assume a dominant position. Again, what they achieved beyond their eulogistical exercises is not easily resolved. Poems on spiritual and related themes were often composed on the Trinity, over-indulgence and other sins of mankind, and the Godhead, all interspersed with statements on the frailty of life. Whilst poems of this kind betray moderate Puritan traits, as did several of the *cwndidau*, their main aim was to reflect how religious change and formal statutory commandments sorely affected the religious customs practised by illiterate parishioners in rural communities. The more conventional *awdlau* and *cywyddau* presented to privileged regional leaders and church dignitaries, were chiefly intended to buttress the interaction that had already emerged between gentry and the Crown. Religion and the 'political nation' in this context were regarded as being inter-related entities vital to the formation of the organic unity of the state. The realpolitik which characterized the gentry order was applied to the role of religion in preserving the sovereign state.

Early seventeenth-century bishops in Wales, who collectively have not received the attention they deserve, were figureheads in endeavouring to maintain the 'wholeness' and 'wholesomeness' of the Church. They were regarded as pastors as well as diocesan administrators. Bent on increasing and improving the publicizing of religious mission by advocating the need for an effective preaching ministry, their efforts broadly were directed towards performing charitable acts, becoming actively engaged in preaching the Word, fostering piety in public and private life and extending patronage and hospitality. While it is true that Bayly, for example, exaggerated his difficulties, doubtless the condition of the Welsh diocese militated against effective missions and administration. In these respects Welsh bishops, in the early decades of the century, followed the example of some of their godly counterparts in English dioceses, being actively engaged in diocesan affairs, initiating and conducting an evangelical programme and associating themselves with charitable and hospitable conduct. Notable in this respect was Henry Rowlands but Lewis Bayly, John Hanmer and Anthony Rudd might also be added as advocators of piety in their dioceses. Among them Bayly is outstanding only in that he published a pietistic work, *The Practice of Piety*, which had tremendous repercussions on the spiritual life of communities in many countries besides England and Wales. In a period when the new Protestant Church was in the process of establishing itself, maintained by a strong group of scholarly higher clergy, the Welsh episcopacy was dutifully engaged in tackling the issues inherited from the previous century. The old problems remained and were to persist, and all that Stuart bishops could do was to reside in their sees, offer hospitality, promote education, improve spirituality, at times coloured with a moderate Puritanism, and suppress Roman Catholic recusancy. In the 1630s, notably during the episcopates of John Owen and William Murray, an effort was made to improve the Church's reputation by adhering to the anti-Puritan policy introduced by Archbishop Laud to strengthen the divine concept of episcopacy, ensure uniformity of ritual and assert the king's absolute power, thereby maintaining the inter-relationship between the Crown and the established Church. They have been described as 'a valuable buttress to monarchical power' which, in turn, assisted in increasing their authority and prestige and enabled them to administer their dioceses more effectively. Despite their shortcomings, efforts were made to restore to the Church, in matters regarding religious worship and ecclesiastical property, the reverence and respect which Protestant divines considered essential to maintaining its spiritual welfare. Since their presence at court did not count for much in their episcopal careers they appeared not to have cultivated the skill to manage property matters to the extent that they might, thus allowing assertive and crafty landed gentry to take advantage of the situation.

Although the Elizabethan Church was abolished by law in the 1640s much of its defiant spirit persisted, particularly among clergy and gentry, since the majority who had in the past functioned in the public domain remained stalwartly supportive of the Stuart Crown in the wars and the following decade. What those wars brought in their trail in terms of disruption and devastation was increased by the introduction of radical changes in religious organization and worship. The Puritan regime which was established after the execution of Charles I created more deep-seated resentment than upheaval in Welsh community life. It is evident that the new order was almost totally rejected in Wales because old patterns of unity and uniformity under the Crown continued to be the basis of order among the politically aware sections of the Welsh community. The Act for the Propagation of the Gospel and all that it entailed to 1653 revealed little that brought permanent success to the Commonwealth besides being an experiment in devolution. The experiences in one Welsh county, namely Caernarfonshire, for which some valuable evidence survives for that decade, illustrates how insecure and unpopular Puritan governors were and how difficult they found their mission to be – reforming 'one of the dark corners of the land'. In this context the role of local government is a focal point. Quarter Sessions and allied legal and administrative records provide the historian with the proof that is needed to show that a decade of stern Puritan rule could never have penetrated sufficiently to have any lasting impact on sparsely-populated, remote and conservative communities. Regardless of the policies that were imposed, there remained an inalienable allegiance to the old order. Neither Approvers nor Triers found themselves comfortably in control, and Major-General James Berry, despite his honest dealings in Wales and the borderland, pursued a policy that was at best arduous and unfulfilling.

What a revolutionary government attempted to achieve was hindered by ignorance and reluctance to co-operate, and the few ministers appointed to promote the Puritan order were severely restricted by their own inadequacies in not being able to make an effective breakthrough in their spiritual mission. What Wroth, Cradock and Oliver Thomas, among others, achieved in promoting the preaching of the gospel in certain areas of Wales, particularly in the eastern borderlands, was heavily outweighed by a partially fulfilled and unrewarding spiritual mission in most others. It is clearly the case that some Puritan activities were to have lasting effects for the future in the history of religious dissent but the hard-core policy of puritanization left very little which the authorities could be proud of in their religious mission. Remote though most areas of Caernarfonshire and adjoining areas were, the evidence clearly points to what was experienced in most other parts of Wales, namely the rejection of heavy-handed tactics employed in imposing the will of the few on the many. It is true that the new Protestant Church had gained immensely from some Puritan beliefs during its period of growth, as emerged in the leanings of a sizeable proportion of its clergy and enlightened laity whose experience of the world in pursuing their occupations and professions had drawn them closely to a pietism which was to have a deep impact on their lives. Conversely, the Puritanism which burgeoned in the 1640s and 1650s also left an indelible imprint on the subsequent development of the post-Restoration Church.

Despite the growth of sectarianism both religious traditions served to enrich each other in the pietistic and philanthropic energies that were to be released by them. This development followed on from the natural advancement of the Protestant faith. The Church was, from its inception, an institution which depended on propaganda and a close interaction between clergy and laity to achieve its aims. Small though that output was it contributed significantly to the promotion of Christian values, aiming to achieve spiritual regeneration among the lower orders. The role of bardic output, in its various forms, adds a crucial dimension to an understanding of views and opinions expressed at grass-root level and among privileged families who were in the process of identifying their allegiance to the Crown with their religious convictions. In the early seventeenth century the Church, through its bishops and higher clergy, placed greater emphasis on mission and on restoring the church to its appropriate status in the state. The strength of the alliance established between the clergy and laity endured even in the period of Puritan rule. That challenge did not destroy what had, in previous generations, become the cornerstone of unity and good order. Despite its vulnerability and further difficulties in the post-Restoration era, through educational endeavour, increased literary propaganda and a deepening pietism, it served, in co-operation with a minority group of dissenting activists, to lay firm foundations and promote a reforming spirit in the half-century before the Methodist Revival.

BIBLIOGRAPHY

Original Sources
BODLEIAN LIBRARY, OXFORD
Jesus MS.18

British Library
MS. 14892; 15003; 31056
Harleian MS. 280
Royal MS. 18.13

Cardiff City Library
MSS. 2.277; 2.68; 3.68; 4.58; 4.101; 4.110; 5.44; 19.527; 84

Gwynedd Archive Service
Caernarfonshire Quarter Sessions Records c.1650-1660

National Library of Wales
Add. MSS. 466E.;16129
Brogyntyn MSS. II.56; 3;6;530.
Chirk Castle MSS: Denbighshire Order Book, 1655
Cwrtmawr MS. 238
Llandaff Cathedral Chapter Act Book, 4
Llanstephan MSS. 82; 118; 123; 125;133; 157; 164
Llanfair & Brynodol MSS. 94; 227-9
Mostyn MSS. 1;131;145;152
MS. 5269B
Panton MSS. 9052E; 9053E; 9054E; 9056E; 9057E; 9058E; 9059E; 9060E; 9061E; 9062E; 9064E
Peniarth MSS. 61; 96; 100; 114, 313
St Asaph Misc. Doc. 835-9
St David's Cathedral, Chapter Act Book, 4

Public Record Office
C(hancery) 193/12 (no.3). 193/13 (no.3).

University of Wales, Bangor
Bangor Mostyn MS. 9

Printed Sources

Acts of the Privy Council of England 1542-1630, ed. J. R. Dassent (London, 1890ff.)

A Funerall Sermon preached...by the Reverend Father in God, Richard...Bishoppe of Saint Dauys at the Buriall of the Right Honourable Walter Earle of Essex and Ewe (London, 1577).

'A discoverie of the present Estate of the Byshoppricke of St Asaph', *AC* (5th Ser.), I, 1884, 53-8.

Ballinger, J (ed.), *Calendar of Wynn of Gwydir Papers, 1515-1690* (Cardiff, 1926).

Bayly, L., *The Practice of Piety* (London, 1630 and 1640 eds.).

Bliss, J., and Scott, W. (eds.), *The Works of William Laud*, III, V (Oxford, 1853).

Bowen, G., *Y Drych Cristianogawl: astudiaeth*, JWEH, 1988.

Bowen, G. (ed.), *Y Drych Kristnogawl: LLAWYSGRIF CAERDYDD 3.240* (Cardiff, 1996).

Bowen. D. J., *Gwaith Gruffudd Hiraethog* (Cardiff, 1990).

Bradney, J., 'The speech of William Blethin, bishop of Llandaff, and the customs and ordinances of the church of Llandaff (1575)', *Y Cymmrodor*, XXXI, 1921, 240-6.

Bruce, J. and Perowne, T. T. (eds.), *Correspondence of Matthew Parker* (Parker Society, Cambridge, 1853).

Bunny, E., *Christian exercise appertaininge to resolvtion...*(London, 1584).

Calendar of Letters and Papers, Foreign and Domestic, Henry VIII 1509-47 (London, 1962-1932).

Calendars of State Papers, Domestic Series, 1509—1674, (London, 1858 ff.) *1547-80; 1581-90, 1603-10; 1611-18; 1622; 1627-28; 1628-29; 1629; 1629-30; 1633-34; 1634-35; 1636-37; 1637; 1639-40; 1640; 1640-41; 1649-50; 1650; 1651; 1654; 1655-56.*

Catalogue of Tracts of the Civil War and Commonwealth Period relating to Wales and the Border (NLW Aberystwyth, 1911).

Catley, S. R., *The Acts and Monuments of John Fox*, V (London, 1838).

Clark, G. T. (ed.), *Cartae et Alia Munimenta...*, IV, 1215-1689 (Cardiff, 1893).

Corbet, J., *A True and Impartial History of the Military Government of the City of Gloucester, repr. in Bibliotheca Gloucestriensis*, I.

Cradock, W., *Glad Tydings from Heaven: To the Worst of Sinners on Earth* (London, 1648).

Davies, C. (ed.), *Rhagymadroddion a Chyflwyniadau Lladin, 1551-1632* (Cardiff, 1980).

Davies, J. H. (ed.), *Hen Gerddi Gwleidyddol, 1588-1660* (Cymdeithas Llên Cymru, Cardiff, 1901).

Davies, J., *Llyfr y Resolusion neu Hollawl Ymroad* (Caernarfon, 1885).

Davies, W. T. P., 'Baledi gwleidyddol yng nghyfnod y chwyldro Piwritanaidd', *Y Cofiadur*, XXV, 1955, 3-22.

Dent, A., *The Plaine Man's Pathway to Heaven* (repr. Belfast, 1994).

Dwnn, L., *Heraldic Visitations of Wales*, ed. S. R. Meyrick, 2 vols. (Llandovery, 1846).

Ellis, H. (ed.), *Original Letters Illustrative of English History*, (2nd Ser.) III, (London, 1827).

Ellis, M., 'Cyflwyniad Rowland Vaughan, Caer-gai, i'w gyfieithiad o *Eikon Basilike*', NLWJ, I, 1939-40, 43-4.

Erbery, W., *Apocrypha* (London, 1652).

Erbery, W., *The Grand oppressor, Or, The Terror of Tithes...*(1652), in *The Testimony of W. Erbery* (London, 1658).

Evans, A. O., *A Memorandum on the Legality of the Welsh Bible and the Welsh Version of the Book of Common Prayer* (Cardiff, 1925).

Evans, J. D., 'Kitchin's return (1563)', *Gwent Local History*, LXVII, 1989, 11-18.

Fasti Ecclesiae Anglicanae, ed. J. Le Neve, 3 vols (London, 1854)

Fincham, K. C. (ed.), *Visitation Articles and Injunctions of the early Stuart Church* (London, 1998).

Firth, C. H., and Rait, R. S., (eds.), *Acts and Ordinances of the Interregnum* (London, 1911).

Flenley, R. (ed.), *A Calendar of the Register of the Queen's Council in the Dominion and Principality of Wales and the Marches of the same, 1569-1591* (London, 1916).

Furnivall, F. J., *Ballads from MSS. on the Condition of England in Henry VIII's and Edward VI's Reign* (Hertford, 1868).

Griffiths, J., *The Two Books of Homilies appointed to be read in Churches* (Oxford, 1859).

Hadley, A (ed.), *The Registers of Conway* (London, 1900).

Hall, E., *Chronicle, containing the History of England...*(1548)) (London, 1809 ed.).

HMC *Salisbury (Hatfield House) MSS* (London, 1883-).

Holland, R. 'Ymddiddan Tudur a Gronwy', in T. Jones (ed.), *Rhyddiaith Gymraeg: Detholion o Lawysgrifau a Llyfrau Printiedig, 1547-1618* (Cardiff, 1956), 161-72.

Hooker, R., *Of the Lawes of Ecclesiastical Polity*, ed. R. Bayne (London, 1907).

Hopkin-James, L. J. and Evans, T. C. (eds), *Hen Gwndidau, Carolau a Chywyddau*, (Bangor, 1918).

Howell, J., *Epistolae Ho-elianae (The Familiar Letters of James Howell)*, ed. J. Jacobs, 2 vols. (London, 1892).

Howells, B. E. (ed.), *Calendar of Letters relating to North Wales, 1533-c.1700* (Cardiff, 1967).

Hughes, G. H. (ed.), *Rhagymadroddion, 1547-1659* (Cardiff 1951).

Hughes, P. L. and Larkin, J. F. (eds.), *Tudor Royal Proclamations* (London, 1969).

J. Wynn, *History of the Gwydir Family and Memoirs*, ed. J. G. Jones (Llandysul, 1990).

Jenkins, D. Lloyd, (ed.), *Cerddi Rhydd Cynnar* (Llandysul, 1931).

Jewel, J., *An Apologie or Aunswer in defence of the Church of England, 1562* (Scolar Facsimile, Menston, 1969).

Jones, D., *Cydymaith Diddan* (Chester, 1766 ed.).

Jones, E. D.,'The Brogyntyn Welsh manuscripts', *NLWJ*, VI, 1949-50; VII (3), 1952.

Jones, J. (ed.), *Cynfeirdd Lleyn* (Pwllheli, 1906).

Jones, J. G., 'Cyfieithiad Rowland Vaughan, Caer-gai, o *Eikon Basilike* (1650)', *Studia Celtica*, XXXVI, 2002, 99-138.

Jones-Pierce, T. (ed.), *Clenennau Letters and Papers in the Brogyntyn Collection* (National Library of Wales Journal, App. Ser. IV, no. 1 (Pt.1), 1947.

Journals of the House of Commons, 1547-1628 (London, 1803).

Kennedy, W. P. M., *Elizabethan Episcopal Administration* (Alcuin Club, 1929).

Larkin, J. K. and Hughes, P. L. (eds.), *Stuart Royal Proclamations*, I (Oxford, 1973).

Letters of Bishop William Morgan, Bishop of Llandaff, and afterwards of St Asaph... and Richard Parry (privately printed 1905).

Lewis, H. (ed.), *Hen Gyflwyniadau* (Cardiff, 1948).

Lewis, J., *The Parliament Explained to Wales* (Cymdeithas Llên Cymru, Cardiff, 1907).

'Llanllyfni papers', *AC* (3rd ser.), IX, 1863, 280-5.

Lloyd, N (ed.), *Cerddi'r Ficer: Detholiad o Gerddi Rhys Prichard* (Cyhoeddiadau Barddas, 1994).

McClure, N. E. (ed.), *Letters of John Chamberlain* (Philadelphia, 1939).

Martin, L.C., (ed.), *Henry Vaughan: Poetry and Select Prose* (London, 1963).

Mathew, D., 'Some Elizabethan documents', *BBCS*, VI, 1931, 70-8.

Matthews, J. H. (ed.), *Cardiff Records* (Cardiff, 1898).

Merrick, R., *Morganiae Archaiographia*, ed. B. Ll. James (Cardiff,1983).

Morgan, M. (ed.), *Gweithiau Oliver Thomas ac Evan Roberts* (Cardiff, 1981).

Morrice, J. C. (ed.), *Barddoniaeth William Llŷn* (Bangor, 1908).

Morrice, J. C. (ed.), *Detholiad o Waith Gruffudd ab Ieuan ap Llewelyn Vychan* (Bangor, 1910).

Notes and Queries: A Medium of Intercommunication for Literary men, general Readers etc, 5th ser., vol. V, January-June, 1876.

Owen, G., 'The dialogue of the government of Wales', in H. Owen (ed.), *Penbrokshire*, III (London, 1906).

Owen, G., *The Description of Penbrokshire*, ed. H. Owen, 3 vols. (London, 1906).

Owens, B. G., 'Un o lawysgrifau Cymraeg y Diwygiad Catholig', *NLWJ*, I, 1939-40, 139-41.

Parry-Williams, T. H. (ed.), *Carolau Richard White* (Cardiff, 1931).

Parry-Williams, T. H. (ed.), *Canu Rhydd Cynnar* (Cardiff,1932)

Paulin, T., (ed.), *The Faber Book of Political Verse* (London, 1986).

Pennington, D. H. and Roots, I. A., (eds.), *The Committee at Stafford, 1643-1645: The Order book of the Staffordshire County Committee* (Manchester, 1957).

Penry, J., *Three Treatises concerning Wales*, ed. D. Williams (Cardiff, 1960).

Peter, H., *A Word for the Armie* (London, 1647).

Phillips, J. R. S., (ed.), *The Justices of the Peace in Wales and Monmouthshire, 1541 to 1689* (Cardiff, 1975).

Powell, V., *Common-Prayer Book No Divine Service* (London, 1660).

Prichard, R., *Y Seren Foreu neu Ganwyll y Cymry*, ed. R. Rees (Wrexham, 1897).

PRO Lists and Indexes, no. IX: *List of Sheriffs for England and Wales* (New York, 1963 ed.).

Prys, E., *Llyfr y Psalmau, wedi ev cyfiaethv, a'i cyfansoddi ar fesvr cerdd yn Gymraeg* (London, 1621).

Pryse, J., *Yny lhyvyr hwnn*, ed. J. H. Davies (Bangor, 1902).

Read, C. (ed.), *William Lambarde and Local Government* (Cornell U.P., 1962).

Rees, B. (ed.), *Dulliau'r Canu Rhydd, 1500-1650* (Cardiff, 1952).

Robert, G., *Gramadeg Cymraeg*, ed. G. J. Williams (Cardiff, 1939).

Roberts, E.(ed.), *Gwaith Siôn Tudur*, 2 vols. (Cardiff, 1978).

Rutt, T., (ed.), *The Parliamentary Diary of Thomas Burton*. 4 vols. (London, 1828).

Smyth, R., *Theater du Mond (Gorsedd y Byd)*, ed. T. Parry (Cardiff, 1930).

Statutes of the Realm, 1547-1885, 11 vols.(London, repr. 1963).

Strype, J., *The Life and Acts of Matthew Parker* (London, 1711).

The Releife of the Poor. Thomason Tracts. A Remonstrance by Leonard Lee [E.273(8)].

Thomas, D. A. (ed.), *The Welsh Elizabethan Catholic Martyrs* (Cardiff, 1971).

Thurloe, J., *A Collection of State Papers* (London, 1742).

Traherne, J. M. (ed.), *Stradling Correspondence* (London, 1840).

Twyne, T., *The Breuiarie of Britayne* (London, 1573).

Vaughan, E. W., *The Arraignment of Slander Perivry Blasphemy and other malicious sinnes* (London, 1630).

Vaughan, R., *Ymddiffyniad Rhag y Pla o Schism neu Swyn gyfaredd yn erbyn neulltuaethau yr Amseriad* (London, 1658).

Werdmüller, O., *A spyrytuall and moost precyouse pearle* , trans. M. Coverdale (London, 1550).

Williams, D. H., 'Fasti Cistercienses Cambrenses', *BBCS*, XXIV, 1971, 189-229.

Williams, G. A.(ed.), *Ymryson Edmwnd Prys a Wiliam Cynwal* (Cardiff, 1986).

Williams, G., *The Rightway to the Best Religion* (London, 1636).

Williams, G., *VII: Golden Candlesticks holding the Seven greatest lights of Christian Religion* (London, 1635).

Williams, I (ed.), *Casgliad o Waith Ieuan Deulwyn* (Bangor, 1909).

Williams, R. (ed.), *The Cambrian Journal* (Tenby, 1863).

Williams, W.G., 'Dau gywydd o waith John Gruffydd, Llanddyfnan', *TAAS*, 1938, 50-6.

Willsford, T., *The Scales of Commerce and Trade* (London,1659).

Wood, A., *Athenae Oxonienses*, ed. P. Bliss, 4 vols. (Oxford, 1813-20).

Wright, T. (ed.), *Three Chapters of Letters relating to the Suppression of the Monasteries* (London, 1843).

Yardley, E., (ed.), *Menevia Sacra*, *AC* (supplement), 1927.

Secondary Sources (volumes and articles)

Ashley, M., *Cromwell's Generals* (London, 1954).

Ashton,R., *Reformation and Revolution 1558-1660* (London, 1985).

Ballinger, J., *The Bible in Wales* (Cardiff, 1906).

Barber, H. and Lewis, H., *The History of Friars School, Bangor* (Bangor, 1901).

Bebb, W. A., *Cyfnod y Tuduriaid* (Wrexham, 1939).

Bell, H. I., *A History of Welsh Literature* (Oxford, 1955) [trans. of T . Parry's *Hanes Llenyddiaeth Gymraeg hyd 1900*).

Berry, J. and Lee, S. G., *A Cromwellian Major-General: The Career of Colonel James Berry* (Oxford, 1938).

Booty, J. E., *John Jewel as Apologist of the Church of England* (London, 1963).

Bowen, D. J., 'Detholiad o englynion hiraeth am yr hen ffydd', *Efrydiau Catholig*, VI, 1954, 5-12.

Bowen, G., 'Gwilym Pue "Bardd Mair", a theulu'r Penrhyn', *Efrydiau Catholig*, 1947, 11-35.

Bowen, G., 'Roman Catholic prose and its background', in R. G. Gruffydd (ed.), *A Guide to Welsh Literature c.1530-1700* (Cardiff, 1997), 210-40.

Bowen, G. (ed.), *Y Traddodiad Rhyddiaith* (Llandysul, 1970).

Breese, E., 'Dervel Gadarn', *AC*, (4th ser.), V, 1874, 152-6.

Breese, E., *Kalendars of Gwynedd* (London, 1873).

Cameron, E., *The European Reformation* (Oxford, 1991).

Charles-Edwards, T., 'Pen-rhys: y cefndir hanesyddol, 1179-1538', *Efrydiau Catholig*, V, 1951, 24-45.

Clark, D. S. T and Morgan, P. T. J. 'Religion and magic in Elizabethan Wales', *JEH*, XXVII, 1976. 31-46.

Collinson, P., 'The Elizabethan church and the new religion', in C. Haigh (ed.), *Reign of Elizabeth I* (London, 1984), 169-94.

Collinson, P., *The Elizabethan Puritan Movement* (London, 1967).

Cornwall, J., *Revolt of the Peasantry* (London, 1977).

Cressy, D., *Literacy and the Social Order: Reading and Writing in Tudor and Stuart England* (Cambridge, 1980).

Cross, C, *Church and People: 1450-1660: the Triumph of the Laity* (London, 1987 ed.).

Cross, C., 'Churchmen and the royal supremacy', in F. Heal and R. O'Day (eds.),- *Church and Society in England: Henry VIII to James I* (Basingstoke, 1977).

Cross, C., *The Royal Supremacy in the Elizabethan Church* (London, 1969), 15-34.

Davies, C., *John Davies o Fallwyd* (Caernarfon, 2001).

Davies, C. S. L., *Peace, Print and Protestantism, 1450-1558* (London, 1984).

Davies, C. T. B., 'Y cerddi i'r tai crefydd fel ffynhonnell hanesyddol', *NLWJ*, XVIII, 1973-4, 268-86, 345-73.

Davies, G., *Noddwyr Beirdd ym Meirion* (Dolgellau, 1974).

Dickens, A. G., *The English Reformation* (London, 1964).

Dickens, A. G., *Thomas Cromwell and the English Reformation* (London, 1959).

Dictionary of National Biography, ed. L, Stephen and S. Lee, 63 vols. (London, 1885-1900).

Dodd, A. H., *A History of Caernarvonshire, 1284-1900* (Wrexham, 1990 ed).

Dodd, A. H., 'Lewes Bayly, c.1575-1631', *TCHS*, XXVIII, 1967, 13-36.

Dodd, A. H., *Studies in Stuart Wales* (Cardiff, 1952).8-91.

Dodd, A. H., 'The pattern of politics in Stuart Wales', *TCS*, 1948.

Dodd, A. H., 'Wales and the Scottish succession, 1570-1605', *TCS*, 1937, 201-25.

Doran, S., *Elizabeth I and Religion, 1558-1603* (London, 1994).

Durston, C., *Cromwell's Generals: Godly Government during the English Revolution* (Manchester, 2001).

Eames, A., 'Sea power and Caernarvonshire', *TCHS*, XVI, 1955, 29-51.

Ellis, T. P., *The Catholic Martyrs of Wales* (London, 1933).

Elton, G. R., *England under the Tudors* (London, 1974 ed.).

Evans, A. O., 'Edmund Prys, archdeacon of Merioneth, priest, preacher, poet', *TCS*, 1922-3, 112-68.

Evans, A. O., 'Nicholas Robinson (1530?-1585)', *Y Cymmrodor*, XXXIX, 1928, 149-99.

Evans, W. G., 'Derfel Gadarn – a celebrated victim of the Reformation', *JMHRS*, XI, 1990-3, 137-68.

Everitt, A., *Change in the Provinces: The Seventeenth Century* (Leicester, 1969).

Fincham, K, *Prelate as Pastor: The Episcopate of James I* (Oxford, 1990).

Fincham, K., 'Ramifications of the Hampton Court Conference in the dioceses, 1603-1609', *JEH*, XXXVI, 1985, 208-27.

Fincham, K., (ed.), *The Early Stuart Church, 1603-1642* (Basingstoke, 1993).

Fletcher, A., *Reform in the Provinces: The Government of Stuart England* (London, 1986).

Flower, R., 'William Salesbury, Richard Davies and Archbishop Parker', *NLWJ*, II, 1941, 7-13.

Fuller, T., *The Church History of Britain*, ed. J. S. Brewer, X (Oxford, 1845).

Fychan, C., 'Y canu i wŷr eglwysig sir Ddinbych', *TDHS*, XXVIII, 1979, 115-82.

Gaunt, P., *A Nation under Siege: The Civil War in Wales, 1642-48* (London, 1991).

Gleason, J. H., *The Justices of the Peace in England, 1558 to 1640: A Later Eirenarcha* (Oxford, 1969).

Gray, M., 'The diocese of Bangor in the late 16th century', *JWEH*, V, 1988, 31-72.

Green, V. H. H., *Renaissance and Reformation* (London, 1956).

Greenleaf, W. H., *Order, Empiricism and Politics: The Traditions of English Political Thought, 1500-1700* (Oxford, 1964).

Griffith, J. E., *Pedigrees of Caernarvonshire and Anglesey Families* (Horncastle, 1914).

Griffith, W. P., 'Anglicaniaid a Phiwritaniaid: myfyrwyr a diwinyddion prifysgolion Lloegr, 1560-1640', *LlC*, XVI, 1989, 23-39.

Griffith, W. P., *Civility and Reputation: Ideals and Images of the 'Tudor Man' in Wales* (Bangor, 1985).

Griffith, W. P., 'Humanist learning, education and the Welsh language, 1536-1660', in G. H. Jenkins (ed.), *The Welsh Language before the Industrial Revolution* (Cardiff, 1996), 289-316.

Griffith, W. P., *Learning, Law and Religion: Higher Education and Welsh Society c. 1540-1640* (Cardiff, 1996).

Griffith, W. P., 'Merioneth and the new and reformed learning in the early modern period', *JMHRS*, XII, 1994-7, 334-47.

Griffith, W. P., 'Schooling and society', in J. G. Jones (ed.), *Class, Community and Culture in Tudor Wales* (Cardiff, 1989), 79-119.

Griffith, W. P., 'William Hughes and the "descensus" controversy of 1567', *BBCS*, XXXIV, 1987, 185-99.

Griffith,. W. P. (ed.), *'Ysbryd Dealltwrus ac Enaid Anfarwol': Ysgrifau ar Hanes Crefydd yng Ngwynedd* (Bangor, 1999).

Griffiths, D. R., 'Four centuries of the Welsh prayer book', *TCS*, 1975, 162-90.

Griffiths, P., Fox, A and Hunter, S (eds.), *The Experience of Authority in Early Modern England* (Basingstoke, 1996).

Gruffydd, R. G., *Argraffwyr Cyntaf Cymru: Gwasgau Dirgel y Catholigion adeg Elisabeth* (Cardiff, 1972), 1-23.

Gruffydd, R. G., 'Bishop Francis Godwin's injunctions for the diocese of Llandaff, 1603', *JHSCW*, IV, 1954, 14-22.

Gruffydd, R. G., 'Gwasg ddirgel yr ogof yn Rhiwledyn', *JWBS*, IX, 1958.

Gruffydd, R. G., *'In that Gentile Country...': the Beginnings of Puritan Nonconformity in Wales* (Bridgend, 1975).

Gruffydd, R. G., 'Michael Roberts o Fôn a Beibl bach 1630', *TAAS*, 1989, 25-42.

Gruffydd, R. G., 'Richard Parry a John Davies', in G. Bowen (ed.), *Y Traddodiad Rhyddiaith* (Llandysul, 1970), 175-93.

Gruffydd, R. G., 'The Renaissance and Welsh literature', in G. Williams and R. O. Jones (eds.), *The Celts and the Renaissance: Tradition and Innovation* (Cardiff, 1990), 17-39.

Gruffydd, R. G., *The translating of the Bible into the Welsh language by William Morgan in 1588* (London, 1988).

Gruffydd, R. G., 'Y cyfieithu a'r cyfieithwyr', in *Y Gair ar Waith: Ysgrifau ar yr Etifeddiaeth Feiblaidd yng Nghymru* (Cardiff, 1988), 27-39.

Gruffydd, R. G., *'Yny lhyvyr hwnn* (1546): the earliest Welsh printed book', *BBCS*, XXIII, 1968-70, 105-16.

Guy, J., 'The Tudor age 1485-1603', in K. O. Morgan (ed.), *Illustrated History of Britain, 1485-1789* (London, 1985), 1-70.

Guy, J., *Tudor England* (Oxford, 1990).

Hague, D. B., 'Rug chapel, Corwen', *JMHRS*, III, 1957-60, 167-83.

Haigh, C., *English Reformations: Religion, Politics and Society under the Tudors* (Oxford, 1993).

Haller, W., *Foxe's Book of Martyrs and the Elect Nation* (London, 1963).

Hasler, P. W. (ed.), *The History of Parliament: The House of Commons, 1558-1603*, (London, 1981).

Heal, F., *Of Prelates and Princes: A Study of the Economic and Social Position of the Tudor Episcopate* (Cambridge, 1980).

Heath, P., *The English Parish Clergy on the Eve of the Reformation* (London, 1969).

Hemp, W. J. (ed.), 'Commonwealth marriages', *TCHS*, XI, 1950, 103.

Hill, J. E. C., *Economic Problems of the Church from Archbishop Whitgift to the Long Parliament* (Oxford, 1956).

Hill, J. E. C., 'Propagating the gospel', in H. E. Bell and R. L. Ollard (eds.), *Historical Essays, 1600-1750, Presented to David Ogg* (London, 1963), 35-59.

Hill, J. E. C., *Society and Puritanism in Pre-Revolutionary England* (London, 1969).

Houlbrooke, R. A., 'The Elizabethan episcopate', in Heal, F. and O'Day, R. (eds.), *Church and Society in England: Henry VIII to James I* (Basingstoke, 1977), 78-98.

Howells, B. E., 'The kidnapping of Griffith Jones of Castellmarch', *Trivium*, XV, 1980.

Hughes, A. Ll., 'Rhai o noddwyr y beirdd yn sir Feirionnydd', *LlC*, X, 1968-9, 137-205.

Hughes, G. H., 'Y Dwniaid', *TCS*, 1941, 115-49.

Hughes, W., *The Life and Times of Bishop William Morgan* (London, 1891).

Hurstfield, J., 'County government *c*.1530-*c*.1660', in *Victoria County History (Wiltshire)*, V, ed. R. B. Pugh and E. Crittal (Oxford, 1957), 80-110.

Inderwick, F. A., *The Interregnum (A.D. 1648-1660): Studies of the Commonwealth Legislative, Social and Legal* (London, 1891).

Ingram, I., 'Reformation of manners in early modern England', in Griffiths, P., Fox, A.S. and Hunter, S (eds.), *The Experience of Authority in Early Modern England* (Basingstoke, 1996),47-88.

J. E. Lloyd and Jenkins, R. T. (eds.), *Dictionary of Welsh Biography down to 1940* (London, 1959).

James, B. Ll., 'The evolution of a radical: the life and career of William Erbery (1604-54)', *JWEH*, III, 1986, 31-48.

James, M., and Weinstock, M.,(ed.), *England during the Interregnum* (London, 1935).

James, M., *Social Problems and Policy during the Puritan Revolution* (London, 1966).

Jarvis, B., 'Welsh humanist learning', in R. G. Gruffydd (ed.), *A Guide to Welsh Literature, c.1530-1700* (Cardiff, 1997),128-54.

Jenkins, G. H. , *The Foundations of Modern Wales, 1642-1780* (Oxford, 1993).

Jenkins, G. H., *Protestant Dissenters in Wales, 1639-1689* (Cardiff, 1992).

Jenkins, P., *A History of Modern Wales, 1536-1990* (London, 1992).

Johnson, A. M., 'Politics and religion in Glamorgan during the Interregnum 1649-1660', in G. Williams (ed.), *Glamorgan County History*, IV, *Early Modern Glamorgan* (Cardiff, 1974), 279-309.

Johnson, A. M., 'Wales during the Commonwealth and Protectorate', in D. Pennington and K. Thomas (eds.), *Puritan and Revolutionaries: Essays in Seventeenth-Century History presented to Christopher Hill* (Oxford, 1978), 233-56.

Jones, B., 'Beirdd yr uchelwyr a'r byd', in J. E. Caerwyn Williams (ed.), *Ysgrifau Beirniadol*, VIII (Denbigh, 1974), 28-42.

Jones, D. G., *Y Ficer Prichard a 'Canwyll y Cymry'* (Caernarfon, 1946).

Jones, E. D. ,'The Brogyntyn Welsh manuscripts', *NLWJ*, VI, 1949-50,1-42,223-43; VII (3), 1952, 165-98.

Jones, E. G., 'Catholic recusancy in the counties of Denbigh, Flint and Montgomery, 1581-1625', *TCS*, 1945,114-33.

Jones, E. G., *Cymru a'r Hen Ffydd* (Cardiff, 1951).

Jones, E. G., 'Hugh Owen of Gwenynog', *TAAS*, 1938, 42-9.

Jones, E. G., 'Robert Pugh of Penrhyn Creuddyn', *TCHS*, VII, 1946, 10-19.

Jones, G. E., *The Gentry and the Elizabethan State* (Swansea, 1977).

Jones, J. G., 'Bishop William Morgan – defender of church and faith', *JWEH*, V, 1988,1-30.

Jones, J. G., 'Bishop William Morgan's dispute with John Wynn of Gwydir, 1603-04', *JHSCW*, XXII, 1972, 49-78.

Jones, J. G., 'Caernarvonshire administration: the activities of the justices of the peace, 1603-1660', *WHR*, V, 1970, 130-63.

Jones, J. G., *Concepts of Order and Gentility in Wales, 1540-1640: Bardic Imagery and Interpretations* (Llandysul, 1992).

Jones, J. G., 'Cyfraith a threfn yn sir Gaernarfon c.1600-1640', *TCHS*, XLVII, 1986, 25-70.

Jones, J. G., *Early Modern Wales c.1526-1640* (Basingstoke, 1994).

Jones, J. G., 'Gentry in action: the Plas Iolyn experience, c.1500-1600', in *Conflict, Continuity and Change in Wales c.1500-1603; Essays and Studies* (Aberystwyth, 1999), 39-79.

Jones, J. G., 'Governance, order and stability in Caernarfonshire c.1540-1640', *TCHS*, XLIV, 1983, 7-52.

Jones, J. G., 'Henry Rowlands, bishop of Bangor, 1598-1616', *JHSCW*, XXVI, 1977-8, 34-53.

Jones, J. G., 'John Penry: government, order and the "perishing souls" of Wales', *TCS*, 1993, 47-81.

Jones, J. G. 'Rhai agweddau ar y consept o uchelwriaeth yn nheuluoedd bonheddig Cymru yn yr unfed a'r ail ganrif ar bymtheg', in J. E. Caerwyn Williams (ed.), *Ysgrifau Beirniadol*, XII (Denbigh, 1982), 201-49.

Jones, J. G., 'Richard Parry, bishop of St. Asaph: some aspects of his career', *BBCS*, XXVI (ii), 1975, 175-90.

Jones, J. G., 'Rowland Vaughan o Gaer-gai a'i gyfieithiad o *Eikon Basilike* 1650', *Y Traethodydd*, CLVI, 2001, 18-40.

Jones, J. G., 'Sir John Wynn junior of Gwydir and Llanfrothen and the "Grand Tour", 1613-14', *JMHRS*, XI, 1990-93, 379-413; XII, 1994-7, 17-28,116-21.

Jones, J. G., 'The defence of the realm: regional dimensions c.1559-1604', in *Conflict, Continuity and Change in Wales c.1500-1603: Essays and Studies* (Aberystwyth, 1999), 113-53.

Jones, J. G., 'The Reformation bishops of Llandaff, 1558-1601', *Morgannwg*, XXXII, 1988, 38-69.

Jones, J. G., 'The Reformation bishops of St Asaph', *JWEH*, VII, 1990, 17-40.

Jones, J. G., *The Welsh Gentry: Images of Status, Honour and Authority, 1536-1640* (Cardiff, 1998).

Jones, J. G., 'The Welsh poets and their patrons, c.1550-1640', *WHR*, IX, 1979, 245-77.

Jones, J. G., *The Wynn Family of Gwydir: Origins, Growth and Development c.1490-1674* (Aberystwyth, 1995).

Jones, J. G., 'Thomas Davies and William Hughes: Two Reformation bishops of St. Asaph', *BBCS*, XXIX, 1980-2, 320-35.

Jones, J. G., 'Yr eglwys Anglicanaidd yn oes Elisabeth I: ei phwrpas, ei phryderon a'i pharhad', *Cristion* (September/October, 1988), 4-8.

Jones, J. G., 'Y "tylwyth teg" yng Nghymru'r unfed a'r ail ganrif ar bymtheg', *LlC*, VIII, 1964, 96-9.

Jones, J. M., 'Walter Cradoc a'i gyfoeswyr', *Y Cofiadur*, XV, 1938, 3-48.

Jones, N. L., *Faith by Statute: Parliament and the Settlement of Religion, 1559* (London, 1982).

Jones, R. T. and Owens, B. G., 'Anghydffurfwyr Cymru, 1660-1662', *Y Cofiadur*, XXXI, 1962, 3-91.

Jones, R. T., *Hanes Annibynwyr Cymru* (Swansea, 1971).

Jones, R. T., 'Mantoli cyfraniad John Penri', *Y Cofiadur*, 58, 1993, 4-41.

Jones, R. T., *Vavasor Powell* (Swansea, 1971).

Jordan, W. K., *Edward VI: the Young King* (London, 1968).

Kelso, R., *The Doctrine of the English Gentleman in the Sixteenth Century* (Gloucester, Massachusetts, 1964).

Ker, N. R., 'Sir John Prise', *The Library*, 5th ser., X, 1955, 1-24.

Kerr, R. M., 'Siôn Brwynog – un o feirdd cyfnod y Diwygiad Protestannaidd', *Ysgrifau Catholig*, II, 1963, 28-30.

Knight, L. S., 'Welsh cathedral schools to 1600 A. D.', *Y Cymmrodor*, XXIX, 1919, 76-109.

Lake, P., 'The Laudian style: order, uniformity and the pursuit of the beauty of holiness in the 1630s', in K. Fincham (ed.), *The Early Stuart Church. 1603-1642* (Basingstoke, 1993), 161-86.

Lewis, C. W., 'The decline of professional poetry', in R. G. Gruffydd (ed.), *A Guide to Welsh Literature*, III, c.1530-1700 (Cardiff, 1997), 29-74.

Lewis, C. W., 'The literary history of Glamorgan from 1550 to 1770', in *Glamorgan County History*, IV, *Early Modern Glamorgan*, ed. G. Williams (Cardiff, 1974), 535-639.

Lewis, C. W., 'The literary tradition of Glamorgan down to the middle of the sixteenth century', in T. B. Pugh (ed.), *Glamorgan County History*, III (Cardiff, 1971).

Lloyd, D. M., 'William Salesbury, Richard Davies and Archbishop Parker', *NLWJ*, II, 1941, 14-32.

Lloyd, J. E. and Jenkins, R. T., (eds.), *Dictionary of Welsh Biography to 1940* (London, 1959).

Loades, D. M., *The Reign of Mary I* (London, 1979).

Maltby, W. P., *The Black legend in England: The Development of Anti-Spanish Sentiments, 1558-1660* (Durham, NC, 1971).

Marlowe, T. *The Puritan Tradition in English Life* (London, 1956).

Mazzeo, J. A., *Renaissance and Revolution: The remaking of European Thought* (London, 1967).

McConica, J. K., *English Humanists and Reformation Politics* (Oxford, 1965).

McGinn, D., *John Penry and the Marprelate Controversy* (Rudgers U.P., 1966).

Merchant, W. M., 'Bishop Francis Godwin, historian and novelist', *JHSCW*, V, 1955, 45-51.

Morgan, I., *The Godly Preachers of the Elizabethan Church* (London, 1965).

Morgan, J., *Coffadwriaeth am y Gwir Barchedig Henry Rowlands, D. D., Arglwydd Esgob Bangor* (Bangor, 1910).

Morgan, W. T., 'The cases concerning dilapidations to episcopal property in the diocese of St. David's', *NLWJ*, VII., 1951-2, 149-98.

Morrill, J. S., *Cheshire, 1630-1660: The County Government and Society during the English Revolution* (Oxford, 1974).

Morrill, J. S., 'The Stuarts', in K.O. Morgan (ed.), *Illustrated Oxford History of Britain*, III (Oxford, 1992), 71-144.

Naphy, W. G., *Calvin and the Consolidation of the Geneva Reformation* (Manchester/New York, 1994).

Neale, J. E., *Elizabeth I and her Parliaments, 1584-1601* (London, 1957).

Newell, E. J., *Llandaff* (London, 1902).

Nuttall, G. F., *The Welsh Saints, 1640-1660* (Cardiff, 1957).

Owen, B., 'Rhai agweddau ar hanes Annibynwyr sir Gaernarfon o'r dechrau hyd y flwyddyn 1776', *Y Cofiadur*, XX, 1950, 3-71.

Owen, B., 'Some details about the Independents in Caernarvonshire', *TCHS*, VI, 1945, 32-45.

Owen, G. D., *Wales in the Reign of James I* (London, 1988).

Parry, G., 'Hanes ysgol Botwnnog', *TCS*, 1957, 1-17.

Parry, T., *Hanes Llenyddiaeth Gymraeg hyd 1900* (Cardiff, 1953).

Peter, J and Pryse, R. J., (eds.), *Enwogion y Ffydd*, 4 vols. (London, 1880).

Pierce, W., *John Penry: His Life, Times and Writings* (London, 1923).

Powicke, F. M. and Fryde, E. B. (eds.), *Handbook of British Chronology* (London, 1961).

Prichard, T. J. 'The Reformation in the deanery of Llandaff, 1534-1601', *Morgannwg*, xiii, 1969, 5-46.

Pryce, A. I., *The Diocese of Bangor during Three Centuries* (Cardiff, 1929).

Pugh, F. H., 'Glamorgan recusants, 1577-1611', *South Wales and Monmouth Record Society Publications*, no.3, 1954, 49-68.

Pugh. F. H., 'Monmouthshire recusants in the reigns of Elizabeth I and James I', *South Wales and Monmouth Record Society Publications*, no. 4, 1957, 57-110, 471-506.

Rannie, D. W., 'Cromwell's Major Generals', *English Historical Review*, X, 1895, 471-506.

Rees, W., *The Union of England and Wales* (Cardiff, 1948).

Richards, T., 'Eglwys Llanfaches', *TCS*, 1941, 150-84.

Richards, T., 'Henry Maurice: Piwritan ac Annibynnwr', *Y Cofiadur*, V-VI, 1928, 15-67.

Richards, T., *Religious Developments in Wales, 1654-1662* (London, 1923).

Richards, T., 'Richard Edwards of Nanhoron: A Restoration study', *TCHS*, VIII, 1947, 27-34.

Richards, T., *The Puritan Movement in Wales, 1639-53* (London, 1920).

Ridley, J., *Thomas Cranmer* (Oxford, 1962).

Roberts, D. H. E., and Charles, R. A., 'Raff ap Robert ac Edwart ap Raff', *BBCS*, XXIV, 1970-2, 282-99.

Roberts, E., 'Teulu Plas Iolyn', *TDHS*, XIII, 1964, 40-110.

Roberts, G., 'The Glynnes and Wynns of Glynllifon', *TCHS*, IX, 1948, 25-39.

Roberts, R. F., 'Dr John Davies o Fallwyd', *LlC*, II, 1952-3, 19-35, 97-110.

Roberts, S., 'Deddf Taenu'r Efengyl yng Nghymru (1650) a diwylliant Cymru', in J. G. Jones (ed.), *Agweddau ar Dwf Piwritaniaeth yng Nghymru yn yr Ail Ganrif ar Bymtheg* (Lewiston, New York, 1992), 93-110.

Roberts, S, 'Godliness and government in Glamorgan, 1647-1660', in C. Jones, M. Newitt and S. Roberts (eds.), *Politics and People in Revolutionary England* (London, 1986), 225-52.

Roberts, S., 'Welsh Puritans in the Interregnum', *History Today*, XLI, March 1991, 36-41.

Roots, I. A., 'Swordsmen and decimators', in R. H. Parry (ed.), *The English Civil War and After, 1642-1658* (Basingstoke, 1970), 78-92.

Royal Commission on the Ancient and Historical Monuments in Wales and Monmouthshire:Inventory, VI, *County of Merioneth* (Cardiff, 1921).

Scarisbrick, J. J., *The Reformation and the English People* (London, 1984).

Shankland, T., 'Anghydffurfwyr cyntaf Cymru', *Y Cofiadur*, I, 1923, 32-44.

Sharpe, J. A., 'Disruption in the well-ordered household: age, authority and possessioned young men', in P. Griffiths, A Fox. and S. Hunter (eds.), *The Experience of Authority in Early Modern England* (Basingstoke, 1996), 187-212.

Skeel, C. A. J., *The Council in the Marches of Wales* (London, 1904).

Stone, L., 'The educational revolution in England, 1560-1640', *Past & Present*, 18, 1964, 41-80.

Stone, L., *The Family, Sex and Marriage in England, 1500-1800* (Oxford, 1977).

Strype, J., *Annals of the Reformation* (London, 1725).

Strype, J., *The Life and Acts of Matthew Parker* (London, 1711).

Tawney, R. H., *Religion and the Rise of Capitalism* (London, 1929).

Thomas, D. R., *A History of the Diocese of St. Asaph*, 3 vols. (Oswestry, 1908).

Thomas, D. R., *The Life and Work of Bishop Davies and William Salesbury* (Oswestry, 1892).

Thomas, H., *A History of Wales, 1485-1660* (Cardiff, 1972).

Thomas, I., *William Morgan and his Bible* (Cardiff, 1988).

Thomas, L., *The Reformation in the Old Diocese of Llandaff* (Cardiff, 1930).

Thompson, G. S., 'The origins and growth of the office of deputy-lieutenant', *TRHS*, V, 1922, 150-60.

Trotter, E., *XVIIth-Century Life in the Country Parish* (Cambridge, 1919).

Tucker, N., *Denbighshire Officers in the Civil War* (Denbigh).

Tucker,N., 'Civil War Colonel: Sir John Carter', *TCHS*, XIII, 1952, 1-8.

Tucker, N., 'The royalist Hookes of Conway', *TCHS*, XXV, 1964, 5-12.

Tucker, N., 'Wartime brawl in Llannor churchyard', *TCHS*, XXVI, 1965, 50-2.

Underdown, D., *Pride's Purge: Politics in the Puritan Revolution* (Oxford, 1971).

Underdown, D., *Revel, Riot and Rebellion: Popular Politics and Culture in England, 1603-1660* (Oxford, 1985).

Underdown, D., 'Settlement in the counties, 1653-1658', in G. E. Aylmer (ed.), *The Interregnum: The Quest for Settlement, 1646-1660* (London, 1972), 165-82.

White, F. O., *Lives of the Elizabethan Bishops* (London, 1898).

Williams, D. G., 'Syr Owain ap Gwilym', *LlC*, VI,. 1960-1, 179-93.

Williams, G. 'Sir John Pryse of Brecon', *Brycheiniog*, XXXI, 1998-9, 49-63.

Williams, G., 'Bishop Richard Davies (?1501-1581)', in *Welsh Reformation Essays* (Cardiff, 1967), 155-90

Williams, G., 'Bishop Sulien, Bishop Richard Davies and Archbishop Parker', *NLWJ*, V, 1948, 215-32.

Williams, G., 'Bishop William Morgan (1545-1604) and the first Welsh Bible', in *The Welsh and their Religion* (Cardiff, 1991), 173-229.

Williams, G., 'Breuddwyd Tomas Llywelyn ap Dafydd ap Hywel', in *Grym Tafodau Tân: Ysgrifau Hanesyddol ar Grefydd a Diwylliant* (Llandysul, 1984), 164-79.

Williams, G., *Bywyd ac Amserau'r Esgob Richard Davies* (Cardiff, 1953).

Williams, G., 'Crefydd a llenyddiaeth Gymraeg yn oes y Diwygiad Protestannaidd', in G. H. Jenkins (ed.), *Cof Cenedl: Ysgrifau ar Hanes Cymru*, I (Llandysul, 1986), 35-64.

Williams, G., 'Cymru a'r Diwygiad Protestannaidd', in *Grym Tafodau Tân: Ysgrifau Hanesyddol ar Grefydd a Diwylliant* (Llandysul, 1984), 87-101.

Williams, G., 'Dadeni, Diwygiad a Diwylliant Cymru', in *Grym Tafodau Tân: Ysgrifau Hanesyddol ar Grefydd a Diwylliant* (Llandysul, 1984), 63-86

Williams, G., 'Education and culture down to the sixteenth century', in J. L. Williams and G. R. Hughes (eds.), *The History of Education in Wales*, I (Swansea, 1978), 9-27.

Williams, G., 'Edward James a Llyfr yr Homilïau', in *Grym Tafodau Tân: Ysgrifau Hanesyddol ar Grefydd a Diwylliant yng Nghymru* (Llandysul, 1984). 180-98.

Williams, G., 'John Penry: Marprelate and patriot?', *WHR*, III, 1967, 361-80.

Williams,G. 'Landlords in Wales: the Church', in J. Thirsk (ed.), *The Agrarian History of England and Wales*, IV 1500-1640 (Cambridge, 1967) 381-95.

Williams, G., *Reformation Views of Church History* (London, 1970).

Williams, G., 'Religion and Welsh literature in the age of the Reformation', in *The Welsh and their Religion* (Cardiff,1991), 138-72.

Williams, G., *Renewal and Reformation: Wales c.1415-1642* (Oxford, 1993).

Williams, G., 'Some Protestant views of early British church history', in *Welsh Reformation Essays* (Cardiff, 1967), 207-19.

Williams, G., 'The dissolution of the monasteries in Glamorgan', in *Welsh Reformation Essays* (Cardiff, 1967), 91-110.

Williams, G., 'The economic life of Glamorgan, 1536-1642', in G. Williams (ed.), *Glamorgan County History*: IV *Early Modern Glamorgan* (Cardiff, 1974)., 1-72.

Williams, G., 'The Elizabethan Settlement of religion in Wales and the Marches, 1559-1560', in *Welsh Reformation Essays* (Cardiff, 1967), 141-54.

Williams, G., 'The Protestant experiment in the diocese of St. David's, 1534-55', in *Welsh Reformation Essays* (Cardiff, 1967), 111-40.

Williams, G., *The Welsh Church from Conquest to Reformation* (Cardiff, 1962).

Williams, G., 'Unity of religion or unity of language? Protestants and Catholics and the Welsh language, 1536-1660', in G. H. Jenkins (ed.), *The Welsh Language before the Industrial Revolution* (Cardiff, 1997), 207-34.

Williams, G., *Wales and the Reformation* (Cardiff, 1997).

Williams, G., 'Wales and the reign of Mary I', in *WHR*, X, 1980-1, 334-58.

Williams, G., *Welsh Reformation Essays* (Cardiff, 1967).

Williams, G., 'Yr hanesydd a'r canu rhydd', in *Grym Tafodau Tân: Ysgrifau Hanesyddol ar Grefydd a Diwylliant* (Llandysul, 1984), 140-63.

Williams, G. J., *Traddodiad Llenyddol Morgannwg* (Cardiff, 1948).

Williams, J. G., 'Rhai agweddau ar y gymdeithas Gymreig yn yr ail ganrif ar bymtheg', *Efrydiau Athronyddol*, XXX, 1968, 42-55.

Williams, P., *The Council in the Marches of Wales under Elizabeth I* (Cardiff, 1958).

Williams, P., *The Later Tudors: England 1547-1603* (Oxford, 1998).

Williams, P., *The Tudor Regime* (Oxford, 1979).

Williams, R., *A Biographical Dictionary of Eminent Welshmen* (Llandovery, 1852).

Williams, Rh., 'Wiliam Cynwal', *LlC*, VIII, 1964-5, 197-213.

Williams, W. G., *Arfon y Dyddiau Gynt* (Caernarfon, 1915).

Williams, W. G., 'Dau gywydd o waith John Gruffydd, Llanddyfnan', *TAAS*, 1938, 50-6

Williams, W. G., 'Hen deuluoedd Llanwnda' IV, 'Teulu'r Gadlys', *TCHS*, VII, 1946, 20-3.

Williams, W. G., 'Llanwnda yn 1655', in *Moel Tryfan i'r Traeth: Erthyglau ar Hanes Plwyfi Llanwnda a Llandwrog* (Penygroes, 1983), 34-51.

Williams, W. G., *Y Genedl Gymreig*, 29 May – 26 June 1923.

Williams, W. O., 'The county records', *TCHS*, X, 1949, 79-108.

Williams, W. R., *The Parliamentary History of the Principality of Wales, 1541-1895* (Brecknock, 1895).

Willis, B., *A Survey of the Cathedral Church of Bangor* (London, 1721).

Willis, B., *A Survey of the Cathedral Church of Llandaff* (London, 1719).

Willis, B., *A Survey of the Cathedral Church of St Asaph* (London, 1720).

Willis, B., *Survey of the Cathedrals of York, Durham, Carlisle...Hereford...etc.* (London, 1727).

Wynne, R. O. F., 'Y Cymry a'r Diwygiad Protestannaidd', *Efrydiau Catholig*, VI, 1954, 13-20.

Yates, W. N., 'Rug chapel, Llangar church, Gwydir Uchaf chapel' (London, 1993).

Yorke, P., *The Royal Tribes of Wales* (Liverpool, 1887 ed.).

Unpublished Dissertations

Bassett, T.M., 'A study of local government in Wales under the Commonwealth with especial reference to its relation with central authority' (unpublished University of Wales M.A. dissertation, 1941).

Bowen, D. J., 'Y gymdeithas Gymreig yn niwedd yr Oesoedd Canol fel yr adlewyrchir hi yn y farddoniaeth uchelwrol' (unpublished University of Wales M. A. dissertation, 1951).

Bowen, Ll. 'Wales in British politics, c.1603-42' (unpublished University of Wales Ph.D. dissertation, 1999).

Davies, C. T. B., 'Cerddi'r Tai Crefydd' (unpublished University of Wales M.A. dissertation, 1972).

Isaac, H. M., 'The ecclesiastical and religious position in the diocese of Llandaff in the reign of Elizabeth' (unpublished University of Wales M.A. dissertation, 1928).

Kerr, R. M., 'Cywyddau Siôn Brwynog', (unpublished University of Wales M.A. dissertation, 1960).

Phillips. E. M., 'Noddwyr y beirdd yn Llŷn', (unpublished University of Wales M.A. dissertation, 1973).

Phillips, T. O., 'Bywyd a Gwaith Meurig Dafydd a Llywelyn Siôn' (unpublished University of Wales M.A. dissertation, 1937).

Rowlands, J., 'A critical edition and study of the Welsh poems written in praise of the Salisburies of Llyweni' (unpublished University of Oxford D. Phil. dissertation, 1967).

Sanders, V. C., 'Elizabethan Archbishops of Canterbury and public opinion' (unpublished University of Wales M.A. dissertation, 1979).

Saunders, E. J., 'Gweithiau Lewys Morgannwg' (unpublished University of Wales M. A. dissertation, 1922).

Stephens, R., 'Gwaith Wiliam Llŷn' (unpublished University of Wales Ph.D. dissertation, 1983).

Williams, B, 'The Welsh clergy' (published Open University Ph.D. dissertation, 1998).

INDEX

Buckinghamshire, 61, 267
Bulkeley, Jane, 155
Bulkeley Sir Richard II, 147, 155
Bulkeley, Sir Richard III, 93
Bulkeley, Thomas, 145
Bulkeley, Viscount, 295
Bull, Papal (1570), 35
Bunny, Edmund, 105
Burton-Latimer, 209

C

Cadoxton-juxta-Barry, 236
Cadwaladr the Blessed (Cadwaladr Fendigaid), 158
Caerhun (Caerns), 18, 276
Caernarfon, 268, 274, 280, 289, 291, 293
Caernarfonshire, 7, 89, 254, 255, 257, 260, 262, 263, 264, 267, 268, 269, 273, 279, 280, 293, 294, 302
Caernarfonshire, quarter sessions court of, 254, 262, 263, 265, 268, 268, 269, 270, 301
Caerwent (Mon), 217
Calais, 98
Calvin(ism), 7, 171, 181, 183-4
Cambridge, 11, 42, 250
Cambrobrytannicae Cymraecaeve Linguae Institutiones et Rudimenta (1592), 91
Camden, William, 225
'Cân am y waredigaeth a gadd y Brytanieid...' (1588), 159
Canwyll y Cymru, 201-4
Cardiff (Glam), 246
Carleton, George, bishop of Llandaff, 210, 217, 246, 250
Carlisle, diocese of, 209
Carmarthen, 132
Carmarthenshire, 216, 244
carolwyr, 146
Carter, Colonel John, 267, 268, 270, 274, 275
Cartwright, Thomas, 42, 51, 53
Castell Caereinion (Mont), 18
Castellmarch (Caerns), 263, 266, 274
Catalogue of the Bishops of England (1601), 218
Catherine of Aragon, 151
Catholic League (1585), 59
Cecil, Sir Robert, 1st earl of Salisbury, 223-4
Cecil, Sir William (Lord Burghley), 13, 15, 17, 22, 42, 45, 64, 90, 100
Cefnamwlch (Caerns), 221, 238, 265
Cefn Brith (Brecks), 40
Cefnllanfair family (Caerns), 266
Ceri, 236
Chancery, court of, 220
Chantries, 133

Charles I, 103, 108, 221, 234, 242, 248, 249, 258, 260, 264, 267, 270, 288, 291
Charles II, 293
Charles, prince of Wales, 228
Cheshire, 282
Chester, 119, 169, 219
Chichester, diocese of, 209, 217
Chirk (Denbs), 155
Christian Directorie, A (1585), 59
Christian preparation to the Lord's Supper, A (1624), 229
Christ's College (Ruthin), 18
Chrysostom, John, 104
Civil marriages, 275, 276
Civil Wars, 4, 6, 245, 253, 255, 258, 260, 262, 264, 265, 267, 269, 270, 275, 285, 301
Clenennau, Y (Caerns), 108, 264
Clocaenog (Denbs), 232
Clynnog (Caerns), 274, 284, 291
Clynnog, Morus, 99
Cochwillan (Caerns), 265, 289
Coedymynydd (Flints.), 190
Commission(ers) for the Approbation of Public Preachers, 257
Convocation, 10
Conwy (Caerns), 12, 266, 267, 268, 275, 282, 283
Conwy valley, 12
Cope, Sir Anthony, 61
Corbet, John, 258
Cornwall, 134
Corsygedol (Mer), 238
Corwen (Mer), 237
Council in the Marches, 44, 50, 51, 90, 93, 94, 144, 154, 241, 242, 244-5, 261, 279
Council of State, 269, 270, 275, 277, 293
County Committees, 256, 262, 264, 292
Coverdale, Miles, 19, 123, 181, 229
Cradoc, Lleision, 137
Cradock, Walter, 249, 248, 259, 271
Cranmer, Thomas, archbishop of Canterbury, 124, 131, 134
Cressy, David, 121
Cricieth (Caerns), 264
Cromwell, Oliver, 261, 266, 268, 269, 270, 277, 278, 279, 293, 295
Cromwell, Richard, 289, 291
Cromwell, Thomas, 10, 100, 123, 124, 126, 127, 144
cwndidau(cwndidwr), 133, 138, 156, 168, 299
cymortha, 89
Cymydmaen (Caerns), 282
cywydd(au), 4, 179, 191, 193, 196, 299

D

'Dadl ynghylch yr Hen Ffydd', 164
Dafydd ab Owain, 129
Dafydd Benwyn, 27, 196
Davies, Dr John, rector of Mallwyd, 3, 27, 105,
193, 198, 208-9, 229-31, 252
Davies, Dr John (Siôn Dafydd Rhys), 3, 68, 69,
88, 91-2
Davies, Humphrey, 252
Davies, Richard, bishop of St David's, 3, 11, 12,
13, 14, 15, 16, 23, 36, 38, 43, 44, 45, 46, 66, 67,
68, 73, 74, 75, 80, 86, 118, 176, 179, 185, 211,
222, 298
Davies, Thomas, 269
Davies, Thomas, bishop of St Asaph, 12, 14,
18, 22, 176-7, 178, 181, 222
Davies, William, 154
Day of Hearing...The, 27
Decimation Tax, 286
Defence of the Government established in the
Church of England, 57
Deffynniad Ffydd Eglwys Loegr (1595), 75, 87
Deganwy (Caerns), 266
De Imitatione Christi, 243
Denbigh, 147, 265
Denbighshire, 46, 144, 241
Deneio (Caerns), parish of, 18, 274, 292
Dent, Arthur, 46, 84, 86, 224, 226
Deputy-Lieutenants, 261
Derfel Gadarn, 100
Devereux, Robert, 2nd earl of Essex, 162, 163
Devon, 134
Dictionarium Duplex (1632), 229
Dictionary in Englyshe and Welshe (1547), 114
Dilyniad Crist (1684), 243
Dinas (Caerns), 265
Dinllaen (Caerns), 293
Directory for the Publique Worship of God, 269,
292
Disce Mori, Learne to Die (1633), 231
'Discoverie of the Present Estate of the
Byshoppricke of St Asaph, A' (1587), 25
Diserth (Flints), parish of, 28
Dod, John, 255
Dodd, A. H., 254, 261
Dolben, David, 238
Dolwyddelan (Caerns), 214
Douai, 157
Drake, Sir Francis, 160
Drych Cristianogawl, Y (1586), 59, 96, 114, 154
Dudley, John, duke of Northumberland, 144,
147, 150
Dudley, Lord Guildford, 150
Dudley, Robert, earl of Leicester, 36, 144, 175
Dwnn, Gruffudd, 148, 175

Dwygyfylchi (Caerns), 223, 291

E

Ecclesia Anglicana, 10
Edeirnion (Mer), 238
Edern (Caerns), 282
Edward ap Ieuan ab Ithel, 141
Edward VI, 64-5, 130, 133, 134, 138, 145, 147,
150, 151, 165
Edwards, John (father and son, Plas Newydd,
Chirk), 88, 241; family, 241
Edwards, Richard, 265, 266, 274
Edwards, Thomas, 220
Edwart ap Raff, 152, 184, 299
Eifionydd (Caerns), 108, 264, 276, 282, 287
Eikon Basilike (c.1650), 108
Elis ap Siôn ap Morus, 222
Elizabeth I, 1, 2, 9, 10, 25, 32, 42, 50, 60, 64, 65,
72, 94, 143, 152-3, 158, 162, 164, 166, 182, 184,
187, 196
Elizabethan Church, 1, 2, 14, 39-40, 42-3, 71,
77, 195, 207, 247
Ely, 211
Elyot, Sir Thomas, 70
englyn(ion), 137, 148, 149, 168, 175
Epistol at y Cembru (Epistle to the Welsh,
1567), 73, 74, 179
Erasmus, Desiderius, 22
Erbery, William, 247-8
Eucharist, 135, 171
Evans, Evan, 280
Evans, Hugh, dean of St Asaph, 23, 25, 192
Evans, William, 27, 189, 196
Evesham, 213
Exhortation vnto the Governours of Wales, An
(1588), 51, 52, 54

F

Faenol (Caerns), Y, 268, 274
'Feoffees for impropriations', 5
Field, John, 54, 61
Field, Theophilus, bishop of Llandaff and St
David's, 211, 214, 218, 221, 220, 226, 229, 239,
246, 249, 250
First Booke of Christian Exercise Appertayning
to Resolution, The (1582), 59, 105
Fleming, William, 96
Flintshire, 128, 157, 155, 168, 241
Forty-two Articles, 42
Foundation of the Christian Religion, 249
Foxe, John, 15, 152, 194
France, 129
Friars School (Bangor), 33, 238, 264
Funeral Sermon (1577), 80

321

G

Galfridian myth, 197
Gardiner, Stephen, 132
Gauden, William, 108
Geneva(n), 50, 62
Gerald of Wales, 76
Gerizzin, mount 119
Gethin, John, 264
Glamorgan, 138, 248, 266; vale of, 241, 272
Glascomb (Rads), 236
Gloucester, 258
Gloucestershire, 248
Glynllifon (Caerns), 265
Glynn, William, 16
Glynne, Colonel Thomas, 265
Glynne, Edmund, 265, 280, 293
Glyn(ne) family (Lleuar, Caerns), 267
Glynne, John, 295
Godwin, Francis, bishop of Llandaff, 30, 32, 212, 213, 217, 218, 224, 225, 232, 251
Goldwell, Thomas, bishop of St Asaph, 190
Goodman, Christopher, 246
Goodman, Dr Gabriel, 208
Gower, Stanley, 247
Gramadeg Cymraeg (1567), 98
gravita riposata, 72
Great Sessions, court of, 258, 268
Greeham, Richard, 31
Grey, Lady Jane, 145, 147, 150
Griffith, Edmund, bishop of Bangor, 217, 220, 226, 238
Griffith family (Cefnamwlch), 220
Griffith, Gwen, 280
Griffith, Huw (Cefnamwlch), 265
Griffith, William, 283
Griffiths, Paul, 108
Gronw Wiliam, 173
Gruffudd ap Ieuan ap Llywelyn Fychan, 138, 169
Gruffudd ap Rhisiart, 29
Gruffudd Hiraethog, 101, 145
Gruffudd Phylip, 197, 198-9
Gruffydd, John (Llanddyfnan), 275
Gruffydd, William, Cemais, 88
Guise, family, 59
Gunpowder Plot (1605), 195, 244
Guto'r Glyn 128
Gwent, 159, 241
Gwilym Tew, 124
Gwydir (Caerns), Wynns of, 37, 220, 219
Gwylmabsant, 287
Gwynedd, 100, 150, 257, 289, 294
Gwynn, Hugh (Berth Ddu), 88
Gwyn, Richard, 155, 156, 157, 164
Gwyn, Robert (Penyberth), 21, 59, 69, 96-7,

114, 115, 118, 154
Gyffin, Y (Caerns), 18

H

Hall, Edward, 126
Hamburg, 85, 228, 256
Hampton Court Conference (1604), 211, 229
Hanmer, John, bishop of St Asaph, 46, 209, 215, 225, 226, 231, 232, 234, 300
Hanson, Thomas (Llanllyfni), 293
Harley, Lady Brilliana (Brampton Bryan, Herefds), 248
Harley, Sir Robert, (Brampton Bryan, Herefds) 247, 248
Harrison, Thomas, 270
Haverfordwest (Pembs), 236, 246
Hawarden (Flints), 236, 295
Hendreforfudd, 20
Hendre, Yr, 265
Henllan (Denbs), 224
Henry VII, 185
Henry VIII, 64, 65, 123, 124, 130, 135, 136, 137, 138, 146, 151, 190
Herbert family of Powys Castle, 81
Herbert, Henry, 2nd earl of Pembroke, 51, 52, 53, 89, 154-5
Herbert, Sir John (Neath abbey), 95
Herbert, William, 100
Herbert, William, 1st earl of Pembroke, 36, 88, 98-9, 144, 174-5
Hereford, 146
Hereford, diocese of, 66, 209, 214
Herefordshire, 146, 242, 244, 247, 246, 248, 278
Heylin, Rowland, 102, 105, 246
High Commission, court of, 247
Historia Gruffyd vab Kenan, 13
Hityn Grydd, 143
Holland, David, 208
Holland, Robert, 32, 88
Holywell (Flints), 244
Homily of Obedience, 73
Hooker, Richard, 78, 92, 116, 186, 232, 298
Hookes, John, 295
Hookes, William, 268, 295
Hopcyn Tomas Phylip, 168
House of Commons, 65
House of Lords, 65, 245
Howard, Thomas, 4th earl of Norfolk, 13
Howard, William, Lord, of Effingham, 160
Howell, James, 289
Huet, Thomas, 32, 43
Hughes, Richard, 195
Hughes, William, 12, 13, 14, 15, 18, 25, 26, 27, 28, 32, 34, 43, 176, 227

Humphreys, Humphrey, bishop of Bangor, 222
Huw Llŷn, 222
Huw Machno, 155, 186, 197, 202, 222, 299
Huw Pennant, 192, 228
Hywel Swrdwal, 128

I
Ieuan ab Wiliam ap Siôn, 140
Ieuan Deulwyn, 129
Ieuan Llwyd Sieffre, 162
Ieuan Tew Ieuanc, 180
Ifan ap Hwlcyn Llwyd, 128
Ifor Hael, 27
imperium, 78
impropriations, 6
Instrument of Government (1653), 269, 277
Intendants, 285-6
Ireland, 129, 162, 243, 244, 263
Is-Gwyrfai (Caerns), 282
Italy, 59
Itinerarium Kambriae, 76

J
Jabin, 185
James I, 195, 197, 207, 227, 241, 249
James, Edward, 5, 23, 24, 27, 32, 298
Jenkins, Hugh, 238
Jenkins, Thomas, 23
Jessey, Henry, 248
Jewel, John, bishop of Salisbury, 15, 77, 186
Johns, David, 27
Jones, Colonel John, 266
Jones, Colonel Phylip, 266
Jones, Edmund, 248
Jones, Edward, 223
Jones, Griffith, 263, 264, 268-9, 274, 280, 288, 293, 295
Jones, Hugh, bishop of Llandaff, 23, 44
Jones, John, 292
Jones-Parry, family, 266
Jones, Robert, 274
Jones, Sir Thomas (Abermarlais), 93; family of, 213
Jones, Sir William, 263
Jones, Thomas, 27, 159, 160, 180
Justices of the peace, 262, 263, 268-9, 276, 279, 280-4, 288-9, 294-5

K
Kelsey, Thomas, 294
Kempis, Thomas à, 243
Kent, 91, 182
Ket, Robert, 134
Kilfenora, diocese of, 209

Kitchin, Anthony, bishop of Llandaff, 10, 23, 153
Knights of St John, Ysbyty Ifan, 144
Kyffin Edward, 82, 232
Kyffin, Maurice, 3, 44, 75, 77, 82, 87, 298
Kyffin, Rhosier, 158, 162, 182, 184
Kynniver llith a ban, 22, 130

L
Lambarde, William, 91, 93, 182
Lancashire, 282
Lasco, John à, 133
Laud, William, bishop of St David's and archbishop of Canterbury, 209, 210, 211, 232, 233, 234, 235, 236, 237, 239, 240, 250, 256, 286, 292, 300
'Lecture system', 246
Lee, Edward Donne, 61
Lee, Leonard, 285
Le Theâtre du Monde, 96
Lewis, Dr David, 93
Lewis, Edward, 196
Lewis, Hugh, 3, 19, 20, 32, 44, 45, 82, 181, 206, 298
Lewis, John, 269
Lewis, Thomas, 196
Lewkenor, Sir Richard, 242
Lewys Morgannwg, 124, 125, 129, 135-6

Lhuyd, Humphrey, 113, 117
Littleton, William, 270
Llanbadarn Fawr (Cards), 269
Llanbeblig (Caerns), 276
Llanbedr-y-cennin (Caerns), 277
Llanbeulan, 264
Llandaff, diocese of, 9, 23, 31, 32, 36, 37, 38, 45, 66, 132, 209, 212, 213, 217-8, 234, 238, 241, 248, 250
Llandudwen, 194
Llanddeiniolen (Caerns), 19, 274
Llandderfel (Mer), 100
Llanddwywe (Mer), 176, 238
Llandeilo Fawr (Carms), 244
Llandudno (Caerns), 18, 59
Llandwrog (Caerns), 274
Llandygái (Caerns), 18
Llaneilian (Caerns), 290
Llanengan (Caerns), 266
Llaneurgain (Flints.), 190
Llanfaches (Mon), 248
Llanfairfechan (Caerns), 291
Llanfechain (Mont), 21
Llangathen (Carms), 216

Pryse, Sir John, 3, 17, 20, 22, 32, 44, 73, 111, 112, 118, 122, 123, 126, 130, 132, 146
Prytherch, William, 290, 291
Pugh, Gwilym, 153, 154
Pugh, Robert, 88, 155
Puleston, Rowland, 247
Puritanism, 1, 2, 3, 4, 5, 7, 8, 27-9, 231, 240-9, 254-60, 290-4, 301-2
Pwllheli (Caerns), 265, 287
Pym, John, 240

R

Radnorshire, 248
Raff ap Robert, 141
Raglan (Mon), 242
Receiver-General of North Wales, 256
Renaissance, 70-2, 94-6
Rhan o Psalmau Dafydd Brophwyd (1603), 83, 232
Rhisiart Cynwal, 155, 193, 204, 222, 227, 299
Rhiw (Caerns), 280
Rhiwledyn (Caerns), 59, 154
Rhydolion (Caerns), 266, 274, 287
Rhys Cain, 199, 219
Rhys Wynn ap John Fychan, 'Sir', 128
Richards, Dr Thomas, 254, 273
Richelieu, Cardinal, 284
Roberts, Evan, 119, 249
Robert, Gruffydd, 3, 85, 98, 99
Roberts, Dr Stephen, 271
Roberts, Gruffydd, 257
Roberts, Michael, 75, 102, 206, 231
Roberts, William, bishop of Bangor, 209, 211, 214, 234, 236, 238, 251, 270
Robinson, Hugh, 277
Robinson, Nicholas, bishop of Bangor, 3, 11, 12, 13, 14, 16, 22, 23, 44, 90, 100, 118, 176, 216
Rogers, John, 123
Roman Catholicism, 1, 4, 91, 94, 114-5, 124, 141-52, 153-7, 229
Rome, 60, 139, 168, 179
Rowland, Ellis, 257, 274, 291
Rowlands, David, 231
Rowlands, Henry, 12, 13, 14, 16, 28, 33, 40, 193, 194, 200, 210, 209, 215, 216, 222-3, 234, 250, 251, 257, 265, 300
Rudd, Anthony, 11, 14, 209, 216, 218, 239, 244, 250, 251, 256, 300
Rug chapel (Mer), 237
Rump Parliament, 268, 270
Ruthin (Denbs), 18

S

Sacred Principles, Services and Soliloquies (1649), 108
Sail Crefydd Gristnogawl (1649), 119
St Asaph, archdeaconry of, 223
St Asaph, diocese of, 12, 14, 18, 23, 28, 31, 37, 43, 144, 208-9, 223, 229, 234
St Asaph (Flints), parish of, 28
St Asaph, school at, 28
St Augustine, 76, 128
St Benedict, 128
St David's (Pembs), diocese of, 13, 14, 31, 36, 42, 43, 211, 218, 239-40
St Dubricius, 217
St George, parish of, 28
St Gregory, 128
St Guthlac priory, 146
St John's College, Cambridge, 155, 177
St Joseph of Arimathea, 74
St Mary's church (Cardiff), 248
St Mary's church (Haverfordwest), 236
St Mary's church (Oxford), 236
St Patrick, 128
St Paul, 104
St Paul's, 13, 214, 235
St Tudwal's island (Caerns), 266
St Tudwen, church of (Caerns), 29
St Winifred's Well (Flints), 169, 244
Salesbury, Colonel William, 237
Salesbury, William, 3, 15, 22, 39, 53, 74, 101, 113-4, 131-2, 150, 175, 177-8, 230
Salesbury, William (Bachymbyd), 237
Salisbury, Thomas, 232
Salusbury family, 81
Salusbury, Sir John, 88, 175
Salusbury, Thomas, 88
Sanhedrin, Jewish, 74
Scales of Commerce and Trade, The (1659), 284
Selatyn (Salop), 209
sermon against fleshly lusts, ...a, 27
Seymour, Edward, duke of Somerset, 19
Shipston-on-Stour, 213
Shirenewton (Mon), 12, 217
Shoebury (Essex), 83, 226
Shrewsbury (Salop), 278
Shropshire, 209, 227, 249, 274
'Sidanen', 158, 166
Sidney, Sir Henry, 76, 155
Sidney, Sir Philip, 76
Simwnt Fychan, 128
Siôn ap Rhisiart Lewys, 128, 137
Siôn Brwynog, 20, 128, 135, 140, 143, 144, 145, 146, 150, 156, 190, 229
Siôn Cent, 129, 188

326